THIS IS HIP

Popular Music History

Series Editor: Alyn Shipton, Royal Academy of Music, London, and City University, London

This series publishes books that challenge established orthodoxies in popular music studies, examine the formation and dissolution of canons, interrogate histories of genres, focus on previously neglected forms, or engage in archaeologies of popular music.

Published

An Unholy Row: Jazz in Britain and its Audience, 1945–1960
Dave Gelly

Being Prez: The Life and Music of Lester Young
Dave Gelly

Bill Russell and the New Orleans Jazz Revival
Ray Smith and Mike Pointon

Chasin' the Bird: The Life and Legacy of Charlie Parker
Brian Priestley

Handful of Keys: Conversations with Thirty Jazz Pianists
Alyn Shipton

Jazz Me Blues: The Autobiography of Chris Barber
Chris Barber with Alyn Shipton

Jazz Visions: Lennie Tristano and His Legacy
Peter Ind

Lee Morgan: His Life, Music and Culture
Tom Perchard

Lionel Richie: Hello
Sharon Davis

Mosaics: The Life and Works of Graham Collier
Duncan Heining

Mr P.C.: The Life and Music of Paul Chambers
Rob Palmer

Out of the Long Dark: The Life of Ian Carr
Alyn Shipton

Rufus Wainwright
Katherine Williams

Soul Unsung: Reflections on the Band in Black Popular Music
Kevin Le Gendre

The Last Miles: The Music of Miles Davis, 1980–1991
George Cole

The Godfather of British Jazz: The Life and Music of Stan Tracey
Clark Tracey

The Long Shadow of the Little Giant (second edition): The Life, Work and Legacy of Tubby Hayes
Simon Spillett

The Ultimate Guide to Great Reggae: The Complete Story of Reggae Told through its Greatest Songs, Famous and Forgotten
Michael Garnice

Trad Dads, Dirty Boppers and Free Fusioneers: A History of British Jazz, 1960–1975
Duncan Heining

This is Hip

The Life of Mark Murphy

Peter Jones

eQuinox

SHEFFIELD UK   BRISTOL CT

Published by Equinox Publishing Ltd

UK: Office 415, The Workstation, 15 Paternoster Row, Sheffield, South Yorkshire,
       S1 2BX
USA: ISD, 70 Enterprise Drive, Bristol, CT 06010

www.equinoxpub.com

First published 2018

© Peter Jones 2018

British Library Cataloguing-in-Publication Data

A catalogue record for this book is available from the British Library.

ISBN-13 978 1 78179 473 9   (hardback)

Library of Congress Cataloging-in-Publication Data
Names: Jones, Peter (Peter Douglas) author.
Title: This is hip : the life of Mark Murphy / Peter Jones.
Description: Sheffield, UK ; Bristol, CT : Equinox Publishing, 2018. |
    Series: Popular music history | Includes bibliographical references and
    index.
Identifiers: LCCN 2017029131 (print) | LCCN 2017030803 (ebook) | ISBN
    9781781796627 (ePDF) | ISBN 9781781794739 (hb)
Subjects: LCSH: Murphy, Mark, 1932-2015. | Jazz singers—England—Biography.
Classification: LCC ML420.M7795 (ebook) | LCC ML420.M7795 J66 2018 (print) |
    DDC 782.42165092 [B]—dc23
LC record available at https://lccn.loc.gov/2017029131

Typeset by S.J.I. Services, New Delhi
Printed and bound by Lightning Source Inc. (La Vergne, TN), Lightning Source UK Ltd.
(Milton Keynes), Lightning Source AU Pty. (Scoresby, Victoria).

Contents

	Acknowledgements	vii
	Foreword: It's Compromise, Don't Bother	ix
1	That's When It Bit Me	1
2	Dues-Paying Days	11
3	All the Bases Were Loaded	22
4	Many Shades of Blue	31
5	That's What I Like About London	39
6	He's As Good As I Am	48
7	Ready for Anything	62
8	Where Fountains Drip in a Forgotten Tempo	80
9	It's Hot, It's Red Lights, It's Exciting!	91
10	I Remember Less and Less, Except You Baby	103
11	A Wild Animal, Or a Child	114
12	Age Only Matters If You're a Cheese	124
13	The Mother of All Love Songs	137
14	Much to Do and Not a Moment to Spare	150
	Appendix A: A Jazz Singer Is a Singer Who Sings Jazz	165
	Appendix B: I Don't Want to Stamp Out Singers Like Cookies	178
	Discography	186
	Notes	204
	Index	230

Acknowledgements

This book needed to be written for a number of reasons, the first being that Mark Murphy deserves greater recognition than he achieved in his lifetime. He mastered the art of jazz singing to an extraordinary degree, taking it to levels appreciated only by those few who knew about him and understood what he was doing. The book includes a chapter that, through interviews with a number of singers, focuses on the techniques and innovations that he brought to jazz singing. Murphy was not only a peerless performer of music, but one who loved to collaborate with jazz instrumentalists all over the world, and who was revered by them for his vast knowledge and understanding of jazz. He took great risks, both personal and professional, in the furtherance of his chosen art form.

He was also for many years a teacher of singers; his prowess in this department through classes and workshops across the globe earned him numerous friends and admirers. Again, I have devoted a separate chapter to Murphy the teacher.

However the book is mostly concerned with the story of his life, a narrative that has been pieced together from interviews with those who knew him best. It would not have been possible without the help of the extended Murphy and Howe families, who supplied stories and family photographs: Nancy Murphy, Kate Murphy, Kathy Hinkhouse, Mark E. Murphy and Allan Howe. The latter also generously transferred home movie footage to DVD and sent it to me – some of it dating back as far as the 1930s.

Another essential resource has been the 74 quarterly issues of *Mark's Times*, the fanzine devoted to him, produced continuously from 1981 to 1999 by Norbert Warner. It's worth mentioning at this point that I have retained Mark Murphy's idiosyncratic spelling, punctuation and grammar from his letters to the fanzine, as well as that of its various contributors. I am deeply grateful to Graham Langley for his hospitality and for letting me borrow his complete set of *Mark's Times*.

A major part of the process has been listening to Murphy's recorded output – 48 albums under his own name and still rising, as well as singles and EPs, collaborations and guest appearances. Heartfelt thanks are due to Mike Elliott for lending me his large collection of Mark Murphy albums. I am also grateful to Francesca Miano for permission to reproduce her eulogy to Mark.

Others who generously gave up their time to be interviewed, emailed and generally pestered, or who sent me valuable materials, include Albert Amaroso, Esther Bennett, Ken Bloom, Michael Bourne, Till Brönner, Pete Churchill, Charles Cochran, Richie Cole, C. Tom Davis, Randy Dempsey, Kathleen Dickson, Lily Dior, Amy Duncan, Larry Dunlap, Ann Dyer, Spiros Exaras, the late Joe Fields, Nancy Galusha Thomas, James Gavin, Andy Hamill, Colin Hogan, Bill Holman, Duncan Hopkins, the late John Jack, Theo Jackson, Sheila Jordan, Greetje Kauffeld, Nancy Kelly, Kathryn King, Samir Köck, Jean-Pierre Leduc, Lance Liddle, Amy London, Kitty Margolis, Dave Matthews, Tina May, Bill Mays, Barbara Nies Mezzatesta, Karlheinz Miklin, Lesley Mitchell-Clarke, Lee Musiker, David Nathan at the National Jazz Archive (UK), Bobbe Norris, Paul Pace, Gilles Peterson, Misha Piatigorsky, Dave Pistoni, Les Reed, Ack Van Rooyen, Mike Rose, Holli Ross, Steve Rubie, Ellyn Rucker, Sebastian Scotney, Ian Shaw, Kirby Shaw, Darrel Sheinman, Ari Silverstein, Sean Smith, Tessa Souter, Peter Stretton, Roger Treece, Jonny Trunk, Norbert Warner, Oliver Weindling, Ronny Whyte and Val Wilmer.

Thanks also to the book's early readers – Bridget Jones, Jim Trimmer and Andrew Cartmel – all of whom corrected mistakes both large and small, and made invaluable suggestions for improvements. I would also like to thank Alyn Shipton for commissioning this project, Thomas Cunniffe for copy-editing, and Janet Joyce and Valerie Hall at Equinox for all their help.

Inevitably, in the absence of previous biographies, and because of Murphy's largely undocumented gypsy lifestyle, there are some gaps in the story. In addition, many of the tales told by Murphy himself varied considerably at different times; working out which version is nearest to the truth has not always been easy. However, for any errors of fact, the responsibility is mine alone. Any corrections or clarifications should be sent to thisiship@icloud.com.

Peter Jones
London, January 2018

Foreword: It's Compromise, Don't Bother

Athens, April 2008: the Gazarte Club, on Gazi central square, with its grand view of the Acropolis. The modern 500-seat concert hall is packed with the top echelons of Athenian society – musicians, artists, composers and politicians, including George Papandreou, soon to become Greece's prime minister. It's perhaps because he was born in St Paul, Minnesota, that Papandreou has come to see the large American in a shiny pale blue shirt who is now ambling slowly on to the stage. His name is Mark Murphy. He's recently turned 76, and although he spends much of the evening perched on a stool, in many ways he seems a younger man, with a full head of shaggy hair and a friendly, confident manner.

Before the applause has died away, bassist George Giorgiadis starts playing a simple two-note phrase – C and the octave above – as Thomas Rueckert ripples through a few plangent piano chords. Meanwhile Murphy introduces himself, name-checks Homer and Socrates, and slips straight into "My Funny Valentine", as Alex Drakos sidles in with the brushes and guitarist Spiros Exaras lightly sketches in the gaps between voice and piano.

This hoary old ballad, regularly murdered by novice jazz singers everywhere, suddenly sounds as fresh as paint, with vocal swoops, falsetto lines, scatting, swinging, riffing, and some good jokes: *Is your figure less than Greek?* "Excuse me, that's the lyric!" and *Don't change your hairdo for me*, and *Your looks are laughable*, tossed away with an affectionate chuckle. It's all a lot of fun, and just as the song seems to be subsiding to a close, *Each day is Valentine's Day* becomes *day-to-day, day-to-day, day-to-day, day-to-day*, and suddenly "My Funny Valentine" has mutated into a samba. After dancing through the lyric again with this new rhythm, Murphy unleashes a volley of scat so hip and inventive, it makes his voice sound like some yet-to-be-invented instrument. Nearly ten minutes pass before he brings the song to a close on a long, soft falsetto note that extends into the intro of the next number, "All Blues". Having

Mark Murphy at the Gazarte, Athens, 2008, with (left to right) Thomas Rueckert, Spiros Exaras, George Giorgiadis, Alex Drakos (courtesy Spiros Exaras).

first dispatched Oscar Brown Jr.'s lyric, he takes another couple of choruses, first improvising on the lyric, then scatting.

The songs fly by in rapid succession, with barely a pause for breath between them. After "All Blues" it's straight into the verse of "On Green Dolphin Street", sung rubato and unaccompanied right through the first chorus, immediately followed by another *a cappella* chorus in which Murphy goes into time, scatting again and fracturing the tune and its lyric, before the band finally drops into place behind him.

Tension and release, tension and release. The audience has never heard anything like it. Despite his years of globe-trotting, Murphy is virtually unknown in Greece, but so assiduously has the club's promoter Manos Tzanakakis plugged this three-night, six-show engagement that every house is sold out. Guitarist Exaras, who has organized the trip, could not be happier.

...

By the time he played these Athens dates, Mark Murphy had been a professional jazz singer for over half a century. He had performed thousands of gigs all over the world and recorded nearly 50 albums, both under his own name and as a guest artist. Yet he was still almost unknown to listeners outside the jazz world. An ungenerous headline from a 1986 newspaper may have said it best: "30 LPs and still obscure". However, many inside jazz regarded him as the greatest male jazz singer there had ever been. Even after his death in

October 2015, his influence on other singers had never been greater: without Mark Murphy there could have been no Kurt Elling or Curtis Stigers – both far more successful in their careers than Murphy ever was. Jazz instrumentalists, who sometimes view singers as little more than a necessary evil, were in awe of him. "The recordings I did with Mark belong to the greatest moments of my life," said German pianist Frank Chastenier. "I wish I could play the piano the way he sings!"

On a good day, Murphy was at ease with his obscurity. "I sometimes wonder what it would have been like to have been extremely famous… and I'm not sure I would have liked it. Because this way I have a lot of freedom… social freedom, musical freedom. I call my own shots… I do what I want… I would have had a very difficult time trying to appeal to anybody else besides the people I do appeal to." Still, he spent a lot of time wondering why he wasn't able to attract a wider audience, or to scale the heights of popular success achieved by singers with a quarter of his talent. Small as his public was, Murphy treasured it. "People who come to jazz are an audience of a higher intelligence. Jazz just does not attract dumb people. Dumb people don't have the patience to sit and listen."

To him, jazz singing, like jazz playing, was Art. He constantly used the word to describe what he did. But his choice to be "an artist" in a despised and overlooked musical genre, rather than the popular entertainer he certainly could have become, consigned him to the outer fringe of popular culture. One of Murphy's immediate predecessors, Nat King Cole, made a different choice, evolving from a dazzling and innovative bebop pianist to a mainstream crooner. After years of scraping a living from jazz, Cole saw a chance to make serious money.

It could be argued that Murphy never really got the breaks he needed. But he began his career recording for two big, mainstream record labels at a time when jazz was at its zenith in popular culture, which was hardly a handicap. The real reason for his lack of mainstream success was that he was unwilling to take career direction from managers and other business insiders. In spite of all his efforts to win the approval of the mainstream entertainment industry, he remained outside it for his entire career. This was partly due to his personal eccentricity: some of his close associates dubbed him "Marf Murky". But it was also his attitude to the business as a whole. "Office people, it's office thinking," he said. "Anything that smacks of a group, group's thinking, or committee thinking – that's why I like to work with a smaller company. No office, just take me out of the office, that's office thinking. It's compromise, don't bother."

However his legacy as an innovator is beyond dispute. The jazz writer Will Friedwald has identified two distinct streams in contemporary jazz singing: the "retro counterrevolution" of conservative younger singers headed by Diana Krall and Jane Monheit; and those who have been profoundly influenced by the eclectic, risk-taking strategies of Mark Murphy and Betty Carter – Cassandra Wilson, Dianne Reeves and Kurt Elling.

Mark Murphy could sing a tune straight better than almost anyone. But simply bookending the band's solos was never enough for him. He played his voice like an instrument, making it a point of principle to perform songs differently every time – perhaps singing sections *a cappella*, or with only the drums or the bass for accompaniment, or linking up with these instruments for a specific melodic and/or rhythmic improvisation. He used the spoken word; he created extraordinary wordless sounds with his mouth. He told jokes and made musical jokes while singing. And while many singers are limited to a narrow vocal range, Murphy could sing anywhere from basso profundo to high falsetto. This voice of his wasn't – isn't – to everybody's taste. In an otherwise approving review, one writer described it as an "unpretty, subterranean baritone – an acquired taste, like raw oysters and aquavit." Another, reinforcing the "acquired taste" idea, compared it to "beluga and snails".

"I don't compromise," Murphy admitted in 1992. "By that I mean I don't bend toward the audience, but rather I try to grab the audience and bring it with me. And I only sing what I like. I don't have to sing 'New York, New York'. Since the early 70s, I've sung only my own repertoire. That's not bad for a guy who's not a household name."

Neglect and obscurity are of course the norm for practitioners across all the arts; fame and success are the exceptions. But considering the fanatical loyalty he inspired among his own audience, Murphy's absence from jazz writing is extraordinary. Shortly after the latter's death, blogger Kevin Lynch conducted an informal survey and discovered that many jazz reference books fail to mention Murphy at all: it amounted to a "4,530-page desert of critical neglect".

His near-contemporary Betty Carter (1929–1998), one of the very few singers who rivaled him for virtuosity, knowledge and sheer inventiveness, experienced major problems in sustaining her career. Both she and Murphy struggled to maintain their musical integrity in the face of commercial pressures. Growing up in the 40s and 50s, being both female and black, and with children to support, Carter faced – and overcame – considerably greater barriers than Murphy. But unlike him, she won a Grammy, was invited to perform at the Newport Jazz Festival and at the White House, and was awarded a National Medal of Arts by President Bill Clinton.

The career of another singer offers another interesting contrast to that of Mark Murphy. Mel Tormé, six years older, improvised alongside jazz's greatest instrumentalists. Yet brilliant and successful as he was, he may have come second to Murphy in at least two respects: 'cool' and 'hip'. These were epithets that clung to Mark Murphy throughout his career. In fact, they were – and remain – so much a part of his appeal to those who appreciate him that it is worth considering what the terms actually signify, because although closely associated, they are not the same.

A person (nearly always male) is considered "cool" when he can make what is difficult seem easy, such as jazz singing or playing the saxophone. Cool also indicates a certain emotional detachment or understatement, and hence an absence of conventional reactions. If Mark Murphy was cool, it was only to the extent that he made what he did seem easy; but he was too passionately engaged in his art to be truly cool.

Hip is a more interesting, more elusive quality than cool. Its etymology has been traced back to Africa, to the Wolof language spoken by slaves brought to the United States from Senegal and coastal Gambia. Hip is thought to derive from the verb *hepi* – 'to see' – or *hipi* – 'to open one's eyes'. Crucially, the hip person knows something you probably don't.

When Mark Murphy appeared on *Marion McPartland's Piano Jazz* radio show, she said: "*I* know what hip is and you know what hip is, but have you ever been asked to explain it?" Mark replied: "Yes, I'm afraid I have. But I don't know, Harry the Hipster's no longer with us, so he can't be any help, but I suppose when you get it all together and tie it up and then you call the ribbon hip, that's what it is. So maybe when you've finally got it all together, that's hip, right?... Hip means ready, fully prepared, and this is the hardest music to get altogether because there's so much you have to know and feel and be able to express, because you can't really express it until you tear the walls down." Unclear as this explanation is, Murphy probably meant that a 'hip' artist must be free from all conventional constraints.

The late 1940s and early 1950s, when Murphy was reaching adulthood, were a time of maximum cool *and* hipness in jazz. Miles Davis's *Birth of the Cool* sessions took place on the cusp of the 1950s. And Miles was the musician Mark Murphy admired the most; like Betty Carter, he wanted to make his voice sound like Miles's trumpet. Jazz defined Mark Murphy to such an extent that in later life he would tell audiences, "You can divide your life into two parts: Before Jazz and After Jazz. You had a life before jazz, but once you heard jazz, you knew that your life would never be the same again."

He lived much of his life below the radar; as he criss-crossed the world, from San Francisco to London, from Japan to Australia, and throughout Europe, even his family and close friends often had no idea where he was. His nomadic life included long periods with no fixed address, living in a camper van or sleeping on people's sofas.

The truth is, Mark Murphy never fitted in. He grew up gay at a time when being gay was literally unspeakable – a crime both legally and socially. He didn't fit in with the sexually straight world, nor – since he was never fully 'out' – with the overtly gay world. He was white when many thought that jazz singers ought to be black. You could be white and a crooner, but Murphy wasn't a crooner. He was an eccentric beatnik-cum-hippie whose distrust of the straight world of business was such that it restricted his career, even as it allowed him artistic freedom. He didn't fit in with the jazz establishment. He was a genuine, dyed-in-the-wool rebel, who identified closely with the acid jazz "kids" he met in London in the late 80s, because, like him, they were part of an underground culture – subversive, passionate, devoid of cynicism.

1 That's When It Bit Me

Mark Howe Murphy grew up in a solidly middle-class family in the far north of New York State. He was born at a hospital in Syracuse on March 14, 1932, after which his father, Dwight Louis Murphy, and mother, the former Margaret Howe, took him back to their home in the nearby town of Fulton. Mark was their third child: the eldest, Dwight Jr., was then aged four, his sister Sheila three. The last child, younger brother Richard Kevin, came along in 1940.

Then a small mill town, Fulton is on the banks of the Oswego River, just 11 miles south of Lake Ontario, which forms the USA's border with Canada. Mark's childhood home still stands, three blocks east of the Oswego, at 351 Highland Street. Built around 1900, it's a substantial grey weatherboarded dwelling in the typical New England style. When the Murphys lived there, it was painted white with green shutters. Its 5,000 square foot lot certainly provided space enough for Dwight, Margaret and all four kids.

Mark always referred to his family as "Scots Irish." By that he meant that despite their Irish name, they were not Catholics but Protestants, with a strong presence in Fulton's Methodist church – particularly its music: Dwight Sr., a trained singer, was choir director. Not only did Mark's parents, uncles, aunts, brothers and sister all put on their church robes and sing together each Sunday, but his grandmother played the organ until arthritis forced her to quit. Afterwards his aunt, Mary Woodruff, took over the job, and carried on doing it for the next 40 years.

Family tradition has it that the Murphys came originally from Ballycastle on the northern tip of Ireland. During the Great Famine, in which a million died of starvation, a million more emigrated, nearly all of them to Canada and the USA. Several members of the Murphy family fled the country and immigrated to North America. Among them was Mark's great-grandfather James Murphy, then aged 14. Along with James's father Patrick Murphy, then 40, and Ann and Mary Murphy, aged 20 and 18 respectively, James sailed from Liverpool aboard the ship *Abeona*, arriving in New York on

The Murphy family home at 351 Highland Street, Fulton, NY.

December 7, 1849. Also in the group was ten-year-old Althea Nichol, the future Mrs. James Murphy.

There had been a strong Irish immigrant community in the Fulton area since the construction of the Erie Canal began in 1817. Like the Murphys, many of the laborers engaged in building the canal were Protestants from the north of Ireland, about five thousand of whom had recently arrived in the United States.

About 20 years after their arrival, James and Althea apparently lived in Stamford, Connecticut, where their youngest son Richard D. Murphy was born. As an adult, Richard lived in Worcester, Massachusetts, where he eventually became president of the Worcester Manufacturing Company. The family also helped found the Bethel Baptist Church. Richard was superintendent at Bethel, before moving to Fulton to lead the Methodist congregation there.

In the early years of the 20th century, despite its modest size, Fulton was a thriving manufacturing center, the base for Nestlé, Birds Eye, Hunter ceiling fans, Miller beer and the American Woolen Mills – the largest woolen mill in the USA. As a result, most residents managed to cling on to their jobs, even during the Depression. In 1936, the *New York Sun* published a lengthy article describing Fulton, its residents and the strong local economy: it was headlined "Fulton, the City the Great Depression Missed."

Mark's father Dwight, the son of Richard D. Murphy, attended Clark University, near Boston, to study law, and after graduating duly entered the legal profession. By June 1941, he was an assistant county attorney. Four years later, soon after the Second World War had ended in Europe, he was sent to Germany to serve as an assistant judge at the Nuremberg Trials. Later, as city attorney, he represented Fulton in legal cases, and was extremely proud that he had successfully sued the state of New York on two occasions.

Despite Mark's self-identification as Scots Irish, the other half of him was of solid English descent. Online census records show that his mother Margaret's family, the Howes, is one of the oldest in the USA. According to these records, their patriarch – the appropriately named Abraham Howe – embarked with a group of other Puritan settlers from Devon, England. He is recorded as living in Marlborough, Massachusetts, soon after 1630. The records describe him as a "farmer, having bought 6,000 acres from the Indians," and that in 1660 "the name of Abraham Howe appears among the proprietors [landowners] of the town," where he opened a pub, the Howe Tavern. The family lived in Marlborough for five more generations until at some point during the early nineteenth century they moved to Granby, a short distance from Fulton.

It seems that the Howes had always been well-to-do. "My mother's family resembled *The Magnificent Ambersons*," Mark Murphy told one interviewer. The term "pillar of the community" hardly seems adequate to describe Mark's maternal grandfather, John Harroun Howe: in 1887 he went into the paper business and was highly successful, buying the Granby mill, on the west bank of the Oswego, and running it for over a quarter of a century. He belonged to the Fulton Rotary Club, the Pleasant Point Club, and the Oswego Country Club; he served on the local board of education, was director of Emerick Park Association and superintendent of the First Methodist Sunday School. Around 1900 he married May Rugg, known to Mark's generation as "Nana" Howe.

At some point in the late 1920s May, who was the church organist, advertised for a choir director. When Dwight Louis Murphy showed up, she was shrewd enough to invite him back to the house for Sunday dinner: there were, after all, four unmarried daughters at home. It was Margaret, the eldest, who caught the young lawyer's eye, and it wasn't long before they were married.

In 1929, the year after the birth of their first child, Dwight Louis Jr., Wall Street crashed. The resultant Depression may have left Fulton relatively unscathed, but the same could not be said for the Howe family fortunes. John Harroun Howe owned two mills outright and another in partnership with two other businessmen. Panicked by the Crash and its aftermath, all of them lost money. Howe went bankrupt, and was forced to downsize to a more modest property on the other side of Voorhees Park. But at least there was now a lawyer in the family to take on the job of administering the bankruptcy. And despite his financial woes, John Howe managed to hang on to the summer home he'd bought at Fair Haven on Lake Ontario for May and the children. None of the Howe kids were known by their given names – Margaret ("Markey"), Elizabeth ("Betty"), Katherine ("Katie"), Priscilla ("Sally"), and little Elliott ("Billy"), the youngest.

Fair Haven (present population 741, according to the 2013 census) overlooks Little Sodus Bay, a small inlet off the Lake. Fringed by mature trees and timber buildings, it's ideal for sailing and other water sports. Murphy family 8mm home movies are full of sailing boats, motorboats, people swimming, diving, water-skiing, or just relaxing on the grass; there are many dogs and many children. The fuzzy magenta-tinted footage is dominated by shots of Dwight and Margaret's own children – smiling, bespectacled Sheila, Dwight Jr. and little blond Kevin playing on the concrete jetty, as the family dog swims past. We see the kids climbing trees and marking out the tennis court with a paint roller; a small flock of Canada geese splashes down near the shore. In later footage people clamber into a camper van, off on some road trip; Margaret's sisters Sally and Betty play tennis; and there's a boat full of people, *The Singing M*, towing a water-skier.

So where was little Mark in all this activity? In one of the home movies a caption appears: *Mark gives us an eye full*. There's a brief close-up of a shy kid on a boat, nestling against his mother, trying to hide. He pulls a face at the camera. And that's it.

"I was not the mover and shaker of the family," Mark said years later. "My father was, first of all. I never met a man with so much frantic energy. He wanted to learn everything and he practically did... If [something] was broken he could fix it. He learned how to remake sailboats and made my grandfather's lake yacht to sleep six people... Beyond that he knew gun craft and could go into the woods and bang, bang, bang the pigeons, you know. He crammed more into that life than most people do if they live until they're ninety."

Dwight Sr., known in the family as "DL", was a hunter and fisherman, and loved to take the boys camping. Shy, sensitive Mark didn't like camping and would ask if he could stay at home, but his father would insist. So Mark would take a sketch pad and slide off into the woods to draw or read. Of the three boys it was Kevin, the youngest, who ended up spending the most time with DL, sometimes accompanying him on fishing trips to Canada.

Father and middle son could not have been more different. People loved DL's openness and energy, always outdoors, holding parties for friends on his boat. But Mark found his dad intimidating, while DL found his son a source of embarrassment and frustration.

The one thing they did have in common was a fine singing voice. At Clark University DL had been a member of the Varsity Quartet, and a soloist in the glee club. He would grab any opportunity to sing in public, even if it was just the National Anthem at sporting events. Speaking of his own vocal prowess, Mark said, "The voice is my father's voice. I inherited it... he supplied the vocals but he didn't have any concept of jazz. He was a concert singer. He had done the old Chautauqua circuit around New York way back when. I'm talking around 1910 – around those days." Mark was able to pinpoint the exact quality of his father's singing voice: it was, he said, almost identical to the one the audience hears in John Huston's film *The Dead*, as Anjelica Huston comes down the stairs and, off camera, an Irish tenor starts singing "The Last Rose of Summer".

Mark must have unconsciously absorbed his father's experiences: the travelling, the singing and the charisma were the template for his own future life. Although he told one interviewer that he rebelled as a child against the whole idea of singing, he more often said that he started at the age of four or five. "My grandmother, my Nana, used to call me the soprano God of the bath. I used to sit on the potty for hours singing."

On Sunday afternoons Grandfather Howe would make the kids listen to the Metropolitan opera on the radio: Milton Cross with *The Firestone Hour*. This may explain Mark's apparent antipathy to opera in later life. It was the women in his family who really inspired him to sing jazz. Unlike DL, Margaret was a jazz fan, a 1920s flapper and jitterbugger at heart, who would head down to Syracuse whenever Duke Ellington came to town. Once, when Mark was old enough, she took him with her, pointing out trombonist Tyree Glenn, and saying, "Don't you see, son – he's talking to you!"

Sexual equality may have been largely unknown to the wider world at the time, but it was the norm in the Howe family: some of the girls went to Bryn Mawr, the elite women's college on the outskirts of Philadelphia. Betty later joined the staff of the Memorial Cancer Hospital in New York, then studied at Oxford, after which she worked as a doctor in London. Margaret attended Shipley School in Pennsylvania, then studied music at Columbia University in New York, and taught it in Wilmington, N.C., for a year or two.

Margaret was a small, rather reserved woman, whom some found lacking in warmth. In Mark's opinion she bore a striking physical resemblance to the Duchess of Windsor, the American divorcée at the center of the UK's 1936 abdication crisis. It was Margaret who had to deal with Mark's childhood traumas. Her son was so shy and sensitive at school that he would sometimes start sobbing uncontrollably in class, and his teacher would have to call Margaret to come and sit with him until he calmed down. Mark preferred spending time with his mother, rather than playing rough and tumble with the other boys.

Like most of his generation and social class, DL had high expectations of his sons and believed it was his duty to toughen them up. As future breadwinners they were expected to learn the masculine skills of hunting, fishing and sailing. When he returned home from the horrors of the Nuremberg Trials, Dwight was furious to find his middle son was still such a milquetoast, a timid little fellow who would as a younger child hide behind the sofa while the rest of the family talked. According to Mark this became the source of 'heartrending conflicts' with his father.

Summers and weekends at Fair Haven provided some relief to the family tensions. Margaret would tune the radio to CBC from Toronto – *1010 Swing Club* and *Jazz Unlimited* with Dick MacDougal, and Bing Whittaker's *Small Types Club*. Back in Fulton, Mark's aunt Mary, the church organist, also played in a swing combo. "That's where I learned most of the early gems of music," Mark told an interviewer. "My aunt played a little piano and she showed me the basics on 'Lullaby of Rhythm'." As a child he would ask her to play popular jazz pieces over and over again.

One day, when Mark was about 14, his uncle Bill, Margaret's brother, beckoned him out to the porch and played him a 78rpm record of Art Tatum's "Humoresque". Young Murphy was transfixed, just as Charlie Parker had been on first hearing Tatum's harmonic ingenuity at the piano. "If you remember, he plays [it] sort-of semi-classical first… and then he swings it in the middle. It absolutely fascinated me and I've been hooked ever since," Mark recalled.

Before long, he was regularly riding his bike across the park to listen to his uncle's other jazz records – Benny Goodman, Stan Kenton, and June Christy. Meanwhile older brother Dwight Jr. had started buying records too, by Ella Fitzgerald and others. Mark investigated further, listening obsessively to the radio and discovering Arthur Prysock, Lee Wiley, Anita O'Day, Sarah Vaughan, Billy Eckstine and Dick Haymes.

But the singers he loved the most were Nat King Cole and Peggy Lee. Cole, popularly remembered today as a silky 1950s balladeer, had come to prominence in the early 1940s as a radical jazz pianist who, as his biographer Daniel Epstein observed, invented "advanced voicings and harmonic substitutions of a kind and quality that some of the early boppers, even Charlie Parker, were using only sporadically or tentatively at the time." Young Mark Murphy was absorbing as much from modern instrumental jazz as he was from vocalists. He first heard Peggy Lee's "Don't Smoke in Bed" on the car radio aged 16, in 1948. "You had to wonder, what were these songs about? Peggy liked to do that to people; she wanted to be serious, to think of herself as a far-out artist. She was the first singer of her level to go into slightly abstract songs."

Mark began to find like-minded friends with whom to share his new-found love of jazz. "There were three or four of us in Fulton at the time… Sometimes at night the sounds would drift up to us, starting at about midnight. We'd listen as long as we could, and then fall asleep, and whoever fell asleep last would wake up the other one – 'Well, I stayed up til 4 a.m.!' So it was kind of an exciting time in that kiddie sense."

Bitten by the jazz bug, emotionally connected to the music, and surrounded by singers and musicians in his own family, Mark was performing in public by his second year at Fulton High School. It was only a matter of time before he began to consider a professional singing career.

But drama also fascinated him. "There was a travelling show that came through town, when I was just a kid… I can't remember, but it was either sponsored by the Kiwanis or the Rotarians or someone. Some of the roles

One of Mark's first gigs in Fulton.

were open to local people." Mark applied for and won a small speaking part in it. "The thrill of being able to say a few lines and get a response from the audience was incredible. That's when it bit me."

Back at school, he was soon being given solos to perform. At first it was simply a matter of listening and copying what he heard. "Everything I have is Yours" by Burton Lane and Harold Adamson was one early favorite. Perhaps relieved that his son was finally taking an interest in something, DL made an effort to help, buying Mark a little 66-key piano, at which he would practice at least two hours every morning, learning tunes. "I still remember more of those early learnings than something I learned yesterday," he told Marian McPartland in 1999.

Although he usually told people he'd never had any voice training, at other times Murphy said he had received some singing lessons, but didn't enjoy them. "My father started me out and then I went to voice teachers who gave me half-ass opera training as it was the only way they knew how to teach."

One of Mark's school friends was Jim Galusha, a trumpet player. Together with another friend, Phil Lambrinos, who played clarinet, and with Mark on piano, they set up an informal jazz group. The three of them would practice together in each other's homes. One evening, in the living room at Galusha's house on Cayuga Street, the boys enlisted Jim's sister Helen as their "canary". The tune for the evening was "Sentimental Journey". "Somehow," recalled another sister, Nancy, "I have no idea how – they got hooked into the tiny Fulton radio station and the next-door neighbors called to say they were listening to them ON THE RADIO. Much excitement. Then one of the guys had the bright idea to lift up the window blinds and wave at our neighbors and proclaimed what they had was – TELEVISION. Hilarity all 'round."

Mark's brother Dwight Jr. had taken up the double bass and put together a six-piece dance band. Mark would sometimes sit in, playing piano and singing. One day the regular pianist was ill, and Mark was asked to sub for him. Before long he was playing gigs with the band, and – judging by the dancing – went down well whenever he sang. According to a handwritten note from the group's original pianist Alan de Line, the other members of Dwight's group were Fred Greco and Leonard Youmans on tenor saxophones, Jac Petino (or Retino) on alto sax, Hugh Burrett on trumpet and a young man called Dutch on drums, with Mark as the vocalist. "[We] joined the musicians' union, and played for many of the high school dances. Most of us were members of the Fulton High School Marching Band. We played mostly big band classics," recalled de Line.

A little bop scene was flourishing in Fulton. In later years Mark remembered standing in a music store downtown, listening to records by thrilling new artists like George Shearing. The hipness of Murphy and his friends was unusual, even then. "You'd be surprised at what a little town like Fulton had for a cultural life. We had a small nucleus of musicians, some in my brother's swing band. This is in a town of 15,000 people. We'd gather in one of the two record stores [and] listen to Charlie Parker and cool stuff." Murphy was already developing those abstruse tastes in music that would place him outside the mainstream in later years. But he also learned Ella Fitzgerald's version of "Lady be Good," "and then I went through a real heavy voice period of Sarah Vaughan and Billy Eckstine in my high school days. Then for years I didn't listen to anybody but Peggy Lee."

The once desperately shy little boy now couldn't get enough of the attention he received whenever he got up on stage. The uniform of the nascent Syracuse bohemian scene was black shirts and dark glasses, and the centre of it all was a club called the Casablanca, near Clinton Square, owned by Teddy Genovese. Teddy's sister Annamarie was wheelchair-bound, having contracted polio soon after birth. She also had an exquisite voice, and soon the 16-year-old Mark began singing Billy Eckstine-Sarah Vaughan duets with her. Poignantly, in the light of Mark's sexuality, Annamarie would often joke about how the two of them were engaged to be married.

He and his friend George Tortorelli once entered a singing contest at Suburban Park hosted by Syracuse radio talk host Jim Deline. They both sang, but lost to an eight-year old girl. At weekends Mark would continue working with his brother's band in Fulton and the Lake Ontario resorts, but even then he travelled as far as Buffalo, to clubs like the Zanzibar and the Royal Arms.

Years later he told the *Buffalo News* that he had learned to work around his shyness. "If you're not naturally gregarious, you have to invent another personality to deal with this work," he said, "and so you have to be careful that you're not always performing, in the performance mode. So sometimes I am back in the shadows. In my lyrics, there are references to being in the shadows, coming out of the shadows. That's what it means. That some people are just born to be in shadow land."

In 1949, after graduating from high school, now certain he had found his vocation in life, Mark enrolled in the Bachelor of Science in Speech and Dramatic Arts course at Syracuse University. Drama was his main focus. During his four years at college he studied everything from Shakespeare to musical reviews, and acted in summer stock productions of *Song of Norway*, *Guys and Dolls*, and Gilbert and Sullivan operettas. And whatever he may later have claimed about his lack of formal tuition, classical singing was also a part of the course. But for years afterwards, the notion of acting appealed just as much to him as singing.

While at Syracuse he would sit in with local jazz musicians, playing piano and singing. "The bop musicians liked my sense of rhythm, which is pure Celtic-Irish. They asked me up to sing because I swung!" He expanded on this idea in another interview: "You see, it's my Celtic roots that give me that ability. Like, Annie Ross was the timekeeper of Lambert-Hendricks-Ross. Have you ever seen a Scottish marching band? Well, they get out there, these plain-looking people, and they get a hypnotic... It's intense! There's very deep Celtic roots in the formings of jazz, too."

Murphy realized in retrospect that he had come on the jazz scene during a period of transition: younger audiences were beginning to turn away from big band music in the Stan Kenton and Woody Herman style. He saw himself the last of the "developed" singers. As time went on he came to love the bluesy style of Joe Williams, who sang with Lionel Hampton's Orchestra in the 1940s, and with Count Basie in the 50s. He learned about ballads as well as bop and blues, particularly the way Peggy Lee sang them. "I send out a beam of attention, like radar. I learned this from Peggy Lee. I used to watch her on Steve Allen's show. Peggy would sit there very still; she never took her eyes off the camera. You'd feel as though she was singing just to you. I see inside the song I'm singing as though I'm watching in a movie, always drawing the picture with my words and sounds. This is art."

One night in 1953, he was singing at the dimly-lit Embassy Club on Harrison Street in downtown Syracuse, whose clientele were mostly black. Halfway through a scat solo, he noticed Sammy Davis Jr. lounging in the doorway, tapping his foot and clearly enjoying the performance. Afterwards the star complimented him on his singing, and mentioned that he was currently appearing at the Three Rivers Inn, between Moyer's Corner and Phoenix. Would Murphy like to come along and sing a tune?

He would, and he did. The approval of a legend like Davis confirmed in Murphy's mind that he was on the right track, and the contact eventually led to him to TV host Steve Allen. There are many variations to this story. In some he claimed that the night after he was invited to sing at Sammy Davis's gig, he was watching *The Steve Allen Show* on TV, and Sammy was a guest. In other versions, it was some time afterwards. At any rate, sensing a tenuous opportunity, Murphy wrote to Allen and told him he had recently met Davis 'and he likes my work'. Allen sent an encouraging response. In an earlier version of the story, Murphy said he sent a demo recording he had made to Davis, asking him to play it to Allen, and the exchange developed into a correspondence between Murphy and Allen.

After graduating from Syracuse, Mark tried to get his professional singing career started, securing an engagement in Magog, Quebec, as the pianist in a trio. "It was a disaster. The other two musicians didn't like my playing, and the feeling was mutual. They were worst two musicians I ever worked with." Temporarily defeated, he ended up back in Syracuse, selling Lionel toy trains in a department store, and managing a doughnut shop. Straight jobs. Jobs he hated. It was time for a re-think.

Mark (left), with his mother and brother Kevin, early 1950s (courtesy Kathy Hinkhouse)

2 Dues-Paying Days

Mark's brother Dwight, who had now acquired the handle "Doc", had been a postgraduate student at the Manhattan School of Music in New York since 1953. He covered his tuition fees between semesters by playing bass in a band on the cruise ship Independence, which plied a course between New York and Naples, Italy. Doc, an accomplished sailor from his summers in Fair Haven, was one of the few musicians on board who never got seasick.

For Mark, the dull days selling toys were sheer frustration. Inspiring music was all around him: Peggy Lee's seminal 10-inch album *Black Coffee* had come out the previous year. Shortly afterwards came "Bouquet of Blues", which became "a kind of hit among the bopsters and the hipsters," he said, finding in it an echo of his own melancholy. "Peggy was the girl of great regret."

In February 1954, when he could stand the drudgery of life in Syracuse no longer, he decided to quit the shop job and join Doc in New York to try his luck again at acting or singing. Despite, or perhaps because of, their very different personalities, Mark and Doc were close. Sheila Jordan described Doc as being very much the big brother, "a warm and intelligent human being, but very straight ahead – the total opposite of Mark."

The brothers shared a tiny cold-water flat on 11th Avenue near the cruise ship dock, for which Mark contributed the princely sum of $8 per month. The third member of this cosy ménage was a trumpet-player called Little Willie Waymans, who slept on the windowsill. A number of Russians lived in the same building. When Margaret came down from Fulton to visit her sons and asked the cab driver to let her out, he said: "Are you sure you want to go in there, lady?"

The apartment was at the northwest edge of Greenwich Village, home to artists, poets, musicians and wannabes. It had a character all of its own. South of 14th Street, Manhattan's grid system of streets and avenues breaks down; the roads have names instead of numbers. Down towards Battery Park on the southern tip, some of them even curve. Concrete skyscrapers gave way to smaller brick houses. In short, the Village then felt less like the rest of Manhattan and more like the Europe from which most of New York City's founders had arrived.

Among the hang-outs of choice were Chumley's in Bedford Street, a restaurant-bar that didn't put its name on a sign outside; Louis', off Sheridan Square, where you walked down a small flight of steps and drank at the bar or sat a small table and ordered the house special of spaghetti and meatballs with tomato and lettuce for sixty-five cents; the White Horse Tavern on Hudson Street, a gathering place for writers and those who thought of themselves as underdogs and rebels, where you could learn and sing songs of Irish rebellion, and the beer came in pints, just as they did back in the old country.

Once settled in, Mark set off in search of acting or singing work, but soon found it wasn't so easy to escape the sort of day jobs he'd left behind in Syracuse. The rent still had to be paid, so he waited tables, worked on Wall Street as an office junior and in hotels as a bellhop. Whenever he could he boarded the subway up to Minton's Playhouse in Harlem which, although past its bebop prime, still hosted the top jazz stars of the day. Murphy entered the singing contests a little further north at the Apollo Theatre, twice winning second place. He appeared with the Gilbert & Sullivan Light Opera Company. At one point he even won a part in a television opera called *Casey at the Bat*, and this led to acting in summer stock in Wallingford, Connecticut.

But the competition for roles was intense, and after a while he decided to concentrate instead on jazz singing and playing. He started hustling for work as a singer-pianist in East Side bars, "But that's a lonely life, baby," he told the writer James Gavin. He began sitting in at jazz clubs and after-hours joints. "I was playing piano for myself, and I don't play well, never did, but I could get a few gigs. Most of the time I got paid. One time the guy said, 'Come here a minute,' and he gave me some money and said, 'I'm going to take you to the railroad station.' I was sitting there in a tuxedo, and he just left me there, and I had to wait all night for a train. So once in a while that would happen. But New York was a pretty brutal town in those days. You know the movie *Sweet Smell of Success*?" (The film painted 1950s New York as a cynical, dog-eat-dog world.) "It was those days.... I used to play at a joint called The Toast, which was over on First Avenue a little bit up from the Living Room, one of those rooms where you could sit in easy chairs. Those were big then, with piano-singers and piano trios."

Asked many years later about the cloud of melancholy that seemed to follow him around, he said, "It goes with my jazz territory. I trace it back to my dues-paying days in New York City where I knew nothing, except that the music inside me had to come out... I walked around Manhattan like a child with his nose pressed against the window of some fabulous restaurant. I saw Frank Sinatra's impossibly blue eyes... Then I saw the blue eyes again – ice blue, ocean blue – on Maureen Stapleton on Eighth Avenue. Searching for an apartment, I ran into Paul Newman. There were those same eyes."

Stuck at the bottom of the jazz food chain, he was at least living the life. "I can remember so many things, like the time I was walking down 54ᵗʰ Street when I did my year as a night clerk at the Gotham Hotel, screwing up all that typing. And I saw Lena [Horne] and Billy Strayhorn walking along hand in hand and I was walking along 51ˢᵗ Street another day and Billie Holiday came bursting out of a bar like giving this guy hell she was with and things like that. I got there just in time to see the end of 52ⁿᵈ Street and the beginnings of Birdland."

Though it was tough for a newcomer like Murphy, the mid-1950s must have seemed like the ideal time to forge a career in jazz. It was, after all, the dominant genre of popular music, and singers were enjoying unprecedented popularity. But in other ways his timing was a little off. Too late for the big swing bands, he was also too early for rock and roll, and bebop singing was (and remained) out on the margin, thinly inhabited and way too niche for the mainstream audience. Nevertheless the established singers, most of whom had started out with big bands, had succeeded in becoming mainstream stars, their sales boosted by the popularity of the vinyl albums which were now replacing shellac 78rpm records. Most of the music that sold well was jazz-influenced pop rather than jazz per se, but it was enthusiastically embraced by radio stations, by upmarket magazines like *Esquire, Life* and *Playboy*, and even by the new medium of television, which hosted shows like Art Ford's *Jazz Party* on the East Coast and, on the West Coast, Bobby Troup's *Stars of Jazz* series.

If Mark had learned anything from his father, it was the virtue of persistence. In New York he was buying sheet music, building his repertoire. This was almost certainly how he came to know the verses to so many of the songs on which he built his later career. Gradually he learned the difference between pure jazz singing and the more showbiz conventions of Broadway and cabaret gigs.

There was live work for jazz singers and musicians at venues like The Embers, the Royal Roost, Famous Door and Kelly's Stable. Even for singers without a gig there was the Amato Opera House, a converted movie theatre where they could perform to the accompaniment of a piano, and audience members passed the hat. Then there was Marie's Crisis Café, on Grove Street, and the Café Bohemia on Barrow Street, where Miles Davis and Art Blakey sometimes appeared.

Another club was the Page Three on 7ᵗʰ Avenue near the Village Vanguard. It was here that Murphy first met his lifelong friend, the singer Sheila Jordan. "God was he handsome!" Jordan told her biographer Ellen Johnson. "I'll never forget when he got up on the little bandstand and sang 'Willow Weep for Me'. I was so impressed with his singing and I thought he really had heart and sang from his soul. There weren't many male jazz singers around at that time, at least not the way Mark sang."

Murphy and Jordan began meeting regularly at the Page Three. "It was usually a variety club, but on Mondays the whole scene was jazz. At eight, when the jazz band came on, the vibe changed and the people changed. Even their clothes changed. It was part of this wonderful mystery." Murphy gradually came to know other singers who hung out there, including Ernestine Anderson and Morgana King. They only got paid $10 a night but it was essential experience, learning new tunes and discussing ideas for song arrangements.

One of the club's habitués was the eccentric gay artist Helen Meyer, the Toulouse Lautrec of Greenwich Village, whose murals adorned the walls of the Page Three. For some reason Meyer had decided to rename herself Junior Morrow. "She was a walking show," Mark later recalled, "Jet black hair piled high; theatrical masks of cosmetics like a second skin; body to die for; and a *rap* that kept me and a lot of others in stitches. Not jokes, but just stories and Damon Runyan-esque tales about life… in the 'old' Village that we all loved."

Ever since moving to New York, Mark had yearned to record. "I was a small-town guy, very shy but single-minded as hell – it took me three years to get a record contract… I just learned by doing." With the help of his brother Doc, he made a four-track demo and began hawking it around the record companies.

In the liner notes to *Meet Mark Murphy*, he relates the painstaking process of making contacts in the business. "My older brother Dwight was playing in the Fort Dix army band when I first came to New York in 1954. A friend of his introduced me to Mrs. Elsie Kirk, mother of Lisa Kirk, who seems to thrive on helping to get kids started in show business, and she introduced me to her niece Polly Magaro, singer and actress, who introduced me to publicist Richard Hoffman, who introduced me to vocal coach Joric Livingston, who introduced me to jazzman Tony Scott, who introduced me to *Downbeat* music critic Nat Hentoff, who introduced me to Monte Kay and Pete Kameron, my managers, who introduced me to Milt Gabler [Decca's head of A&R], who introduced me to Decca and my first records."

Decca liked the demo and signed Mark, deciding to promote him as a light entertainer rather than a jazz singer. "They were concerned, first of all, with hiding the word jazz and putting tracks in that they hoped would lift out of singles *[sic]*. Other than that, you could do pretty much what you want. It's funny, they called me up, 'You got a record deal.' I said, my God, what should I record. So I just picked a bunch of tunes that I like. I might have done it by instrumentation. I probably would have thought in terms of what will fit the big band thing."

The story he often told of three years' hard labor before anyone gave him a break is undercut by intriguing evidence that he was recording for Decca as early as 1955. According to Tom Lord's definitive *Jazz Discography*, Murphy cut 12 tunes with an orchestra at Decca that year, a session that was given a catalogue number, but which has never seen the light of day. The tracks included a very early version of one of Murphy's favorite songs, "Detour

Ahead", and standards and pop tunes he never recorded again, including "Isn't It a Pity", "There is No Greater Love" and "Try a Little Tenderness". Even discounting these unreleased recordings, the 'three year' chronology doesn't quite stack up: Murphy began making his first album in June 1956, considerably less than three years after his arrival in the Big Apple.

Whatever the truth of the matter, one major attraction of a Decca contract, from Mark's point of view, was that in 1952 Milt Gabler had signed Peggy Lee. Gabler enjoyed a big reputation. As well as Lee, he had recorded Jack Teagarden, Bud Freeman, Pee Wee Russell, Lester Young, Coleman Hawkins, Edmond Hall, Hot Lips Page and Billie Holiday. He was also working with an unknown band, Bill Haley and his Comets, having recently produced their single "Rock Around the Clock". Gabler seemed genuinely excited by Mark's potential, comparing him to Mel Tormé and predicting that his impact would "scare Frank Sinatra". As a producer, Gabler was relatively hands-off, trusting his acts to know what they wanted: Murphy said he "just wanted me to sing the way I sing."

He teamed with arranger Ralph Burns, a bebop pianist who had been working with Woody Herman's big band since 1944, and who later became a successful composer for film and television. According to Murphy's old friend, the singer and pianist Charles Cochran, "Ralph was very versatile... He was a jazz wunderkind [from] when he was in his teens." Burns was certainly a hipster: a marijuana smoker since the 1930s, he was also gay, and a close friend of Billy Strayhorn, another closet homosexual. When Gene Lees asked Burns years later why he and Strayhorn were so secretive about their orientation, he said, "In those years, if Billy or I had ever admitted it, our careers would have been over immediately." Lees suggested to him that jazz musicians were likely to be more tolerant of homosexuality than the public at large. "No, they're not," said Burns, "They're far less tolerant. Billy and I would have been ruined if it had been known."

Mark Murphy was very particular about his musical arrangements, never wanting to place this aspect of the music entirely in the hands of others. He claimed that Ralph Burns made no changes at all to his own arrangements of "Fascinatin' Rhythm", "Exactly Like You" and "A Nightingale Sang in Berkeley Square".

The first recordings for *Meet Mark Murphy* were made on June 26, 1956. The album opens with "Fascinatin' Rhythm". Mark's voice bounces along in a light and effortless baritone, with clear diction on a song which, as its title reminds us, makes demands on a singer's sense of rhythm. The second time through the head he starts playing with the words – juggling the rhythm of the lines and finishing with a bit of scat on the fade-out. It's clear that, technically at least, everything came very easily to the 24-year-old Mark Murphy. And on Jule Styne's "I Guess I'll Hang My Tears Out to Dry" and "Irresistible You" he demonstrates his early mastery of the ballad.

There was no question that he had the chops. But there were also some signs of trouble to come. Here and there he makes the mistake of overdoing it: on "A Nightingale Sang in Berkeley Square" he shows off his impressive range in the verse, plunging from E-flat above middle C to A-flat an octave and a half below. But his operatic technique detracts from whatever sincerity was possible with the song's rather Edwardian sentiments. Gabler and Burns might have advised him against the inclusion of "I'm A Circus", with its excruciating lyric, and "Two Ladies in de Shade of de Banana Tree", complete with Murphy's attempt at a "humorous" Caribbean accent.

In retrospect, there is no consistent style on this, his debut album. Was Mark Murphy a romantic young heart-throb, or a dizzy young dude about town, or a family entertainer? Whatever persona he thought he was projecting, he often seems reluctant just to sing a good song straight. Nor were the album's title and cover much help to the casual record-store browser who wanted to know which Mark Murphy he was meeting. Inadvertently, the sleeve hints at the shy, awkward reality behind the confident-sounding hipster you heard in the grooves: Mark poses in front of a black, slightly crumpled backdrop, one foot up on a stool, gazing anxiously off-camera.

Radio host Michael Bourne later told Murphy he hardly recognized him from the cover picture because his hair was naturally straight. Murphy told him he'd had it permed. But this wasn't true, and the evasion was one he maintained until he was an old man. "I believe he was wearing a toupée on the cover of the first Decca album," said Murphy's friend James Gavin, "because he had lost his hair very, very early. He was bald, man! He was the proverbial billiard ball, and just had a little tiny fringe of hair round the sides."

And what was the reason for the subtitle, *The Singing M*? It was said to have been Gabler's idea, perhaps to invest Murphy with some sort of identifiable trademark. Part of the image problem was Decca's unease with jazz as a genre. "Their main concern was not to sell it as a jazz record," Murphy explained, "And yet, the first time I ever heard myself on radio was on this station in Chicago. They said, 'Here's a new jazz singer, Mark Murphy.' So there you were."

Nonetheless, on release *Meet Mark Murphy* was well received by the record trade. *Billboard* reported: "Young Murphy – a 'Deejay Programming Spotlite' a few weeks ago – sings up a swing storm on his first Decca LP, which should get plenty of jockey attention. Relaxed, distinctive phrasing in a highly stylized jazz vein with unusually tasteful backing by Ralph Burns' ork. Two sides ("Fascinatin' Rhythm" and "Exactly Like You") are already out as singles, and the rest spotlight equally good show material." Elsewhere *Billboard* commented: "Murphy sings with a modern jazz feeling, and like an instrument. His unorthodox phrasing and sophisticated manner will register especially with hip deejays."

Before the year was out, Mark recorded another 12 tracks which have never been released, including "Easy to Love", "Isn't It a Pity?", and "I'm Glad There is You".

The release of his first album meant more to him than simply marking the beginning of his career as a professional singer; it showed his father that he could make his way in the world, that he was tough enough to support himself after all. Up until now, DL had remained baffled by his son's style of music. "I used to see him sometimes," Mark said. "I'd do a gig at Birdland and look down and there was my dad. Later on, I realized he was trying to figure out what the hell I was singing. He didn't understand jazz like my mother did."

All that changed with the release of *Meet Mark Murphy*. In December, 1956, Mark was honored by the Kiwanis, Rotary, Lions and other civic groups at the Fulton Chamber of Commerce for the achievement of making his first album. DL is missing from the local newspaper photograph, despite the presence of Nana Howe, Mark's mother, his sister Sheila and her husband, his uncle Bill, aunt Katie, brother Kevin and aunt Mary. The next day Mark was to be found signing copies of *Meet Mark Murphy* in the record section at Home Appliance on 1st Street.

Cuttings from the Oswego Valley News announcing the release of Meet Mark Murphy.

Whatever the reason for DL's absence that day, he seems to have accepted that his son had achieved something in life. "He was very thrilled because about the same time my first LP came out... they had the first decent hi-fi sets and he really enjoyed sitting next to it and listening to classical music, and when my record came on he was really thrilled and he sent it to his old voice teacher and it was very, very touching." And Dwight Sr. was certainly proud enough of his middle son to name a motor boat after him: *The Singing M*, a Chris Craft, featured in family home movies from the late 1950s, carrying family members around the lake near Fair Haven.

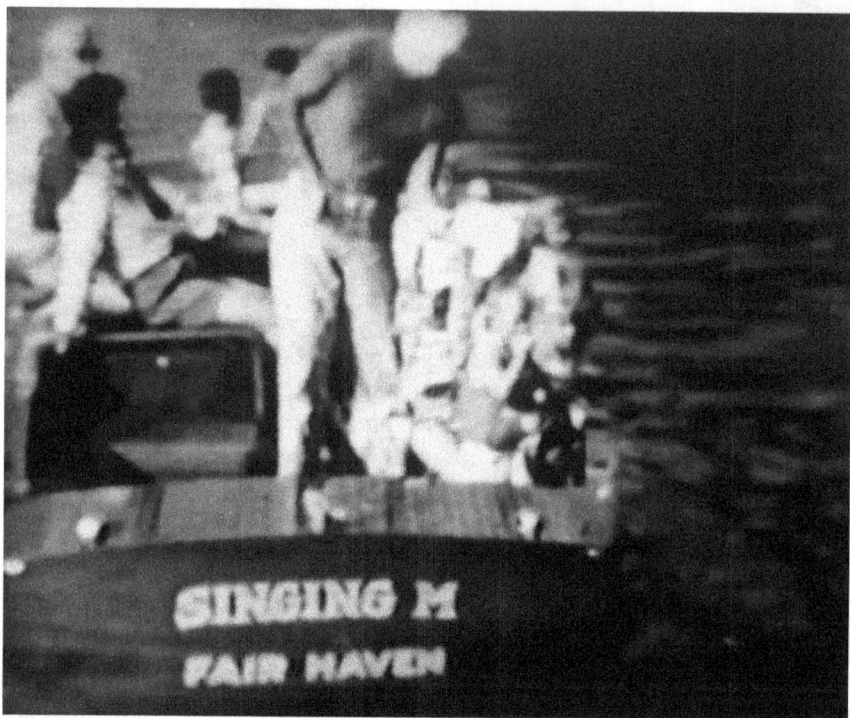

The Singing M, named after Murphy's debut album. The children include Kathy Hinkhouse, her sister Diane and cousin Nancy Jean Howe (video courtesy Allan Howe).

Unfortunately, sales of *Meet Mark Murphy* failed to take off. "I remember when my first record came out," he said. "Johnny Mathis and I were reviewed in the same issue of *Downbeat*. And now he's making millions..."

Mark was still learning his trade, particularly when it came to performing. Charles Cochran remembers seeing him on stage in 1957. "Although he was a wonderful singer, in person I thought he was a little bit stiff. He did not move very much."

On 23rd April, 1957, Mark was back in the studio to record his second album, *Let Yourself Go*, again with Burns and his orchestra, cutting "I Got Rhythm", "Taking a Chance on Love", and "T'ain't No Sin"; then, on 3rd May, "Ridin' High", "Crazy Rhythm", "Elmer's Tune", "The Lady in Red"; and on the 22nd, with a smaller ensemble, "Little Jazz Bird", "Robbins' Nest", "Pick Yourself Up", and "Lullaby in Rhythm"; and finally on the 15th, the title track. There was an additional session for the single "The Right Kind of Woman" and "Goodbye Baby" on 26th June. According to Mark, Doc played bass on some tracks.

The Mark Murphy of *Let Yourself Go* sounds a little more relaxed, less anxious to show off his versatility. It was another highly competent collection, the highlights including the Jerome Kern/Dorothy Fields tune "Pick Yourself Up", with a sweet guitar accompaniment to the verse; the old show tune "Crazy

Rhythm", which works well for a singer like Murphy, whose ear was always so attuned to the underlying nuances of the beat; and Vernon Duke's "Taking a Chance on Love", taken at a beautifully slow tempo, with a restrained rendition of the melody, despite an uncharacteristic off-key moment at 2:56.

Yet Murphy's ongoing image problem is painfully clear from the cover photo. This time looking more sophisticated in a sports jacket and tie, he lies atop a piano. Posed next to him are two slinky-looking females – a brunette with a knowing sidelong look, and a blonde with her hands on Mark's shoulders, apparently trying to get his attention. Murphy, looking straight at the camera, wears a panic-stricken expression, his outstretched hands suggesting helplessness. Given his sexuality, there may have been more truth in the photograph than anyone suspected at the time.

Billboard's review was lukewarm: "Uninhibited patter and scat singing by versatile Murphy. 'Elmer's Tune', 'T'ain't No Sin' and 'I Got Rhythm' are among the best, with discerning support by Ralph Burns' group. Fans will like." Decca's failure to release anything from the three further 12-track sessions recorded later that year may explain why Murphy left the label after only two albums.

He said he first met Bill Evans at around this time, at the Newport Jazz Festival. If true, it must have been either the one in July 1957, when Evans had a trio slot within Don Elliott's set, or the following year, by which time Evans had joined Miles Davis's band. Mark told an interviewer that when he arrived in New York he was eager to hear Miles perform, and also hoped to meet him. But we do not know when or in what circumstances Mark did finally meet Miles, only that "the eventual encounter with the notoriously prickly trumpeter was not a happy one."

Evans features in an apocryphal tale told by the Murphy family. The walls of Mark and Doc's apartment were originally painted black, so the brothers redecorated them in green and blue. One night, so the story goes, Mark played a gig with Evans (who later contributed to his *Rah* album). When Evans came to the apartment the next day to get paid, he noted the color scheme and wandered off muttering, "Hmmm, blue and green, blue and green..."

Doc was playing a gig up north at Lake Placid one night when a young woman approached him and asked if he could give her bass lessons. Her name was Nancy Purcell. In the event she only had two lessons, but by then they were dating, and by the Summer of 1957 Doc was asking Mark to be best man at their wedding, on 13th July. Doc moved out of the apartment, but Mark stayed on for another eight years.

One of the singers Mark came to know around this time was Dave Lambert, and it was at the latter's apartment on Cornelius Street that he first encountered Jon Hendricks. Lambert and Hendricks were planning to record an album of Basie tunes on which a choir would replace the trumpets, saxophones and trombones. It was the beginning of the experimental project that

Mark (right) is best man at his brother Doc's wedding to Nancy Purcell, July 1957 (courtesy Allan Howe)

eventually turned into *Sing a Song of Basie*, and Murphy was invited to join the choir.

To keep costs down, they recorded at night. As the charts were handed out, Lambert's professional backing singers took one look at the chord clusters, found their parts, and sang them straight off the page. Murphy realized as soon as they started that he was out of his depth. But Hendricks, who couldn't read music at all, recognized that Murphy was the only one who understood what they were trying to do: the others just didn't swing.

The choir idea was abandoned, and Lambert and Hendricks recorded all the voices themselves with Annie Ross, building them up in layers, in one of the first ever multi-track recordings.

On Saturday September 21, there was grim news from Fulton. Just two months after his eldest son's wedding, DL was dead. He had gone out hunting in nearby woods with 16-year-old Kevin, and blown his brains out with a shotgun. Mark rushed home, but found that no one wanted to talk about what had happened. As time went on, he came to believe that his father had been suffering from multiple sclerosis, and his death was a tragic accident, a result of visual or muscular degeneration. "His mind was just gone... He was an expert gunsman and woodsman. He would never have done it intentionally. His mind was affected, it just goes blank. You just become a vegetable, little by little."

Many years later, however, an alternative version of events emerged when Kevin Murphy, who had never discussed his suspicions with Doc, Mark or Sheila, finally told his wife Kate what had happened. According to this account, Dwight Sr. was not suffering from MS but had had a stroke. Any flickering light, such as candlelight, would cause him to have a seizure or a migraine, and he was terrified of having another stroke and becoming a helpless invalid.

On that fateful Saturday, there had been a change to the usual bird-shooting routine. Usually DL and Kevin would walk on opposite sides of a grove of trees. If either saw something he wanted to shoot at, he would yell "Fore!" The other person would yell "Here!" In this way they would know not to shoot in that direction and thereby avoid accidentally shooting the other person. Kevin heard a gunshot, but his father had not yelled 'Fore!' Realizing something was wrong, he began calling his father, and when there was no response, plunged into the brush to find him. He discovered Dwight lying dead with his brains strewn across the railroad tracks. Yet the shotgun's safety catch was in the on position.

Turning the incident over in his mind in the days that followed, Kevin finally concluded that it had been no accident: his father had committed suicide. The only explanation that seemed to make sense was that Dwight had been practicing pulling the trigger and the safety at the same time. The insurance company would not pay out in the event of a suicide; but if Dwight could make it look like an accident, his wife and family would get the money. The fact that the safety catch was on looked like proof, and it was sufficient for his desperate plan to work.

3 All the Bases Were Loaded

Sales for both *Meet Mark Murphy* and *Let Yourself Go* had been anemic, to say the least. Mark, still reeling from his father's violent death, felt the relationship with Decca had gone sour. He'd had enough of New York, and decided that relocating to the west coast would enable him to start again.

Accordingly, in 1958 he moved to Los Angeles, staying at the YMCA to save money while he looked, mostly in vain, for singing work. Instead what he found was a piano-playing gig with the notorious "insult comedian" Don Rickles. The engagement was at the Slate Brothers, a 100-seater nightclub owned by Jack, Henry and Sid Slate, a physical comedy act. Rickles had been booked after Lenny Bruce was banned for using offensive language. Being the pianist set Mark up as the nearest and most visible target for the comedian's barbs, and it marked a new low in his career. "It was ridiculous," he said. "Somehow I stuck it out. But after that, nothing."

Not quite nothing. Murphy was prone to dramatize his desperation in those years, often claiming that he couldn't afford to eat ("I starved to 149lbs in 58"). James Gavin, who interviewed him about this period in his life, considered this an exaggeration: Mark had, after all, made two well-received albums, and although they had not sold well, he was a bona fide recording artist with a major label. There were also plenty of jazz clubs in LA in those days, where he could have found enough singing work to avoid literal starvation.

And then there was television. Far from being ignored, Murphy made two appearances that year on the Channel 7 KABC series *Stars of Jazz*. This show is the story, in microcosm, of television's attitude toward this music: a few years earlier, ABC's executive in charge of programming, Selig J. Seligman, had found himself under pressure from several jazz enthusiasts on the staff to add a jazz show to the schedule. Not convinced that this would appeal to the great American public, Seligman resisted for a long time, but eventually, with great reluctance, gave in. He allowed producer Jimmie Baker to make four initial shows, but warned him there would be no money for writers or sets.

He could only commandeer a studio when it was not being used by another production, and would have only a skeleton crew to work with. Musicians, even stars like Dave Brubeck, who usually got paid in the hundreds of dollars per appearance would have to do the show for union scale: in those days, $21.

Somehow, Baker and his team made it work, and the run of four was extended. Mark Murphy was booked for February 10, 1958, backed by Shelly Manne and His Men. This debut TV appearance was described by British Murphy fan John Wood: "A very youthful Mark, looking more like a Big Apple lawyer in his smart lounge suit complete with tie, sings two numbers. Starting with Mark finger-clicking his own intro and backed by a trio of piano, bass & drums, singing a beautiful version of George and Ira Gershwin's 'Fascinatin' Rhythm' which he had just recorded on his very first album *Meet Mark Murphy*. Between numbers Mark is interviewed by Bob Goop *[sic]*, who was presenting the TV show, and they discuss Mark's career to date, and also how he got his Decca recording contract, then they plug Mark's new and second album *Let Yourself Go*. Finally Mark once again in his snappy lounge suit and surrounded by the most fantastic props (typical late 50s style), including tremendous close-ups of 6/8 dining chairs, sings the most seductive male version I have heard of Johnny Mercer and [Harold] Arlen's 'Blues in the Night'. Intro is accompanied by drums only, then in walks the bass for a couple of bars, before the piano joins the trio on the remainder of the performance. Simply tremendous. Boy, I bet Mark was overwhelmed with phone calls after this broadcast from the girls just dying to show him their etchings."

'Bob Goop' was, in fact, Bobby Troup. Murphy was sometimes compared to Troup, a fellow hipster, singer, pianist, composer of, among other tunes, 'Route 66' – and the husband of singer Julie London.

Murphy was invited back for a second appearance on November 24, and sang "That Old Black Magic" and "Body and Soul". These recordings were released on one of the 36 compilation albums known as *Sessions Live*, on the specially created Calliope label, which featured recordings from *Stars of Jazz*.

A few weeks after his first TV appearance, and a mere five years after beginning his correspondence with Steve Allen, Mark was finally invited on to his show. In the episode broadcast on March 16, 1958, he shared the bill with Lena Horne, Keenan Wynn, Jack E. Leonard and boxer Carmen Basilio. His contribution was the novelty song "Two Ladies in de Shade of de Banana Tree", from *Meet Mark Murphy*.

Steve Allen was a modern renaissance man. As well as an urbane and witty radio and TV broadcaster, humorist, actor (playing the title role in 1956's *The Benny Goodman Story*), pianist and a prolific songwriter, he is usually, albeit wrongly, credited with inventing the TV talk genre with *The Tonight Show*, of which he was the first host in 1954. He rebooked Mark several times: on 12th April, 1959, guesting with Diana Dors and Don Elliott, Mark performed Allen's composition "This Could be the Start of Something"; he was back again a year later, this time reprising "Two Ladies in De Shade of De Banana

Tree", with Charles Laughton as a fellow guest; there were further appearances on both August 6 and 7th, 1962, on a new show called *The Steve Allen Playhouse*.

Apart from appearing on TV and looking for other singing work, Murphy wrote some songs at around this time, including "Come and Get Me". But he was still without a record label. Then one day the phone rang. It was Tom Morgan, a producer with Capitol Records. Morgan was a big fan of Murphy's work for Decca, and he was calling to make him a three-album offer with Capitol. Morgan was an old-school A&R man, who cherished his artists and tried to help them develop a solid career that would make money for the label. He was popular with his artists, and was considered a safe pair of hands by the company. His knowledge and good taste were well known; Capitol had given him the freedom to sign artists if he believed in them. And although it was a money-making enterprise like any other, the company had been founded by songwriters, and it was still possible then to take on a new act and sign them on purely artistic grounds. With the profits they were making from their established roster, Capitol could afford to take a punt on someone like Mark.

"As soon as I signed the contract," he recalled, "I went over to this cafeteria, sliced that turkey, and ate an enormous meal." Capitol had promised to make him a star, and he was thrilled: it was his biggest break so far. He would be recording for the same label as Frank Sinatra, June Christy, The Four Freshmen, Kay Starr, Dakota Staton, Sue Raney... and Peggy Lee. Peggy had somehow managed to finesse a career as both a sophisticated pop star and a serious jazz singer; Mark had been working the pop end of jazz with Decca. What was to stop him becoming a male version of his idol?

In mid-June, he arrived at Capitol's Vine Street studios for a singles session with the pianist and arranger Evelyn Roberts and her Singers. They cut five guitar-based tracks: "I'll Never Be Free" and "Makin' Whoopee", neither of which was issued, "Looking for Somebody", "Don't Cry My Love" and "Daddy Must Be a Man". That autumn, Mark made three more sides, this time with guitarist and arranger Jack Marshall – another stab at "Don't Cry My Love" (this version was never issued), plus "Blacksmith Blues" and "Belong to Me". The first single, "Looking for Somebody" and "Daddy Must Be a Man" hit the record stores but made no impact. The follow-up, "Don't Cry My Love" and "Belong to Me", was released that December but similarly failed to dent the charts. "Blacksmith Blues", meanwhile, moldered in the vaults for nearly 40 years until finally it was exhumed as a bonus track on *The Best of Mark Murphy: the Capitol Years*.

For Murphy's first album on the new label, Tom Morgan allowed him to choose his own musical director. The man to get the nod was Bill Holman who, as well as playing tenor saxophone, was best-known for injecting some much-needed swing into the Stan Kenton band's arrangements. James Gavin quotes André Previn, who wrote that Holman's "true instrument is the orchestra, and he plays it with musicianship, honesty and brilliance."

Crucially, Holman was also one of Peggy Lee's favorite arrangers. One of his greatest gifts was his ability to write voicings for small band charts so that they sounded like orchestras.

As with the Decca sessions, Murphy had his own ideas about how the material should be presented, and made demo recordings of all the tunes in advance with just piano and voice. "He knew the exact feeling he wanted on each section of the tune," said Holman. "For example, he was able to indicate where the conga drum should or should not be used to get the sound he wanted... equal arranging credit should go to him."

By the time they were ready to record in Capitol's 'B' studio, Morgan had secured Peggy Lee's rhythm section: pianist Jimmy Rowles, bassist Joe Mondragon, and drummer Mel Lewis, plus trumpet-playing brothers Pete and Conte Candoli. Rowles was in great demand from top-drawer female singers including Billie Holiday, Ella Fitzgerald, Jo Stafford, Anita O'Day and Julie London, due to his sensitivity at the keys. Murphy, Holman and the band recorded the seven-song medley that would become Side 2 of *This Could Be The Start of Something*; two weeks later, with a slightly reduced line-up, they recorded six more tunes for Side 1, including the title track.

As one would expect, the album overall has a more informal, stripped down feel than the Decca recordings, but it is also rather uneven, and on some tunes one feels that Mark's heart isn't in it. But Holman and Murphy's arrangements work well. On the title track, written by Steve Allen, the backing is light and sympathetic, full of space – there's very little going on much of the time except for bass, brushes and congas. When the muted trumpets come in on the first bridge they play a counter-melody to Murphy's vocal, ending with an unmuted flourish that makes them sound like a different instrument. The bridge on the second chorus is accompanied by nothing more than handclaps. Mark sings nonchalantly about life as a wealthy playboy, more concerned about his waistline than his stomach. The lyrics may have been an accurate reflection of Steve Allen's well-padded lifestyle, but at the time Murphy would have been more than happy with the rich French food he was singing about.

As a single, "This Could Be the Start of Something" became a minor hit. But there are some misfires on the album: on "Falling in Love with Love", Mark strangles the first chorus with a silly comedy throat voice. On "The Lady is a Tramp", the band sings *tramp tramp tramp tramp* like a troop of exhausted soldiers. Otherwise Murphy doesn't do much with the song that Sinatra didn't, apart from relocating Harlem to Beverly Hills and stumbling over his Sunset Strip barons and earls. But on another tune made famous by Sinatra – "Just in Time" – he serves up the verse, whose reference to lying comfortably in the gutter speaks more accurately about his own recent experiences.

The idea of doing a 20-minute medley was bold, and Mark swings comfortably through the numbers without a break, sounding relaxed throughout, ending with a clever restatement of all six.

Publicity shot, 1950s.

This Could Be the Start of Something was released in May 1959, and Capitol duly cranked up their publicity machine. "In those days", Murphy said, "Capitol had offices in all the big cities, and people would take you around all the DJs. It was kind of like a family. At that time the Kingston Trio were doing 25 per cent of Capitol's business… I was lucky to get any attention at all from the local distributors, because I had to compete with Frank, Peggy, Dean Martin, George Shearing."

Again the reviewers were friendly and encouraging, but they did not rave. *Downbeat* called Murphy a musician's singer with a "shrewd sense of phrasing" and "interesting ideas" but decided he lacked a "strong flavor of individuality, projection of verbal meaning and a feeling of believing in the words. Nonetheless", the review concluded, "here is a young man who could become quite a singer." But is not yet one, it seemed to imply.

He was certainly gaining a higher profile on radio: in *Billboard*'s 1959 poll of jazz disc jockeys he came in third behind Joe Williams and Frank Sinatra. Nevertheless, Morgan, Holman and Murphy had a re-think about the next album, deciding to feature jazzy versions of recent pop hits, with the title *Mark Murphy's Hip Parade*. Perhaps he could yet give the likes of chart favorites Frankie Avalon and Fabian a run for their money. And surely there was no need for all those boring instrumental solos?

In late August they went into the studio with many of the same musicians as before, plus the Jud Conlon Singers. Three days later *Mark Murphy's*

Hip Parade was in the can. The album is less awful than its detractors suggest (there was a worse one to come), but there are plenty of wince-inducing moments. The worst problem is over-production: "Come to Me", for example, had been a hit for Johnny Mathis, whose dramatic, impassioned version was drenched in reverb. Murphy's rendition, despite the frenzied bongos and other Latin percussion, just doesn't put over the emotion as effectively. His attempt at Avalon's recent hit "Venus" starts with more bongo fury, after which it becomes a kitchen-sink-throwing exercise.

Some good basic songs are often over-embellished: Tony Bennett's hit "Firefly" from a couple of years earlier is done faster, with the cheesy Jud Conlon Singers joining in, and an irritating variety of stop-start tempos. "(You've Got) Personality", Lloyd Price's R&B hit, has the Singers going *shaaah bubadoo-bubba-boop*, but although Murphy's is supposed to be the hip version, it sounds more like the square version. "It's Not for Me to Say" was another song made famous by Johnny Mathis, who did it as a gentle ballad. Again the Mathis version works better, because this time Mark sounds too perky. But there are some fine renditions too, including a slow, drummerless "Witchcraft", and a bluesy version of the Nat King Cole hit "Send for Me".

Mark eventually learned that sincerity was the key to a great recording. Peggy Lee's best ones, he told Stan Britt in 1964, "turn out to be those where she was just herself... She gives deep readings to fascinating songs... She sits on the time like a drummer playing his hi-hat. Another thing that gasses me is her unbelievable versatility. Through all the fads and different influences that come along, she is always able to dig something out of herself."

He had also noticed that Lee understood the intimacy made possible by the television close-up. Just as the best radio broadcasters imagine they are speaking to one person, Lee kept her smoldering glance on the camera constantly, mesmerizing the susceptible viewer. Although no classic beauty, she surrounded herself with glamour – white candy floss hair, heavy make-up, clothes so tight she could barely move in them.

In fact, Murphy knew more about Lee than he let on to Stan Britt. In his book *Is That All There Is? The Strange Life of Peggy Lee*, James Gavin describes Murphy's traumatic encounter with the object of his veneration in the spring of 1960. Mark had long wanted to meet Peggy, and now, signed to the same label, was as good a time as any. Lee, a well-known sexual predator, had her own reasons for wanting to get to know the tall, handsome, talented young star in the making. A few months earlier, Murphy had been in the studio audience of ABC's *Bing Crosby Show*, on which Peggy sang "Baubles, Bangles and Beads", shimmering in front of a giant candelabra in a bejewelled, tightly-fitting dress. Snapping her fingers to the bass, hi-hat and rimshot intro, and staring all the while into the camera, Peggy made it seem like the jewelry was *all* she was wearing.

Having made Murphy's acquaintance, she invited him to visit her at home. He had already heard rumors that she was unstable and prone to let fly at those whom she felt had disappointed her. But he liked her, and was flattered to be asked. When he arrived, he found her wearing a bathing suit. Peggy suggested they go out to the pool. Before he knew what was happening, she had grabbed his hands and put them on her waist, asking, "Like the pretty view?" Mark ran for his life.

Such was the story, but Lesley Mitchell-Clarke, Murphy's publicist in later years, believes that what really happened went further and was even more mortifying. He told her he had idolized Peggy Lee, and when the "romantic overture came, he went right along with it. But perhaps more due to hero worship than anything else, he was just not able to perform. He was overwhelmed by her as a star and unfortunately instead of being compassionate or sensitive or anything in that neighborhood, Peggy Lee berated him and chastised him and made him feel like the lowest thing on the earth. And I think that that had a big impact on his sexuality.... Perhaps because he was always looking for acceptance from his mother, which he never got, there's a whole Barnum and Bailey room of neuroses, I think, with Mark."

Feeling spurned, Peggy decided to get her revenge. Capitol had asked her to write the sleeve notes to the *Hip Parade* album, thereby lending him some much-needed star credibility.

> *Those of us who love music,* she wrote, *say "bravo" ...or "hurray" ... or perhaps a more modern expression of approval when a singer like Mark Murphy comes along.*
>
> *Mark Murphy sings for the sheer joy of singing and then he listens critically and, at times, almost painfully. This is only one of his admirable musical traits. It is obvious in observing him that he hears so much, wishes to express so much that he has begun to express it. When something is done for the love of a job well done, the listener can hear it; and Mark sings for the love of it...*
>
> *Listen closely to the soloists, please, and you'll find it a pleasing experience. (They are listed separately and you may wish to start your own fan club.)*
>
> *The talent for singing is one of life's finest gifts and about Mark, personally, it can be said that he appreciates that gift and works diligently to uphold what is good in the "old" and to bring out the "new."*
>
> *He phrases at times like a horn; and a horn with a modern sound. As the expression goes, you might say, "He blows"... and he's attractive, single.*

It was a peculiar endorsement, at best, that scrupulously avoided praising Mark and offered little more than description. He was horrified. "*He blows... and he's attractive, single*"? The hints were obvious to anyone except, it seemed, Capitol Records. As Ralph Burns had found, jazz was not kind to homosexuals, and this nudge in the ribs must have been especially painful for Murphy, who had always been careful to keep his orientation in the closet.

And that wasn't all. In itself, describing someone as "single" sounds harmless enough. But it may have had some painful resonance for Peggy Lee: back in 1937, shortly after a North Dakota radio station manager had rebranded the former Norma Deloris Egstrom as Peggy Lee, her bio read, "Of course, you know Peg is single" – an ambiguous aside, at the very least. Did it mean she was sexually available, or on the shelf?

Murphy was aware of the schizophrenia that could result when performers like her created an alter ego for public consumption. "She was a woman horribly not at peace with herself... When she was Peggy Lee, not so many problems – but when she was Norma it was problem city."

A few days after the incident by the pool, a delivery arrived for Ms Lee – a box with a ribbon tied around it. Inside was a bunch of long-stemmed roses with the buds cut off, and with them a note from Mark Murphy: "Dear Peggy, I think you know what to do with these."

Despite misnaming the album *Hit Parade*, *Billboard* approved, albeit with reservations, dubbing it a "quality item": "Murphy has chosen a group of tunes – hits of this and recent seasons. His approach has jazz overtones. Support from Bill Holman, who did the arrangements, is first rate. The album is an excellent jockey programming item." *Downbeat* called him "a pleasant, Sinatra-ish singer with a broad tone, a self-conscious manner, and a tendency to be overly mannered... He might make it but he needs direction and seasoning."

Like *This Could Be the Start of Something*, the *Hip Parade* album failed to take off. "I had tried to compromise, which of course was a mistake," Murphy explained in later years. "People who wanted those songs didn't want to hear me, and people who liked me didn't want to hear those songs. They printed too many copies and it sank. We were kind of traumatized."

The deal Murphy had signed with Capitol in 1958 was for three albums; it was now 1960, and there were only two flop LPs and one minor single hit to show for it. He had one more chance, one more album, to justify the label's faith in him. *Playing the Field* was not that album. In fact it was probably his worst to date, with several sub-two minute tracks, presumably in hopes of some easy radio play. The mood is relentlessly upbeat, but much of the material is forgettable, and there is too much insincere showbiz sparkle and showing off. He holds the final note of "Put the Blame on Mame" for 21 seconds – for no better reason, apparently, than to prove he can. The title track, another Steve Allen composition, may have been chosen for its cool, carefree "This Could Be the Start of Something"-style nonchalance, but it's unmemorable, complete with tuneless whistling. From the laddish title to the cover, Murphy was again being sold as a babe-magnet-cum-man-about-town, depicted in various sophisticated poses with four different females.

Murphy and Morgan tried to convince Capitol to release "Put the Blame on Mame" as a single, but they declined. "By that time they had given up on me," Murphy said. "They had released the album at the beginning of '61, and said Goodbye Murphy." Considering his elation at securing the deal, and the thought of sharing the roster with so many household names, it was a bitter end to his contract.

So what went wrong? James Gavin opines that despite Murphy's complete command of singing technique, not to mention good looks and determination, it was an uphill struggle for him to make an impression. "He was not a fully-formed artist at that time. There were tons of singers like that who were being recorded by major labels and getting a lot of attention... Of all the jazz singers that were being recorded with great arrangers, great orchestras, very few of them came forward. I have sometimes wondered whether being gay might have been a factor in all this. Mark was not out to anyone except his friends until the last few years of his life."

The one thing Murphy hadn't yet tried was just being himself. He had grown up excited by bebop and swing, yet from the beginning with Decca, and now with Capitol, he had gone all out for popular acceptance by the mainstream market. That seemed to mean presenting himself as a young hipster, a swinging cool dude around town, toying with the affections of innumerable women, and having a whale of a time.

Once again he found himself in limbo. He and Jack Jones were both briefly courted by Kapp Records, but in the end it was the crooner Jones who signed the deal. "I had to invent ways of doing things differently. Because every time I would start over again, I'd find that all the bases were loaded, so I had to go out somewhere where they couldn't go, and so I had to go, say, far out on the edge of jazz. People say I'm a risk-taker, I'm on the edge. But I had to be there, because that was the only place that wasn't overcrowded."

New York beckoned once more.

4 Many Shades of Blue

Murphy wasted no more time in LA. For some time he had been going back and forth from the coast, building a club and college audience back east, before finally deciding to quit LA for good. In New York, he made his way to the West 51st Street offices of the jazz label Riverside Records – smaller than Decca or Capitol, but perhaps a more logical home for him and his particular talents and interests. Founded by Bill Grauer and Orrin Keepnews, Riverside had an impressive modern jazz artist roster including Thelonious Monk, Kenny Dorham, Cannonball Adderley, and Wes Montgomery, but also issued classic blues and jazz sides, new recordings by aging jazz giants, and novelty albums such as *Vintage Sports Cars in Stereo* and *Coney Island In Stereo: The Thrilling Sounds Of The World's Greatest Amusement Park*.

The modern jazz artists who recorded for Riverside were not the type to chase singles chart success or worry about appealing to the teenage market, and as his 30th birthday approached, this must have looked very appealing to Mark Murphy. Riverside was also the home of Bill Evans. At the time Murphy appeared on the scene, Keepnews had just produced two classic Evans albums – *Everybody Digs Bill Evans* and *Portrait in Jazz*, the latter featuring Paul Motian on drums and 25-year-old Scott LaFaro on bass.

The first Riverside release to feature Mark Murphy was a sampler album. *Everybody's Doin' the Bossa Nova* featured tracks from bandleader Art Mooney, guitarist Charlie Byrd, conga-player and bandleader Ray Barretto, and guitarist Billy Mure with his 7 Karats. Murphy's two short tracks, recorded with an orchestra conducted by Al Cohn, were "Fly Away My Sadness", written by the young pianist and Bill Evans protégé Warren Bernhardt, with lyrics by *Downbeat* editor Gene Lees; and "It's Like Love", by Galvis and Young. We can't be sure, but Murphy's later love affair with Brazilian music probably had its genesis here: bossa nova was a perfect vehicle for his rhythmic style of singing, and these were two good songs. Neither recording suffers from the self-consciously ornamental flourishes that had marred much of his previous vocal output. He sounds relaxed, and sings the songs straight.

It was agreed that for his own first full album with Riverside, he would work with the writer-arranger and saxophonist Ernie Wilkins, a Count Basie alumnus whose composition "Every Day I Have the Blues" had been a huge hit, bringing its singer Joe Williams to national prominence. As was his habit, Murphy began planning the album by recording demos, accompanying himself on piano. "Frankly, I don't know how singers do it the other way," he told Gene Lees, "going into the studio to face a completely new orchestration. I have to feel comfortable in the arrangement. The first time you hear an orchestration, it's distracting." His approach to arranging varied according to a tune's tempo. "In the fast ones, I emphasize the music more than the lyrics and try to bring out both the melodic character of the song and the chord changes. I try to isolate the melody and then bring in the changes, maybe scatting a chorus to further point up the changes. But in a ballad, I try to emphasize the lyrics."

Before he made it into the recording studio, there was a nasty shock in store. Murphy always believed he was the last person to see Scott LaFaro alive. On Wednesday July 5, 1961, as he told the story, he was in a New York piano bar when LaFaro walked in, looking for Bill Evans. Murphy told him Evans had already left town. LaFaro said he planned to drive upstate that evening to see his parents in Geneva, a five-hour drive away. Four days earlier he had been accompanying Stan Getz at the Newport Jazz Festival, and a few days before that, he had made the legendary Village Vanguard live recordings with the Bill Evans Trio. Murphy could see that the young bass-player was exhausted, and urged him to stay over at his place and leave in the morning. But LaFaro was adamant. That night, his car skidded off the highway and hit a tree as he was heading east between Geneva and Canandaigua on Route 20, an unlit rural road in those days. In the car with him was a high school friend, Frank Ottley. Both men were killed instantly. Even by jazz standards, this was an early death, and LaFaro was an exceptionally talented and original bassist.

Murphy always blamed himself for LaFaro's death, feeling he should have been more insistent that Scott stay the night before making the journey. However, Murphy's account only squares with another detailed version of the story if the piano bar encounter took place relatively early that day. According to this other narrative, LaFaro was already in Geneva by early evening. He and Ottley then drove to Warsaw, 90 miles west, to see a friend of Ottley's, arriving at around 10.30pm. After a couple of hours, the friend – just like Murphy – urged them to stay over because they seemed tired, but again they declined, and headed back to Geneva, crashing the car on the way. If this account is accurate, Mark had nothing to reproach himself for, nor was he the last person to see Scott LaFaro alive.

Murphy's new album was titled *Rah*, and Murphy found Ernie Wilkins a congenial collaborator. "Each arranger I've worked with has been completely different," Murphy said, "yet they've all given me great arrangements. Burns has been marvelous. He never minded my tugging at his shoulder on the date and asking for changes in an arrangement. Bill Holman was very kind when I recorded with him for Capitol. He's such a poet with a big band. Al Cohn is wonderful. He's so relaxed on a date – such a down stud, as they say."

The musicians who assembled at New York's Plaza Sound were the cream of the session crop, including Clark Terry and Blue Mitchell on trumpets, Urbie Green on trombone, Wynton Kelly on piano and Jimmy Cobb on drums. There were four sessions, Kelly playing on the first three during the second half of September. Producer Orrin Keepnews brought Bill Evans in on piano for the fourth and final session. Evans was still mourning the death of LaFaro three months earlier. His inclusion was less a matter of supplying Murphy with extra firepower, more a ruse to get Evans back into a studio – any studio – in an effort to lift him out of his depression: he had not recorded anything since June. For Murphy, the break with Capitol had also meant a break with Tom Morgan as manager; he was now with Helen Keane, who shortly afterwards began managing Evans.

Rah began life as a twelve track LP which included the popular ballad "I'll be Seeing You" by Sammy Fain and Irving Kahal, with some dark Mark Murphy lyrics added, as well as his own hipster version of "My Favorite Things". The release ran into copyright trouble straight away. Murphy thought Riverside had simply forgotten to obtain clearance from the copyright owners. The problem with "I'll be Seeing You" was that, as he freely acknowledged, the lyrics he had written for the second chorus turned the song into a parody of itself.

> *I'll be seeing you in all the old familiar places, all the horses at the races*
> *All year through in that damp café, the parking lot across the way*
> *That beat-up carousel where we used to sell cheap Muscatel*

The case of "My Favorite Things" was more serious, since Murphy's lyrics offended the mighty Richard Rodgers: the latter felt that they sullied the memory of the recently-deceased Oscar Hammerstein, whose original words were written for Mary Martin.

> *John Coltrane talkin', Miles and Gil blowin', Mulligan's walkin', the Hi-Lo's hi-lo'ing, Ray Charles and Basie and Garner with strings, these are a few of my favorite things...*

> *When some square goofs, when the blues come, when I'm feeling sad....*

In the face of Rodgers's complaints, Riverside agreed to withdraw the first pressing of *Rah* and issue a new version without "I'll be Seeing You", and with "My Favorite Things" retaining its original lyrics. This, of course, reduced the overall running time, so the re-issued album (RLP 395) included a track titled "Like Love", which was in fact "It's Like Love" from the *Bossa Nova* sampler. But this too vanished from later pressings.

The Jazz Discography states that on October 16th, 1961, Murphy recorded "Out of This World, My Favorite Things (long ver.), and My Favorite Things (short ver.)" If two different versions were indeed recorded on the same day, this suggests that the copyright issue was already known about – begging the question of why Riverside went ahead and released the album with Murphy's own lyrics. Whatever exchanges took place with Riverside's legal representatives, Murphy was unimpressed when they caved in to Rodgers. "It brings the whole question of parody up. It's legal to do parody isn't it? If my father had been alive and well, we would have fought the case. I got the idea of doing it from Anita O'Day's jazz lyrics and nobody sued her for insulting Cole Porter..."

Although Murphy himself didn't think he really found his voice until he hit 40 (i.e. in 1972), many of his fans regard *Rah*, his sixth album, as his best. Certainly, he seems at last to have found a style of his own. Ernie Wilkins's light, crisp backings sound hipper than those devised by Burns or Holman. The singer sounds relaxed, unburdened by the need to show off. Good material almost sings itself, and on this occasion he doesn't destroy it by over-emoting. In fact, he sounds like he's having a wonderful time. The production mix also gives more space to his voice, which in the Decca years sometimes seemed to be battling against the orchestration. Murphy also sounds as if he has been more closely miked.

Ballads like "Spring Can Really Hang You Up the Most" suggest a new maturity – no melodrama, simply a grown man looking back and wondering how things might have been. On "No Tears for Me", Murphy's love of theatricality hits exactly the right tone: *Bap!* (on the snare). *Miss O'Malley, take a letter!* as if he's in a stage play, and after the verse, he slides beautifully into the ballad proper, with its opulent Wilkins horn lines. There's also a rich, sensuous take on Neal Hefti's "Lil Darlin'", and a gloriously lunatic delivery of Annie Ross's lyrics to "Twisted", but it's when the needle bites into side two that the change really becomes apparent.

By now Murphy had fallen under the spell of Miles Davis' recordings with Gil Evans, and his version of "Milestones" is truly something new. His friend Jimmy Britt had written the lyrics to the tune, which had originally appeared on Davis's eponymous 1958 album. Murphy's increasingly distinctive scat is beautifully showcased by the fast-walking double bass which almost drops out in the bridge to increase the tension, rather like the 'drop' in house music, providing a certain euphoria when it comes back in. The ride has been such a thrill that we even forgive the slight wobble on his final note.

For the first time, the cover of *Rah* depicts Mark as a mature adult. He sits outside a college building, with cropped hair, wearing a pink shirt, black waistcoat, chin in hand, unsmiling, facing the camera, his eyes hidden behind shades. His left hand supports a placard bearing the word *Rah*, while his right elbow rests on a book with the title *Economics*. The body language is casual, thoughtful – no more helpless gestures, and no more puppy dog eyes pleading to be loved. And no supporting cast of women. As a visual statement, it all gives the impression that he is no longer interested (if he ever was) in pandering to the market. *Rah*, a college cheer, looks ironic, to say the least. Perhaps Murphy had learned that the economics of the clean-cut college-boy image, of trying to please the youth audience, weren't working, either for him or for his record labels. Many years later, Murphy told WBGO's Michael Bourne that 'Rah' should be spoken softly. "It's supposed to be a *cool* Rah. I would just like to say I was not into Economics, I was late for the picture session up at Columbia University and I grabbed a book off the shelf."

Did the influence of Miles Davis, jazz's prince of darkness – the man who famously played with his back turned to the audience – have anything to do with this less crowd-pleasing image? Certainly it is difficult to overstate the significance of Miles in Murphy's development as a singer. The seriousness of the Davis project was in contrast to Murphy's career to date, which had been consumed by the sheer effort of surviving as a professional singer.

For all the subsequent acclaim lavished on *Rah*, Murphy himself was lukewarm towards it. "I had a cold on four of those tracks and I didn't sing 'Out of This World' at all like I wanted to sing it," he told Bob Rusch. But it was, finally, an album that gained some traction in the jazz world. In his review, *Downbeat* critic John A. Tynan said: "Murphy should thank his lucky stars for, among other things such as his talent, Ernie Wilkins. Wilkins has written a set of arrangements for the young jazz singer that should turn Frank Sinatra green with envy. Much of the album's success is due to the arranger's pen." This was somewhat dismissive of Murphy's input, but Tynan probably wasn't aware of it.

According to Bert Warner, later the founder of the International Mark Murphy Appreciation Society, "[Rah] did not sell too well. At the time Mel Tormé found this with his own jazz albums. Very few jazz fans buy vocals and for the most part, people who do buy vocals buy Sinatra, Bennett, Damone, etcetera and this was far too way out for them, as they do not buy or understand jazz."

Murphy continued to sit in at gigs around New York. In 1961, when pianist and singer Ronny Whyte was just starting out, Murphy turned up at the Showplace in Greenwich Village and sat in for a couple of tunes. "I was lucky," said Whyte. "I had steady jobs all the time. Back in the Sixties, and into the Seventies, we worked six nights a week, six hours a night in saloons. The steady night-after-night jobs hardly exist any more. Then I proceeded to see him in several places around town. He was still playing the piano for himself too. There was an abundance of jobs – if you could play and sing, you could work all the time. On the East Side of New York, almost every restaurant had a piano. Some of them were pretty awful and not in tune." After Chuck Israels replaced Scott LaFaro in the Bill Evans Trio, Mark would sometimes sing a few numbers with them at Sunday matinées at the Village Vanguard.

At some point in 1962, he recorded four sides for single release, with tenor sax, piano, bass, drums, bongo, strings and a female vocal group. They were: "Love", "Come and Get Me", "Why Don't You Do Right" and "Fly Me to the Moon". The latter, written by New York cabaret pianist Bart Howard, was originally entitled 'In Other Words', but Peggy Lee, who had sung it on the Ed Sullivan show in 1960, had suggested Howard change the title to something more catchy. Complete with heavenly choir, spoken word intro and verse, it became a minor hit for Mark Murphy, and a much bigger one for Frank Sinatra two years later.

Murphy recorded his second album for Riverside, *That's How I Love the Blues!*, in late 1962 with an orchestra arranged and conducted by Al Cohn. As a long-time devotee of Nat King Cole, Murphy would have been well aware of Cole's *St Louis Blues* album, the soundtrack to the W.C. Handy biopic of the same name. In that case, all the tracks were Handy compositions. Wisely, Murphy avoided those songs.

The arrangements are certainly sensitive to Mark Murphy's voice on this, his last American album for a decade. It features a specific style of blues – spacious, sophisticated, urban, in the commercially successful Joe Williams/ Basie manner. There's a lightness of touch here, in an instrumental line-up distinctive for the absence of woodwind. Murphy's voice sounds even better than it does on *Rah*, particularly on the Johnny Mercer/Harold Arlen song "Blues in the Night", where it is soft, liquid and intimate, to a perfect minimal backing, and on "The Meaning of the Blues", which Miles Davis and Gil Evans had recorded on the *Miles Ahead* album. The loose, relaxed style of his singing again demonstrated how versatile he was – at home with pop, mainstream jazz, ballads, bebop, and now a natural blues singer too. Tunes such as Horace Silver's "Señor Blues", Big Joe Turner's "Wee Baby Blues", and the sexy Billy Eckstine/Earl Hines ballad "Jelly Jelly Blues" continued to feature in Murphy's live shows for years afterwards. And he maintained his tradition of including a bit of light comedy with the vaudeville-style "Everybody's Crazy 'Bout the Doggone Blues". A few years later, having made it clear that he didn't consider himself a blues singer per se, Murphy explained the album's title: "I stressed the pronoun in the title – 'How *I* Like [sic]... It may not be how someone else likes them, but it is how they appeal to me... I wanted to do an album of many shades of blue, azure, indigo and so forth."

Billboard said, "Singer Mark Murphy has been on the scene for a good spell but he has seldom had a better showcasing than this... Good wax that can easily make a dent." The following year Gene Lees interviewed him again about *That's How I Love the Blues!*, this time for *Downbeat*: "It surprises me that the blues album has been accepted the way it has, both by critics and the public – and the Negro public in particular," said Murphy. "The critics could have thrown up their hands and said I shouldn't have done the album, but they didn't, with only one exception I can think of... I wasn't trying to do an album of Negro blues. It was my conception of the blues, and it has been accepted as such." *That's How I Love the Blues!* always remained one of his own favorite recordings.

Although ABC had by now kicked *Stars Of Jazz* off the schedules, Steve Allen had the industry clout to continue flying the jazz flag on network television. Through his company Meadowlane Enterprises, he was now executive producer of a syndicated show called *Jazz Scene USA*. Recorded in Los Angeles, with Oscar Brown Jr. as host, *Jazz Scene* ran to 26 episodes in 1962. Murphy was extensively featured in episode 21 on November 12, 1962 with the Jimmy Rowles Quartet, performing "'S Wonderful", and a medley of "Old Folks" and "God Bless the Child". These were followed by a *West Side Story* medley – "Something's Comin'", "Tonight", "Maria" and "Somewhere".

Interviewed by Brown on the show, Murphy had clearly forgiven Peggy Lee for her sleeve notes. "She's the most interesting singer of jazz alive, and certainly one of the most creative, from a lyrical, emotional standpoint. Then, in a lyrical, vocally astounding way, the singer who gasses me most is Betty Carter, the gal who made that album with Ray Charles. Then there's Blossom Dearie, Lee Wiley, and of course, Lady Day." "And on the male side?" prompts Brown. "So many. Ray Charles, Dick Haymes, Johnny Hartman, Mel Tormé, and Joe Williams for blues. And the best scat singing – Dave Lambert."

By this point in his career, Murphy had enjoyed enough media exposure to attract the attention of other jazz singers. His relationship with the more commercially successful Mel Tormé was ambivalent, and despite obvious mutual respect, over the years each directed waspish comments at the other. At some point during 1963, Murphy and Tormé appeared on the same bill in Philadelphia. Interviewed the following year by *Perfectly Frank*, the fanzine devoted to Sinatra, Murphy said, "When I listen to [Tormé] I don't listen for too much depth of emotion because that doesn't seem to be the way he sings." Tormé hit back: "Murphy's remarks about the fact that I am purely a technical and creative singer, and don't sing from the heart, are nothing more than stupid, in my opinion." He added that he found Mark inconsistent as a singer, and he had a point. Mark Murphy was more than capable of singing in a technically perfect way when he chose to, as had been obvious ever since *Meet Mark Murphy*. But he didn't choose to. The Tormés, Bennetts and Sinatras of the smooth professional type could build successful singing careers because their acts varied hardly at all, and over the years, the audience came to know what to expect. Murphy had other ideas. He knew that if as a jazz singer you wanted to scale the heights of performance, you had to take risks, and that meant that consistency was not always possible.

His old friend Charles Cochran, who knew him well for over 20 years, and remained in touch for 20 more, described him as "mercurial... he was a man of many colors." Anita O'Day, Cochran said, was a similar personality. "Sometimes Mark's inventiveness went a little bit haywire."

The jazz writer Francis Davis has coined the term "outcats" for those hipsters who can never settle comfortably into the mainstream. "By virtue of the marginal status of jazz in contemporary American culture, all jazz performers, including the most famous, influential and housebroken, are outcats." And in 1964, years before Davis invented the term, Mark Murphy transformed himself into the archetypical outcat.

5 That's What I Like About London

On the face of it, things seemed to be going well. Mark had finally found a record label that catered for musicians like him. He'd had a hit single with his romantic pop version of "Fly Me to the Moon", backed with another strong tune, the earthy R&B-inflected "Why Don't You Do Right". He was getting booked at the Village Vanguard and the Village Gate in New York. And, no doubt helped by Gene Lees's support, he was voted New Star of the Year by the readers of *Downbeat*. But something wasn't right. He felt restless.

"In a way… I guess I was still trying to be a cabaret singer in a tuxedo, but singing the things I liked. It just didn't work," he recalled in 1980. The biggest problem was that public enthusiasm for jazz was on the wane in America, squeezed between the militantly anti-commercial free jazz movement and the new heavily promoted pop music. Jazz singers and players had enjoyed mainstream success in the previous decade, but now pop was snapping at their heels. Some of the biggest stars had started to feel the heat: in 1962 both Anita O'Day and Mel Tormé lost their Verve contracts, and the same happened to Chris Connor at Atlantic. By 1964, when Beatlemania swept the USA, pop was in the driver's seat. The change in popular audience taste had become all too clear by the mid-Sixties, and it was increasingly hard for the more bop-oriented players to attract interest from either the public or the music industry. As Betty Carter put it at the time, "I'm in real trouble now, because I haven't gotten nowhere in the first place."

Social change was, of course, the underlying factor, rather than the mere sudden appearance of a new, less sophisticated musical genre. And socially, it was a difficult time for jazzers to carry on as if nothing had happened. It wasn't just musical forms and instrumentation that were changing, it was the very thoughts and feelings expressed in song. Up until the mid-Fifties, men were men, and marriage was forever; women provided men's comfort and cooked their meals. But once the tectonic plates started to grind, love and marriage no longer went together like a horse and carriage. The sentiments of the jazz repertoire had changed little since the dawn of the popular song beloved of Alec Wilder but, lyrically at least, they were finally going out of style. As a result, singers like Tony Bennett were beginning to sound nostalgic for a lost era.

The New York club scene was changing too. In 1962, the original Five Spot was demolished to make way for a housing development for senior citizens, and the club moved three blocks north to St. Marks Place. By the autumn of the following year, its audience was falling away, and all the excitement seemed to be centered on Gerde's Folk City, where the featured performers were stand-up comedian Bill Cosby, and folk singers Richie Havens, Odetta and Bob Dylan. The latter had arrived in Greenwich Village a couple of years earlier. One 1950s hipster, Mike Harrington, pinpointed the moment the old bohemia ended: it was "the night a gawky kid named Bob Dylan showed up at the [White] Horse in a floppy hat." Harrington had previously heard him give an impromptu concert at McGowan's restaurant, and commented, "I heard the future and I didn't like it."

In her autobiography, Anita O'Day wrote, "When I turned on the radio I didn't even hear my kind of music. It was all Elvis, Jerry Lee Lewis, Little Richard and Bill Haley, or Pat Boone, Perry Como, Frankie Avalon and, of course, The Beatles." The Fab Four's debut on the Ed Sullivan Show came on February 9, 1964. That was the year O'Day took up hairdressing to survive. In 1968, Betty Carter accepted a job bagging groceries at a Detroit supermarket.

As for Mark Murphy, the promising early TV appearances had given him the profile he needed to stay afloat, but it had not built a substantial new audience. It would have been surprising if it had: apart from Johnny Carson's *Tonight Show*, jazz no longer featured in any substantial way on American television. In a 1980 interview with Bill Moody, Murphy offered an explanation for this neglect. "Money, greed and paranoia that someone might change the channel for even a minute and you'd be the cause of it... You can get on *The Tonight Show* if you're lucky, and they do have a fantastic band. But on all those shows there's no reason not to have a jazz artist once a week – and maybe every third week a jazz vocalist. But they don't. It's not their policy. But I don't kid myself. America is geared on money success. You just have to find a way to survive."

Record companies were no better, in his experience. "You get into these New York offices and they get on that machine gun trip they're into and you're lucky if you get three minutes of their time, and during that three minutes they're on the phone to somebody else. Those people are on such a speed trip, I can't tell you. Give a guy a telephone and a secretary, and he becomes a different person."

And management? Murphy claimed to have hired and fired no fewer than 13 managers by 1963. "I tried everyone," he said. "None of them got results." This was probably an exaggeration: it is unlikely there were 13 people in the US who even wanted to manage him. But to people who knew him well, it wasn't surprising that he got through a lot of managers. "Mark was always very defensive, very easily hurt, took things very personally, and would have been quick to blame a manager if something didn't go the way he wanted it," said James Gavin.

And of course, the times were a changing politically. The situation in Vietnam, from an American perspective, was deteriorating fast. In early 1963 President John Kennedy sent additional troops to shore up the corrupt South Vietnamese regime. Mass draft-dodging was just around the corner. Many American jazz musicians came to the conclusion that the USA was no longer the place to live, let alone make a living. Large numbers packed up and crossed the Atlantic, among them Phil Woods, Mal Waldron, Slide Hampton, Philly Joe Jones, Art Taylor, Steve Lacy, Ben Webster, Dave Pike, Maynard Ferguson, Red Mitchell, Leo Wright, Carmell Jones, Jon Hendricks, Cecil Taylor, Ornette Coleman and Ed Thigpen. Arrangers too, including Thad Jones and Ernie Wilkins, made their homes in European cities like London, Paris, Stockholm and Copenhagen, where they believed they could once again find sympathetic audiences. "It was a bad time for all the boppers," Murphy told Leonard Feather. "All the undergrounders had surfaced in the late '50s and early '60s; then we had to scatter again and wait."

To cap it all, in December 1963, Riverside's Bill Grauer dropped dead from a heart attack on his way to the bank. The company's accounts proved almost impossible to disentangle, because Grauer kept everything in his head. The following July, the company filed for bankruptcy, but it took years to clear up the mess. It also left Mark Murphy without a record company. But by then, he had already made his move.

His first trip to London had been in 1961. "My first time in England wasn't all that great. I was booked into the Astor," he told *Crescendo* magazine three years later. "They told me in the States it wasn't a jazz club, so I brought over a completely commercial program... Have you ever watched television when the sound's broken down? It was just like that. As though I'd got up to sing and there was no mike. I might as well have stood silent for all the attention I got." But he went back in autumn 1962 and this time found enough support to show up at a nightclub and, during the course of this trip, managed to get himself on to BBC radio.

Before London, however, there was Paris. And here we come to another tangled story. "I was getting pissed off with the States and just then a friend of mine knew somebody who was writing a musical and wanted me to star in it on Broadway. Michel Legrand was interested in writing the music at that time. She said: 'Send me to Paris and I'll make arrangements for you to come over.' I paid her way to Paris, then I got over there and she got into the Beaujolais wine and nothing got written. Everything went poof!"

This was a tale he regularly told to explain his relocation to Europe. However it has proved impossible to verify the facts – particularly the identity of the woman in question. At other times he said she was a friend of his, and that the problem was drugs rather than Beaujolais. James Gavin is skeptical about the whole business, pointing out that it was a little early for a Broadway show featuring the music of Michael Legrand, who didn't really come to international attention until 1964's *The Umbrellas of Cherbourg*. There were also some curious variations to the story. In a late interview with *The Huffington Post*, he said, "I was brought over there by some Australian scam artist who told me there was a Jacques Brel show lined up for me. She just fell into a bottle of wine and never got out."

Whether he was genuinely stranded in Europe, or whether he simply chose the Old World as the backdrop to another career relaunch, we may never know. At any rate, Dutch promoter Fred Burkhardt came to his rescue with offers of recordings for the Philips label in Holland, and provided him with contacts for work around the continent. And although the stateside release of *That's How I Love the Blues!* had fallen into a void due to Riverside's collapse, in Europe the album had been well distributed. This gave Murphy a toehold, enabling him to find work in Scandinavia before heading for London – again at Burkhardt's suggestion.

It was in 1963, on his third visit, that he fell in love with London. "It was cheap, very charming, and yet to be discovered by the masses. It was fantastic!" And as luck would have it, his aunt Betty, the doctor, was working in a London hospital and had a flat there, providing Mark with a place to stay. "All this green! So many open spaces," he enthused. "That's what I like about London. Soho Square... great! Beats Washington Square to pieces. You can sit down without feeling you've got to dust the seat first. They were talking of closing Washington Square just before I came across, and doing it over. It's dirty and run down..."

Asked in an undated mid-60s conversation with fellow singer Matt Monro how long he had been over this time, he said, "About six months, and I'd like to stay forever. London, to my way of thinking, is a much nicer place to live than New York, because New York is a business city. It's exciting, it's fast, and everything is open late, but when it comes right down to living, there's no comparison."

It was also in London that he began to feel a little more comfortable in his own skin. Speaking of his life in the States, he told an interviewer years later, "I was a drag, man... Always sitting in the corner with my head down and not a nice person. Then I started drinking... then I stopped that... And then I came to Europe and I really learned to like myself mostly when I was in England, expanding my brain."

He soon became excited by the possibilities opened up by the imminent extension in broadcasting in the UK. In 1963, there were only two TV channels – ITV and BBC, which also ran three radio services. But a new upmarket BBC TV channel was planned for launch in April 1964. In the same month Radio Caroline, the first of the "pirate" radio ships moored just outside British territorial waters, broke the BBC's official broadcasting monopoly by playing pop music around the clock, joined a few months later by Radio London.

By January 1964, Murphy was booked in London's premier jazz club, Ronnie Scott's, located in a basement below a gown manufacturer on Gerrard Street, Soho. Due to a long-standing Musicians' Union ban, American performers were still a relatively new phenomenon at the club. But over the years that followed, every American jazz artist of note appeared at Ronnie's, including former Riverside artists Bill Evans and Wes Montgomery.

At his debut gig on Monday 27th, Mark appeared with the Stan Tracey Trio — Tracey on piano, Ronnie Stephenson on drums and Malcolm Cecil on bass. The set included "A Lot of Living to Do", "Jelly Jelly Blues", and "My Favorite Things" — complete with the lyrics that had so upset Richard Rodgers. According to a reviewer, Murphy also did a "savage" "Nobody Knows You When You're Down and Out" in a medley with "Brother, Can You Spare a Dime?" And he was already singing Oscar Brown Jr's lyrics to Miles's "All Blues".

A contemporary reviewer picked up on certain tropes in Murphy's singing: "He has three main emotional forces with which he imbues his songs. He gave them full vent at his 1964 opening night at Ronnie Scott's.... First there is the mean, racy, abandoned mood — storming through numbers like 'Goody Goody' or a hipped-up 'Hello Young Lovers'. Then he can sing with a sensitive, soft-pedalled poignancy, as for example, on 'I've Got You Under My Skin'. Murphy's interpretation of this is utterly different from all the others you've ever heard, all the way from its feelingful, pianissimo start to its high-powered climax. Third, Mark Murphy is a singer with a great sense of humor. He had us all grinning throughout his rendering of "Doodlin'" and guffawing at his cod version of 'Mack the Knife.'"

Mark loved the club, and became a regular there during the Sixties. "The way the people are seated and handled at Ronnie's... the way it's run... you feel you're in control. You can't get that kind of attention in the States." London, he told Benny Green that year, was proving to be good for his ego, whereas in New York no one seemed to know who he was, and he couldn't get a gig.

"Friends helped," he said years later, "Cleo Laine, Johnny Dankworth. And there were good moments, playing opposite Monk at Ronnie Scott's, where I met Mick Jagger and inadvertently said, 'Congratulations on keeping your career going so long.'" And Annie Ross, who had left Lambert and Hendricks back in New York, invited Mark to play at a new club she was opening, Annie's Room, in Russell Street, Covent Garden.

All in all, it was an ideal time for Murphy to appear on the UK scene. Working at Ronnie's helped him get back on to BBC radio, and occasionally TV, on a steady basis. Although a minority interest, jazz was not yet a dirty word at the BBC. For musicians, the work was plentiful because at the time the Musicians' Union was all-powerful: broadcasting rules said that for every hour of records played ("needle time"), a corresponding amount of time had to be given over to live music – which was more expensive to produce, but provided work for musicians.

In the same month as his first appearance at Scott's, Murphy made his debut on BBC radio's *Jazz Club* with the Scott quartet, baritone sax star Ronnie Ross and piano legend Bill LeSage. This was followed by further appearances, on *Jazz Session* with the Stan Tracey Trio, *The Jazz Scene*, and *Roundabout*. As the Sixties went on, Murphy became a frequent guest on many other BBC radio shows, particularly those in whose title the words "Midnight" and "Music" were combined with some random preposition, e.g. *Music Before Midnight*, again with Stan Tracey and his trio; *Music Around Midnight*, introduced by himself; *Music to Midnight*, with Alan Dell, featuring the Tony Kinsey Trio; and *Music from Midnight*, eventually retitled *Music Through Midnight*. If any radio show was billed as 'late', Murphy was usually on it. He appeared on *Late'n'Lazy*, with the Brian Dee Trio; *Stay Late*, with the Midnight Strings; *Jazz at Night* on the BBC's upmarket Home Service, and *Night Beat*, with the Jack Dorsey Big Band and the Anglo Saxes.

No jazz purist in those days, he was equally happy in the world of pop, appearing in September 1964 on Brian Matthew's *Top Gear* show on the Light Programme, the BBC's easy listening radio service, along with Gerry and the Pacemakers. In fact, Mark embraced "swinging London" with enthusiasm. Before long, the shy American was the hippest of the hip, a dedicated follower of fashion, dressed in a black velvet suit with wide lapels and flares. He also found in London a cultural life that deeply appealed to him. The world seemed full of possibilities. Interviewed between sets at Scott's in 1964, he said, "I really love going to art museums and the legitimate theatre. I love to go and see brilliant actors, especially English actors. I sit on the edge of my seat throughout. I'm also a sort of archaeologist… love digging up things and finding old fossils, buildings, pots and stuff like that." He was still thinking about acting. "I'd like to get a role in the movies. As an extra. An off-beat role. Some sort of weird part. Something like Elvis Presley's elder brother who takes dope!"

But it was a while before he regarded London as his permanent home. In a *Crescendo* interview that year, he was still talking about the performing scene in the US. "I have had to develop two acts. One is for places like Birdland and contains most of my jazz material. The other I keep for places like [Jack's] in San Francisco, The Crescendo in LA and The Desert Inn at Palm Springs, where you have to aim at a more commercial late supper crowd." And he grumbled about the quality of the musicians he had to work with: "You know the standard of house bands is far from satisfactory. In point of fact, it's still a discouraging picture in many areas. On the whole, I'm not too keen on working in saloons. I much prefer doing concert work. There are only a handful of clubs I really enjoy working in. People are people wherever you go. Some are hip, but the majority are the squarest… Then there is Europe. I would like to do some work over there... It would give me a chance to reach some different audiences."

It wasn't long before he attracted the attention of the UK recording industry in the shape of Jack Baverstock, head of A&R for Fontana Records. A subsidiary of the Philips record company, Fontana was primarily a pop label. But in the late Fifties it had also recorded Ronnie Scott and his sextet, and in the early Sixties alto saxophonist John Dankworth, his wife, singer Cleo Laine, and tenor man Tubby Hayes.

Given Murphy's subsequent reputation as a hardcore bebop singer, it's easy to forget that from the beginning of his career with Decca, he had recorded singles in the pop vein, starting with 1957's "The Right Kind of Woman". The pianist, composer and arranger Les Reed remembered meeting up with him before recording the Fontana album to discuss some songs Reed had written with his partner Barry Mason, with a view to single releases. One of them was "And Now You've Gone", a pop soul dance number in Murphy's jazzy supper club style. Later there were other pure pop singles for Fontana, such as the string-laden mid-tempo ballad "Broken Heart".

In April 1964, almost certainly at the Philips Studios in Stanhope Place, he recorded an album – *Mark Time!* It was decided to use three different arrangers: Tubby Hayes, Johnny Dankworth, and the 28-year-old Les Reed. Each worked with the singer on four tunes, giving the main voicings in their arrangements to different parts of the orchestra: Hayes with brass, Dankworth with woodwind, and Reed with strings. 'The contrast in the studio was interesting... the way each [arranger] set about the sessions,' said Murphy shortly afterwards, "Johnny Dankworth, rather like a professor of music. Cool, competent, collected. Maybe he knew they were going to call him *John* on the sleeve. Tubbs... more like a friendly bartender. Completely relaxed. Amiable. And then, at moments, like a John Bloom. Wondering if the deal is going to get through after all."

Murphy also shed a little more light on his relationships with arrangers. "I don't get on all that easily with [them]. I always warn them in advance... I hear it one way, and if I can't feel they've got the right background, it doesn't move me. Often it's come down to the guy demanding: 'Who's the arranger? Me or you?'" Mark's rather withdrawn off-stage personality didn't help. Les Reed found him uncommunicative, and felt that he was a very lonely man. But Mark enjoyed collaborating with him. "I'd worked with Les before, but only on singles. I didn't know what his string writing was like. But it's beautiful!" Reed added, "Mark was always of the opinion that we should do our own thing, which we did and he was quite satisfied with the results. A nice man generally and incredibly complimentary."

And indeed the tracks arranged by Les Reed are by far the strongest on *Mark Time!*, which was released in the US as *A Swingin' Singin' Affair*. But overall it sounds like a step back to Ralph Burns, with brash, over-confident cuts like "Ballyhoo", an obscure number written by Charles Aznavour. And despite the combined jazz pedigrees of Dankworth and Hayes, some of the arrangements can only be described as misjudgments, including a hiccupping Hayes arrangement of the Beatles' "She Loves You". Here, and on many of the other tracks, such as a slow waltz-time take on "Happy Days Are Here Again" and a shouty "Hard-Hearted Hannah", Murphy's vocal performance sounds brash and insincere, and the arrangements equally overcooked.

According to Murphy, his interpretation of "She Loves You" was the first Beatles tune to be recorded "out of context". "Shortly after I recorded it I heard Ella was in town and she recorded 'Can't Buy Me Love'. Because of who she was, she got it out before me and of course national exposure." There seems to have been some ambivalence about the Beatles in his mind: his live version of "She Loves You" was deemed "subtly insulting" by one reviewer who heard it.

Producer Jack Baverstock inadvertently gave away the cause of the problem with *Mark Time!*: "I have tried to retain enough of the jazz content in Mark's singing to bring home his unique and dynamic style. But I have sought to give the album a commercial 'edge' in order to interest people outside the jazz sphere." Once again, in other words, there seems to have been a loss of nerve, and a blurring of Mark's musical identity, so that he ended up straddling jazz and the mainstream. But it was a sign of the times: jazz was falling through the cracks opened up by the pop earthquake. As recently as 1961, trad bandleaders Chris Barber, Acker Bilk and Kenny Ball had scored unexpected chart hits, while Dankworth and his orchestra had also reached the top 10 with "African Waltz". This naturally encouraged Baverstock into thinking that jazz could still be commercially successful.

Mark changed his story about rock and pop later in life, maintaining that he had been forced to abandon jazz throughout the Sixties. But in 1964 he told *Crescendo*'s Pat Brand, "Good tunes are getting into the top 40... I'd like to do a complete album of good new material... I think it's wrong, too, for musicians to condemn the newer music so quickly and completely. Because songs like 'She Loves You' and 'Walk On By' have got originality. They've broken away from that eight-eight-bridge-eight that I got so bored with."

So Fontana tried to market *Mark Time!* to jazz fans, while simultaneously attempting to broaden Murphy's appeal. A curious advertisement in *Crescendo* bears this out the label's confusion: "He has suddenly been discovered as a superlative performer of quality pop or 'jazz fringe' material (it's funny how there isn't a single word for good music any more) and bids fair to becoming *the* popular male singer of the decade." It described the album as "great popular music laced with jazz", adding, "For years he squandered his musicianship – he plays piano as well as sings – on inattentive American night club audiences."

Previewing the album in the *Sunday Telegraph*, Peter Clayton was warm in his approval of Mark Murphy, if slightly less so of *Mark Time!*: "Not an out-and-out jazz record, it could nevertheless only have been made by jazz musicians... I still don't know whether Mark Murphy is in fact that rare bird, the jazz singer. But even in his commercial vein, Mark Murphy will do for me until, as the song says, the real thing comes along."

BBC2, the new television channel, came on the air in April, and with it a promise by the broadcaster that it would be a platform for the arts, including jazz. Sure enough, a show called *Jazz 625* soon emerged. Britain's premier modernist, Tubby Hayes, was an obvious choice for inclusion on the new show, and on March 22nd his quintet pre-recorded two *Jazz 625* episodes live at Soho's Marquee Club, with guest vocalists Mark Murphy and Betty Bennett. After a couple of instrumentals, Mark sang "Where Are You?", "Kansas City", "I Believe in You", "'S Wonderful", "Hey Look Me Over" and "A Lot of Livin' to Do". The show was aired in August.

Murphy made a second appearance on *Jazz 625* in February 1966, this time with the Stan Tracey Trio and Ronnie Scott. His chosen tunes were "My Favorite Things", "Blue Monk", "Someone to Love", "For Heaven's Sake", "Happy Bachelor", "The Great City", "On Broadway", and "Secret Love." Sadly, like so much of the BBC's Sixties output, both recordings have been lost.

In later years Mark Murphy told interviewers that for ten years he "put his jazz book away", but it was another of his self-created myths. A date in Manchester at Ernie Garside's Club 43 was a case in point. Mark had made the trip north in late 1964 to see John Dankworth's quintet play to an appreciative audience of serious jazz fans, and afterwards commented, "I guess the jazz things will be all right for this audience." Two weeks later he was back as a performer, backed by the Brian Dee Trio, with Freddie Logan on bass and Jackie Dougan, drums. The repertoire that night included "Straight No Chaser", "All Blues", "Bijou", "Señor Blues", "Doodlin'", "Milestones", "Body and Soul" and "Wee Baby Blues".

A perceptive reviewer saw exactly what Murphy was up to: "[The gig] made one realize why Murphy is so insistent on having the right backing," wrote Steve Voce, "using, as he does, a majority of numbers intended for big bands, the accompanying group has to provide a more complex than usual support, and this was particularly evident in numbers like 'I Remember Clifford' and 'Whisper Not'. Murphy's idea of the jazz things baffles me a little, for I have seen what he calls his commercial night club act – which is total jazz. I have never heard him sing anything which couldn't be described as a jazz performance." The audience at Club 43 was stunned into an "awed silence which was to persist throughout each number of his two-hour show," added Voce.

Two years after Mark Murphy first arrived in London, it still didn't seem to be his permanent home. "He is an avowed anglophile, and his ambition is to live in London permanently," reported *Jazz Journal* in mid-1965. "His recent stay was terminated only by the expiry of his Ministry of Labor work permit, and there seems little doubt that he will make further extended trips to this country."

But a successful singing career was not the only reason why Murphy spent so many years in London: it was there that he found the love of his life.

6 He's As Good As I Am

We don't know exactly when Mark Murphy met 24-year-old Eddie O'Sullivan, but it may have been in the spring of 1964, at a record shop in King's Road, Chelsea, owned by Alan Strickland. It was one of a small chain of stores specializing in jazz and big band music, specifically LPs. Eddie was the manager of Strickland's Soho Record Centre in 1963/4, and managed other shops at different times. In those days, Strickland would host in-store personal appearances by the biggest music stars of the day, including Frank Sinatra, Shirley Bassey, Sammy Davis Jr., Johnny Mathis, Andy Williams... and Mark Murphy. It is possible that Murphy was at the Chelsea branch to promote *Mark Time!* However, Eddie also at one time ran his own business, known as Town Records, at 402 King's Road, and the meeting may have taken place there.

The true history of Mark's relationship with Eddie is difficult to establish in retrospect because of the very real need for secrecy in those days: homosexuality was illegal. Only a decade earlier, computer pioneer Alan Turing, who had been convicted of "gross indecency", agreed to be treated with female hormones (so-called chemical castration) as an alternative to prison. He committed suicide two years later. Even after 1967, when the passing of the Sexual Offenses Act permitted homosexual acts under very limited conditions, the courts interpreted these strictly: the sex had to be proven consensual, it had to take place in private (this excluded hotel rooms and houses in which other people were present), and the participants had to be over 21.

The importance of Eddie O'Sullivan in Mark Murphy's life is difficult to over-state. Not only were they lovers, but Mark found in him an intellectual equal, a cultured and knowledgeable Englishman whose background in selling records had made him aware of many kinds of music. Eddie's areas of musical knowledge included the Brazilian songs that later formed such a crucial part of the Murphy repertoire. They even wrote a tune together – "Do You Wonder If I Love You" – for the B-side of the "Just Like A Woman" single release on Fontana.

Mark Murphy was all too well aware of the effect that it would have on his career, his liberty, and his permission to remain in the UK, if his orientation became generally known. Well into the 21st century, long after there had been major changes in public attitudes, and subsequently in the law, he remained discreet about his sexuality. Despite knowing Mark for 40 years, Michael Bourne was surprised when he learned of Eddie's existence for the first time at Mark's memorial service in 2016. "I never knew him in a couple. He never talked about that. He once told me a story that began, 'You know when you're with a chick...' And I looked at him and thought, 'You were never with a chick!' He was being metaphorical, [he meant] like when you're with a lover."

In 1966, three years into his UK sojourn, Mark still presented an intriguing picture to those who sought him out. Gloria Bristow, who worked in music press and promotions for Philips, wrote in the liner notes to *Who Can I Turn To?*: "Off stage one finds a reserved, well-rounded personality, a young man who can discuss with equal facility everything from Cole Porter to Respighi, Sophocles to Dylan Thomas, world politics to moral responsibility in the Arts, and therapeutic fruit juices to cucumber salad!"

By this time, Mark and Eddie were living together in a small first-floor flat at 40c Cornwall Gardens, South Kensington, a few blocks west of the Natural History Museum. It was one of seven flats in the building, old-fashioned and high-ceilinged, with a balcony that looked out over an elegant square filled with mature trees and shrubs. A modest single-bedroom flat like theirs sells today (2018) for well over a million pounds. Back then, long before the property boom, the area was cheap enough for students.

John Jack, who worked at Ronnie Scott's for much of the Sixties, saw Murphy quite often around this time. "I knew and liked his work from his Riverside recordings, so I enjoyed being able to come in contact personally with him. At one point an old friend and I started to become 'a decorating company' – a rather short-lived venture for various reasons, but Mark had the honor of

The London flat (with balcony) shared by Mark and Eddie O'Sullivan (author photo)

being one of our first clients. He had taken a flat over in Kensington/Chelsea area... and wanted the décor changed, which was fine by us, but he sailed off to Harrods of all the places he could have gone to, and bought a load of extremely expensive wallpaper. Very classy, complete with an overriding pattern in gold!! Beautiful Mark. BUT the damned stuff was not fixed to the surface properly and as soon as one put paste on the back to fix the paper to the wall, you could not smooth it out without the gold dust coming off, [a] total waste of pricey paper. 'Johnson and Jack' packed up ladders and pots for a swift exit!"

Leonard Levesley, who visited in March, described Mark as "a tall, withdrawn, intellectual American of 33 who can (and does) sing 'Doodlin'' better than Annie Ross, 'Spring Can Really Hang You Up the Most' better than Sinatra and 'Who Can I Turn To?' better than Shirley Bassey... He lives in less than luxury in a small Kensington flat, surrounded by antiques, paintings, works of history and philosophy, and every record that Peggy Lee and Anita O'Day ever made." Murphy must have been feeling a little down at the time. In his sympathetic piece, Levesley continued, "His first agents also handled the Modern Jazz Quartet, and since then he has caused roughly the same reaction as them: doted on by connoisseurs and eggheads, enjoyed but largely ignored by a wider public. Three years ago he came to England, where he has no difficulty in getting cabaret dates or supporting bits in television shows. This makes him mournful. 'I'm the kind of guy producers keep ringing up and saying "Mark, old chap, we've got two minutes to fill." And that's my lot.'" And Levesley spotted something that most of Mark's record companies had missed. "Realistically a publicist would find it an impossible job to fit Mark Murphy into any of the moulds of current pop idols. His hair is thinning slightly. He has a serious, shy, donnish look about him. He finds it difficult to make the judgments of instant slickness that 30-second television interviews demand."

Mark sometimes returned to the States to see his family. Doc's wife Nancy remembers a visit from him and Eddie in the mid-Sixties when she and Doc were living in Lake Placid. In 1966, after Doc and Nancy moved to Altamont, NY, Mark and Eddie arrived driving a camper van. In the autumn of the following year, Mark played host at Cornwall Gardens to his brother Kevin and Kevin's wife Kate. "What a thrill it was to hear Mark's music all over London," Kate remembered in 2016. "Even when we went shopping in Harrods, we heard him on the Muzak."

Since Mark had never come out as gay to his family, as far as they were concerned, Eddie was his "flat-mate". So first, there was the tricky problem of explaining the sleeping arrangements. Said Kate, "My new husband... and I stayed in their lovely apartment, and Mark offered us the story of him sleeping in the living room, while Eddie slept in the bedroom. Me: 'Yeah, right.' Kev: 'Well if he says it's that way, then it's that way.'" At dinner one night, the mild-mannered Eddie suddenly unleashed a tirade against marriage, saying that every couple he ever knew lost all the love in their relationship as soon as they got married – it squelched everything. Mark laughed nervously and said, "Eddie, I've never heard you go off like this about marriage!" Kate felt he was embarrassed, she and Kevin being only recently married, and in fact on their second honeymoon.

"A year later, Doc's wife, Nancy Murphy, and I stayed up the whole night, and with the help of a little gin, convinced the two brothers of Mark and Eddie's deep commitment to love, and to each other. It wasn't so much that the brothers held unkind feelings about gay people, as it was... well, they just couldn't believe their Mark was gay. When Mark's mother passed away... she still hoped he'd find a nice girl to marry, because she thought that was the only way to true happiness. I think she was the last one standing who still thought he was straight."

Charles Cochran, with whom Mark used to stay when he visited New York, also visited him at Cornwall Gardens. "The apartment was shabby-chic, as they say nowadays. It had a lot of old things in it. There was a nice old-fashioned elegance about it, with high ceilings and a pull-out sofa-bed." Murphy took Cochran on a visit to Sissinghurst Castle because he was a big fan of Vita Sackville-West, who created a famous garden in the grounds, and Virginia Woolf – both writers admired by his hero Jack Kerouac.

Around the middle of 1965, David Platz of publishers Essex Music was looking for a recording project in which some of the songs he represented could be used. He was prepared to finance it, and to arrange its release through a major label. Platz liked to encourage new talent: he brought rock acts The Move, Joe Cocker and Procol Harum to EMI, and signed up an array of Sixties acts including John Dankworth, Dudley Moore, and David Bowie.

Whenever he found a writer with potential, Platz would set up a new company for them, which gave his clients a financial incentive to stick with Essex. At one time, Platz was a director of over 30 such companies. Among his clients were musical theater songwriters Anthony Newley and Leslie Bricusse. Essex had originally been established in the UK by American music publisher and manager Pete Kameron, who along with Monte Kay had managed Mark Murphy in New York ten years earlier, when he was signed by Decca.

Together with his friend Kenny Napper, bass player in Ronnie Scott's house band, and some top UK jazz talent including Kenny Baker (trumpet), Tony Coe (tenor sax) and Alan Branscombe (piano), Murphy started working on a new album, with Napper as arranger and conductor. Eight of the 12 songs were published by Essex Music. Platz convinced Rolling Stones manager Andrew Loog Oldham and his partner Tony Calder to include the new Murphy album among the first releases on their new Immediate record label.

Immediate was an independent operation, with a maverick, punk-type ethic *avant la lettre*. The new Mark Murphy album, entitled *Who Can I Turn To?*, was only the fourth to be released on the new label, in early February, 1966. Record Retailer announced: "To coincide with the disc's release, Mark, who is currently starring at Ronnie Scott's Club, will be featured on several TV shows. Among the latter are *The Mark Murphy Show* (BBC2 – February 6), *Five O'Clock Club* (ITV – February 8) and on February 25 he stars on one of BBC TV's late shows. A *Bernard Braden Show* appearance is also planned."

As before, Murphy seemed only too ready to "put away his jazz book". Although a marked improvement on *Mark Time!*, *Who Can I Turn To?* once more falls awkwardly between pop and jazz. It was one thing to freshen up the jazz repertoire by incorporating the best of contemporary pop writing, but many of the tracks had recently been recorded by Murphy's contemporaries. Four were Leslie Bricusse compositions, including the title track, from the Bricusse/Newley musical *The Roar of the Greasepaint – The Smell of the Crowd*. Both Shirley Bassey and Tony Bennett had recorded versions of the title track that year. In its Murphy manifestation, it's arranged as a slinky Latin shuffle, dominated by strings and Kenny Baker's trumpet.

In an era where all forms of popular culture were still produced within rigid genre categories, the world wasn't yet ready for Murphy's experiments with non-jazz material. On hearing the album, the reviewers failed to rave. What was a jazz singer doing recording tunes like "My Kind of Girl", a 1960 pop hit for Matt Monro? And why was it arranged like a George Fame-style driving blues? His version of Charles Aznavour's "Le Temps" would have made little sense to many listeners – it never settles into any solid rhythm, starting with ballad strings, and then quickly switching between Latin and swing.

However, there is much to like about *Who Can I Turn To?* Kenny Napper's arrangements sound smoother and more contemporary than those on *Mark Time!* Murphy's bossa nova take on Johnny Mercer's "Star Sounds", complete with cool vibes, is a foray into the Brazilian music he always loved. The traditional spiritual "This Train" was first recorded in 1922, the locomotive in question being "bound for glory". Mark's organ-driven, second-line-beat train, by contrast, is more notable for its passenger list. It "don't carry no phonies" and "don't have no Mersey sound, it "just carries the swingers... Stan Getz, Ray Charles, Peggy Lee and Sarah Vaughan... Count Basie, Woody Herman, Miles Davis, Dave Brubeck..." And Mercer's slow swinger "Talk To Me Baby" opens with sophisticated Big Apple strings, muted trumpet and Tony Coe's cool saxophone fills.

In spite of his natural introversion, Murphy's public profile was high. In 1965/6, and again in 1966/7, he was voted no.2 male vocalist – second only to Frank Sinatra – in the *Melody Maker* readers' poll. The paper described him at the time as "an ultra-cool male version of Annie Ross". His sheer ubiquity on radio and television probably had a lot to do with this: he did not limit himself to music shows. Twice in 1964, he appeared on a BBC2 afternoon magazine show called *Open House* ("People-Places-Pops") introduced by Irish chat host Gay Byrne, and on November 6, he even turned up on *The Benny Hill Show*.

Today this all sounds distinctly odd, but at the time jazz singers were a common sight on mainstream television – Cleo Laine, Annie Ross and Salena

Jones also made appearances with Hill. With only two television channels to choose from, plus one highbrow newcomer, shows like these regularly enjoyed ratings above five million. In April 1965 Mark had been a guest on ITV's Millicent Martin show, *Mainly Millicent*, singing with the Jack Parnell Band and cantering through "Stablemates" from the *Mark Time!* album, and reprising his single hit "Fly Me To The Moon". These were among the top-rated light entertainment shows of their era. The children's show *Five O'Clock Club*, with its puppet stars, provided another opportunity for Mark to show off his jazz chops, in February 1966. If that sounds like an even more bizarre mismatch than Benny Hill, it should be said that George Fame and the Blue Flames and the Dudley Moore Trio were also featured on *Five O'Clock Club* at different times. In August 1969, Murphy was part of the "cabaret" for the BBC1 coverage of Miss United Kingdom in glamorous Blackpool. In August 1970 he even appeared on *The Golden Shot*, a teatime show which involved members of the public firing a crossbow while blindfolded.

Was Mark Murphy a middle-of-the-road entertainer or a serious jazz artist? In November 1966, the jazz critic Benny Green witnessed his gig opposite Freddie Hubbard at Ronnie Scott's, which had by now relocated to its present base in Frith Street. Green, whose rasping "East End" delivery made him an instantly recognizable voice on radio, was a highly knowledgeable critic with a forensic brain. His insight into Mark Murphy's singing style was pointed, and it highlighted an issue that many had noticed before, but few of whom had articulated with such precision.

In his book about the early days of Ronnie's, Green described the singer as "an intensely devoted artist with a good musical knowledge and almost limitless ambition. Murphy's chief fault seems to be connected with his desire to cram into every vocal all the harmonic complexities that one would normally look for only in the work of an instrumentalist. In reducing his voice to an instrument through which to express the words, Murphy sometimes complicates his material to the point where it disappears entirely. There is another end result of this kind of vocal daring. Each song, composed of chords, is given the same degree of intensity, so that the weightiness of one lyric is equated with the triviality of another. If Murphy were to lend a lighter touch to some of the lighter songs, the value of his recitals would immediately double. As it was on his debut at Scott's, admiration for the vocal gymnastics was always tempered by the regret that he was reducing the words too often to mere sounds."

But throughout his life, all attempts to cast Mark Murphy from some pre-existing mold were doomed to failure. He was an educated middle-class man who never showed the slightest interest in money or the pursuit of a conventional career. He was a white man whose entire being was consumed with his love for jazz, which despite its hybrid origins has long been considered a "black" art form. For whatever reason, he felt he had been rebuffed by Miles Davis, and usually worked with white musicians. But in May of 1967, he took the unusual step of spending three weeks in South Africa, the first jazz musician to do so since Tony Scott ten years before. In a letter to *Downbeat*, he said he "was just plain curious" about the country and wanted to get to meet its people and see how they were affected by their "strange environment", a reference to the apartheid regime then firmly in control.

As the magazine reported, "the tour turned out to be far more than a satisfaction of this curiosity. The singer found that although his tour schedule included only performances before white audiences (which he had expected), it was possible also to perform for non-whites if one really wanted to and was persistent enough." Murphy duly applied for a permit to perform for a black audience. Predictably this was turned down, but he was finally allowed to give a concert at the Dorkay House in Johannesburg. Accompanied by guitarist John Fourie, bassist Midge Pike and drummer Selwyn Lissack, he played to an audience of more than 600 black Africans.

Murphy's decision to visit the country was at odds with the prevailing wisdom in both the UK and the US that a complete boycott was the only way to end the apartheid regime. He may have been inspired by the principled stand taken by Dusty Springfield in December 1964. After Dusty and her group The Echoes performed for an integrated audience at a theatre near Cape Town, their tour was abruptly terminated, and she was deported – despite her contract specifically excluding segregated performances.

In his letter to *Downbeat* Mark Murphy urged fellow musicians to follow his example, which they could do by contacting a Johannesburg DJ called Lowell Johnson. "[Murphy] points to the need for music books and study materials, but most of all for personal contact," explained *Downbeat*. "While he empathizes with those American musicians who refuse to go to South Africa to play for segregated audiences, he feels that they might go to give lectures or seminars. '[Black audiences] would be so damn glad just to see you and shake your hand."

Murphy's later publicity often claimed that while in the UK "he worked mainly as an actor". Although that was not actually the case, he did make a number of forays into drama, albeit often as a singer. One of these was a cameo in the 1967 Swinging London comedy-drama *Just Like A Woman*, written and directed by Robert Fuest, who specialized in cartoony productions like TV's *The Avengers* and the 1971 horror film classic *The Abominable Dr Phibes*. *Just Like A Woman* is the story of a wealthy couple, played by Wendy Craig and Francis Matthews. The latter is a hard-drinking, womanizing television director. There's the obligatory moronic pop star, and a number of funny foreigners, including a monocle-wearing German inventor played by Clive Dunn. Mark, in the not-too-taxing role of a swinging, black-clad jazz singer, appears in two nightclub scenes. He duets with Craig on the song "Let's Take A Chance", and later performs the film's title song. The film probably came Murphy's way thanks to the involvement of Kenny Napper, who had been hired to write and conduct the music.

Just Like a Woman (Dormar Productions Ltd 1967): Mark with Wendy Craig

BBC Radio was radically reorganized in September 1967, when the Corporation finally claimed victory over the North Sea pirate stations by hiring their star DJ's, who had captured the Light Programme's younger audience. In belated recognition that pop music was indeed popular, the Light Programme now split into Radio 1, a new pop station, and Radio 2, devoted to MOR and easy listening. The classical Third Programme became Radio 3, and talk network the Home Service became Radio 4. With all the upheaval, it was more than a year before Murphy got himself back on the air, albeit at the familiar hour of midnight or even later, making weekly appearances with the Gordon Beck Quartet on Radio 1's *Night Ride* ("swinging sounds on and off the record"). The show later migrated to Radio 2, its more natural home under the new regime.

Norbert Warner, a serious fan of vocal jazz who lived in the north-east of England, had bought a copy of *Meet Mark Murphy* in 1959 and liked it so much that he bought every subsequent Murphy album. Eight years later, he saw from his local newspaper that the singer was appearing at Greys in Newcastle, a club considered discreet enough for local businessmen to bring their girlfriends and/or secretaries. Warner, who often made his own recordings of live gigs, had permission to haul his battery-powered Revox into the club but was firmly told that cameras were not allowed: the clientele were understandably publicity-shy.

Murphy was astonished when Warner appeared at the gig with copies of every album he had ever recorded, asking him to add his signature. He told Warner he would be working in Newcastle for the next couple of weeks. Soon the two were getting on so well that they arranged for Mark to visit the Warners' home in nearby Whitley Bay. Bert offered to pick him up from his hotel in Sunderland. "Outside, Mark asked where my car was. I pointed to my Lambretta motor-scooter. We had a great run in the country that afternoon."

The two became firm friends, and Murphy would stay with the Warners whenever he was playing in the north-east. "He liked looking at stately homes," recalled Bert, "so I would take him around on the back of my Lambretta." On one occasion, Mark and Eddie came up by car to look at a stately home in Scotland. In the course of this jaunt they found a curiously shaped dead tree washed up on the beach, tied it to the roof of the car and carried it back to London.

In every public place in the UK at the time, smoking was rife – an occupational hazard for singers. Mark had always taken great care of his voice, and now fretted about losing it. "The rooms in the clubs are so thick with cigarette smoke that you couldn't see across it. I almost had a nervous breakdown worrying about my voice." Sometimes if he thought the air in a club was too smoky he would go around the room opening all the windows. He began employing a bizarre array of protective measures, including electric fans positioned on the stage to blow the smoke back at the audience, a flying saucer-shaped steamer on top of the piano to keep his vocal cords lubricated, and a row of potions as well as honey and water.

At one point the smoke became such an obsession that he seriously considered a change of career. "I had this fantastic masseur. Here was this guy who whizzed around on his bicycle to his clients during the day, made good money and didn't have to declare more than half of it. He came and went as he pleased and worked when he wanted to work. If he didn't want to work, he just had to say he was busy. I literally almost went off to a school to learn massage, then I looked at an anatomy chart and thought, how in the hell would I memorize all that! I stuck with the only thing I could do, and that is to sing and act."

On a cold December day in 1967, after a trip to Prague to play in a major jazz concert at the Lucerna Hall, Mark flew to Köln to record at Lindström Studios for the German label MPS. His backing group consisted of key members of the Kenny Clarke-Francy Boland Big Band, with whom he had toured several times. The resulting album, *Midnight Mood*, is one of the best he ever made. For over a decade the Clarke-Boland band were perhaps the most impressive jazz orchestra outside the United States, with an international line-up that included Ronnie Scott on tenor and Francy Boland (who wrote the arrangements) on piano.

Murphy is in devastatingly fine voice on these tracks, relaxed and swinging with the kind of material he loved and knew well. And although he often said that his true voice didn't emerge until he was 40, that voice is here, and this album prefigures the golden era of his mid-Seventies Muse recordings.

The cuts on Side A include the sublime "Why and How", written by Jimmy Deuchar and Murphy himself, powered by Clarke's groovy backbeat and cowbell, with a terrific horn arrangement from Boland. Suddenly, we feel we are in the present, far away from the BBC and the tatty old England of the Sixties. The track was rediscovered in the Eighties, when it became a soul jazz rare groove track beloved of DJ Gilles Peterson. The laid-back second side is devoted to ballads of a type suggested by the album's title, including the beautiful, dark Murphy/Boland composition "Hopeless", Jimmy Woode's "Sconsolato", Murphy's first proper foray into slow Latin groove, with meandering flute from Sahib Shihab, and a version of "My Ship", which Murphy delivers with controlled passion and some lovely glissando work.

At some point in early 1968, a friend of Murphy's got him on ABC's reality TV show *The Dating Game*. It had become a vehicle for exposing rising young stars, including Lindsay Wagner, Tom Selleck, Arnold Schwarzenegger, and even Michael Jackson. Murphy was chosen by actress Susan Strasberg to be her date on a trip to Greece, and won a camera as a prize. "Susan Strasberg turned out to be four feet tall," said Mark. "She was working, I was working, and I'd been to Greece before, so I just took the camera and ran. The emcee introduced me by holding up my album (*Midnight Mood*) so I got national publicity even though it wasn't released yet." And of course nobody on *The Dating Game* mentioned that Mark was gay.

For many years, his appearances were trailed with a "quote" from Ella Fitzgerald – "He is my equal". The origin of that not-100%-accurate endorsement was one Friday evening at Ronnie's, during a week-long Mark Murphy residency. Just before his final set, there was a commotion in the reception area. Ella Fitzgerald, accompanied by her manager, had entered the club, having just played a sell-out concert at the Royal Festival Hall. Buoyed by its success, she was in a bubbly mood, stopping to sign autographs and waving as she recognized friends in the audience.

The jazz diva sat down at a table. Soon afterwards a bottle of Dom Perignon arrived, courtesy of Ronnie Scott. Mark, sensing the theatrical possibilities of the moment, welcomed her to the club. Then, as the applause died down, he invited her to join him on stage. Ella declined, feigning bashfulness, so Mark continued with his set. Not so bashful, however, when it came to showing her appreciation for him, yelling "Isn't he terrific?" and "Isn't he wonderful?" for the next three or four numbers, and generally enjoying herself hugely.

Once again Mark urged her to get up on stage, but Ella continued playing hard to get. Then he sang "Blues in the Night", and to the delight of the crowd, changed the lyrics to include such lines as "That Ella's no good, a wearysome thing, who'll teach you to sing the blues in the night" and ending with "Every Day I Have the Blues": "Ell-a Fitz-gerald, sure is good to see you,

Ell-a Fitz-gerald, sure is good to see you, why don't you come up here and sing some jazz songs too?"

Having enjoyed the Dom Perignon as well as the music, Ella at last stood up and began weaving her way towards the stand. Mark, ever the gentleman, leapt down and escorted her to the mic. Laughing, with their arms around each other, they debated what to sing. Everything Mark suggested was met with, "No, that's too difficult" or "Why don't we do something easy?"

Eventually she agreed to sing "Tea for Two". Mark took a step back to let her go first. Ella had a fit of the giggles, and after several attempts, couldn't remember the words beyond the first two lines. Mark stepped in to help. As he was singing, Ella got in the mood, snapped her fingers and began harmonizing behind him. According to one eyewitness, she then took over for what became "the most mind-blowing scat-duet that had ever been heard. Following extended improvisations from both singers, they traded fours and eights, mesmerizing their audience with quickfire wit and ending with Ella's memory fully restored." Afterwards Mark asked her to sign a picture. She refused, asking on her way out, "How can I give him my autograph? He's as good as I am."

Along with the work he was starting to get around continental Europe, Murphy made his bread and butter from live recordings for the BBC. Needletime rules meant that the Corporation had built up an enormous library of jazz arrangements, which Murphy was at liberty to browse for his own sessions. Since 1967 he had also been making regular trips to Hilversum to work with producer Joop de Roo for Dutch radio.

Some time during 1969, Murphy made his most mysterious and hard-to-find album, *This Must Be Earth*. According to the sparse information provided

With Ella Fitzgerald at Ronnie Scott's, 1968. Guitarist is George Kisch.

on the liner, the album was produced "in association with Eddie O'Sullivan", although its actual producer was Ken Barnes, a Middlesbrough-born journalist and record producer. Barnes had also worked with Bing Crosby, Peggy Lee, Fred Astaire and Gene Kelly, as well as popular UK entertainer Roy Castle. Not surprisingly, he was an aficionado of the Great American Songbook – but on this occasion the traditional canon of vocal jazz was very far from what Mark Murphy had in mind.

This Must Be Earth is a strange, mellow collection of songs from various non-jazz genres – pop, folk, soul, Latin – many of which had been recent hits for other artists. The album's characteristic sound is flute and acoustic guitar. Although by no stretch of the imagination could one call it jazz, there is a pastoral warmth and gentleness to it. Between the tracks are the sounds of waves or wind, which Murphy and Barnes had gone to record on Hampstead Heath early one Sunday morning. With a sound suspiciously like a low-flying vacuum cleaner, the album opens with a spaceship landing on earth, and then dramatic strings introduce Richard Rodney Bennett's title song, in which Murphy imagines himself travelling in a time machine.

Elsewhere there are some Brazilian-influenced tunes, including "Cinnamon and Clove", a lovely Johnny Mandel samba with lyrics by Marilyn and Alan Bergman. Sergio Mendes and Brasil '66 had recorded the song in 1967, but Murphy's version is slower and more ballad-like. Another song – "Salt Sea" – was written by Mendes for his just-released *Crystal Illusions* album, which seems to have been an important influence on Murphy: it also contained a version of "Dock of the Bay" – which Murphy also recorded for *This Must Be Earth* – and Milton Nascimento's "Vera Cruz", which became "Empty Faces" after Lani Hall added her English lyrics. Murphy recorded it six years later for *Mark Murphy Sings*.

The album contains a strong environmental theme: the liner note reads, "Perhaps the most important event of the Apollo moon missions was the 'discovery' of the most beautiful planet in our solar system... EARTH. P.S. Let's keep it that way."

Decades later, British vinyl archaeologist Jonny Trunk was delighted to spot a rare copy of *This Must Be Earth* for sale in London's Spitalfields Market, and negotiated with the dealer to swap it for a rare record of his own. He discovered that CBS was the original distributor of the album, and that Ken Barnes owned the rights. By chance, Trunk knew Barnes, who told him he had no objection to giving him the digital rights, as long as Mark Murphy himself agreed. Trunk duly contacted Murphy and asked him about the recording. Mark told him, "That session was going really well, and then I pissed all over it." Asked what he meant by that, Trunk said, "I have the strong impression he was off his tits at the time."

By the end of the Sixties, Mark was beginning to tire of performing in clubs and on radio across Europe, where sometimes the language barrier bothered him. "I'm somewhat limited with audiences in Europe because of the language problem," he told Bill Moody. "I don't work in France. So of course my best audience is in England or Holland, where English is understood by the majority of people... Living and working in Europe is nothing to be that envious of. There are certain situations, like Herb Geller in Hamburg or Leo Wright in Berlin have, working with state radio orchestras. Now we don't have that in America. But you also run into the European educational system with jazz fans. There is too much concern for disciplines and categories. They want a certain kind of jazz, and two world wars have not erased the class system in England. Try to get out of your category, whatever they think it is, and they treat you like a bad soprano in Milan. They booed Anita O'Day and me in Bremen and Jon Hendricks and Annie Ross when they appeared with Georgie Fame instead of doing their Lambert, Hendricks & Ross bit. Now that's just a lot of spoiled brat nonsense. They don't even have jazz festivals there anymore because they couldn't control the audiences. Believe me, man, jazz fans can be dangerous."

He began making exploratory trips back to North America. In 1971, Charles Cochran, who hadn't seen him perform for years, went to a Murphy gig at the Cava Bob in Toronto. "I was blown away. He was completely transformed. He moved like a dancer, and I thought to myself that something psychological had happened to Mark. No question." The positive influence of Eddie probably had a lot to do with this, as had the hard-won experience of performing day and night during his long stay in Europe. And perhaps too, as he approached 40, Mark had simply become more at ease with himself.

But work in the UK had become scarce. The problems had begun the year before, when the BBC made cutbacks to its expensive radio orchestras, and then Murphy's Dutch radio producer Joop de Roo got transferred to another network. Worried about how he was going to make a living, Mark decided that now might be the time to brush up his acting chops. Back in 1964, he had been cast as "The Singing Voice" in a radio play by Leo Goldman for the BBC's highbrow network, the Third Programme. *Still Small Softcell* was "a gentle satire for radio in which the still, small inner voice proclaims the commercial and political dictates of modern American life."

The roles that now came his way included, in October 1970, a dramatized BBC1 version of the notorious Chicago 7 Conspiracy Trial of 1969–70, in which he played the chief witness for the prosecution; on BBC2, in Brecht's *The Resistible Rise of Arturo Ui*, subtitled *The Gangster Show*, Murphy played a gangster called James Greenwood; then there was a promo film about London Tara Hotel, a voice dub for a film called *Pablo's Place*, and a song in the film version of Herman Hesse's *Steppenwolf* ("that was me with the French accent singing a song dubbed in for the actor Pierre Clementi in the cabaret scene"), with music by avant-garde composer George Gruntz.

In April 1972 he joined Annie Ross, Jane Manning and Isabelle Lucas in a BBC Radio 3 play *Radiance and Death of Joaquin Murieta*, by the Chilean poet Pablo Neruda. "The work takes the form of a dramatic cantata," explained the

Joop de Roo in the 1960s.

Radio Times, "of which Neruda has said that it is intended to be 'melodrama, opera and pantomime' as well as a tragic poem. It tells, in chorus, verse, song and dramatic scenes, the story of a Chilean who came to California in the gold rush of 1849 but turned into a bandit when he saw that his countrymen were treated as second-class citizens by the Yankees." In an otherwise sniffy review, *Guardian* radio critic Gillian Reynolds wrote, "Miss Ross and Mr. Murphy came out of it much the best, understandably since jazz singers in the course of careers spent doing standard Tin Pan Alley ballads, have the edge on most dramatic performers when it comes to endowing clichés with significance."

But soon even the acting work dried up. By the early 1970s, the Murphy/O'Sullivan finances were in steep decline. According to Bert Warner, Mark and Eddie had been renting their London flat for a while, until eventually Eddie decided to buy it. Now he put it up for sale, later telling Warner that he had accepted "cash from an Arab". Soon afterwards Mark could be found living in a trailer in a parking lot on London's South Bank, where the National Theatre was under construction. An even more alarming indicator of his dire situation was a rumor picked up by Warner that Mark and Eddie had been dealing drugs, and the police were on their tail. Mark was also being pursued by the Inland Revenue for unpaid tax.

It was then he learned that his mother had died.

7 Ready for Anything

On October 1, 1972 Margaret Howe Murphy called 911 and was taken to Fulton Hospital in an ambulance. No one in the family knew what was wrong, nor indeed had anyone suspected there was anything wrong. On arrival she asked for a cup of tea, and by the time the nurse returned with it, Margaret was dead. She was 71. Her daughter-in-law Nancy believes she died from either an aneurysm or a heart attack.

Mark returned from England for the funeral. "I expected Mark to be devastated," said his sister-in-law Kate, "because he had doted on her so. But he wasn't! He and I were sorting her stuff and packing up and all that, and he would come running into the living room. 'Look what I found, Kate! I found pictures of her old boyfriends!' And he'd be showing me old hidden love-letters and pictures that she had before she married the father. And he was just enamored of that."

Mark's sexuality and the ambivalence of his relationships with both parents would go some way to explaining this curious reaction. His bruising battles with DL seemed to leave him with a self-esteem problem, causing him to react against his father's patriarchal values, whilst at the same time craving his approval. Mark told his publicist, Lesley Mitchell-Clarke, that his mother was "incredibly cold and aloof", and his sister-in-law Nancy found her intimidating. Mark's delight at finding the pictures and letters may have been an expression of relief – that Margaret had been a real human being of flesh and blood after all.

Margaret Murphy clearly loved her son, even if she found it difficult to show it. Kate remembered, "When he was coming she'd get her nails done and her hair done and always would wear fine clothes. Mark liked that old English thing about getting dressed for dinner, and there being a formal affair. And whenever he was visiting she would always be dressed for dinner, and serve a really good dinner on the fine china and all that. When his mother died, she left him her wedding ring, and one of them [sic – presumably a different ring] was a platinum ring with 20 diamonds around it... And he brought that to me in the kitchen, and said, 'I want to give this to you because you're the closest thing to a wife I'll ever have.' When Kevin and I broke up, Mark wanted me to drop his name and take back my maiden name and really strike out and do wonderful things for myself."

No doubt Mark wanted the best for the newly-independent Kate. But Mark and Eddie had forged a successful and long-standing relationship in London, proving that it was possible to achieve happiness and intimacy in a state of complete freedom, without being tied down by the legal obligations of marriage or the conventions of heterosexual married life. Mark's comments to Kate, and Eddie's earlier outburst on the subject, suggest that the two of them shared this view. "At the time we weren't talking about him being gay, although I think he knew that we knew, but it wasn't an open discussion," added Kate.

Mark, disillusioned with life in London, decided to stay and try again in America. For the time being, Eddie would have to remain behind, since he had no right of residence in the USA. People in the north-eastern cities still remembered Mark from the Fifties and early Sixties, played his records and offered him gigs, and so were the logical places for him to begin what was now his fourth career relaunch.

He settled initially in Buffalo, finding work there and in Cincinnati, Cleveland, Providence and Boston, albeit performing top-40 material. In Cincinnati he had worked in the past with a *simpatico* trio led by the drummer Dee Felice, and he picked up with them again. In Buffalo he worked with another trio formed by pianist John Hasselback, whose drummer was Albert Amaroso. For four weeks a year they would play St George's Table, and at a short-lived downstairs club called The Scene. Albert remembers Mark sending the band members little notes after gigs, written in different colors – green or brown. "He would write, 'Hey man you did fabulous on this tune', or, 'You were a little too busy on the bridge of "Empty Faces". I know you love that song, but listen to the phrasing."

To save money, Mark lived in a camper van dubbed Big Bertha – a bland-looking vehicle in beige and pale green, with matching curtains and bed-cover. "He was not fussy about his living situations," recalled Charles Cochran. Murphy kept all his music in Big Bertha, something that alarmed Albert Amaroso. "I said, 'What happens if you get in an accident, or there's a fire?' He had Dave Matthews's beautiful charts in there! I used to say, 'Why don't you keep 'em locked up somewhere safe?' And he'd say, 'Oh no, Albert, they're fine.'"

Whenever possible, the impecunious Murphy would stay with friends. Cochran had a one-bedroom apartment at 230 Central Park West, New York City, with a fold-out bed in the living room. "From 1973 to 87 I only had one bedroom, and he would sleep soundly on that pull-out couch and never complain. He was a very easy house-guest. For his entire life, Mark was struggling

Mark with Charles Cochran in Big Bertha, 1970s.

financially. I don't think he ever had any appreciable money at all." Though he indeed made few demands as a house guest, Murphy's presence could sometimes become an irritation: the two or three days he said he was going to stay would turn into ten, which tried even the patience of the easy-going Cochran. However, he had learned tolerance with overstaying house guests before: in the mid-Sixties Anita O'Day had occupied the apartment for nine months.

While in New York, Mark looked up his ex-manager Helen Keane, who had been managing Bill Evans for the past nine years. Gene Lees, who knew Keane well, described her as "the archetypal New York woman", tough, clever, perceptive, realistic, but with a sensitivity she kept well hidden – especially from the macho world of jazz. One of her contacts was Joe Fields, who had just started a new jazz record label called Muse.

By 1972, Fields was already a music business veteran, who had been to see Sarah Vaughan "when she was skinny and had a space between her front teeth." Growing up in Brooklyn, where most of the kids obsessed over basketball and baseball, he and his friends were avid record collectors. "We would go to old jukebox places that would play the A sides to death, until they were grey, but it was the B sides that I was looking for." Beginning as a salesman for Columbia, Verve and Prestige in the 1950s and 60s, he later served time with the bubblegum pop label Buddah. "I have a hundred gold singles at home, and a dozen gold albums, from all the Yummy Yummy Chewy Chewy, from Curtis Mayfield to Gladys Knight. They were the hottest singles label in the US. I knew the business, and I knew the radio business. I wasn't an absolute

Joe Fields.

purist; I was looking to sell records. I dug what Mark was doing, but you always think that maybe you could tweak it a little bit, and get a little more airplay, and maybe break something through. That was always the thought in the back of my mind."

Muse Records, which Fields launched without financing ("I rubbed two matchsticks together," he told *Downbeat*) was both prolific and diverse. It functioned for a quarter of a century, releasing well over 200 albums in the Seventies alone, from soul jazz and hard bop to Latin and fusion.

Fields knew about Murphy's *Rah* album from hearing it on the radio, and he also knew Helen Keane. "We were quite friendly. She was one of the first tough bitches that walked around in the jazz business... which wasn't exactly a minor-league feat. We got along just great. So she said, 'Come to lunch, I want you to see Mark in person.' I don't remember the exact occasion, but he was the act that was singing for this particular luncheon. And I liked it, it knocked me out. As tough a broad as Helen was, she had great taste... she worked very hard to promote Bill Evans."

For his new venture, Fields had already recorded James Moody, Sonny Stitt and a handful of other artists, and he quickly decided he wanted to record Mark Murphy too. In fact, vocal jazz was one area in which the label became particularly strong. "That was something I always had a great feel for and there were always great singers around me. So early on [I worked] with guys like Eddie Jefferson and Mark Murphy, and even Morgana King, who wasn't strictly a jazz singer, but she was a great singer."

Fields called Dave Matthews, who had already recorded a couple of albums for the label. Matthews was immediately interested in working with Murphy. Back in the early Sixties, Murphy had taught Matthews something important about the jazz business. "I went to music school in Cincinnati, which was one of the towns Mark would come and play in maybe twice a year, playing with local musicians for about a week, then he'd move to the next place. If you have ten towns where you're popular, that's twenty weeks of work every year, and you can pretty much live on that."

It was agreed that Helen Keane would co-produce the new album with Matthews, while he would write the arrangements and assemble the musicians. A week before the recording date, the three of them assembled at his E. 58th Street apartment to thrash out the overall concept for what became *Bridging a Gap*. In some ways Matthews was a curious choice to work with Mark Murphy: despite making several albums with James Brown, and spending four years on the road conducting his band, Matthews had always maintained that he didn't like singers. "I don't think of James Brown as a singer, I think of him more as an instrumentalist. On his biggest hits, most singers would not like the singing quality. But the point is there is so much feeling and groove in it, that you can't ignore it. Mark was certainly very rhythmic. And anyone who considers themselves a jazz singer must have very good time. A lot of singers are difficult and temperamental, but we never had any problem at all, and his artistic vision was so clear that it was really quite easy for me to make an accompaniment to his artistry."

Certainly, Muse was a good fit for Murphy. Joe Fields liked to give his artists their head. "My philosophy's always been, from day one: how could I tell an artist, that has his own style and his own approach, what the hell to record? I can't. I wouldn't have the balls to do it, because he or she knows what they want to do more than I do." And there was another, more down-to-earth reason why the canny Fields took a shine to his latest signing. "He was a very fast worker. That was another big criteria from where I sat, having to do with money. I didn't want anyone who would drop a note and say, OK, take 22. None of that crap. He was an improviser, and he got through it very, very quickly. He had six hours. If he couldn't cut it in six hours, I couldn't do it."

Other Muse artists learned to cope with the pressure of this punishingly tight recording schedule. Saxophonist Richie Cole always made sure he rehearsed with his band before they went into the studio, because once in there, from noon till six, there was no time for mistakes – "for an album you had to live with for the rest of your life," as he put it.

But Fields was also a genuine and unabashed Mark Murphy fan. "[Mark] had great taste in songs. He heard songs that when I heard it from him, and when it was the first time that I'd heard the song, and then went back and listened to the original version, he was amazing. He was a real tune maven. He knew great lyrics. And when I heard him do them at the recording, I would go, whoa, where did he get that from? He absolutely killed them." Fields appreciated Murphy's deep knowledge of the Great American Songbook, in particular his frequent revival of some long-forgotten verses. "People [had] stopped doing verses, which was a crime, because some of the verses are as beautiful as the songs themselves, sometimes better, sometimes they'd tell a story."

On November 20, Mark Murphy arrived at Basement Studios, New York, to meet the Rolls Royce band that Matthews had assembled: the Brecker Brothers, then playing with Horace Silver, plus experienced session men Pat Rebillot on organ, Sam Brown on guitar, Ron Carter on bass and Jimmy Madison on drums. Murphy had already proved his mastery of blues, soul, ballads and fine swingin' jazz. On *Bridging a Gap*, he brings all of this multi-faceted experience to the fore. Matthews's horn charts, drawn from his years with James Brown, are strong throughout, particularly on his funked-up "Sunday In New York" and express-train arrangement of "As Time Goes By", with Murphy's soulful improvised lyrics over the extended coda. The album begins with a new version of "Come and Get Me", with prowling bass and chilly high-register organ, and continues with another of his own compositions – "Sausalito", like a darker, more satisfying "'I Left My Heart in San Francisco", with a strong melody, terrific dynamics, and tasty guitar fills from Brown.

Murphy's partially re-harmonized 12/8 version of Jimmy Dorsey's standard "I'm Glad There Is You" begins with a long verse, backed only by Brown's reverberating guitar. The rest of the band comes in halfway through it, with gorgeous swelling organ, and a passionate vocal from Murphy. And despite an egregious fumble by Sam Brown at 4:19, the coda fade is a dark, moody masterpiece, with a Phrygian mode guitar solo over spectral midnight chords. This track made a big impression on broadcaster Michael Bourne, who became a lifelong fan. "[It] opens with Mark singing the verse quietly, tenderly, with only a guitar, floating freely. Some chords from the keys enter with a pulse, and Mark sings into and around the pulse. Like Icarus flying skyward, Mark's voice swirls up to the sun, up to the height of his chops, and then, with his wings melting, with a cry in his voice, he falls down to the bottom register, dark and deep into the song... lovingly caressing '*you*.'"

But not everyone loved *Bridging a Gap*. "Good music, enjoyable, fine singing, but with the lack of good male jazz vocal records, why bridge a gap between jazz and pop, especially when this is constantly being done and over done?" complained *Downbeat*. Of course the album also bridged a gap in time and space: some three years had passed since the recording of *This Must Be Earth*, not to mention 3,500 miles of ocean.

While working to revive his career in the States, Mark stayed in touch with radio producer Joop de Roo back in Hilversum, Holland, and for four years he returned there regularly to record with the Louis van Dijk Trio. Murphy's association with the Dutch Metropole Orchestra was longer; he recorded many sessions with them for Radio Nederland between 1969 and 1993. And although he seems to have left the UK under something of a cloud, until 1975 he continued coming back to see Eddie in London, and to do BBC radio work on shows such as *Music to Midnight* and *Dancing to Midnight*.

In the dying days of December 1973 he recorded *Mark II* for Muse, again with Keane and Matthews at the helm. Although it has its defenders, this is not the most fondly remembered of his recordings. This time, the idea was not so much to bridge a gap between rock and jazz, but to make a slightly jazz-influenced rock album. The addition of a second guitarist, John Tropea, made obvious the effort to reach the rock generation. The music of the era is represented by tunes like Stevie Wonder's "Lookin' for Another Pure Love", Joni Mitchell's "Barandgrill" and David Crosby's "Triad", previously recorded by the Jefferson Airplane. The strong country influence suggests Murphy was floundering, looking for something – anything – that would resonate with the public. *Mark II* is a fascinating oddity, and there are some intriguingly obscure song choices. These include the opener 'Chicken Road', a slice of southern gothic with great story lyrics that sound as if they were written by Joni Mitchell. In fact the song was originally recorded in 1955 by country star Tennessee Ernie Ford, of "Sixteen Tons" fame. "Triad", Crosby's sensitive plea for a threesome with a pair of nubile young ladies, was written in 1967, before he was ejected from The Byrds. Murphy sings this queasy, cloying ballad with a slightly wheedling tone. Most extraordinary of all is "They", a Murphy composition which, as Peter Keepnews's liner note points out, is "probably the first romantic Latin-tinged ballad ever written about flying saucers."

As a sequel to *Bridging a Gap*, *Mark II* was curious, having more in common with *This Must Be Earth* in its choice of material. It may have represented the kind of music Murphy was now performing live, but this time *Downbeat* was frankly disgusted. "Vocalist Murphy has nothing to offer the readers of this magazine. Despite ludicrously overblown liner commentary claims to the contrary, he is little more than a polite supper club singer who decided, this time, to record tunes by the likes of Joni Mitchell and Stevie Wonder instead of by Irving Berlin or Bacharach/David. His versions add nothing to the originals."

Many singing stars of the Fifties had experienced similar helplessness in the face of pop and rock's continuing onslaught. No one was immune. As James Gavin has pointed out, in 1974 Frank Sinatra released an album called *Some Nice Things I've Missed*, which included such bland fare as "Tie a Yellow Ribbon 'Round the Ole Oak Tree" and Neil Diamond's "Sweet Caroline".

Despite the failure of *Mark II* to ignite popular enthusiasm for Mark Murphy, Joe Fields kept the faith, with one important change of tack: by the time the same production team reassembled at Basement for a third attempt the following June, the rock experiment had been ditched. *Mark Murphy Sings* was going to be a big jazz sound, Murphy working with an octet for the first time since *Midnight Mood*. Having previously insisted that he didn't usually like singers or care about the lyrics they sang, Matthews wrote in the liner notes, "On this album, we chose real jazz tunes, Herbie Hancock, Freddie Hubbard. [Murphy's] voice fills the place of Freddie Hubbard's horn, and I treat his voice as the trumpet player. It's like a trumpet with words."

Interviewed in 2016, he added, "When Dave Sanborn came to New York, and I needed a small, funky, poppy horn section, I used the Brecker Brothers and David Sanborn. So when we did *Mark Murphy Sings*, I recommended to Helen that we try to get a more contemporary sound, which Mark agreed with... The musicians were those I was working with on pretty much every studio recording I made during that time period: Mike Moore, Jimmy Madison and I were all from Cincinnati and we went to New York at about the same time, and I was using them as the rhythm section on jazz recordings."

Basement was booked for mid-June. And this time the result was one of the greatest jazz vocal albums in history, although cover artist Hal Wilson did his best to disguise the fact with one of the worst designs in history, featuring a yellow rubber glove in an abstract landscape. Several timeless Mark Murphy classics burst from the grooves of *Mark Murphy Sings*: Freddie Hubbard's "Red Clay" becomes "On The Red Clay", with Murphy's own lyrics, inspired by a phone conversation with the trumpet player. "I called Freddie in LA," said Mark in the liner notes, "and said I didn't know what 'Red Clay' was. 'What had you envisioned?'" It transpired it was about remembering Indiana, where Freddie grew up – "the earth we're born upon, play upon, and finally return to." It was a tune Murphy returned to time and again in live performance, even recording a new version in 2012. John Coltrane's ballad "Naima" is a spine-chiller, with spooky organ and blaring horns, but the killer is David Sanborn's alto, piping like an ancient ram's horn. There's something eerie and incantatory about this track, Murphy's voice soaring like a pagan priest calling down the goddess.

"Body and Soul" is rendered in slow, magnificent 12/8, re-harmonized in the bridge, with a gorgeous extended coda. Beautiful Randy Brecker trumpet and Harvie Swartz's electric bass add contemporary polish to a revered standard. "Young and Foolish", once a ballad, is rendered at a suicidal tempo (310 bpm) against Murphy's relaxed vocal. He relishes the excitement, riding the rhythm in his inimitable style. The coda fades out with him and Michael Brecker tearing it up together. Another iconic track, Milton Nascimento's samba "Empty Faces" is driven by Don Grolnik's growling Hammond, with bouncy Harvie Swartz bass. This cut features a wonderful suspended section in the middle, making the release of tension all the more powerful when the rhythm section comes back in (an idea he had used before when the bass briefly dropped out in "Milestones").

"Cantaloupe Island" was, according to Murphy, "the first in a projected series of songs from the music of Herbie Hancock, and again they're visions... I had just read a book about sailing and mining in prehistoric times, and there's so many references to mysterious islands in the West, which were North and South America. So I had in my head already a lot of images for that. The whole first part of 'Cantaloupe Island' is a discovery – first you don't see the island, then you do, through the mist. In my mind, I saw the island. I really see what I'm singing about. That's one reason I get so tired at the end of the evening. I don't cheat. I really do the songs. I really experience the songs."

Joe Fields asked Michael Bourne to write the liner notes. It was the first time Bourne had met the singer, who was then sporting a reddish-brown pirate wig with a moustache, "like Tyrone Power standing there with the ocean breeze blowing through his curly locks. He was living in a trailer that was parked somewhere on the street downtown, and there were power cables crossing the sidewalk into someone's basement, and we sat on folding chairs on the sidewalk and did the interview." Asked what he thought defined a jazz singer, Murphy made the oft-quoted, apparently flippant reply, "A jazz singer is a singer who sings jazz."

Downbeat was mildly approving this time: "*Mark Murphy Sings* is a solid musical effort by a fine singer... Overall, Murphy projects a sophisticated yet fresh viewpoint."

But for Murphy, there was no big payday. Money was hard to come by, as always, because it was so hard to market him – a problem that dogged his entire career. Some of his relative penury appears to have been self-imposed: according to Albert Amaroso, he was once offered $10,000 by a wealthy fan to make a commercial for IBM. All he would have to do was fly to Dallas, do the whole thing in an hour, and get back on the plane. But IBM was The Man, and Murphy wanted nothing to do with it. On another occasion, a Midwest promoter wanted to put together a package of 14 one-nighters, including a couple of college concerts. It would be easy for Murphy – he could drive between the dates in Big Bertha. "But three weeks beforehand," said Amaroso, "Mark decided to go to England to be Jesus. That was really weird." Mark told Michael Bourne how this came about: while performing in a club in Wimbledon, southwest London, on one of his return visits, he noticed someone in the audience with a casting directory open at the Mark Murphy page. Why, the singer inquired, was he looking at it? "Because you have the face of Jesus," came the alleged reply.

The Passion of Christ was conceived as a 12-part series, to be shot in Spain and directed by Kenneth Talbot. Unfortunately it got no further than the pilot. The project was abandoned after finding itself up against the star-studded Anglo-Italian TV blockbuster *Jesus of Nazareth*, with pin-up actor Robert Powell as the rival Savior. Financed by UK TV mogul Lew Grade, this six-hour epic was directed by Franco Zeffirelli, with an international cast that included James Earl Jones, Stacy Keach, Anne Bancroft and Ernest Borgnine.

Albert Amaroso also recalls going with Mark to a bizarre lunch meeting in Buffalo with some executives from Warner Brothers. After some discussion of how much it would cost to acquire Mark's master tapes from Joe Fields, it dawned on Amaroso that Warners were trying to get Mark to sign with them. "One of them says, 'I see him in brown and green!' Mark didn't say a damn thing, he just sat there. I said, 'What are you talking about, brown and green?' And one of them said [to me], 'You'd be fine, because you could pass for Hispanic.' So Mark gets up from the table, and I thought he was going to the bathroom. But he just walked right out of the place. He left the building. So that night, we're at the gig, and I said, 'What happened?' And he said, 'They're not going to tell me what I'm gonna look like, Albert.' I said, 'Mark, they can probably give you $50,000 right now to sign with them, man!' 'No,' he says, 'We're not going to do that.'" Integrity was not the path to riches, in Mark's case.

Eddie came over from London whenever he could. Mark's niece Kathy Hinkhouse recalled a visit from the two of them in 1975. "I remember Mark was relaxed, he was wearing his little *toque* – that's a Canadian expression – a little hat that he always wore because he was bald from pretty young. They came to our house in Kansas City and stayed overnight in their camper in our yard, and left the next day." Later Kathy repeated to her mother, Mark's sister Sheila, a comment that David, Kathy's husband, had made about Mark being gay. And Sheila said "Do you *think* so?"

Alongside his groundbreaking work on albums like *Mark Murphy Sings*, Mark was sometimes able to show a more conventional side of his jazz persona. In 1972, the composer Alec Wilder had published what quickly became a standard reference book, *American Popular Song: the Great Innovators 1900–1950*. In it he analyzed 17,000 pop tunes, explaining precisely how they worked melodically, harmonically and rhythmically. In Wilder's view, few songs of value had been written since 1950, hence the date in the title, and he argued passionately in defense of his ideas.

Dick Phipps, a producer for South Carolina Educational Radio, felt that the songs, the singers and the author could, in combination, make an excellent series for National Public Radio, and in late 1976 he launched *Alec Wilder and Friends: American Popular Song*. The guests, who included Mabel Mercer, Tony Bennett, Bobby Short and Johnny Hartman, would chat with Wilder and his pianist Loonis McGlohon in the comfort of Phipps's living room on Lake Murray, Lexington, South Carolina, and sing a selection of the tunes under discussion. The whole idea was to create a relaxed and informal atmosphere, even to the point of hiding the microphones in large houseplants.

After the first season of shows, Wilder became fed up with the whole thing and wanted to stop, but when McGlohon played him a Mark Murphy album, he had a sudden change of heart. Shocked that he had never heard of the singer, Wilder demanded to know who he was. He duly went to see Murphy play at Carnegie Recital Hall, but flounced out, hating the jazz-rock style that made the whole experience sound decidedly post-1950. But he soon got over it, and Murphy was booked to appear on the radio show in September 1977. His focus was the songs of Dorothy Fields and Cy Coleman, separately and together. "I run into people every few years, thank God, that are just instant friends," said Murphy, "and it was like that with Alec. So many people don't relax me, but with him the talk flowed so freely, and I was just able to be myself." It had become a mutual admiration society. "I honestly consider him one of the very few great singers I have ever heard", announced Wilder. "Thank the good lord that he's alive, healthy, and stubbornly insistent on singing *what* he sings and *as* he sings." Ever afterwards Wilder declared that Mark Murphy was one of the greatest interpreters of ballads and standards he had ever heard. "I was quite literally amazed. Mark's musicianship, range, intonation, diction, inventiveness, and incredible rhythmic sense are all of a piece and all marvelous."

Murphy's show was broadcast in February, 1978. So popular had *Alec Wilder and Friends* become that the record label Audiophile released the best performances, including *Mark Murphy Sings Dorothy Fields and Cy Coleman* the following year.

Given Murphy's subsequent visits to the outer fringes of jazz singing, this album comes as something of a surprise, and a delightful one. With clear, sympathetic backings from McGlohon and his trio, the album reveals Murphy as a peerless straight-ahead interpreter of standards. The old singer's maxim "Let the song sing you" applies here, because these are high quality bittersweet romantic tunes, and Murphy sees no reason to mess with them. The renditions of such classics as "I Walk a Little Faster", "I'm In the Mood for Love" and "Alone Too Long" are low-key, warm and intimate, many of the songs played straight through without solos.

Although Mark and Eddie were making regular trips between the US and England to see each other, it was hardly a satisfactory arrangement. And Mark was by now tired of living in a vehicle, his home for the last five years. While useful for travelling around the country and getting to gigs, Big Bertha lacked the creature comforts a man in his mid-40s might expect. The winter of 1976/7 was the last straw: in late January, five days of snow combined with high winds battered western New York State. The snowdrifts were five feet deep, and the mayor of Buffalo declared a state of emergency.

A plan was hatched to relocate to San Francisco, this time with a more permanent residence. "The blizzard of 77 blew me out to California, and there, for the first time, I saw sunlight," said Mark, speaking both physically and metaphorically. "It happened in Tiburon, just over the Golden Gate Bridge – a club, a steady gig, a growing following. Newer jazz singers... were kind enough to call me an influence, and suddenly I was a veteran, a musical model."

According to Albert Amaroso, by now Mark had reached the conclusion that the only way he and Eddie could be together permanently was if Eddie found himself an American wife, so that he could apply for US residency. The lucky lady was a plain woman in her fifties named Irene Firestone, a fan who had a massive crush on Mark. Irene agreed to marry Eddie, on condition that she was allowed to spend more time with Mark. At first this condition was satisfied by the fact that, for appearances' sake, she lived with them. Subsequently, it seems that Mark found himself rather too busy to hang out with the new Mrs. O'Sullivan. At a party Irene complained to Kate Murphy that the men were trying to distance themselves from her. Kate recalls that they eventually found her somewhere else to live, but she was not happy. Mark wanted her to agree to a divorce. But being married, Irene now decided she wanted to stay married – even though her husband was gay, at least a decade younger than her, and already in a relationship. "I never met Eddie," said Amoroso, "but the first time I ever saw Mark get very angry was when we were at somebody's house in San Francisco having dinner. Mark was on the phone with Irene. She was refusing to divorce Eddie. I said, 'Come on, Mark, she's gotta be seventy years old, for crying out loud!'"

Whether Mr. and Mrs. O'Sullivan ever did get divorced, no one seems to know. But Mark and Eddie did finally move into apartment #7, 2344 Van Ness Avenue, San Francisco. Kate and Mark's brother Kevin lived nearby, in the Santa Cruz Mountains. "We began the ritual of getting together once a month – sometimes at our house, but with Mark's busy schedule, mostly we went up to San Francisco. When our daughter Heather was little, we used to let her buy evening gowns in the local thrift store and wear them to Mark and Eddie's for dinner. Years later, when she asked why I let her do that, I said, 'Well you enjoyed it, and your Uncle Mark enjoyed it even more, so why not?' Eddie was the cook and I usually hung out with him in the kitchen, while Kevin and Mark talked in the living room. An avid reader, Eddie was always interested in what my book club was reading that month. Usually he had read it, and would give me great tidbits along with his insights to take back to my club. Sometimes he recommended books – great books such as Carson McCullers's *The Heart is a Lonely Hunter*."

1977 was also the year Mark was inspired by a new album entitled *The Main Man* by bop singer Eddie Jefferson, which featured a fat five-horn nonet led by the young alto player Richie Cole. Jefferson had made a minor splash back in the early Fifties through his close association with James Moody, in particular his lyric to "Moody's Mood for Love", a vocalese number based on the tenor man's solo on "I'm In the Mood for Love". Since then Jefferson's career had merely sputtered along, and while doing gigs with Cole in Washington DC and at the Tin Palace in New York's Bowery, he earned his daily bread by driving a cab and working in a haberdasher's shop. Jefferson introduced Cole to Joe Fields, for whom they recorded the album *Still on the Planet* in 1976.

Thanks to this and the new album, suddenly Eddie Jefferson was back and getting radio play. Mark Murphy saw it not merely as a return to form for Jefferson, but an uncompromising and joyful return of bop singing – from which he himself hoped to benefit. Murphy and Richie Cole had become good friends when, by coincidence, both were living in their vehicles – Murphy in Big Bertha and Cole in a small Dodge van. At night they would drive down to the marina in San Francisco and park next to each other. But Eddie Jefferson never lived to reap the rewards of his new-found popularity. In the early hours of May 9, 1979, he and Richie were walking out of Baker's Keyboard Lounge in Detroit when a green Lincoln Continental drew up and four shotgun blasts were fired, one of them hitting Jefferson in the chest, killing him instantly. The killer, Eddie's former professional dancing partner, was arrested but got off on a technicality in court.

Leafing through his charts in the camper one day, Mark came across some lyrics he had written for the Oliver Nelson tune "Stolen Moments" years earlier, and took another look at it. "I started to do it at the clubs, and the kids liked it, and were always asking, 'Can you do that 'Stolen Moments' again?'" He called Joe Fields. "He said, 'I want to do a big band album on the west coast.' I said, 'Well, who's going to do the arrangements?' And he said Mitch [Farber] knew the tunes, and I flew to the west coast with Mitch, and we went through the money, arrangements, what the studio was going to cost, what the guys were going to get."

The album that ended up as *Stolen Moments* was originally intended as a showcase for Joe Zawinul's tune "Birdland", for which Murphy had written a lyric. But Zawinul had other ideas: two days before Murphy was due to record it, Zawinul's lawyer called to nix the idea. Even without "Birdland", the result, recorded in June 1978 at Filmways/Helder Studios in San Francisco, was a relaxed, joyful album, which found Murphy once again in great voice, with tight horn support from the line-up which included Richie Cole on alto, Warren Gale on trumpet and Mark Levine on valve trombone, Smith Dobson on piano and Vince Lateano on drums. "The guys that he had known in San Francisco were great players," said Joe Fields. "Mitch wrote the arrangements, in many cases, on the spot. If he didn't have enough players, he voiced the horns so that they would play a little higher and a little lower so that it sounded bigger than it was."

If the horns are somewhat fewer than on Eddie Jefferson's *Main Man*, Murphy more than makes up for it by becoming a part of the section himself, as Farber – like Dave Matthews before him – had planned. On the title track, this voice-like-a-horn was never more in evidence, as he sings the whole first chorus as part of the horn section, followed by a scat chorus, then unleashing

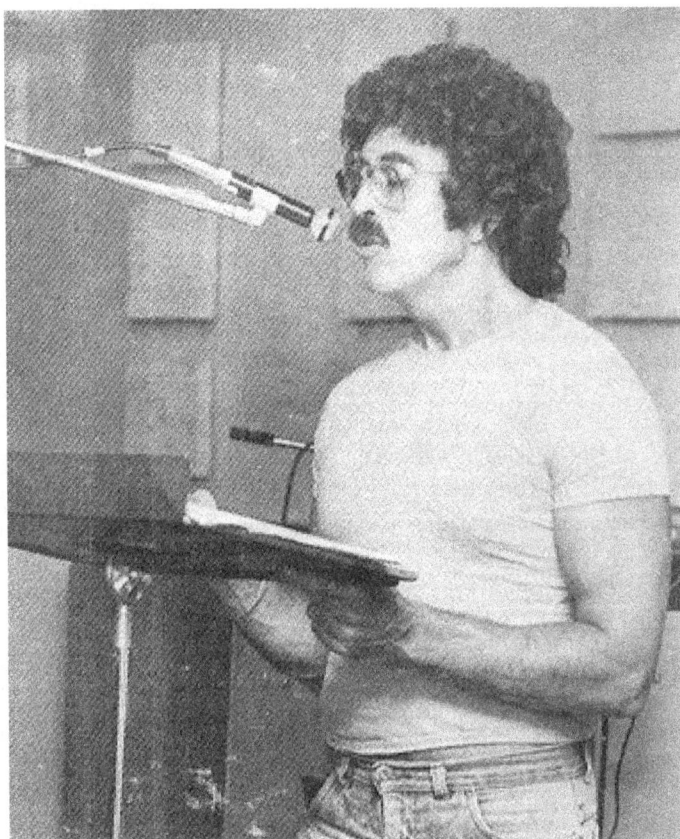
Recording Stolen Moments, June 1978 (publicity shot).

his rhythm chops in response to Lateano's drums. "Farmer's Market" was a tune he had recorded many times but which had never made the final cut before. His extraordinary verbal facility is on show in this tricky all-vocal/no solos Art Farmer/Annie Ross vocalese number, its big range requiring flips into falsetto. The ballad "Again" was another number he frequently performed live. It was the tune Ida Lupino sings in the film *Road House*, a favorite of Murphy's. "I use a 12/8 feel on the drums on the ballads, allowing me to do it incredibly slow. Yet it doesn't drag," he told Herb Wong.

He left the studio worrying about what a rush it had been to get the album finished within Joe Fields' six-hour straitjacket. When he heard Mitch Farber's mix, he didn't like it, and fretted over the details he'd been too busy to notice on the day. But to his astonishment, *Stolen Moments* received solid airplay across the USA, and began to climb the charts. WRVR in New York played it constantly. Mark told an interviewer many years later, "To this day I have no idea why [it] started to sell... I was completely unprepared that this lyric of mine would get over to the young people of that day."

The key *Stolen Moments* personnel, Farber and Cole, reconvened at New York's Nola Studios in November 1979 to record the *Satisfaction Guaranteed* album. Among the session players this time was Mike Renzi on piano, whose immaculate pedigree as an accompanist included work with Peggy Lee, Lena Horne, Mel Tormé, Cleo Laine, Blossom Dearie and Jack Jones. The occasion also marked the return of Jimmy Madison.

Although Murphy dedicated the album to "the living genius of Eddie Jefferson", in fact it bears little of Jefferson's stylistic imprint, but is a relaxed, accessible, warm, and – as promised in the title – satisfying recording, on which Murphy is at his least self-indulgent. Quiet, scuttering piano and drums accompany the first head of "Waltz for Debby", the celebrated Bill Evans tune with lyrics by Gene Lees, whose rhythm parts were arranged by Richard Rodney Bennett when Murphy was living in London. Alec Wilder was invited to the session to observe the recording of his poignant ballad "Welcome Home", introduced by Gene Bertoncini's guitar, with a lyrical solo by Richie Cole. Cole's empathy with singers was partly due to his instinctive understanding of when *not* to play: over the years he had heard too many saxophonists trampling on lyrics. But he also had his own lyrical style. "I'm a singer on the saxophone. When I play I tell a story, and I know every word of every song I'm playing."

The album was nominated for a Grammy in the category Best Jazz Vocal Performance (Male) – the first time Murphy had been recognized by the Recording Academy – but in the final run-off *Satisfaction Guaranteed* was beaten by George Benson's album *Moody's Mood*. Despite the nomination, and the success of *Stolen Moments*, it also failed to achieve much airplay except from supporters like Rosetta Hines at WJZZ and WBUR's Tony Cennamo.

Throughout the late Seventies, Murphy continued to make regular trips across the Atlantic. In November 1975 he flew to Oslo to record a program of Harold Arlen songs with the Norwegian Radio Orchestra. It was one of the entries for the annual Nordring Radio Prize, competed for by seven northern European countries. The Harold Arlen personnel went on to record a series of six shows at AVRO TV studios in Hilversum in 1975/6, each dedicated to a separate Broadway composer: Jule Styne, Jerome Kern, Cole Porter, Richard Rogers, Jimmy Van Heusen and Jimmy McHugh. Producer Joop De Roo's wife, the singer Greetje Kauffeld, was also booked for the date.

Mark became excited by the prospect of staging the Arlen segment as a live event in the USA, and asked de Roo to lend him the score. He eventually premiered it at Edmunds Community College near Seattle, and again with the Buffalo Philharmonic with Ernestine Anderson and Richie Cole, with Frank DeMiero conducting. In 1980 de Roo asked Murphy back to AVRO to record a special with the 60-piece Dutch Metropole Orchestra, along with Blossom Dearie and pianist Roger Kellaway, and every year Mark also worked on *Metro's Midnight Music*, another Dutch radio show.

With Greetje Kauffeld, Hilversum 1971 (courtesy Sonorama Records).

From 1978 to 1986, he was a regularly featured singer with Dutch radio big band The Skymasters, whose show on AVRO Radio's weekly jazz program *Swingtime*, was broadcast from Nick Vollebregt's Jazzcafé in Laren. Murphy was following in the illustrious wake of many other American soloists who guested with The Skymasters, including Dizzy Gillespie and Mel Tormé.

It is not clear exactly when Mark Murphy began teaching his craft, but he may have got the idea in 1979 at the College of the Siskiyous, a public community college that had a jazz choir. Run by Dr. Kirby Shaw, an accomplished trumpet player and scat singer, the College was in the hill town of Weed in the far north of California. Shaw loved "Stolen Moments", and had written a vocal arrangement for it. In researching the tune, he realized that Murphy lived only a few hours away, and decided to contact him.

Murphy recalled that it was just beginning to snow as he drove up the hill for his first visit to Weed. As he stepped out of the car he was hit by a snowball on the back of the head. But what struck him even more forcefully was the sound of "*doolitidoolitidoolit* – bop lines coming out of the building and kids, twelve year old kids were screaming like it was their basketball team. So I said, OK, I'm ready for anything; what's going on here?" He and Shaw became friends, Murphy even recording the latter's swing composition "I Return to Music" for *Satisfaction Guaranteed*. The following year he recorded a couple of tunes with the students.

Lack of money was another good reason to consider teaching. Interviewed by Bill Moody in London in 1980, Murphy said, "Living, I've never had a problem with. Saving money? Yes! I'm not the kind of person who can pinch pennies all the time. I'd rather live well and let the future take its course."

Norbert Warner, the Mark Murphy fan from Newcastle who had known him since 1967, always went to see him perform when he toured in the UK. In September 1980 Warner managed to catch Frank Sinatra at London's Festival Hall before dashing across the river to Ronnie Scott's in time for Mark's second set. "I had seen two of the world's greatest singers in one night. Sinatra is still one of the greatest entertainers and a legend in his own lifetime. But in no way could he sing jazz like Mark Murphy."

A serious and committed devotee of vocal jazz, Warner had been writing articles for a Sinatra fanzine, conducting interviews with the likes of Mel Tormé, Dick Haymes and Cleo Laine whenever they came to Newcastle. For quite some time Mark had been urging Bert to start up a Mark Murphy fan club. Fans were always pestering him about his records, he said, so there must surely be enough of them out there also to sustain a little newsletter. In fact there was already a fan newsletter called Remarks, run from California by Murphy fan Ron De Armond. But now, since Mark had persuaded Bert to set up the International Mark Murphy Appreciation Society (IMMAS) from his home in Whitley Bay, De Armond and Warner joined forces. This meant

Eddie O'Sullivan, Bert Warner, Mark Murphy and a friend (Mark's Times).

that articles and reviews of Mark-related events could be written on either side of the Atlantic.

The first quarterly issue of *Mark's Times*, consisting of a few stapled-together A4 pages, appeared in March 1981. Its production values rivaled those of the ultra low tech punk rock fanzines of the late Seventies. Over the years, that kitchen-table aesthetic never wavered: it was a fanzine, not a commercial operation, and anyone was welcome to make a contribution. From the beginning, the 'zine did not restrict itself to talking about Mark Murphy. Instead, although anything Mark was doing always took priority, it adopted a wide-ranging brief on jazz singers and jazz in general. As time went on, Warner began to receive reports on Murphy's activities from all over the world, from mainland Europe to Australia and Japan. By issue 20, five years on, *Mark's Times* had ballooned to 142 A4 pages, and its readership had increased from a hardcore couple of dozen in the UK to a genuinely international fan-base: the subscribers' list had been growing quarter by quarter, the more so after the address of the IMMAS began appearing on the covers of Murphy's albums.

The fanzine ran frequent interviews with its spiritual head. The informality of *Mark's Times* meant that Murphy himself felt free to chat discursively about anything under the sun, as if with friends. On one occasion he told Warner he'd been writing a screenplay. "I took my own life experience about being a cult artist who is unknown except to those who know him, and transferred it to another area of show business – how the guy feels trapped. You're not really trained to do anything else, so you keep going. Then he tries other jobs, and he screws up everything. It gets funnier and funnier, and finally he sinks even lower, trying to deal a little dope, and he even screws that up. But then bounces back at the end, marries this older woman that he didn't realize he loved, and so on. It's the saga of a survivor. It's completely out of jazz, but I'm finding ways I can put things of my own in it."

Asked who he'd like to cast in the lead, Murphy said, "I saw *The Pope of Greenwich Village* recently and – I can't think of the kid's name – he could do it marvelously. He just has that instinctive ability, where the person bounces back, because these days, nobody has any guts any more. Nobody rolls with the punches. That's why I think you've got to keep a large part of yourself *to* yourself, and don't let people fool around with it."

8 Where Fountains Drip in a Forgotten Tempo

The hipster bible, Jack Kerouac's *On the Road*, was published in 1957, three years after Mark Murphy first came to New York. Murphy was so obsessed with Kerouac that he dedicated two albums to him, and would often read extracts from his books at gigs. As late as 2008, he recorded a joyous new Kerouac song with the Five Corners Quintet. There was something about the beatnik writer that resonated deeply in him, a footloose man without religion or a family of his own. It meant much to him that the Kerouacs were descended from Bretons – Celts just like the Murphys; and that Kerouac's home town of Lowell, Massachusetts, was very like his own home town of Fulton.

Pointing out that the real-life model for *On the Road*'s Dean Moriarty had been the Irish-descended Neal Cassady, Murphy told an interviewer in 2004 that on a visit to Kerouac's grave in Lowell, he had reached down to put his hand on the stone, and felt it vibrating. "It was kind of a joyous feeling, that he was glad to see me or something... There was a definite kinship there, and I didn't feel this until I came back from England and started finding his books in paperback in the airports and train stations, and began to dig that this was rhythmic writing." As the book's narrator Sal Paradise heads west, he learns how to improvise his life, consciously making use of the open-mindedness, the spontaneity, the unappreciated, unrecognized *how* of jazz.

Without being a musician himself, Kerouac had an intuitive understanding of jazz, its rhythm, flow and phrasing. His poetic prose was the equivalent of the bebop of Parker, Gillespie, Shearing, Powell and Monk that he found so inspiring. As Francis Davis has pointed out, "For Kerouac... Parker's genius was the living proof that excess was the path to wisdom." "Kerouac wrote because he had to," explained Mark Murphy. "He wrote because this stuff was in him and he had to get it out. And I'm not sure that that possibility exists today... Maybe the Kerouac thing's the closest to a self-portrait... Kerouac got to me emotionally as a person-to-person thing."

It may also be significant that Kerouac's first language was not English but the working class Québécois dialect Joual. Before he began learning English at the age of six, the language to him was mere sounds and rhythms, the building blocks of poetry, and in his writing he often seemed to be trying to communicate through sounds alone, as if bypassing the English language altogether and creating pure language. It was scatting in prose.

The structure of *On the Road* resembles that of a jazz performance. Instead of moving steadily from exposition to resolution via conflict, development and climax, like a traditional narrative, Kerouac's story loops back on itself. Like a jazz tune, it states a theme, improvises on the same changes, and ends with a restatement of the theme. The book is full of the verbal riffs and ideas that Kerouac had developed over many years in his letters and notebooks. In this way, although the book appears to be spontaneous and unstructured, it borrowed from jazz the hidden work, the painful wood-shedding and long gestation necessary before there can be any glorious outburst, mirroring an art form that, again to paraphrase Bill Evans, is not a *what* but a *how*.

Chet Baker's pianist, Russ Freeman, talked about the quasi-religious ecstasy of the jazzman's beatnik life, which he said he had experienced himself: "I'm not a religious person at all... but a few times I actually had an out-of-body experience while playing. I was next to or behind myself, watching myself play, totally oblivious to everything around me. And I knew at those moments that the magic was happening."

"I grew to see that Kerouac's writing in books like *On the Road* was very jazz-like in the cadence and rhythms he used and very naturally musical," Mark Murphy told the *Edmonton Journal* in 2007. "So I borrowed that thing. I wanted to get the rush of that contemporaneous style of writing with nerve endings."

The events Kerouac wrote about had taken place in the late Forties, at the birth of bebop. That world was long gone by the time *On the Road* was published, and the book is full of nostalgia for it – "the then vanishing and now, perhaps, disappeared America: that America of old hotels, railroad sidings and lunch counters with steaming coffee urns." The melancholy of it was not lost on Mark Murphy. In some ways the inauguration of Ronald Reagan in 1981 was the perfect moment for the singer to record his Kerouac tribute. Reagan's folksy persona consciously embodied the clean-living family values of the Fifties, reassuring middle America that the social changes of the Sixties and Seventies had been a mere aberration from the norm. With *Bop for Kerouac*, Mark Murphy showed that it was possible to be nostalgic for something that was far from mom and apple pie. In his celebration of the most liberal writer America has ever produced, Murphy offered an alternative vision of both the Fifties and the present.

Pianist, writer and arranger Bill Mays, who was then living in LA, had been to hear Murphy sing a couple of times, and shortly afterwards received a call from Joe Fields. A session man of long standing, Mays had accompanied singers from Frank Sinatra to Al Jarreau and worked with the likes of Shelly Manne, Sonny Stitt and Gerry Mulligan. Now Fields was asking him to collaborate with Mark Murphy on his Kerouac project. But being expected to do so on a Joe Fields budget came as something of a shock. As he wrote in his self-published book *Stories of the Road*, "Tight-fisted with a dollar, the company allotted me just six hours in which to do an entire project..." Later he said, "I hate working that fast really. I mean, even to have just another six hours would take the pressure off... But Mark was very well prepared. Before we went in, he and I rehearsed very thoroughly at my apartment, where I had a nice Steinway piano. Mark had me underscore the readings much like I might do in a film segment. We knocked out an awful lot of music in six hours."

And they weren't lacking in top-flight musicians. Richie Cole came back, along with guitarist Bruce Forman. "Mark had been doing some gigs that Richie would show up at, so it was at his request that Richie be on the date. The thing about that album that I'm proud of is that I had a small group, and I made it sound like a little big band, especially 'Boplicity.'" As his previous arrangers had known, the most effective way to achieve this was through the voicings and harmonizations. "When I write I'm very influenced by orchestral music and big band arrangements... Mark had very definite ideas most of the time about how he wanted the tune to go, the key changes and tempo changes, and so a lot of it was his input and I fleshed it out musically. Mark was really a co-arranger on many of the tracks. He played some piano himself, so he had a sense of harmony, and he had very good, if sometimes unusual, instincts about what to do on a given tune. I remember when we recorded 'If You Could See Me Now' [originally written as a ballad], he said he wanted to do it medium uptempo. I was taken aback, but I think it worked.

"[Mark] gave a lot of room to the sidemen, just as he did in live performance. He was very laid back and accepting of human foibles. If something went wrong he just giggled. I don't think I ever saw Mark get upset about anything. He was very go-with-the-flow, make the best of it, whatever the situation is. A true jazz musician, always improvising, not only with the music but with the matters at hand, whether it was a bad pedal on the piano, or out-of-tuneness, or people talking in the club, he was pretty loose."

Towards the middle of March, on the day of recording at Sage and Sound in Hollywood, the omens didn't look good. First, a video crew filming the session blew out the electrical circuits, delaying the start by an hour. Once they got under way, Forman proved to be a fine soloist but, according to Mays, didn't read very well. And Richie Cole, who had dated Mays's wife in years past, ran into his car in the parking lot. Nonetheless the recording was completed on schedule.

Bop For Kerouac combines the sadness and the euphoria of the intertwined jazz and beatnik lifestyles that Murphy knew from the inside, but it isn't the crazed, ecstatic homage to bebop that one might expect. Despite the opening track's hip rendition of the mid-tempo Miles/Gil Evans number "Boplicity" (retitled "Bebop Lives"), the overall tone is elegiac, and ballads dominate: on "Goodbye Pork Pie Hat", Mingus's lament for Lester Young, with lyrics by Joni Mitchell, Murphy plays with the rhythm, working ahead of the beat at times in a similar way to Bill Evans. The lyrics of most tunes on the album deal with the bebop life. "Boplicity" is a fanfare, a salutation to bebop's iconic figures. Midway through the slow blues "Parker's Mood", Murphy reads an extract from Kerouac's *The Subterraneans,* reporting on a Parker gig at the Red Drum in Kansas City. And there's another reading, from *On the Road* this time, at the start of the heart-wrenching Tommy Wolf/Fran Landesman "Ballad of the Sad Young Men": *"Nobody, nobody knows what's going to happen to anybody, besides the forlorn rags of growing old."* "You've Proven Your Point (Bongo Beep)" is another Parker blues, its lyrics celebrating Sonny Stitt, although you'd never recognize it from the smooth rock intro, before it heads off into swing. David Raksin's ballad "The Bad and the Beautiful" ends on a spine-shivering repetition of 'you', reminiscent of the fade-out of "I'm Glad There Is You" on *Bridging a Gap.*

The sleeve features specially written contributions from leading beat poets Lawrence Ferlinghetti and Gregory Corso (Kerouac himself died in 1969). Others added their thoughts, including Steve Allen, beatnik entrepreneur and publisher Jay Landesman, Kerouac biographer Lawrence Lee, and San Francisco club-owner Fred Kuh. There is also a biblically-inspired quotation from a 1959 Playboy article penned by Kerouac, "The Origins of the Beat Generation".

Richie Cole regarded *Bop for Kerouac* as a jazz concept album. "[Mark] was taking a chance with that, because at the time everyone wanted a hit record. He didn't give a shit about hit records. He just had this fantastic artistic concept... it was something he believed in, and he did it. I admire him so much for that. If it's something that you really wanted to put out there, that you think is worthwhile, then Jack Kerouac was certainly worthwhile. It brought new attention to [him], as an underdog kind of hero."

The album, Murphy's 18th, was the first to catch the attention of young writer James Gavin. *Stereo Review* magazine included it in its "best of the month" roundup: "I was fascinated by the description of the *Bop for Kerouac* album. It sounded as though Mark were a sort of pained, troubled world traveler, who was underground after having been in the business for many years, and had an elite cult following of very hip, very clued-in musicians, singers and fans. And that made it catnip for me, because I'm mistrustful of anything that is too popular. It remains, I think, his greatest achievement on record, and an album that I play to this day. It has all of the best of Mark and none of the worst of Mark."

Murphy told Bob Rusch in 1984 how much he appreciated the freedom he had with Muse to pursue his own creative projects: "I never could have done Kerouac anywhere else." Rusch asked how well the album had sold. Murphy had no idea. He could only say that his albums must have been selling, or Joe

Fields would never have asked him to keep making them. Rusch, taken aback, pressed him on the point. Surely, he said, he must have some idea of sales. No, said Murphy. The reason, it emerged, was that he was not paid royalties: the recordings were done for a flat fee. Why on earth, Rusch wondered, was he prepared to work on that basis? "Oh I don't know," sighed Murphy, "Maybe it's too complicated with accounting, the dribs and drabs coming in. It just seems like a more convenient way to do it." Rusch pointed out the obvious drawback to this financial arrangement – that if he had a serious hit, he would never get the reward.

"Yeah," came the reply, "Maybe it's cynical to say, but I almost know it's not going to be that sort of thing. It's vocal jazz, it's the smallest slice of jazz, which is the smallest of the music business. Like when you go to the Grammys, they get the jazz over with first, the first five minutes, and from there on for two hours you don't hear one word about jazz. I'm kind of a realistic person. I know where I am. I know exactly where this is (pats his heart) and I don't expect too much from it. I think that's really the more mature way to deal with the situation." It hadn't been that way with Riverside, he conceded, from whom he continued to receive royalties via "some funny bank in the Bahamas" even after the back catalogue had been bought up first by ABC Records and then by Fantasy.

In late summer he tried out the *Bop for Kerouac* material live for the first time in LA, at the French restaurant Le Café in Sherman Oaks. The owner, Lois Boileau, had set up an acoustically perfect room upstairs. Murphy decided to premiere the whole album. He was nervous, because he always had trouble memorizing new lyrics, and also because he knew he had produced something a little different, a concept album. If the audience didn't like the concept, what chance was there that they would respond well to the gig? He had no cause to worry. "The two opening tracks, Parker's 'Bongo Beep' and Miles's 'Boplicity', went over just fine," he reported to *Mark's Times*. "The movie song (the most 'in' of all the 'chic' songs of the early fifties when I arrived in NYC – and, my first experience with an 'under-ground' success song-wise 'The Bad and the Beautiful' got good response, as it is the kind of song that takes a little listening to get it all. A similar reaction to Mingus' 'Goodbye, Pork Pie Hat' with Joni Mitchell's lyric – a lot to digest..." He was particularly touched and relieved at the positive reaction to his readings from Kerouac. 'But each night the one they roared for and sometimes stood for was the 8 minute track combining the last page of Kerouac's *On the Road* and the Landesman/Wolfe song (written for Jack's Beat Generation) '"The Ballad of the Sad Young Men."'

Meanwhile, the overseas tours continued. Shortly after his Sherman Oaks success, he made his first trip to Australia and New Zealand, taking in 14 dates from Auckland to Perth, including three nights at Sydney's The Basement. By the start of 1982 he was back in London, opening a tour at The Canteen in Covent Garden. Two nights later, at Leicester's Braunstone Hotel, he performed with tenorman Al Gay and a none-too-inspired local rhythm section. The weather outside was frightful, freezing fog keeping most people indoors. The 20-strong audience insisted on encores, however, and at the end Mark stood by the door like a kindly vicar, shaking hands with everyone, thanking them for coming out on such a terrible evening.

A date at The Bull's Head, Barnes, was followed by the Strathallan Hotel in Birmingham, where he was teamed with a unit known as CDM – John Critchinson (piano), Martin Drew (drums), and Ron Matthewson (bass), who at that time were the Ronnie Scott's house rhythm section. At South Hill Park, Bracknell, the sight of Mark's vaporizer steaming away on top of the piano invoked the ire of guest vibes player Lennie Best, who promptly unplugged it, before an outraged Murphy fan plugged it back in. Then it was back to London for a date at Islington's The Grapes, where Fran and Jay Landesman breezed in, remarking "swell joint you have here". The tour ended where it had begun, at The Canteen.

In March, back in the US, Mark played San Francisco's Great American Music Hall, to a larger-than-usual audience of more than 400. According to a reviewer, he was wearing "a brightly colored purple, fuchsia, [and] brilliant blue short-sleeved shirt, accompanied by beige pleated slacks, brown shoes. His hair and side burns [were] not quite so overpowering as they have been in the past."

True, Murphy was always changing his appearance. His fan club secretary Bert Warner recalled that when he first met Mark, he looked as he did on his Capitol albums, clean-shaven, with short dark hair. His next UK visit up north saw him with a different hairstyle and a beard. When Bert saw the cover of *Bridging a Gap*, he failed to recognize him at all. Not only did he think this artist was black, but now he sported a drooping moustache. "I honestly thought it was another man entirely and it was not until I had read the notes on the back that I realized it was the same Mark Murphy that I knew – only eighteen months previously, he had spent three weeks at my home!!!" he informed the readers of *Mark's Times*. Commented Mark's friend Francesca Miano, "Mark's look kept changing, from Indian cotton shirts, jeans and Afros, then less traditional suits, with his hair styled in a mullet, on to shiny brightly-colored shirts and dress pants or dark suits with turtlenecks, and medium-length hair. As the look changed, the singing became increasingly more adventurous."

The first time Ari Silverstein saw him at SUNY in Buffalo, he was wearing "green sweat pants and a black button-down shirt with roses on it and a long leather trench coat, and a really funny looking disheveled salt-and-pepper wig. There was a mental institution right next to the college and I thought maybe one of the patients had wandered over." He was also very fond of chunky costume jewelry, particularly rings, dozens of which he would carry around in a plastic bag. Mark's get-up caused a minor stir among his admirers when, in July 1982, he appeared on the midnight UK TV show *The*

Muse publicity shot, 1970s

Millionaires' Club, presented by American expatriate Marsha Hunt. "God, those brown baggy pants and 'Jacobs' shirt were just awful, fortunately Mark must have gotten a look at himself because in the second half he was much better dressed in blue shirt and white slacks", tutted an IMMAS member.

Despite the quality of the music, no floor manager had been deployed to warm up the studio audience. "The first program made me wonder if the bodies had come from the local morgue, so still were they – not a foot tapping, not a smile showing. No animation whatsoever. The cameramen seemed confused too – when they should have been zooming in on [pianist] Brian Dee when in solo, they were either out of focus past Mark's left ear, or were focused on the bass player – or anybody." Murphy pronounced himself "most unhappy" with the TV show, but mainly because of the way he looked: "I've embarked on a very serious attempt to lose 10 pounds."

A few weeks earlier, he had been at Sear Sound in New York to record with a septet containing some familiar faces – Gene Bertoncini on guitar, Sue Evans on percussion and Jimmy Madison on drums, joined by Tom Harrell on trumpet and flugelhorn. This was the two-day session that became *The Artistry of Mark Murphy*, the fourth and last of Murphy's collaborations with Dave Matthews. It sustained the mellow, mature feel of *Bop for Kerouac*, but somehow the latter's excitement and creative tension were absent, with a feeling of treading water, and the vocal is often given too much reverb.

Afterwards he spent two weeks performing at the Royal York in Toronto, then toured Finland, visited Holland and the UK, then flew to Miami, and thence to Rio, where he spent two weeks. "We didn't get any introductions there, we just followed our noses," he wrote. "A friend of mine in San Francisco told me that Jobim had a place called Anthony's well there wasn't any we found a place called Antonia's so we went there and that was in a district just behind Equmina beach called the Lagos and all round this lake were all the little places where samba jazz was happening there were singers that we just fell in love with. We stayed there and jammed all night and the dawn was coming up right behind that huge statue of Christ on the mountain and then driving home on that beach promenade all the way down to Copacabana beach it was something else."

In the liner notes to his next album, he gave a further flavor of his South American adventure. Deciding to visit a museum, he took the bus, seemingly with Dean Moriarty at the wheel: "I have taken hold of two hand grips for support, and soon thanks my lucky stars I did. The bus immediately enrolls in a rush hour not very different from what the Indianapolis 500 must be like. We dash past cars, race by taxis, lurch around curves, slide by corners, careen through tunnels and emerge to speed around square where fountains drip in a forgotten tempo. My legs are spread, feet gripping the floor, my eyes closed most of the time except when they are wide open, helping my mouth form the biggest Ooooohhhh ever yelled. But everybody yells in Rio. The bus stops and we fall off – or climb out..." After that he flew back to Miami, stayed a week, returning to California for Christmas. There he spent time listening to the records he had bought in Brazil and planning the album that would become *Brazil Song*.

Mark embarked on another Australian tour in February 1983 ("but it was marred by the strain of having a very bad promoter"), coinciding with the release of *The Artistry*. A few weeks earlier *Billboard* had announced that *Bop for Kerouac* had been nominated for a Grammy. Soon after his return from Australia, Mark motored down from San Francisco to the Shrine Auditorium in Los Angeles for the ceremony in his ancient camper, that did six miles to the gallon in town, eight on the road. Bill Mays also attended with his wife Judy. "Count Basie was the entertainment with his big band. Mark's date for the evening was a singer-pianist called Joyce Collins, and I remember fondly my wife and I and Joyce and Mark dancing to Basie's orchestra." But *Bop for Kerouac* lost out to *An Evening with George Shearing and Mel Tormé*. Mark declared himself "pissed off... the 6,000 vote for the most familiar name!"

Although his disappointment was understandable, he had learned not to expect any recognition for his work other than the applause and congratulations of audiences when he played live. And apart from the occasional decent press review, he had come to the conclusion that the critics didn't really like him. He knew he was not everybody's cup of tea, but put that down to the fact that he was an artist rather than a popular entertainer. Now 50, and in the business for three decades, he knew he would never get rich. His comfort, he said, was that the people who appreciated him *really* appreciated him, and that because they hung on to his old records, and often brought them to gigs for him to sign, he played some small part in their lives.

His mind was now on his new Brazilian project. He had loved Brazilian music ever since seeing Carmen Miranda in the films she made with Betty Grable for Fox during World War II, such as *Down Argentine Way* and *Springtime in the Rockies*, when she became one of the top entertainers in the USA. "That's how it happened," explained Mark. "I saw a black and white film, I just happened to have it on the set... and Carmen comes out, and she starts singing some Spanish number... and right in the middle of it she stops, and then starts mimicking the Brazilian rhythm section sounds out of her mouth... and then it changes into samba... and I would wager you that <u>that</u> is the moment when the samba electrified the world."

In late March, he started work with locally-based band Viva Brasil at San Francisco's Russian Hill Recording. But before the sessions were complete, he traveled to Europe, where he suffered a strange collapse. "Dear Bert, Alma & Everybody," he wrote to *Mark's Times*, "Don't take this too heavily, but I'm here in Holland at the home of Dutch arranger Jerry Van Rooyen, recovering from what seems to have been a complete physical, emotional and nervous breakdown. It occurred Monday May 30 in the studio in Hilversum during rehearsals for the Dutch segment of 1983 Nordring festival. I was OK for about the first hour, and then I started to climb 3 flights of stairs to the canteen and by the time I got to the top I started to feel very weak. I sat down at the table with the musicians, and just like that, 'all my motors' stopped, I couldn't speak or <u>anything</u>. I was terrified – I've always been so disgustingly healthy! I asked one of the trumpet players Ack (Ock?) Van Rooyen, the brother of Jerry, to take me out for a walk and then I collapsed completely and I'm afraid a little hysterical. I asked for the hospital and they put me in Intensive Care for two days. The results were such that I was proven <u>very strong</u> in the heart and blood. So, it was just exhaustion (I believe mainly from the travel stress)! But, my friends, I really thought for a few moments it was the curtain. I felt like I was <u>sinking</u>."

In his letter, he put the episode down, quite reasonably, to exhaustion. He hadn't had a rest since the end of the last Australian tour, during which he had worried constantly about when – or even whether – he would get paid. The 90-degree heat hadn't helped: much as he employed the tanning salon, Murphy was a man of the north, and disliked hot weather.

The day before his collapse there had been more rushing about. "I met my train in Cologne Sunday May 29 – after a week of wonderful work recording for West Deutsches Radio with Bill Holman's big German band – I put my small bags on the train, went to get my two large cases – the train starts up and the damn conductor wouldn't let me on! So I'm furious, shocked, and schlepping my two large cases around Cologne rail station up and down stairs and running with the bags to catch the next train. Once aboard, I thought the heart had had it. That brought on my breakdown I'm sure."

But that hadn't been the half of it. The travelling and recording never stopped: "After Australia I drove right to Los Angeles for the Grammy ceremonies to hear Mel Tormé won – then back home to record my new and wonderful Brazilian LP (it is done but needs finishing touches and mixing)... On top of that I drove to Washington, DC, to work with Ernestine Anderson at Charlie Byrd's club, did a one-nighter in Boston, stopped in NYC, then flew to DC to pick up a car my aunt left me in her will to drive to San Francisco. Once on the New Jersey turnpike near New York, I almost fell asleep twice, so I thought I'd go into Manhattan and drink coffee for an hour and show the car to my friends. On coming out of the Lincoln Tunnel in the city, I promptly had an accident caused by heavy rain, skidding and confusing traffic lights. Luckily, <u>no-one was hurt</u> – not even me! – my car only slightly damaged but the other one <u>clobbered</u>! So the shock of that plus the long X-country drive took a lot out of me. Then I got lost in the Nevada Desert – at night (!) in fog, almost ran into 7 cows – who really are not aware what a road is anyway. I kept awake and going by listening to a hilarious Mexican radio station from Chihuahua, Mexico. They really do have that night-club comic accent, and about three o'clock in the morning there seemed to come on a sort of Chihuahua version of the Gang Show – absolutely terrible singers off-key and out of time and the audience tittering in the background. I was in stitches and it kept me going until I found my next road. Well, I'm a lucky man, eh? And what continually astonishes me is that with such a <u>devoted</u>, but small following, I can make a good living – travel the world – and make so many friends."

In August, after two more days of studio work, the tracks for Brazil Song were finally complete. In the sleeve notes Murphy said he had made the album because he thought that Brazilian songs were not being done correctly – that North American singers were unable to capture the correct musical pulse of Brazil, mainly because when the lyrics were rendered into English, they often became more sentimental. On Nascimento's 'Outubro' (October), Murphy sings in the original Portuguese – the first song he ever recorded in a language other than English. Steve Rubie, a flautist and an authority on Brazilian music, pointed out that many singers prefer to sing Brazilian songs as originally written because Anglicized – or more specifically Americanized – lyrics had tended to change the subject matter drastically: where, for example, the original might be a wistful story about the hardships of a young man drifting to Rio from the north-east of the country, and the poverty and loneliness associated with such a move, the shift into English might turn it into a song about two lovers admiring a sunset. "The rhythmic pulse has a different timing," explained Murphy. "I think that's a quality inherent in the Portuguese language, so I try to sing the English lyrics as though they were Portuguese.... The best songs now are coming from Brazil. It's almost as though they've written into the Brazilian Constitution that it is illegal to write a bad song." He pronounced himself very satisfied with Viva Brasil ("they were most authentic, the best band this side of Latin America"), liking the fact that they were an established working group.

Brazil Song is a short album, the second side running for under 15 minutes, but it marked a distinct change of direction. Murphy had worked with Brazilian or Brazilian-style material before – beginning with *Everybody's Doin' the Bossa Nova*, but also "Star Sounds" from *Who Can I Turn To?*, "Sconsolato" from *Midnight Mood*, a couple of Sergio Mendes numbers on *This Must Be Earth*, and of course "Empty Faces" from *Mark Murphy Sings*; but this was the first time he had concentrated exclusively on this kind of material. Notable from *Brazil Song* are Antonio Carlos Jobim's "Two Kites" and Milton Nascimento's "Nothing Will Be As It Was Tomorrow", dance tracks later beloved of the British club crowd. This was the second time he had recorded Nascimento's "Bridges" ("Travessia") – the first was for Dutch radio in 1970. Gene Lees's lyrics could have been written especially for Mark: *I have always been a stranger and I've always been alone.*

In August 1983 he was back in England for live dates in Manchester, Brighton, Bristol and Leicester, followed by some teaching at a jazz summer school at the Cranfield Institute, Wavendon, sponsored by the Dankworths. Afterwards he drove to London for a recording session at the BBC with Critchenson, Drew and Matthewson. Mark had been looking forward to working with them again. "I've never heard Mark sing better, he was superb," wrote the *Mark's Times* correspondent, who travelled with him. "It is a crime that this session will not be released on an album, and an even bigger crime is that it will go over the air between 3am and 5am! 'No one will hear it,' I said to Mark. 'That's the story of my life!' he retorted."

What no one had predicted was that a new Mark Murphy cult was about to take off – in London.

9 It's Hot, It's Red Lights, It's Exciting!

In 1979, a 15-year-old South London schoolboy was skimming through the racks in the music section of Sutton Public Library when he came across a newly-released Mark Murphy album and decided to borrow it. The record was *Stolen Moments*, and it turned Gilles Peterson into an instant fan. 37 years later he still hadn't quite got around to returning it. As a teenager, Peterson was listening to jazz-influenced rock and soul – Level 42, Earth Wind and Fire, and Central Line – as well as jazz-pop artists like Al Jarreau and Michael Franks, and the music he heard on pirate stations such as Radio Invicta. It inspired him to set up his own pirate station, with an aerial slung between a tree and a phone box, playing a mixture of jazz, funk, reggae, soul and early electro. Soon afterwards, as luck would have it, Radio Invicta needed a new transmitter, so Gilles offered to donate his in return for a regular slot on the station. Other pirate ventures followed – KJAZZ, Solar Radio and Horizon – before, in the grand tradition established by Radio 1, he was hired in 1986 to present a show on BBC Radio London: *Mad on Jazz*.

After establishing an early presence as a London hip-hop DJ, Peterson started looking for a new angle on the dance scene, and found it by going back to the original jazz records sampled by the hip-hoppers. He found his audience very receptive, and acid jazz was born. The high energy jazz recordings of earlier decades enabled him to carve a niche for himself in a DJ-ing field dominated at the time by Danny Rampling and Paul Oakenfold, with their early 80s versions of American-originated acid house music. The Royal Oak pub near London Bridge was Peterson's musical laboratory in the early Eighties, and he played there for three or four years, gradually building an audience for his distinctive choice of rare groove and jazz.

As someone who was now making a career out of sharing his musical taste with the public, Peterson detected a kindred spirit in Mark Murphy. What particularly impressed him was Murphy's selection of material. Upstairs in the Jazz Room at the Electric Ballroom in Camden, he took over from DJ Paul

Murphy (no relation to Mark) at the tender age of 18, often playing Mark's dance-oriented tracks, such as the passionate organ-powered samba "Empty Faces".

Jazz was becoming the focus of the growing London street dance scene. The IDJ (I Dance Jazz) dance troupe, formed in 1984, were regulars at the Electric Ballroom, dominating the floor as they danced to fierce uptempo Latin and hard bop in the Art Blakey style. Once, at a Blakey live show, IDJ founder member Jerry Barry ordered the drummer to up the tempo of "A Night in Tunisia". IDJ became known not merely for the balletic moves they had developed, but for their suits, suspenders and two-tone spats.

Gilles Peterson continued to play Mark Murphy tracks like "Down St Thomas Way" from *Bop for Kerouac*, and "Two Kites" from *Brazil Song*. After leaving Radio London, he started a five-year run of Sunday afternoon sessions with fellow DJ Patrick Forge – Talkin' Loud and Sayin' Something – at Dingwalls dancehall, next to the canal in Camden. Before long he was supplementing these with live appearances by some of the artists his audiences responded to the most enthusiastically. After playing some of Eddie Jefferson's work with Richie Cole, Peterson booked Cole to come over from San Francisco to appear at the Town and Country Club in London's Kentish Town. "Some of his records had become classics on our scene. Richie was hanging out with us, but we were only about 18 or 19, and it wasn't at all like playing the Bull's Head in Barnes, or Ronnie Scott's. These guys would come to an event I'd put on, and there'd be 800 people in there, dancing, and all under the age of 23. So for these artists it was outrageous – because they just hadn't seen that before. They were bewildered by it."

Back in 1981, Colin Kellam's distribution outfit Jazz Horizons had made all of Mark Murphy's Muse albums to date available in the UK. It was good timing, from Murphy's point of view, since it meant younger fans could now go out and buy the music they were hearing for the first time.

When IMMAS member Maurice Dunn went to a rare Jon Hendricks gig in north London in March 1986, he took along a few of Hendricks's albums. To his surprise, some young audience members approached him and asked if any of them were for sale. "Sorry," he said, "I brought these along for Jon to sign." "Can we see what you've got?" "Certainly." "Tell me," he asked, "how come you are at a gig like this? Wouldn't have thought you'd even *heard* of him." "Oh," one of them replied, "we all like this stuff. Bop is IN amongst our lot. We like Eddie Jefferson and Mark Murphy as well... his *Brazil Song* album is very popular down at our club. I think some DJ down in Canvey Island first started playing bop and it's getting more popular all the time."

The next time Mark Murphy came to the UK, it was with his Miles Davis tribute show, and he was astonished to find one of his South London pub gigs packed with young people. What were they doing there? The answer became clear as soon as he counted in "Milestones", and the audience began screaming with joy. Not long after that, he met Gilles Peterson, who took him to the

Electric Ballroom. Again the track of choice was "Milestones", and again the reaction was instantaneous, a large room full of young people jitterbugging and going crazy for a recording he had made a quarter of a century ago.

The renewed interest in his music gave Murphy ideas. "I'm kind of tired of the cool jazz approach. That's why I'm so interested in Latin music. It's hot, it's red lights, it's exciting!" And he felt that the rhythm in his singing was what had turned younger audiences on to his work. "I started singing this music because I'm a rhythm singer. I learned that from Nat Cole and Ella Fitzgerald. I want that to vibrate out. I think the day of keeping it all in, of being too cool, is finished. After I was forty, I became a gregarious person, and I knew I'd wasted a lot of time being introverted. I enjoy the outgoingness of singing hot jazz instead of cool jazz."

By 1987 the Mark Murphy craze was in full swing in England. In March he played two sell-out gigs at the Bass Clef in East London. The little club was packed with young fans, who erupted whenever Murphy sang one of their favorite tunes, particularly "Milestones". "These kids, carried away by Mark, carried us all with them. It was just one wild night," reported an observer. "My new-found popularity in Britain is all down to Gilles Peterson," Mark told *New Musical Express*. "It's a phenomenon to me that a man my age has been taken up by so many young people. The BBC has finally picked up on [Peterson's] radio attitude and this resulted in some 700 people coming to The Wag when I played my last Monday gig there. They were young and enthusiastic and applauded like crazy." The Wag's jazz dancers had created their own Latin-inspired version of jazz dance. "Latin music has got so much feeling, you can do more as there are different layers of beats. So you can dance fast or slow, be more feminine or more masculine," explained one female dancer.

It quickly became clear that Murphy now had two distinct audiences in the UK: older jazz fans, who enjoyed everything he did, including ballads, and youngsters who only wanted to dance to the Latin tunes and the up-tempo swing numbers. He played a Latin Jazz all-nighter at the trendy Scala Cinema near Kings Cross. In the months that followed he returned for more dates at the Wag Club, the Bass Clef and – on Sunday afternoons – Dingwalls. All of them were packed. Mark's tunes, like "Empty Faces", were part of a mix of popular floor-fillers along with tracks by Jack McDuff and Lonnie Liston Smith, Jean Luc Ponty's "In The Fast Lane", "Samba De Flora" by Airto and Jorge Dalto, "You've Got To Have Freedom" by Pharoah Sanders and "Brother John" by Yusef Lateef.

Peterson also introduced Murphy to club venues like the Belvedere Arms in Richmond, and the 606, a tiny after-hours basement club in Chelsea's King's Road. The 606 had been founded by former dentistry student Steve Rubie, who runs it to this day at its present (considerably larger) headquarters just around the corner in Lots Road. Ronnie Scott's hosted three sets a night, the last one finishing at 3am. With too much adrenaline flowing to go straight home to bed, the musicians would often head over to "the Six" to wind down with a few drinks. As property prices soared towards the end of the 1980s, musicians could no longer afford to live in inner London, and the boho scene began to disappear. But Murphy loved to relax at the Six till 4 or 5am, sitting in sometimes with the acts that Rubie had booked. The club later became an important base for one of Murphy's greatest contributions to jazz, his singing workshops (see Appendix B).

He commemorated his wild nights with Gilles Peterson on "Ding Walls" – a track from his 1991 *What a Way to Go* album. Commented Peterson: "That song really just details a week with me. That's basically him going to my parties. He talks about the Emerald Centre – that's about Jazz 90 in Hammersmith, then upstairs at the Electric Ballroom in Camden, which was the Friday night party I used to do which was a hundred black kids literally battling on the dance floor to very fast jazz and crazy afro-cuban music. And then he ends up at Dingwalls on Sunday afternoon."

Back in the States, Mark and Eddie had been living in their 1920s Spanish-style apartment in San Francisco's Marina district for several years. Inspired by their love of English stately homes, the interior was cluttered with the spoils of regular buying sprees in London. There was an antique couch, a great deal of old china and crystal, and formal English portraits, many featuring members of the Royal Family. The walls of the dining room were decorated with fleur-de-lys wallpaper. The living room was painted blue, with a fake electric fireplace, and there were floor-to-ceiling shelves of books, CDs and records. When Bert Warner visited he was kept awake at night by the loud ticking and chiming of the couple's large collection of old clocks. Mark's

Mark at home in San Francisco, 1980s (publicity photo).

friend the singer Ann Dyer found the apartment "elegant, tasteful – very rich. Mark loved Russian aesthetics, 19th Century, deep jewel tones, old mahogany, gilt, that sort of thing. Very masculine."

When not away recording or gigging, Mark was part of a social scene involving local singers and musicians like Kitty Margolis, Bobbe Norris, and Madeline Eastman. He also loved salsa dancing at places like the Montmartre Club, his dancing partner at that time being Ann Dyer. "When he came home from being on the road, the first thing he'd want to do was go salsa dancing," she recalled. "He was a good dancer, and he loved Latin rhythms."

By this time, Irene Firestone was out of the picture, so Mark and Eddie could at last resume their previous life together, with Eddie playing the domestic role in the relationship, cooking and organizing their social calendar. When Mark came home from work he saw no need to concern himself with the domestic arrangements. But he was nowadays able to have an open discussion about homosexuality, at least with Kate Murphy, and she and Eddie became firm friends. The two would stroll around San Francisco, Eddie pointing out examples of his favorite architecture. Although highly intelligent and witty, with a teasing sense of humor, Eddie was a pessimist at heart. Kate believed this outlook was at the root of his past business failures: he lacked faith, and ended up working in an up-market San Francisco men's clothing store.

In 1983 Mark had told Joe Fields he wanted to record a tribute to Nat King Cole, the idol of his teenage years. "Everybody else was a Sinatra freak," he recalled, "but I was a Nat King Cole freak… He was like rhythmic honey." The result was a two-album set, recorded in October and November of that year at Western Sound Studios in Kalamazoo, Michigan. But first there was a musical problem to solve: how to approach Cole's tunes without merely duplicating either the piano/guitar/bass format of the jazz-oriented Nat King Cole Trio or the singer-plus-orchestra format of his solo career? Mark's solution was a brave, perhaps even foolhardy one: he decided to use a trio of musicians – pianist Gary Schunk, guitarist Joe LoDuca and bassist Bob Magnusson – but only one of them at a time: each of the recordings would be a duet. He was attracted by the starkness of this approach, knowing that it would leave his voice very exposed. It was the sort of challenge he relished.

"Do not expect slavish imitations of Nat Cole's voice and style", wrote Neil Tesser in the original album notes. "Even if Murphy were capable of subsuming his own individuality to that degree, what would be the point? This is a tribute, not a copy, a tribute, as Murphy explained, 'to my first influence, and to Nat's taste. Of course, he could make everything sound good, but he also picked such wonderful songs.'" Never one to take the path of obvious commercial opportunity, Murphy avoided most of the hits and instead picked a large number of lesser-known tunes.

These self-denying ordinances produced mixed results. On "Nature Boy", for example, he has only Bob Magnusson's buzzing, scraping arco double bass to sing against. It is thus diametrically opposed to Cole's original 1948 Capitol recording with Frank de Vol and a full orchestra, complete with swooning French horns, lush strings, oboes and flutes. Murphy's version segues into "Calypso Blues", now with plucked bass and a "Two Ladies in de Shade of de Banana Tree"-style Caribbean accent. This track also suffers by comparison with Cole's original version, which in this case was even sparser than Murphy's – just voice and bongos, the two elements perfectly in rhythm. On "Never Let Me Go", accompanied by Gary Schunk's piano, Murphy growls the tender lyrics, rather in the style of his later ballad masterpiece *Once To Every Heart*. Murphy moves the song's bridge to the end, thus creating a lyrical connection with the verse of "These Foolish Things", which follows, and is one of the most affecting songs on the album.

The recordings selected for Volume 2, although cut during the same sessions, are a little more accessible. The ballad "For All We Know" features Schunk's dark electric piano. Murphy concludes his version of the song with these lines: *Why should we waste a night like this? Why should we waste a single kiss? Why can't we laugh at tomorrow? Tomorrow we'll pay what we borrow.* Joe Lo Duca's plangent Spanish guitar accompanies the Mark Murphy version of "Blue Gardenia". This was the title song of a 1953 film noir, in which Cole had made a cameo appearance.

Muse outdid themselves with two more atrocious record sleeves: on Volume 1 the title is stamped in black right across Nat King Cole's face, and unless you look closely, you could be forgiven for thinking that Volume 2 was recorded by Cole himself. The releases were greeted with puzzlement in some quarters. "To no one's surprise," commented *Cadence* magazine, "there is absolutely no attempt made to evoke the breathy Cole voice or his casual phrasing. Murphy makes these songs his own, and he has so much confidence in his own powerful vocal instrument that he needs but one instrument in support, on any single track... Murphy is extraordinary, illuminating each song from within."

The following year, at Rudy Van Gelder's legendary Englewood Cliffs studio in New Jersey, Mark recorded *Living Room*, an album originally pressed in green translucent vinyl, and released with an out-of-focus Eddie O'Sullivan photograph of the artist on the sleeve. The album is one of the hippest things Murphy ever committed to disc, producing it himself along with David Braham, who sticks to organ and bass pedals throughout. The band also includes Peggy Lee's drummer, the famous Grady Tate, who plays on half the tracks. Mark's madcap sense of humor is once again evident on the old Louis Jordan jump-jive tune "Ain't Nobody Here But Us Chickens", which became a live favorite, complete with exuberant, clucky scat solo and chicken jokes.

Mark's continued to perform his Tribute to Miles, with variations, into the late 2000s. He told audiences he would be focusing on "classic Miles", the Miles he remembered from when he was growing up. Typical was a two-night booking in July 1985 at the newly-opened Milestones club at 5th and Harrison,

San Francisco, with the Benny Miller Quartet. He started with "All Blues", segueing into "Summertime", and then "Autumn Leaves". Then came "Bye Bye Blackbird", with some audience participation, "Green Dolphin Street" and "My Ship", which brought applause as soon as he uttered the first note. "Milestones" was also greeted with thunderous approval, followed by his old crowd-pleaser "Twisted" and then "Wee Baby Blues".

With more than 20 albums now under his belt, Murphy was able to range far and wide over a considerable repertoire. The second set at Milestones opened with "Farmer's Market" from *Stolen Moments*, continued with "I Remember Clifford" from *The Artistry of Mark Murphy*, and then his against-the-grain upswing version of "As Time Goes By" from *Bridging a Gap*. "Maiden Voyage" (*Mark Murphy Sings*) was followed by his Etta Jones medley of "Don't Go To Strangers" and "Don't Misunderstand" (*Satisfaction Guaranteed*). He continued with "All The Things You Are", its *a cappella* verse relocated to the middle of the song, "Moody's Mood for Love" and then the Kerouac numbers – "Goodbye Pork Pie Hat", "Bebop Lives", and "Parker's Mood". The ballad "Again" was introduced with a prologue about Ida Lupino and the movie *Road House*, and the evening ended with "Stolen Moments".

For several months, he had been planning an album he called *The Jazz Composers*. In September 1985, recorded it at New York's Classic Sound with Bill Mays, who was confronted with another micro budget to work on. "Again my writing chops were challenged because I only had a rhythm section and two instrumentalists to work with... Lou Lausche the violinist... was a friend of Mark's from Cincinnati... There were two bass players – Steve LaSpina's wife was pregnant so I had Mike Formanek standing by in case she went into labor, which is what happened, so Steve had to leave the session and Mike finished it."

Two tracks came from slightly unconventional sources: Murphy obtained "The Lady who Sang the Blues", a tribute to Billie Holiday, from Edwin Duff, an Australian composer known for his work on programs produced by the Australian Broadcasting Company (ABC). "Vocalise", a Rachmaninoff melody, grabbed Murphy's ear when he heard it while driving around San Francisco. "I had the classical station on, and when I heard it, I had to pull the car over, it sounded so modern."

Beauty and the Beast, as the album was eventually titled, begins with Murphy reading out the lyrics he had written to Wayne Shorter's eponymous tune, backed by the dark ripples of Bill Mays's piano and synth – *The sun shines on a gun, the beast lies low but always waiting...* This is followed by the song itself, with an eccentric, bubbling, semi-falsetto scat, with made-up syllables – *Blom Blom Blom*. The album is littered with other examples of Murphy scat: on "Doxy" – *Swing! Swoh! Swang!* On "Along Came Betty" – *Spots Spoo Dee!*

Beauty and the Beast's release (with a far better sleeve this time) was delayed as Mark awaited approval from Shorter's representatives for the lyrics he'd written to the title track. The months rolled by, but there was no response. Frustrated, he eventually called Shorter himself, who said "Yeah, great, I love it, no problem."

Working with a keyboard specialist of Bill Mays's quality, by now Murphy had very clear ideas about what he wanted from a pianist. "This rambling stuff with no rhythm, I don't consider jazz. I miss Erroll Garner like crazy. I use a lot of wonderful pianists as accompanists all over the world. I get tired of Bill Evans clones who have decided that they're going to lay back all their lives. I look around for a pulse and I don't get it, so I have to do all the work."

Meanwhile *Nat King Cole vol.2* (or, to give it its full resounding title, *Mark Murphy Sings Nat's Choice: The Nat "King" Cole Songbook Volume Two*) was nominated for a Grammy, his third album to get the nod. He wrote to *Mark's Times*: "I tried to make the LA trip for a gig plus the Grammys driving down there and staying in my ancient RV 'Bertha' (She and I have been throhgh it folks) So – first, tune her up. I called a truck garage and took her in. These places usually real BASIC – no frills. You don't expect that. So I left the RV and returned for it later, and drove back to the Navy Yard where I pack. Next day I pack my tuxedo etc and all my music and drive on down only to find that when I start the motor I see smoke! And the heat needle goes crazy. So, back to the BASIC garage – explanations etc – 'leave it we'll fix it.' Returned many hours later to find motor running and a bill that took every bit of cash I had. And all that smoke still happened, it heated up and stalled <u>in traffic</u>. All the control I've learned on stage came in handy as I returned to the garage."

After all those years together, Big Bertha had finally run out of road. Mark ended up flying to LA instead, playing a couple of nights at the Alley Cat in Culver City for good measure. Wearing a pin-striped double-breasted wool suit in the 90-degree heat for the pre-Grammy cocktail party, Mark grew increasingly hot and bothered. Unable to locate a rental car and spluttering with frustration, he calmed down after his friend Judy promised to lend him hers. At the ceremony the winners were declared: Hendricks and McFerrin with *Another Night in Tunisia*, a track from the Manhattan Transfer's album "Vocalese".

For years Mark had wanted to record a tribute to the postwar singer Dick Haymes, but his pleas fell on deaf ears. With no release date in sight for *Beauty and the Beast*, in June 1986 he recorded another Brazilian album – the mellow, melodic *Night Mood*, this time featuring the songs of Ivan Lins – a writer all but unknown outside Brazil, whom Murphy dubbed "the contemporary Jobim". The label was the San Francisco-based Milestone Records, founded by Orrin Keepnews after the demise of Riverside and, like Riverside, since bought out by Fantasy Records. The deal came about, according to Mark, as a result of Fantasy's successful re-release of *Rah*, which had shown that there was a new audience for his work.

Another of Milestone's signings was the Brazilian jazz-funk trio Azymuth, and Mark decided to use them as his backing band, along with alto saxophonist

Frank Morgan and trumpet player Claudio Roditi. Morgan was a notorious junkie who had spent half his adult life in prison, but had resolved the previous year, when released on parole, that he was never going back. The album was widely reviewed, though the consensus was approving rather than rapturous. The *L.A. Reader* noted that Mark's "deep feeling for Brazilian music (and Lins's tunes in particular), his power to express subtle shadings of emotion, and his rich, velvety voice and great range and control, make him the ideal interpreter for Lins's songs." Reflecting the changes in consumer technology at the time, *Night Mood* was released on both CD and LP.

One Sunday in late November, 1986, Mark arrived in Englewood, NJ, to spend two days recording *Kerouac Revisited* (or possibly *Bop for Kerouac Part II* – the title was as yet undecided) with Bill Mays (piano), Steve LaSpina (bass) and Adam Nussbaum (drums). Said Mays, "We recorded it at Tony Bennett's son's house where he had a recording studio [Hillside Sound] with a big nine-foot Bosendorfer piano. He had all these separate isolation booths so you had the piano in one compartment, the bass in another one, the drums in another. But none of us could see one another, we were all spread out. And Mark was in the hallway with the microphone. They didn't have a video set-up either, so we only had earphone contact... it was a little disconcerting." They started with the mid-tempo swinger "If You Could See Me Now", then "Lazy Afternoon", a ballad with a second-line rhythm accompaniment, and the ballad medley "The Night We Called It A Day" and "There's No You".

The following afternoon, LaSpina's place was taken by John Goldsby. Mark's sister Sheila was present for the first time at one of her brother's recordings, along with fan club member Barbara Glass: "Mark and company start to rehearse the first track, 'Blood Count', which Adam tells me was the last song Billy Strayhorn ever wrote," Glass reported in *Mark's Times*. "This is a ballad to end all ballads – exquisite. At 2:05 they get a perfect take... You can hear a pin drop. Mark and men come in to listen to the tape, but Tim [the engineer] has an alarming announcement to make. 'I didn't record it,' he apologizes. Seems that he forgot to turn one of the switches on. The guys take it in such good grace I can't believe it. Adam moans comically, 'Oh no, the perfect take!' Then they all go back inside and do it again..."

When he wrote "Blood Count" in 1967, Strayhorn was in hospital dying from leukemia. Here, arranged as a mini-epic, it is spine-chilling, with recently-added lyrics by San Francisco resident M.B. Stillman. Murphy's first high, keening vocal notes and Mays's glittering piano runs exude a powerful whiff of mortality. As the song progresses, harp and string ensemble effects give way to gothic descending organ, Mark urging the departed to come and meet him in a dream. And then a long, slow fade. Explained Bill Mays: "Mark wanted it to be like a funeral, and I said well we can't get a pipe organ in here, so we used a synthesized version."

Glass continues: "The second track is another Kerouac reading from *On the Road*. It's called 'San Francisco Ride', and is done with bass and drum accompaniment, Kerouac's account of a wild ride down one of San Francisco's steep streets. There are lots of technical sound problems on this one – Mark's voice doesn't carry well over the fast riffs on bass and drums, so it is decided that he will do his reading out in the hallway, while the others remain [in the studio]. This works perfectly, and at 2:50 they get a perfect take." This track, with fast swing bass and drums, is a spoken-word piece, quoting Kerouac's story of a wild ride through the city from his novel *Big Sur*: *I used to drive the getaway car.*

The tracks continue, with salutes to hipsters past, notably "Lord Buckley", another spoken-word piece, in which Murphy revisits Buckley's spoof of Mark Antony's speech from *Julius Caesar*: *Hipsters, flipsters and finger-poppin' daddies, knock me your lobes...* Murphy makes full use of his genius for comedic timing and theatrical voices: *All you cats have goofed to wig city.*

Death haunts the entire album. *Time passes on, and so do the masters of jazz*, he declaims in the elegy for Eddie Jefferson, written with Richie Cole. Mark's voice climbs down to the cellar: *There he goes/There he goes/There he goes/Never to come again.* "I'm not that sophisticated a person," commented Richie Cole, "but I can't believe I wrote that song, it's like Billy Strayhorn or something. I don't know where that came from. It's hard to sing, man, with really large intervals. Mark nailed it."

"You know that song 'September in the Rain'?" said Bill Mays. "Mark said he wanted to a take-off of that, 'I wanna call it "November in the Snow".' So he wrote the lyrics first and then I wrote the melody, and that's why on the album it sounds like a Shearing arrangement. I overdubbed vibes in unison with the piano to get the Shearing sound. We didn't have guitar but it's still got the Shearing sound." In the middle of the track comes another reading from *On the Road* – the scene where Sal and Dean experience quasi-religious ecstasy as they listen to Shearing play at an all-night Chicago jam.

"Lazy Afternoon", from an obscure 1954 musical called *The Golden Apple*, starts with a piano ostinato, rushing water, and birds chirping. Many UK singers discovered this languid song via Murphy's version, although Mark probably heard it on Barbra Streisand's 1975 album, also titled *Lazy Afternoon*. The ballad medley of "The Night We Called It A Day" and "There's No You" begins with sparse piano, bass and the merest dusting of brushes. As the second song begins, these are augmented by a quiet string pad, with a bit of bowed bass, ending on a spacy echo, recalling his old hit version of "Fly Me to the Moon". With no budget for a string section, Bill Mays once again used a synthesizer to achieve the sound Mark wanted.

In September of that year Mark recorded a second album for Milestone with pianist-arranger Larry Dunlap, appropriately titled *September Ballads*. On this occasion, all the songs would be the work of contemporary composers. "'It's a truism that ballads are a singer's biggest challenge," said Murphy in the liner notes. "In fact, it's like you're doing a small movie on the fly – you're in it, you're telling the story, creating the mood and sustaining it. You've got nothing to hide behind."

It's a soft, gentle album, richly melodic, played straight, with no unorthodox arrangements or challenging scat experiments. The songwriters include Pat Metheny and Lyle Mays, whose "September Fifteenth" refers to the day in 1980 when Bill Evans died. Gary McFarland's haunting "Sack Full of Dreams", Richard Rodney Bennett's "I Never Went Away", and "Para Nada" ("For Nothing") by Brazilian singer and pianist Eliane Elias are also featured, along with a gentle, lilting new version of Murphy's own "Sausalito". Larry Coryell and Art Farmer both make guest contributions.

Another five tunes were recorded but didn't make the cut. "For me it was a very expensive album. We ran up huge mixing bills, the sessions were long... but the album was wonderful. I expected some promotion from the company [Fantasy], but they didn't give any," complained Mark.

The liner notes pointed out that he was now hitting his stride as a revered elder statesman of jazz: "Mark Murphy is an international jazz figure who tours Europe several times a year, appearing in clubs, concerts, festivals, and television programs. He was the subject of a TV special in Yugoslavia, Denmark, Sweden, and Britain, and has been seen on PBS stations in this country. Murphy has also played to enthusiastic audiences in Japan and Australia."

It was true. Mark was hardly ever at home these days. When not criss-crossing America, playing dates like the El Morocco in Worcester, Massachusetts, or the Hershey Hotel, Philadelphia, or the Vine Street Bar & Grill in Hollywood, he was criss-crossing Europe. In June 1988 he appeared on the gigantic stage of the Hamburg State Opera in the performance of George Gruntz's three-hour jazz opera *Cosmopolitan Greetings*, described by one bemused journalist as "an eccentric yet big-hearted and affecting avant-garde mixed-media whoozie-whatzit." The performers included the NDR Big Band, Dee Dee Bridgewater, Sheila Jordan, and several well-respected jazz soloists including Don Cherry.

The subject of *Cosmopolitan Greetings* was the life of blues singer Bessie Smith, and the libretto included poetry by beat poet Allen Ginsberg. It was important to Gruntz that the singers chosen to perform the parts were actual jazz vocalists. In his opinion, "Nothing is more horrible than opera singers trying to sing jazz." Another witness described it as "an apocalyptic vision set to a colossal epiphany of sound and solos which sound like the world is, indeed, coming to an end. Then there's the charming poem, set to an African mood, about the tree that complained of having a white car under it because it 'smells of smoke." Murphy made several appearances in 1989 with Gruntz's 19-piece touring outfit, formed from the old Don Ellis Big Band, and including Joe Henderson and Tom Harrell.

In February he had been briefly elated by the news that *September Ballads* had received a Grammy nomination – his fourth in the category Best Jazz

Vocal Performance, Male. This time he was beaten by Bobby McFerrin with "Brothers", a duet with Rob Wasserman.

After a delay of two and a half years, *Kerouac Then And Now* was finally released. But Mark's heart was no longer in it. He was stricken with grief and guilt because back home in San Francisco, Eddie was dying.

10 I Remember Less and Less, Except You Baby

Mark had barely left the USA since recording the Kerouac album, and now the reason became clear: Eddie had contracted AIDS. On tour in Germany with the Gruntz opera, the only person Mark felt he could share his grief with was Sheila Jordan.

Kate Murphy had realized something was wrong when Mark and Eddie came over to her house one day. Such was their long habit of discretion, they did not reveal that Eddie was sick, merely that he was on a special diet of fish and leafy green vegetables. Not until he was already bed-bound did the truth come out. The couple had recently moved to a new and much larger apartment – #601, 2701 Van Ness Avenue, just 3½ blocks north from their old address, on the opposite side of the street, with a view of the Golden Gate Bridge. Mark wanted Eddie to be able to see it when he looked out of the window from his sick-bed.

Eddie died in San Francisco General Hospital on November 9, 1989, aged 50. Mark organized a lavish memorial service the following spring, attended by 200 people, many of them from the city's jazz community. Mourners were invited to read a poem, or sing, or dance. Mark had also asked guests to make a square for a huge quilt, in memory of anyone special to them who had died of AIDS, and bring it to the memorial, which Kate and her daughters did, and then the whole enormous thing was stitched together. Murphy and O'Sullivan had lost numerous friends to AIDS over the years.

"When we lost Eddie, we were all sad, but Mark was devastated. As years went by we encouraged him to take another lover. He tried, God bless him, but Eddie was the one true love of his life. The album and the song lyric he wrote, 'Song for the Geese', was testament to his belief in mating for life. They were quite the couple, those two – Eddie, ever the pessimist, and Mark the consummate optimist." Afterwards there was nothing Mark could do but carry on doing what he had always done.

Until Eddie developed AIDS, Mark had been thinking seriously about relocating to Los Angeles, where he felt sure he could infiltrate the music biz establishment, and finally win himself a Grammy. "I should live in LA, I suppose," he had said at the time, without much enthusiasm. "I'm hardly ever there. I guess when I'm there I love the climate... I was trapped in the Niagara Hilton in the blizzard of '77. That really snapped me, I can't take these winters any more. I guess from travelling so much I never want to move again as long as I live."

"The act of performing has gotten me through some of the darkest years of my life recently," he told Jazz FM's Steve Edwards in 1991, "because we have a place to go to scream it out. I don't know what people do who don't have that... I think they end up in mental institutions, and blubbering on the streets." At the end of gigs, Mark would often dismiss the band and sit alone at the piano to play "For All We Know", the old Nat King Cole song composed by J. Fred Coots and Sam Lewis, in unacknowledged tribute to Eddie. In later years, he would play "Too Late Now", which he would preface by performing the last part of the film *Brokeback Mountain*. "And you would know he was thinking about Eddie when he did that," said Kate Murphy.

In February 1990, after a long absence, he returned to the UK for a two-week residency at the Pizza on the Park at London's Hyde Park Corner. With its excellent acoustics, elegant, dinner-jacketed waiters, black wallpaper and soft lighting, it was a venue beloved of jazz musicians – particularly vocalists, in whom it specialized. Mark then flew to Austria to play a couple of nights at the Nachtkaffee in Vienna, with Allen Praskin on alto, Phil Young on drums and students from the Graz music school, before returning to Pizza on the Park for an added week, such was the success of the original fortnight. A subsequent Nachtkaffee show on May 10, 1990, was recorded live for an album that was eventually released 14 years later as *Bop for Miles*.

Throughout his career Mark Murphy played with a bewildering variety of musicians, and over time he came to realize that when confronted by an unfamiliar pianist, one should avoid ballads. He arrived at Pizza On The Park expecting Brian Dee on piano, but found when he got there that he had Mick Pyne instead – a fine player, who had worked with everyone from Tubby Hayes to Humphrey Lyttelton, but Mark felt he was not Dee's equal with a ballad. In the middle of the week, the venue also switched drummers without telling him in advance.

The presence of unfamiliar players usually meant sticking with standards: one opening set during this residency began with a swinging "All The Things You Are", followed by "Moody's Mood for Love", "It Might As Well Be Spring", which segued into "Spring Can Really Hang You Up the Most", then a couple of Nat Cole tunes – "Route 66", "I Keep Going Back to Joe's". After that came "Lush Life", and finally a Kerouac cameo, with "St Thomas" and "Parker's Mood". In the second set he sang "Stolen Moments", "Blues in the Night", "Skylark", "You Don't Know What Love Is", "Ain't Nobody Here But

Us Chickens", "I'm Old-Fashioned" and "How High the Moon", closing with "Here's That Rainy Day".

In September 1990 he returned to New York to record a new album for Muse – *What A Way To Go*, dedicated to Sammy Davis Jr., who had recently died. In a letter to the fan club, Mark wrote: "Talk about Murphy taking cances!!! *[sic: chances]* This whole thing was a chance since I did not know Larry Fallon the producer/arranger. Joe Fields insisted Larry had the sound of the 90s at his finger tips, and I listened to tape he did with Gloria Lynn that has sold well. I am hear to tell you, the chance paid off. We made a marvelous side." He then listed the tracks, including the so-far untitled "Ding Walls", done as a consciously Kerouac-ian piece, plus something called "Jarrdical", described as "a fusion tune with my words – but lyrics still subject to approval." He went on: "The strings and horns are the best synthesized orchestra sounds I've yet heard with a singer." In early 1991 he sent an undated letter to the fan club, explaining that the album "was really made for a specific market in the USA – the newer, slightly 'new-age' CD stations... I took a chance on the whole thing – I knew only one cat in the studio Pat Rebillot from my 'Bridging the Gap' in 72! But I think you'll like it spcially the lovely ballads."

As well as his mostly-improvised Gilles Peterson tribute, the manic "Ding Walls", Murphy dug out some obscurities for *What A Way To Go*: the virtually unknown songwriters included Seattle-based pianist June Tonkin; Stanley Ellis, a drummer from Boston; and Reuben Brown, whom he later described as "one of the undiscovered geniuses of jazz who plays Monday nights at One Step Down, the super-hip DC jazz club." The critical response was muted, some reviewers, including contributors to *Mark's Times*, not liking the synthesizers.

As a live act, at least, Murphy was considered still to be moving from strength to strength. Perhaps his recent scarcity made his London appearances more of an event, but the Pizza on the Park shows were widely reviewed. "His genius,'" wrote one journalist, "lies in far more than his ability to move in seconds from the deepest baritone to crystalline heights of the kind expected from the top notes of a soprano sax. It lies in the way he can control and play with notes, pull and push them around to create powerful images in sound."

Murphy's now regular trips to Austria had begun as a result of a new association with the University of Music and Performing Arts in Graz, near Vienna. A few years earlier, Karlheinz Miklin, director of the jazz department, had invited George Gruntz to run a big band workshop, followed by a performance of his 1983 oratorio *The Holy Grail of Jazz and Joy*, which – in typical Gruntz style – was to be performed in a cave. In search of some promising young singers to take part, he had enlisted Sheila Jordan and Bobby McFerrin as talent scouts, and this gave Miklin the idea of introducing vocal jazz to the curriculum for the first time. He duly asked Jordan to teach at Graz on a regular basis. But after a couple of years she grew tired of the semester-long absences from home, and recommended the more footloose Murphy as a replacement. So it was that Murphy found himself with a regular teaching gig that lasted from 1990 to 1997, one semester at a time, with a final one in 2001. Murphy's methods impressed Miklin. Other teachers, trained at revered American jazz institutions like Berklee, would come over and show the students what they could do. Jordan and Murphy, by contrast, would start by listening to the students, and then show each individual how to improve.

But in a group context, Mark's on-the-fly approach at first made Miklin distinctly uneasy. After the final rehearsal on the day of an important student concert, many musical issues remained unresolved, and none of the ideas seemed to be working. "I thought, how will this go at the concert in three hours from now? And I remember the piano player Fritz Pauer saying, 'Please Mark, could we play *one* song to the end?' But they did not, and I was really nervous. But the concert was perfect because Mark's presence on stage was incredible. He directed, he led the band. It was so clear; everybody could follow. I never saw anyone else go on stage with so little preparation. But it always worked out."

It wasn't long before the new vocal tutor was also revealing his more personal eccentricities. While teaching at Graz, Murphy occupied rooms in the penthouse flat of the student hall of residence. "Mark didn't like how it was painted," recalled Miklin, "so he organized the students to paint it brown. Without asking anybody! It was some kind of beige brown. And the head of this house came to me and said, 'Herr Professor, do you know what Mr. Murphy did?'"

In keeping with his highly individual dress sense, Mark arrived for one summer semester in shorts. "There's a busy tram intersection where a lot of people sell newspapers – it's the busiest place in Graz at night. He [noticed that] the newspaper sellers... were shouting out the titles they were selling. And Mark started to direct a choir of them. The police came, thinking he was crazy, standing there in his shorts. They asked him who he was, and he said, 'I am Professor Murphy'. They took him to the police station, and he had to stay for [quite] a while." It was years before Miklin's colleagues summoned the courage to tell him about the incident.

On another occasion Miklin, Murphy and some other musicians from the Graz school were booked to play a gig at an ancient castle in Salzburg. "We stayed in a pension [boarding house] nearby. We had some drinks. Mark would always drink bourbon. So we went back to the pension, and the next day at breakfast before moving to the next place, the owner was very upset, because Mark took all the flowers he could see and put them in his room."

Back in the States, after a gig with Sheila Jordan at the Cuyahoga Community College in Cleveland in April 1991, the two long-time friends decided to record an album together for Muse. They met at Jordan's place in upstate New York to discuss material, and in September they recorded it at Sear Sound in New York, a few blocks off Broadway. Kenny Barron (piano), Harvie Swartz (bass) and Ben Riley (drums) had recently played on Jordan's

Lost And Found album. For two George Gruntz compositions – "Avia 18" and "Eastern Ballad" – they were joined by Bill Mays.

Jeff Zygmont was present at the session for *Mark's Times*. The two singers decided to sit on stools facing each other. "Joe Fields was in attendance, sitting up high on a podium. A compact man, balding, serious and dignified in demeanor, he was the only person wearing a suit and tie in this blue-jeans crowd, though once the actual recording began he took off his jacket and worked in shirtsleeves. Music scores were laid out on the desktop in front of Joe, and he followed along during each recording. During rehearsals between takes, he listened with his head down and eyes closed, so still you'd have thought he was sleeping. But he heard all. I take it Joe is the producer of this album. All questions and controversies were ultimately referred to him, the chief judge and decision maker."

On listening back to the take they'd just done of "One for Junior", the title track, all approved except Jordan, who said: 'It seems like I'm screaming here'. The others assured her it was fine, but Zygmont silently agreed with her. "So far I'm not thrilled about what I heard at the studio… I agree with Shiela's assessment: She was shouting maybe too much. In fact the word 'shrill' appears in my notes. In contrast, Mark was much mellower – a combination that didn't sum well."

On the medley "Don't Like Goodbyes"/"Difficult To Say Goodbye", it was Mark's turn to have problems. "The biggest concern seemed to be the song's tempo. Mark insisted that they slow it down, way down, even slower than the blues piece for Junior that they'd just recorded… while he rehearsed his solo part, he seemed to be caressing the lyric tentatively, probing for the right feeling and expression, and I thought that he handled the music very well because of this extra care he gave it. The tape started rolling… Mark… was having a problem reading the music because of the way it was spread out across his music stand – again he regretted forgetting his glasses. He had to weave his head to see it better, and the microphone picked up the changes in his position."

The *One for Junior* cover shows an affectionate cartoon representation of two children, the girl being the older one, the boy with his face mostly hidden by a huge hat obviously borrowed from his mom. The "Junior" of the title was Helen Meyer, the gay painter friend of the pair from New York in the 1950s, who used to hang out at the Page Three. One kind reviewer commented: "[Murphy and Jordan] are complete masters of the material… And both are at an age where their voices are mature enough to put the experience of life into the lyrics."

Mark's other recording that year, made in December, was *I'll Close My Eyes*, again produced by Larry Fallon. Although happy with the album, Mark decided it would be his last for Muse. He told *Mark's Times*, "This turned out better than *What a Way* because that recording date was confused by sceduling problems and Larry couldn't get exactly who he wanted. But this date – and what a <u>whiz</u>

– so slick and yet deep too in the ballads... Muse gave me a lovely discography, But almost succeeded in nullifying that achievement by 'Keeping me hidden in it's pocket' and neglecting to shop me further afield. Catch 22? Uh huh. But I've more prospects for more CDs, so I'm very pleased really."

And as on *What A Way To Go*, he recorded the work of several unknown songwriters: "Happyin'", a hip bop swinger by Flip Nunez, a Filipino pianist living in San Francisco; "Ugly Woman", a comic reggae song by singer and pianist Howlett Smith; and "There is No Reason Why", a sad, pretty ballad about loneliness, reminiscent of Bacharach and David's "A House Is Not A Home", "written by Patti Linardos, a girl from New England who gave me this at my gigs up in Hartford... It's a deep song, very deep."

Alarm bells went off among Mark's fan-base in response to another letter he sent them a couple of weeks later, perhaps prompted by his approaching 60th birthday and the end of his Muse contract. "I'm putting a feeler out to you all that I may not be able to stand this sort of life much longer – I just don't know. You see, NONE of you sweet people can imagine what it is like never to be home!" Looking back over his career, he told a reporter, "It didn't come easy, but I do think I've earned a niche now in jazz history, and that's something that can't be taken away from me... I'm kind of tired. I don't know if I can stand the stress any longer. But as of now I'm planning to give it five more years, then ride off into the sunset and buy a bed-and-breakfast place... I just don't want to become a road zombie."

There were other ways to become zombified, however. Emotionally, Mark had been unraveling ever since Eddie's death, and his previously mild drink and drugs intake began developing into a crack cocaine habit that lasted through the first half of the decade. "He was wracked with guilt," said James Gavin. "Mark felt that if he had been home more with Eddie and paid more attention to Eddie, then Eddie would not have gone out straying, which Mark was certainly doing himself. But he felt responsible for Eddie's becoming ill and dying because Mark was on the road and not home with Eddie. Mark was not a stay-at-home guy. He was a true Kerouacian, On The Road vagabond."

Live performances at this time were often as disheveled as the man himself, as he expressed his anger and grief in the only way he knew how. Gavin went to see him in September 1991 at Birdland. "He was bored, he was tired, he was frustrated. He was taking it out on the audiences and the songs, and a ballad that began beautifully could end up unlistenable, and frequently did... I was so disheartened by what I saw. Mark was so clearly depressed and out of sorts. It was the first time I had seen Mark where I thought something terrible was going on because he was destroying song after song. His scat singing was like the most wild and undisciplined free jazz of the 1960s. It was out of tune – caterwauling, in my opinion. He was disciplined in a studio setting but in live performance things got out of control. There were two shows – I stayed for both – and I thought, What is going on? This is not the Mark Murphy I love. And that would have been early in Mark's drug addiction phase."

Murphy himself freely admitted that he was an addict for three years when work was scarce, and that he had lost control. It was only when he started teaching again that he stopped using crack and began to rebuild his life. The catalyst, he told the singer Amy London, was a hot cinder that flew into his throat while he was smoking. The shock of what it could easily have done to his vocal cords was such that he quit then and there, he said.

Though the going was tough in the States, there were still plenty of opportunities in Europe. He continued to work with the Dutch Metropole Orchestra, and there were gigs and teaching assignments lined up in Denmark, Holland and Austria. And in May, he and Sheila Jordan were booked to record an album of music from George Gruntz's *Cosmopolitan Greetings*.

Even on *The Dream*, his album of generally excellent recordings with the Metropole, one can detect weaknesses in the vocal performances from 1991. Dave Raksin's standard "Laura", for example, suffers from nearly all of Murphy's more annoying mannerisms, a combination of striving for effect, misjudging the mood and failing to trust the song: we find him speaking a word rather than singing it; rushing a phrase or extending it for no discernible reason; then there is the needless glissando on to notes; the sudden fast vibrato at the end of a line; holding a line back; swooping around a note; little bursts of yapping falsetto scat.

In April 1992 he was back to his old enthusiastic self, writing to his fans: "… something WONDERFUL happened to me in Lost Wages (Vegas!). I do one night every 1½ years at the Four Queens Hotel on Alon Gronts [Alan Grant's] Monday night jazz series. I loathe Vegas, so I was really trying to just get through the evening calmly and leave next day. I looked over at my pal and colleague Marlena Shaw, who had just entered, and I was giving her hugs, when I saw over shoulder a guy who looked just like Gregory Hines sitting between two other black men – and it WAS. I went right over and asked him to please make more records because he's a great singer too." At the end of Murphy's set, Hines brought his purple tap shoes up in a plastic bag, sat on the edge of the stage to put them on, then danced while Murphy sang "Farmer's Market". "It was one of the great thrills of my life. And then later on John Rogers at KJAZZ played a track that Gregory had recorded with Jimmy Cobb, the drummer, in some obscure album in the seventies. He did four songs and KJAZZ used to play 'My Old Friend' quite a lot. The first time I heard it I had to pull over and stop the car, because the tears came and I didn't know who it was, at that moment, but then they said Gregory Hines and I said wow, now he's my favorite singer."

Back in London, Pizza on the Park had not responded to his inquiry about more gigs. "I don't think they want me," he groaned. But Malmö in Sweden did, and in a radio interview the presenter asked him about the retirement rumors. "You are not a person for sitting down and waiting… you cannot sit in a house all day and play records," commented the interviewer. "I might be," said Mark, "I'd like to find out! (laughs) I'd like to have some dogs… and a garden… and a fireplace… y'see, these are all the things I give up to come on the road… I don't want to start relying on artificial stimulants to keep me going… and I don't want to become a road zombie… I mean, there are people still travelling – I won't mention their names – who should not sing anymore… I mean, let us remember how great they were because they were the greatest… I don't see myself travelling in about six years."

It wasn't just the creeping weariness; audiences seemed to be thinning out. "Biz was slow at Pizza last time… Biz slow in Vienna… Paris – slow. USA in recession – Australia down the tubes. You can see the difficulty just trying to plan economically for the last part of my life." The music was certainly proving a tough sell in London. The UK's only dedicated jazz radio station, Jazz FM, was under new management, and was beginning its transition into a vanilla-flavored soul-pop operation, while after only two years at its Camden site, the Jazz Café was in the hands of receivers, with imminent closure rumored. The following year, the BBC announced it was axing its big band, effectively cancelling any future appearances with Mark Murphy.

Long-time fan Barry Bendell, who could not believe that no club wanted to book Murphy, arranged a one-night-only show in July 1992 at the Jazz Café. Bendell and some fellow enthusiasts put posters up in the capital's jazz record shops, and got some promotion going on Jazz FM and in *Time Out* magazine. Consequently the date was a sell-out, with both Murphy's older jazz audience and his younger fans in attendance – all of them wildly enthusiastic, greeting each tune with whoops and cheers. The show was hosted by Jazz FM's Steve Edwards, who had recently been fired – whilst still on the air – by the station's new program controller.

Mark came out and read a poem called "The Rays", before introducing the ever-reliable Brian Dee Trio, with Mario Castronari on bass and Ralph Salmins on drums. The set began with "Stolen Moments", followed by "Brother, Can You Spare a Dime" (during rehearsals, Mark said, he had seen four people sleeping in a doorway across the street) segued with "Nobody Knows You When You're Down and Out" – a medley he had performed at Ronnie Scott's in the Sixties. In the second set, over Dee's rumbling piano intro to "I'm Old Fashioned", Murphy remarked that he'd read somewhere that the Earth vibrates in the key of G. Later he embarked on an improvisation of G words: *Good Golly Gosh Gotterdammerung Red Garland* and *Erroll Garner*. After two encores ("Old Piano" and "Farmer's Market") the management promised him a further three-night booking, which he duly fulfilled in early November.

Life and work went on, but Mark was still suffering agonies of grief over Eddie, and constantly questioned what he was doing with his life. The lowest point came in early 1993, when he wrote to the fan club: "Last night the decision formed in my mind to actually Take early retirement at 62 (in 94) because of the financial bender of my big empty apartment is finally just too much to afford. The only way to get out of that is to sell after I'm 62 and then pay everything off and resettle in the east near Sheila Jordan. My nerves just can't take the constant economic insecurity <u>any longer</u>." With a heavy heart, fan club secretary Norbert Warner duly announced the closure of *Mark's Times.*

It was to prove a false dusk. In fact, Murphy was busier than ever: in mainland Europe, no fewer than six album projects, all on different labels, were at various stages of gestation. Shortly before his first Jazz Café engagement, he had set off for the town of Monster in Holland to record an album for the Belgian label September entitled *Another Vision*, a one-off project notable chiefly for its final track, "Never Never Land", originally written for a 1954 Broadway musical version of *Peter Pan*. The song, performed *a cappella*, is preceded by a self-revealing speech from Mark about how "our poor plundered planet is sinking into a swamp of murderous argument, war, hate, disease and general depression. Shouldn't it be the opposite, as we come so close to the new age? The human mind should expand instead of shrink. Are you, like me, perhaps awaiting the arrival of the UFOs to jump on and go away, if possible? Or is another vision what you see, like this song?"

Other projects were queuing up. The 1990 Vienna Nachtkaffee live recording with the Peter Mihelic trio, eventually released in 2004 by HighNote as *Bop for Miles*, was still awaiting a buyer; in 1993 he recorded an album's worth of material with some students from Graz at a studio in Klagenfurt, which appeared the following year on the West and East Music label under the title *Very Early*.

In the absence of any new recorded product from the States, Mark's older UK audience had been following these European adventures with interest. For years, Bert Warner had been selling cassette tapes of Murphy's radio broadcasts as a means of subsidizing *Mark's Times*. The singer was particularly struck by a BBC Radio 2 show that Bert had taped of him singing with the Metropole. Four of these had aired in the UK in August 1982 as *Hilversum Greets Radio 2*. Three years later there were more recordings in a show called *The Metropole Orchestra*, followed in the early Nineties by a series titled *Easy Does It*. It was these, and others, that were compiled by Joop de Roo as *The Dream*, on the Austrian label Jive. Over a quarter of a century, working with the Metropole had given Mark Murphy the sort of large-scale instrumental backing that had been scandalously denied him in the US since the end of his Decca contract. *The Dream* features lush, romantic ballad arrangements of consistently high quality.

Also in 1993 he made yet another live recording, this time with Karlheinz Miklin in Graz at a club called Jazz. The album was released as *Just Jazz* on a Croatian label called Jazzette; both the album and the label permanently vanished from sight during the Bosnian war. And there was yet more Dutch radio material, produced in Hilversum by Joop de Roo at various sessions during the early Seventies with the Louis van Dijk Trio. This finally surfaced in 1997 on the Portuguese Jazz World label with the rather underwhelming title *North Sea Jazz Sessions Volume 5.*

The *Bop For Miles* set, recorded live right in the middle of the year Eddie died, gives some clues to the disintegration witnessed by James Gavin and others. *Why have all my dreams been broken*, he sings, *and where is the hope that was in my heart?* – before launching into a high-velocity rendition of "Autumn Leaves" (after which the same line is repeated). *Just Jazz* contains a 13-minute version of "Stolen Moments", with two wild scat solos, and on "Vera Cruz" (aka "Empty Faces") there is more quite uncontrolled scatting, the track ending with rhythmic panting and grunting, prompting giggles among the audience applause.

Murphy had by now settled into a pattern of performing and teaching in Europe every summer. In England he began working with the Pete Churchill Trio. He had also established regular backing groups in Italy and Germany. In Munich, a key collaborator, in composition as well as live gigs, was the pianist Andy Lutter. Under the influence of Jack Kerouac, who invented the Western (or American) haiku poem, Murphy liked to write "jazz haikus" of his own. These were less formal than the 17-syllable verses of Japan, but composed in a similar spirit of brevity and insight. One was called "Café Paranoia". Another was "Sleepy People (Don't Cause Revolutions)". Then "Less and Less" – a poignant one: *I remember less and less, except you baby.* Then there was a longer, more complete lyric called "The Planet Formerly Known as Moon", about a bar where he used to drink, now sadly changed:

> *...missing just something sort of funky*
> *In this clever franchised saloon bar...*
> *Alas awaste – but keep all that in*
> *the devastated street speed, thanks a lot...*

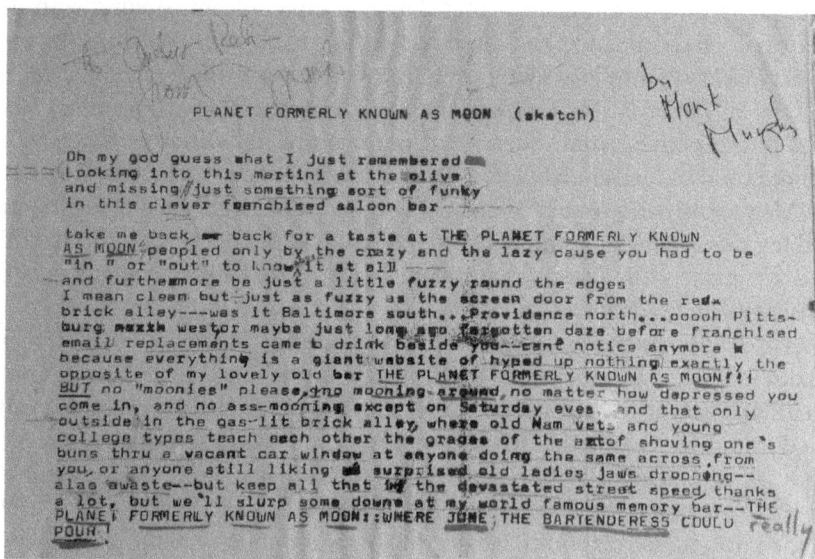

A Mark Murphy 'jazz haiku' annotated with colored felt pens (author photo).

Andy Lutter eventually wrote music for many of these jazz haikus, later recording them with the British jazz singer Tina May.

In London, the big advantage of working with Pete Churchill, from Murphy's perspective, was that the pianist knew a lot of tunes; it gave the two of them an instant shared repertoire. Churchill knew all the piano bar songs, and had played small wine bar gigs with London-based singers like Stacey Kent and Christine Tobin. Soon afterwards he met his future wife, the jazz pianist Nikki Iles, who had played with luminaries like Art Farmer. "My listening changed. She brought a load of music I hadn't listened to. My playing changed too. And the next gig I did with [Mark], I remember so clearly, he put his hand on my shoulder in the middle of the gig, and said, 'Have you met someone?'"

By this time, Murphy was starting to emerge from the depths of misery and self-destruction brought on by the death of Eddie O'Sullivan. In an effort to clean up he was drinking less, but was still prone to snort cocaine in the intervals at gigs, which sometimes made the second set even more of a challenge for his accompanists. But this habit too grew less frequent as time went on.

For a week in early September, Murphy played the short-lived Birmingham Ronnie Scott's in Broad Street to audiences of noisy drunks, and a few days at Pizza on the Park, who had finally relented and offered him a booking. Smollensky's in The Strand was a large American-style bar and grill in a basement, with another rowdy, inattentive audience: the bar area tended to fill up with people who were there to drink and chat rather than listen. The stage was awkwardly positioned so that few people had a clear, uninterrupted view which, in itself, relegated the music to background status for many people. The tables were screened off from each other, which made the viewing conditions worse. In an effort to keep his younger audience interested, Murphy began inviting the Jazzcoteque dancers to some of these gigs – one, two or sometimes three young men clad in black and white – to come and do their frenetic jazz dancing as the band played.

It was a shock to Pete Churchill's system to be tossed into the stormy seas of a Mark Murphy gig, where the improvisation was on a whole new level. "It was an unbelievable awakening. He was throwing things out at me, and long scat solos where I just thought, I don't know how to do the gear change that he wants from me in the rhythm section to take it to the next level. He was the perfect link I'd been looking for between the vocal jazz world and the instrumental world. I'd always seen them as very separate. I did my singers' gigs and then I did my instrumental gigs. And now here was a singer's gig where he didn't want me to be a singer's pianist. That was revelatory. The way he engaged the rhythm section and *played* the rhythm section was unbelievable. I don't know any other singers who did it the way he did it."

Retirement and withdrawal were off the agenda. Mark Murphy was finally ready for a new challenge.

11 A Wild Animal, Or a Child

After playing one evening at Gaye Anderson's New Orleans Restaurant and Jazz Café in Seattle with the group New Stories, Mark had an idea for a quite different kind of album to any he had made before. "It's from some things we improvised on the band stand because they like Latin music and I do... certain songs like 'You Go to My Head'," he explained later.

He had been looking for some new musical direction to revive a career that seemed to be faltering again. Having tried and failed in the early days to become a popular singer, like Tony Bennett or Mel Tormé, he felt that, as a white man, he would never be taken seriously as a jazz singer either. He had slipped through the cracks and ended up nowhere – an aging gay white male, singing jazz, and in the eyes of some people, that disqualified him. And that wasn't all: although highly intelligent and well-informed, Mark was too much of a hipster-poet to be easily understood when he spoke to the mainstream media, too quirky to be pigeonholed by the industry and in the public mind.

Nor was his music easily digestible, like that of Frank Sinatra or Nat King Cole, or Joe Williams, who achieved success by performing pleasant and familiar-sounding music that the average person could listen to at home and feel that they were listening to jazz. Listening to Mark required effort; it was not background music, nor was it easy listening. But his experience of being greeted with joy and reverence by young people in Britain had been profound, and now he was eager to record something that "college kids" in the US would want to listen to.

He decided to enlist the help of vocal arranger Roger Treece, leader of a vocal trio called Full Voice. "He played me a little recording [of "Song for the Geese"] that he had done with Sean Smith and he gave me a lead sheet and said, 'I would really like to have your vocal thing on this song.'" At this stage Murphy only wanted something he could take to record labels to illustrate what he had in mind for the record. Treece made some adjustments to the chords, and the trio recorded their own demo of the song.

The cutting edge technology at the time was ADAT, a digital tape format that allowed the simultaneous recording of eight separate digital or analog tracks. It enabled cheap recording at high quality. Treece owned three ADAT machines, which he had linked together, allowing him to do 24-track recording at home. In essence, the process was not so different from the one Lambert, Hendricks and Ross had pioneered in the Fifties: Treece would build up a choir effect through multi-tracking, plus this time there would be a MIDI jazz trio (piano, bass, percussion), and then Murphy's voice would be added on top.

Mark wanted "Song for the Geese" to be a bolero, although in the end it sounds more like a ballad. Explained Treece, "The vocal arrangement concept was to put a "frame" around his voice. A choir is something that happens on stage, live. It's not as intimate. I wanted this to sound like [you were] in a room with 60 voices totally encircling you, and you were so close together that you could touch them. And that's the way I always wrote and mixed the vocals that I was writing."

In the past Mark's music had been driven by the rhythm section, but this time the vocals were in the driver's seat. In January 1994, he reported to *Mark's Times*, "There are three of them but they overdubbed another three voices and they sound like Take 6. I enjoy the sound of that and I need a completely new sound in back of me to resuscitate my image and career here, in the United States especially. Europe's a different matter and England is a separate thing in itself which we're taking care of." He had obtained a promise of funding for the project from Bud Miller, a businessman from Redding, California, who wanted to support jazz in general and Mark Murphy in particular. 'We were set to go next week and then there was some delay in the finance coming through from Mr. Miller and so now we have decided to wait until May to do it... Even someone as well established on the pop market as Al Jarreau is not finding an easy time of it just now, so we're looking for a way of connecting the old with the new which I've done before, which is exemplified in the title of my album *Bridging a Gap*. I'm always bridging the gap between the old and the new and I'm going to restate that for the 90s. It's a 90s world and I think you all realize that."

It wasn't just the modern audience that he wanted to reach out to, but also the jazz business: he was feeling out of touch. "I gotta somehow reach this new 27-year-old Mafia that runs Jazz now: all the old Promoters, except maybe George Wein who is probably limping around on one foot – are either dead, retired or burnt out... It's going to be very airy and light and cheerful-sounding and a lot of energy and I've written words to a Pat Metheny song that I got approval on."

Jazz as a business was indeed tough going. He was aware that things were changing in California, and not for the better. The public radio station KJAZZ in Long Beach was about to be sold, with the likely changes in format that would entail; Kimball's in San Francisco had closed, and there were rumors that Yoshi's in Oakland was going the same way. By September 1996, in San Francisco, the New Orleans Room at the Fairmont Hotel had switched from jazz to cabaret; Kimball's had reopened briefly as a jazz room but had now become a salsa bar; and two smaller venues – Storyville, on Fulton Street, and Pearls, near Chinatown, were booking mainly local musicians.

There were also changes afoot on the domestic front. After violent storms the previous year, Mark's condo in San Francisco was being refurbished and the residents had bills to pay for waterproofing and repainting. "I want to put this place up for sale if I can and get out of here," said Mark. "I'm a little bit tired of San Francisco and I want to move East I think again if I can just stand the weather. It's about 20 below in upstate New York just now but if you plan your life right, that sort of thing can be livable – with a little bit of luck. San Francisco is a lot of 'wases' to me. It's not what it used to be: it still looks good to tourists, but the jazz is really dead, well the whole west coast is dead. Really where it's happening on the west coast now is Seattle, there's not much of distinction in LA because the music scene in LA has been so decimated with the advent of the keyboard. I mean, if you think what LA was like when all those studios had orchestras, all the television corporations had orchestras, some of the radio stations had bands; it was a real mecca for good musicians. Now a lot of the jazz people are walking around in circles, saying 'what happened?'"

By April 1996 he had decided: he would move north, to Seattle. He was still talking about it at the end of the year. Loneliness had a lot to do with it: "I don't have much to say to people of my own generation who are not in music, you know, because I don't have children or grandchildren or property or a yacht, or you know, things that they talk about: I don't play golf, I don't bowl..." He projected his gloom on to the present state of the world: "I would question whether we'll make it. I mean there's a big question mark whether we'll make it until the year 2001 as a planet. Maybe I'm a little bit dismal on that aspect but some things in society are very good these days but underneath it all it seems in many societies that the mind should be expanding towards the New Age but it's not, it seems to be shrinking into separation, into all that ethnic stuff and tolerance is spit on these days and many sections of different societies should be throwing their arms out to each other; instead they're killing and fighting and hating each other... I wouldn't mind if a ray of light came through the window right now and it was a UFO and it took us all on board and we went somewhere else."

On this occasion, that somewhere else turned out to be Australia. His plan was to tour there, followed by a few gigs in Vienna, then three weeks in Italy, some teaching in Holland, then back to the US in May to record, and play some gigs around the US, before heading to the UK in the summer. Previous trips to Australia had not always gone smoothly, but this time he had more luck, despite an early clash with a noisy audience member. The tour was bookended by dates at the Basement in Sydney. "I even threw a woman out of there on the second night and I've never done that in my life. I mean

I didn't *physically* throw her out, but I said: 'If you don't leave, I won't come back.' So they got her out of there. She was smoking – amazing thing about Australian audiences: they don't smoke. I couldn't get over it. But this woman was obviously out of it on something. I don't know what, and she was singing along with me – a different song – and I just blew up, so they got her out and I continued." In each city he supplemented the gigs with singing classes and private tuition.

Kinsela's in Melbourne, he said, provided the optimum conditions for singing. "I had a sound man, I had a light man. I had the same band – a quintet with Latin percussion – for the two or three weeks I was there, and I'm telling you I grew like a tropical flower. The performer I am today started on that gig in Kinsella's. And this place in Melbourne was called the Café Continental, in a section they call St Kilda, near Melbourne Bay... The stage was in the corner of almost a square room, so that every single person could see you, and then in a semi-circle around the stage, was a line of two tables for eating and then in back of that they could pack in about two hundred people standing (and they did) and business was wonderful."

He was still in demand amongst the hip crowd in London, where he performed live at the huge discotheque Ministry of Sound with a group of Japanese DJ's and an English band, then went into the studio. On May 19, he wrote: "I am now a rapper! You'd never have believed it but my poem "Future Light" – (spoken) came out as the first over 60 rap! The most amazing thing to me was that I was the only musician there! The 3 Japanese guys called UFO were and are not muso's, they are DJs! They tour playing their records at midnite dance hops! Thru sequencing and sampling they reate a backing tape, mainly a sythyn track. Then I read my poem, then we add things Gilyand I put on our own backup vocal track – a repeating phrase – then I did another track singing (actually) words and phrases they liked – inventing a new melody. Over that I added a scat track in certain epodes-ord at the end. Finally I redid my rap and they now will mix. And it looks like the single could come out early this summer. Amazing YEAH!" The recording was a guest appearance on the album *No Sound Is Too Taboo*, recorded in London at Gilles Peterson's suggestion by United Future Organization, aka UFO (not to be confused with the veteran English rock group of the same name).

Far from winding down in his seventh decade, Murphy was stepping on the gas. With Graz as his base, he made his first trip to Indonesia, playing to a thin crowd at the newly-opened Blue Note club in Jakarta on November 5, 1994, accompanied by Larry Dunlap, Scott Steed and Vince Lateano. After a brief return to Graz he flew back and forth to Tokyo, San Francisco and finally to Mombasa in Kenya for a short holiday, before returning to Graz.

And in April 1995, after four weeks of rehearsal, he finally recorded his long-planned Seattle album, although as yet no record label was interested in it. Mark had written the lyrics for the title track, "Song for the Geese", years earlier after he and Bill Mays had been to the upstairs room at the Village

Gate in New York to hear bass player Sean Smith's band. Hearing Smith's composition as an instrumental, he eventually penned the words as a tribute to his family, and in memory of his childhood days at Fair Haven. "These Canadian geese would come. I can't remember if it was mid or late summer... but they'd arrive and we'd just ... a hush would fall, and we'd just watch them." It was also, he told the fan club magazine, a tribute to Eddie O'Sullivan.

> *A child that was me saw two geese / Long ago on a bay at dusk / They'd arrive unannounced / A hush fell as we would watch / They glide side by side / As partners for life ...*

Mark had also wanted to record Steely Dan's hit "Do It Again" for years, and had once called Donald Fagen to ask whether he had sheet music for the song. "Yeah, we got the music," responded Fagen, "Come on over." Murphy duly made his way across town, found the house and knocked on the door. After several minutes the door opened and Walter Becker appeared in a cloud of ganja smoke. Inside, kaftan-clad hippies were sitting around on cushions. "Hey, Donald," said Becker, "Mark Murphy's here, have you got the music?" "Sure," said Fagen, "I've got the music." He disappeared for a few moments and came back with a copy of the album, a sheet of manuscript paper and a pencil. "Here's the music," he said, handing paper and pencil to Murphy. "I'll put it on for you – go ahead."

Mark was delighted with Full Voice. "They sound fantastic... much of what we did on the vocal tracks started out as almost completely electronic stuff on Roger's machine in his house. Then he adds the voices, which of course are not mechanical, then he brings them to the studio... he's done all this on what they call ADAT then the studio transfers it from ADAT to analog tape, which is where the other stuff we recorded – reel-to-reel tape – then we could put them together. And as you'll hear in 'It's Just Talk', at one point the band drops out and it just becomes vocal... now that's got to be remixed... By the time it got to the mix it's all on analog tape. The young people who ran the studio would run in and listen so raptly... and that was the age group I'm aiming to... but not scaring away my more mature fans..."

Roger Treece remembered Mark demonstrating the musical pulse he heard in his head. "Imagine somebody holding their arms out, palms down, and then getting their hands like they were holding two softballs. And then imagine the person making these gestures as if they were going to put the softballs down on a tabletop. So Mark would be making these gestures in the air, left and front and right, mimicking where the instruments are, and he would be making sounds, placing this stuff. There were sessions where I felt like I was dealing with a wild animal, or a child. A child that you could by no means have follow directions. You had to follow him. Not that he was any sort of authoritarian 'my way or the highway' kind of guy, it wasn't that at all. It was just that he was in his world, and you could not get him to come into your world. It had to be his world, because that's where he was. I remember he recorded the overdubs to 'It's Just Talk' laying on the leather sofa in my studio. He was laying with his right leg stretched out, with his left leg on the floor. He was propped up with a couple of pillows. And I had to take the mic so he could lay there and record the vocal that way, get the boom stand and the mic into this awkward position. And as he was singing he would make the same gestures with the softballs, poking the air with his arms."

After the recordings were complete, Roger accidentally erased one of Mark's lead vocal lines: *As years had passed by, when geese to the bay did return alone...* In the end, after much anguish, he managed to extract the line from the DAT tape demo that Mark had recorded in his studio three years earlier. "Talk about a weenie-shrinker, man. That was a very difficult couple of hours." It also turned out that engineer Dave Dysart had pressed the wrong button when they transferred the 24 tracks to the master CD. Worse yet, the master had already been sent to the duplicators, and shortly afterwards Mark took delivery of 300 CD's, all of them in glorious mono. "It's a bit humorous to me," he chuckled, "but anyway the thing is the record company took the blame... the vocal kids wanted to remix their stuff, so they did it. And then I put some more percussion on a couple of the tracks and the whole thing sounds 100% better. It really was manna from heaven and one of those mysterious things that maybe was just supposed to happen and did. So I'm very, very pleased that it sounds so much better as it goes round and we shop it."

A year before the start of the project, there had been an unusual request from the dance company Decidedly Jazz Danceworks in Calgary. Producer Vicki Adams Willis had been a Mark Murphy fan since 1981, while she was teaching at the city's university; she first heard *Bop For Kerouac* when a student "bounded into the studio with a record that 'I just had to hear'". When she heard that Murphy was due to perform at Calgary's Baker Street Jazz Club in May 1994, Willis took her dancers along to hear him, arranged for an introduction, and invited him to one of their rehearsals. Mark, of course, was thrilled, especially when they showed him a videotape of their dances to his music. The following month they asked him back to see the performance, *Rhythm Addiction*, and Mark immediately agreed to return as a guest star in a new show for the next season.

The plan was to select some of his recordings and work them into a unifying storyline. The dancers would rehearse to the recordings, and Mark would come in for two weeks of intensive planning and rehearsal with Willis and musical arranger Tommy Banks to work on his own role. For the show itself there would be a live six-piece jazz group. The production was called *Stolen Moments*, and it was performed at The Martha Cohen Theatre in Calgary Centre for the Performing Arts for most of June, 1995. Mark sang and narrated throughout. The first act, described as "fast-paced, spirited, high energy, boppy and bluesy" was inspired by Murphy recordings including "September Fifteenth", "Empty Faces", "Madalena" and "Ballad of the Sad Young Men", ending with a tightly-choreographed tap and sand-dance sequence called "Living Room". The second act was a live version of film noir, complete with its iconography of trench coats, gangsters, femmes fatales, cigarette smoke and slatted lighting. The story linked songs like "Angel Eyes", "Stolen Moments", "Lady in Red" and "Never Let Me Go", with Murphy's narration providing the transition between scenes. The cast included a character named Angel Eyes, a boxer, and a detective. "Highly athletic, with segments of lightning-fast choreography, syncopated rhythms, steamy love scenes, and a surprise ending, it has all the ingredients of a great detective story!" gasped the press release.

Much as he was enjoying himself in Calgary, Mark found the altitude taxing. "The city is as high as Denver, which is a mile high, and I'm huffin' and puffin'... So I'm going to see a doctor today, perhaps to get some oxygen or maybe an inhaler, so then I can take a blast during my first set. In the second set, where I play a detective, sort of Raymond Chandler style, I have long moments where I can just sit down and just sort of breathe, but in the first act I'm going all the time... I was terrified when I first got to here because of my memory thing... you know I always have to have crib sheets, but I even went to a hypnotherapist for some memory and concentration exercises... and it worked because ... well... I guess the kids like it actually because every night I do something different.. and so almost every other night I forget something.. so they're right on their toes...which is what dancers should be, right?" The show was filmed by three cameras with a view to selling it to a television broadcaster. "We'd love to put that out as a video some day", he told *Downbeat*, "But like everything, we're searching for an angel to help finance the project."

Meanwhile there was a sudden flurry of excitement at *Mark's Times*. The Murphy revival had also revived the spirits of editor Bert Warner, as had the infectious enthusiasm of a new IMMAS member and contributor. Cindy Bitterman, aka Cindy Sigman, aka Cindy Lou Bayes, was a former underwear model and Miss Stardust of 1948. In the Fifties she had worked as a model, and in 1954, stepped out with Frank Sinatra.

And now she was dashing off ecstatic reviews of Mark's recorded output and Stateside gigs. The effect was like that of a lightning bolt on an expiring patient. In the next issue she reviewed *The Dream*, which had just become available, ending with: "MARK MURPHY, take some giant steps to the nearest mirror and look at the greatest singer I have ever heard."

"She was estranged from her husband," explained James Gavin. "They were living in different wings of the house. She loved singers and loved jazz, and she was driving around when she heard Mark on the radio for the first time." This was January 1995, and the tune was "There's No You". Cindy wrote about her epiphany in *Mark's Times*: "I've heard lots of really top singers do this just as you have, but I don't recall holding my breath at the ending as I do with his version. The first time I ever heard him sing this was in my car and it nearly caused me to have a very bad accident." Within four months she had

Cindy Bitterman with Frank Sinatra, 1954.

collected 24 of his albums. This was more than mere fandom; for Bitterman it was a mystical revelation. "I experienced such incredible joy and happiness. I felt more alive, vital, enthusiastic than I had in years... I don't believe much in religion, but I feel renewed. If this is a religion, then its name is Mark Murphy."

Her reactions were more physical than spiritual. Writing about "Laura" on *The Dream*, she commented, "...And speaking of exciting, listen for the longest pause before the word kiss. Is this vocal foreplay?" Reviewing the Austrian release *Very Early*, she wrote, "What a silly name for a CD that is so virile... I need Prozac after this because I want more, more, more... Johnny Green's 'I Cover the Waterfront' at a breathtakingly slow beat is sinful..."

She finally got to experience Mark Murphy in the flesh on Sunday 16 July at the Zanzibar in Philadelphia. That afternoon she'd had a wedding party to attend in New York, but her mind was not on the proceedings. After less than an hour she dashed out, rendezvoused with her friend Peggy King and boarded a train to Philly, armed only with some cash and her Sony sound recorder. They arrived early so they could bag good seats. "Will it suffice for me to tell you that after both sets, during which my brain paralysis probably began with his opening song, I left the Zanzibar with my recorder and Mark inside it, on the bar."

Bitterman soon became much more than a mere super-fan or groupie. At first Mark was suspicious of her, assuming her to be one of the legions of adoring older ladies and wannabe singers who surrounded him these days. In fact, she was like a second Baroness Nica de Koenigswarter, the friend and patron of Charlie Parker, Thelonious Monk, and many other prominent jazz musicians of the Fifties. Not only did she understand with great clarity what Mark Murphy was doing professionally, she seemed to see into his very soul: "Watching Mark work only confirmed what I guessed at after listening to a few of his albums last winter, He reminds me of a little boy who is only happy when playing in his sandbox, and Mark's sandbox is filled with things musical. Just as Mark is. I think his veins are filled with bits of notes, chords, sharps, flats etc. Music is to Mark what water is to a fish. A necessity. Watching him work you can see his knowledge and command of his craft. He toys with a song, not quite like a cat with a mouse, because Mark is not killing, but toying, weaving and winding and bending and leaving me as usual shaking my head in disbelief. Taking two steps away for a drink while the trio continued, Mark is still working. I don't believe I've ever seen any singer so totally involved and in control of his work."

"Over a 15 year period, I cannot begin to tell you what Cindy did and the amount of money she poured into making Mark Murphy's life better," said James Gavin. "I don't think he would have lived as long as he did without the loving care of Cindy Bitterman. She paid for him to stay at Washington Square Hotel when he came to New York so that Mark wasn't staying at places like the YMCA any more. She paid for projects for Mark, she bought him clothes. Mark at some point turned on almost everybody in his life. He did it to me a couple of times – it passed quickly, I got off cheap. But he never turned on Cindy Bitterman; he didn't dare. Because he needed her, but he also really loved her. They were talking on the telephone every day, several times a day, for years. When Cindy got sick, and that petered out, Mark again took it all very personally. But Cindy wanted nothing more than to help nurture Mark, for Mark to feel good about himself, and bring him to a wider audience.

I'm pretty sure she paid for his publicist, Lesley Mitchell-Clark, for two years." Along with Mark's manager Charlie Ellicott, who worked out of Petaluma, near San Francisco, Cindy began looking for US distribution for *The Dream* and a record label for *Song for the Geese*.

Meanwhile *Mark's Times*, which had always featured articles about other jazz singers and jazz in general, published an announcement in its September 1995 issue. "STOP THE PRESSES!!!!!!" wrote US contributor Don Hoffman, "A new jazz singer has suddenly appeared on the scene who extends the idiom and insures the future for male jazz singing. Remember this name: KURT ELLING! A young man from Chicago (27 years old) will continue and advance this art form for many years to come! The freshest and most exciting sounds since M.M. He sent a tape to the top man at Blue Note, who immediately signed him. (KURT ELLING...CLOSE YOUR EYES, Blue Note CDP 724383064526) This guy has it all; a full bodied bartitone, great intonation, passion, creativity, and swing. He sings with total confidence and NO FEAR! His scatting is very original and spontaneous. Ballad singing is unusually mature for such a young man (although not yet at the level of M.M.) But he's got 50 years to go!... He dedicated CD to Eddie Jefferson, Jon Hendricks, and Mark Murphy, 'who taught me how to sing Jazz.' His risk taking is assured and exciting to listen to. Bert, if Mark ever retires we can start an exciting new appreciation society which will live longer than we will! His inspiration is heavy with M.M., and I'm very excited about this development!"

The arrival of Elling was soon to have a double-edged impact on Mark Murphy.

12 Age Only Matters If You're a Cheese

In 1996, Mark recorded *Dim the Lights*, a duet album with the young Bud Powell-influenced pianist Benny Green. As a "rhythm singer", he constantly talked about his desire to work with pianists who approached material in the same way he did. "Benny Green has been playing with Ray Brown, and he's one of the new hot musicians coming out of the newer trends in jazz where they are listening to the later 50s music of rhythmic players like Ramsey Lewis and Ahmad Jamal. And to us it's old but to them it's brand new," Mark told *Mark's Times.* A protégé of Oscar Peterson, Green had made his name as a member of a late version of Art Blakey's Jazz Messengers, and had been in Betty Carter's trio.

Despite Benny Green's rhythmic heritage, many of the tunes on *Dim The Lights* were rendered as ballads. One of its experiments was a medley of "Beautiful Love", "Lullaby of the Leaves" and "Softly as in a Morning Sunrise", songs all written on similar chord progressions. However 'muddley' is perhaps a more accurate term: the new (to Mark) science of overdubbing had got the better of him: he took the decision to overlay the three songs on top of each other, so that one hears all three being sung at once, including three different scat choruses. The album, on a tiny Canadian label called Millennium, remained unreleased for three years.

It was the same story with *Song for the Geese*. In the summer of 1996, a year after recording it, Mark still hadn't found a record label – surprising perhaps, given his, for once, very clear focus on the market he was trying to appeal to. He said he was turned down by every major label in the US, and every minor one, too. Perhaps, he thought, it was something to do with his age, or the absence of any fashionable names in the line-up – a Terence Blanchard or one of the Marsalis brothers. "I was mistakenly expecting a label to say, 'Hi Mark, sign up with us', but they don't do that any more."

But he was still full of ideas for new projects. These included recording an album in Slovenia with Graz colleagues Karlheinz Miklin and Fritz Pauer that was eventually released as *Shadows*. He had already written lyrics to two of Miklin's songs and two of Pauer's. Mark's interest meant a lot to Miklin, since it was the first time a singer had ever added lyrics to music he had written. "One track – 'Hodnik' – we had not planned. Mark just said to the drummer, 'Play a fast time'." This is the number where Murphy simply improvises vocal sound effects while Dusan Novakov plays, and gradually the other musicians join in. "Mark just saw a sign on the wall that said 'Hodnik'. He didn't know what it meant, but that's what he at first wanted to call the album... And another one, 'Humanity Ltd', we also never practiced – it was completely improvised." Murphy this time recites a bleak poem as the band play ominously behind him. "He asked us to play slow to set a mood, then he started to talk... I remember going back to Maribor with Mark after the recording to mix it," said Miklin. "When I saw him mixing his voice, it was great to see the importance [he placed on] one word, to give a little more emphasis to one word. I am not a singer, so I could not hear but when he made a change I could see why he had done it. But Mark was crazy, not just musically, but in his business dealings. He had a contract with Muse, I think, at the same time."

Indeed, there were always ructions whenever Mark became excited by some new project and recorded without Muse's say-so. And this time there was an additional problem: *Shadows* was experimental – even less likely to sell than usual. To no one's surprise, the result was that it stayed unreleased for the best part of two decades.

More frustration was to follow. A regular part of Miklin's professional life at Graz for the past 30 years had been his work with visiting Argentine musicians. This may have been how Murphy first became aware of the music of Astor Piazzolla, and why he conceived the idea of making an album of Piazzolla's slow tangos. The composer was now dead, but negotiations with his widow – who seemed to think there would be money in it for her – had been going on for months.

Given the lack of new product, it now seems remarkable that in late 1996 Mark Murphy won the *Downbeat* readers' poll for Best Male Singer. Interviewed by the magazine's Dan Ouellette, he said, "As soon as the results of the... poll came out, I began to get calls from ... [Murphy lowers his voice to a secretive whisper and dramatically utters one word at a time] ... *very important people.*" Ouellette added: "But the mercurial Murphy, who speaks in machine-gun bursts of energy, spins on a dime and offers a kernel of cautionary advice for would-be contract-seekers: 'Record companies have us by the B-A-L-L-S. You've got to remember that those Monday morning listening parties are full of coffee and Benzedrine and whatever else these guys have been doing on the weekend. You're lucky if you get a two-minute attention span. So you can't program your ballads first, because these guys will toss your demo across the room into the reject pile.'"

The poll result must have helped, but the long-awaited record deal for *Song for the Geese* actually came about thanks to the two-pronged efforts of Cindy

Bitterman in the States and Samir Köck and Werner Geier in Austria. Köck, a well-known club DJ and journalist for daily newspaper *Die Presse*, had first become aware of Mark Murphy at a concert at Jazzland in Vienna. His friend Werner Geier was a radio presenter who had just founded the record label Uptight Records, mainly with the object of releasing electronica. "But he also let me compile jazz, soul and funk albums," said Köck. "The series was called 'The Big Lulu'. We thought it might be good idea to ask Mark if he was interested in singing on one of these electronic tunes. Mark showed interest. He also sent me a CD with the completely produced *Song for the Geese* album. I listened to it and was blown away. I loved the intensity of the ballads, the wonderful singing of the choir. I went to Werner and played it to him. He liked it also."

It was not before time. After two years without a flicker of interest from the American record industry, Bud Miller was becoming increasingly vocal about seeing some return on his investment. "So Werner and me convinced the local manager of major label BMG Ariola to pay the money Mark owed [Miller] and release the CD." The deal was signed in mid-February 1997, with release planned for August or September. It included a "guaranteed" second BMG album for Murphy – his cherished Astor Piazzola project, with the involvement of Danish trombonist Erling Kroner. The best part of the deal with BMG, from Murphy's point of view, was that its releases came out on RCA Victor in the USA.

The latest Mark Murphy revival received another fillip when Joe Fields sold his 600-title Muse and Landmark labels to Joel Dorn's new venture 32 Records. Using the popular format of CD twofers and boxed sets, Dorn planned to re-release a slew of albums that had been unobtainable for years. The artists included Sonny Stitt, Wallace Roney, Eddie Jefferson, and Mark Murphy. Michael Bourne was hired to make the Murphy track selections, which were released in four batches over the next two years.

Joe Fields sold Muse because, he said, he had seen Bob Weinstock do the same with Prestige Records back in 1971, when he sold out to Fantasy. "He put out a lot of records under Prestige... When I worked for him, one of his quests was to ultimately sell the record company. And he did. And he made millions. He had a catalogue that wouldn't quit, not only in jazz but in all kinds of music. He was a unique individual that nobody even talks about because he had a terrible personality, and he's a totally forgotten guy. So I thought, wow, what an ambition. What I'm gonna do, when I grow up, I'll be just like Bob Weinstock. I'll have a record company and I'll make all kindsa records, and somebody will come along and say, 'Bless you, my son, here it is – it's all yours.'"

In January 1997, Mark was booked to perform two nights at Birdland in New York, then stay on for two more weeks to do some teaching in New Jersey. But a few days beforehand, staying in Denver with the singer Ellyn Rucker, he was suddenly wracked with bronchitis, flu and laryngitis. He'd played a gig on the Friday night but hadn't been able to complete the second set, and had cancelled the Saturday altogether. He was due to leave Denver on Sunday for a date in Kansas City, then head to New York on Monday to fulfill gigs on Tuesday and Wednesday. Cindy Bitterman, who had planned the whole thing, told him to cancel Kansas City and, if he felt better by Monday, fly straight to New York. She herself cancelled his Monday evening radio interview.

Murphy duly arrived with mountains of luggage, because after New York he intended to spend the next six months working in Europe. The signs looked favorable: having eaten nothing for two days, he was now ravenous. Bitterman made him two thermoses of chicken soup, and prayed for a quick recovery. By Tuesday, after a couple of hours of rehearsal, Murphy seemed his old self again, telling Bitterman to bring tissues to the gig because his band were so beautiful, they would make her cry. The place was packed with fans, friends and family, and other singers, and Murphy sipped the chicken soup while the band members soloed. Afterwards he was rebooked for three more nights in September.

As a result of his *Downbeat* poll triumph, he was asked to perform with several other singers at Carnegie Hall in a Nat King Cole tribute on July 8, featuring a 16-piece orchestra. There was to be a second show with different performers the next night. Mark was backed by the long-established trio of Mike Renzi (piano, also the musical director of both shows), Jay Leonhart (bass) and Grady Tate (drums), who had worked with Peggy Lee on her ill-fated autobiographical show *Peg* back in 1983. Wearing a green bow tie as part of the required tuxedo get-up, Mark sang "Tangerine" (with solo bass accompaniment) and "Again".

All 2,800 tickets were sold. Reported *Mark's Times*, "Singer after singer offered song after song from Nat's musical life, along with fond and/or funny memories of Nat's friendship and inspiration... Ruth Brown remembered learning from Nat the importance of articulating lyrics, Mark Murphy remembered how Nat's piano and voice encapsulated the whole era of swinging LA in the 40s and 50s. Margaret Whiting remembered bringing Nat's earliest records to Johnny Mercer, then head of Nat's soon-to-be-longtime label Capitol."

In the *Downbeat* interview with Murphy published in April 1997, Dan Ouellette mentioned the up-and-coming Kurt Elling, "the young Chicago vocalist and Blue Note recording artist who some people feel has stolen Murphy's style hook, line and sinker." It was true that Elling had attended Murphy's vocal clinics at the Green Mill in Chicago, but in this interview Murphy defended the newcomer from accusations of plagiarism. "People accuse him of sounding just like me, but I don't think that's true at all. I do know that he likes that Kerouacian space I used to work in. But I've moved on to other places in my vocalizing..."

Elsewhere Murphy described Elling as "my protégé, or one of my protégés. And I don't think he sounds like me at all! He has taken a direction with material that is somewhat similar to where I was when he first met me – not particularly where I am now. But you know, all that reading and Kerouac stuff and poetry and – well, I'm ready to do it if somebody wants it. But he even has that slight razor pitch toward the end of a phrase like Sinatra did – which is not saying he's influenced by that guy, but it's just another dissimilarity to me. So I think that the people who say that he's stealing your set... that's not right...I'm just glad he got a start. I was glad I was able to help him get to Bill Traut in Hollywood who got him on to Blue Note."

But Murphy fans quickly dubbed Elling's 1997 album *The Messenger* "a take-off of Mark's Kerouac albums", with its extended vocalese excursion on Dexter Gordon's "Tanya" (written by Donald Byrd, and here retitled "Tanya Jean"), and its homages to Nat King Cole ("Nature Boy") and Miles ("Ginger Bread Boy" and "Prayer for Mr. Davis"). Modern opinion remains split between those who claim that Elling leans too heavily on the Mark Murphy legacy, and those who see him as a natural inheritor of the mantle. "He got a lot from Mark," commented Australian jazz singer Lily Dior, who received personal coaching from Murphy. "A lot of people didn't know about Mark when Kurt burst on to the scene, and he was using a lot of similar material to Mark in the beginning. Kurt came over to Australia and did a whole Lord Buckley routine, and people would say, 'Oooh that's amazing', and I would say, 'Well, Mark did that first.'"

Whatever the truth of the matter, in 1997 it seemed that Mark Murphy was finally beginning to achieve recognition in his own country. He received news that he'd been voted best male jazz singer by *Downbeat* readers for the second year running. And soon afterwards *Song for the Geese* finally appeared on the shelves.

What Murphy really needed at this point in his career was the help of an experienced professional publicist with wide-ranging contacts throughout the media. In the early Nineties, Lesley Mitchell-Clarke had been working for publicity agency Third Floor Media in New York, with a client list of big jazz names of the time, including Marian McPartland, Diana Krall and Susannah McCorkle. From LA she conducted tours of Liberace's house in the Hollywood Hills. Fleets of limousines would drive up there with 15 women on board at a time, most of them in a state of high excitement. She even recalled one woman from the Midwest rolling around on the pianist's bed. So she was not surprised when taking on the Mark Murphy account, at Cindy Bitterman's request, to find that another gay man in his sixties was capable of arousing straight women to the point of hysteria.

"There was a pattern of women of a certain age who contributed financially to his career," said Mitchell-Clarke. "They were lonely, and believe me, he was charming. He worked it. He knew how charming he was... And on a certain level, Mark was working his mojo on me too. I know he was." Like many who observed the relationship at the time, she believes Cindy Bitterman and Mark Murphy were in love, in some way. "Mark was very lonely and needy and would call Cindy up at night and want to talk on the phone for about four hours."

Lesley started booking interviews with Murphy on New York jazz stations, and arranged for him to perform on a couple of the city's chat shows. She flew him to Atlanta to record music cues in commercials for Turner Classic Movies – work that Murphy relished. "It was so hip," said Michael Bourne, "his singing about old movies, showing clips of Bogart, Bette Davis and whoever. It was like mid-tempo, where he was really swinging."

As soon as review copies of *Song for the Geese* were available, Lesley aimed for as many reviews as possible, despite yet another poor album cover, featuring another out of focus photo of Murphy taken by Eddie O'Sullivan. But radio airplay was good, in the both the US and Europe. The line Lesley pushed was that Murphy was a *contemporary* artist, not just some old groaner from the Fifties.

The album was not universally loved by the critics. One approved the ballads, "but two thumbs down for the percussive r&b sneering on Steely Dan's 'Do It Again' and the slurring lounge-crooner diction ('I sincerely wanna zay...') on 'I Wish You Love'.... I've always found Murphy's autumnal moods more plausible than his exuberant show-biz side, even when his foggy baritone is as velvety as his cummerbund."

Dealing with the artist himself was a challenge. A lifetime of going his own way had made it impossible for Murphy to toe any party line, even when it was for his own good. Lesley remembered, "[Mark] was very stubborn and... could be very difficult to deal with. I had to finesse him into everything, every media appearance... I never knew if he would be loquacious, or dark, or if there would be big silences. And whatever I told him to say or focus on, he would not... Even though he desired it, it was very hard [for Mark] to think in commercial terms."

Then there was the problem of the wigs. As his publicist, it was part of Lesley's job to take account of her client's appearance. "Mark really believed that that wig was his hair... He used to send off to some cheap wig house and get a two-for-one deal." She was appalled by the Rod Stewart-style mullets he wore. "They were a terrible colour, they were a no-colour, made out of plastic. So I said to Cindy Bitterman, 'Let's take him to the best wig-maker in New York and get a proper wig made.' So Cindy said OK. You had to work with Mark without using the word 'wig'. I don't know how, but somehow we got him to a top-flight wig-maker and they took a cast of his skull. So he gets a new wig, and it's styled, and it looks great. That lasted about a week. I don't know what the fuck he did with this wig – put it through a washing machine, but a week or two later it looked like something Phyllis Diller would wear at the height of her career. After that he went back to his mail-order wigs and nobody could do anything about it. The only time he ever acknowledged to me that it wasn't his actual hair was when he was having his CD launch at Birdland – that's what the new wig was about – and he explained to me that he had to have a rest between the soundcheck and the performance because he had to re-tape the wig. The toupée would only last so long." Mark would also smear Vaseline on his wigs, for reasons most of his friends found unfathomable, although Mitchell-Clarke's theory was that it was an attempt to make the fake hair shine just like real hair.

An additional cosmetic problem was Mark's ill-advised plastic surgery, which had probably been carried out in either Mexico or Brazil. Lesley recalled that Mark had linear scars behind his ears and on his temples, as well as evidence of work done under his chin, and lifts of various kinds in various locations.

And then there was the technology. Roger Treece remembers a call from Cindy Bitterman, who wanted him to come to Birdland for the album launch. "She needed me to mix down the vocals on to some sort of media so Mark could perform with it live in New York... It was in mono. They were playing to a DAT tape, and the drummer had to wear headphones so he could hear the click in one ear and the vocals in the other."

The launch was attended by anyone who was anyone – Rex Reed, Susannah McCorkle, Jackie and Roy, James Gavin – and was adjudged a big success. However, reaction to *Song for the Geese* from Mark's most diehard fans was mixed, some loving it, others outright disappointed. Those in the latter camp included Bert Warner. "This is Mark's worst album," he declared in *Mark's Times*. "He's done something I thought he'd never do, kopt out and gone totally comercial. The drummer is pure rock, which must make Buddy Rich turn in his grave." Warner added: "My biggest fear is that we will get more of the same? I really detest those three songs ['It's Just Talk', 'Everybody Loves Me' and 'Do It Again'], and I feel so strong about it. Also are members becoming too fanatical, in that they love everything by Mark? I was connected with the Sinatra Society for many years, until new listeners came along and loved the rubbish as much as the gems, so I left."

Curiously, it had taken Warner more than two years to decide how awful the *Geese* album was. On first hearing the tapes in April or May 1995, he had written: "There are some things on it I'm not too sure about... All I can say is the backing is quite superb..." But by the time *Geese* came out, Bert Warner's anger suffused the pages of *Mark's Times*. "The last time I felt so disappointed must have been when I heard there was no Santa Clause! ... it's mainly Mark singing 'poplike' I can't stand. On *Mark II* he sings pop tunes, but in his own way and it possesses a quiet charm about it and I can sit and listen to it right the way through without kicking the dog."

But Mark was happy. "The year is ending nicely, and the next year looks very promising. *Song for the Geese* is selling!! It's the first time in my career anyone has TOLD me sales figures!" The professionals had done a sterling job: *Song for the Geese* was nominated for a Grammy in the category Best Jazz

Vocal Performance (by this time the gender distinction had been abolished in the jazz vocal category). It was Mark Murphy's fifth nomination, and it came after a gap of nine years. Perhaps this, at last, would be his year. Cindy Bitterman paid for hotels, clothes, including a new tuxedo for the awards ceremony, and a session with photographer John Abbott. But it made no difference: *Geese* was defeated by Dee Dee Bridgewater's tribute album to Ella Fitzgerald.

"These are political awards," explained Lesley Mitchell-Clarke. "Dee Dee Bridgewater... had done everything that politically she should do, short of serving breakfast in bed to all of the members of the Grammy committee. Mark was always the eccentric outsider. None of that lent itself to travelling along the political channels. To be successful in the music business you have to be both right-brained and left-brained. You have to run your career like a business – especially in the contemporary climate of no managers, no real record deals, no development of talent. Kurt Elling is a very political person and he doesn't have the same artistic temperament or eccentricity as Mark. So I suppose people who booked him felt that they were dealing with someone maybe more reliable, in a certain sense. Not that Mark was a no-show for gigs. But he was definitely an unpredictable character..."

Wearily accustomed to professional disappointments, Murphy moved on. In Toronto, where he was booked to play the Top o' the Senator for a week, he worked for the first time with the bassist Duncan Hopkins. As at Birdland, Mark wanted to perform with the recorded Full Voice harmonies. There was only one problem: he had arrived in Toronto without a DAT machine. Young Hopkins, who barely knew a DAT machine from a dishcloth, was dispatched to comb the city in search of one, armed only with Murphy's credit card. When he finally found a store that sold them, the sales people asked what specification he needed, such as how many inputs and outputs. "And I had no idea. And then his credit card failed. So I called up the club and the owner gave me her credit card. In the end, we probably used the DAT machine on one night. It was so awkward because everybody needed headphones, but only the drummer had headphones."

The first gig was equally unnerving for the bass player. Murphy called "Señor Blues" as the opening number. "At the end of the song, it goes into this Afro-Cuban vamp, and he walks up to me while I'm playing and he whispers, 'You finish the song. You just take it now, and finish it.' And I looked at him and I thought, Do you mean *now*? Or do you want me to solo...? And he just walked away and stopped the band. So I was wondering, should I take ten minutes, or finish the song in the next 30 seconds, or what? So I just played the way I thought I should do it. I don't know how long I went on for, but it was several minutes of solo bass. And he loved it, he was glowing the whole time. If you were taking your chances and tried to approach it the way he did, he loved it."

Sometime later, Full Voice came to visit Mark in San Francisco. His car at this time was a rust-coloured AMC Pacer, a model familiar to fans of the film *Wayne's World*, in which it is dubbed The Mirthmobile. Recalled Roger Treece, "The first time we came down he took us on a ride around San Francisco. After the Pinto, the Pacer was probably the worst car in American car history, so it was only fitting that that would be the car Mark would choose to buy. The first stop was to a pub, where Mark consumed several glasses of Wild Turkey, and then we hit the streets again. If you've ever seen films like *The Presidio* or the Clint Eastwood *Dirty Harry* films, that's what it was like. We were literally afraid for our lives because Mark was running red lights. Sandy [Anderson] dubbed it Mr. Toad's Wild Ride." Afterwards Roger took a picture of the car in the underground garage below Mark's apartment, and scribbled 'I drove the getaway car' on the back – a quote from *Kerouac Then and Now*.

In London, on October 8, Mark was interviewed about *Song for the Geese* and his forthcoming shows at Soho's Pizza Express by DJ Helen Mayhew in an hour-long special on Jazz FM radio. It was vintage "Marf Murky", a rambling, distracted performance that left Mayhew nonplussed, to say the least. "Helen seems ill at ease with her guest," commented an IMMAS member who heard it, "and the interview never amounts to much of a conversation. This is compounded by Mark's unusual conversational style. It's almost as if his answers to her questions take on the logic of a scat, as he puts random ideas against

AMC Pacer, Mark's vehicle of choice, 1990s (courtesy Roger Treece).

each other, plays around with words, riffs on a subject etc. You can almost hear him thinking as, pausing for inspiration (and sometimes breath) he goes down another avenue of reminiscence, speculation, enlightenment etc. Helen Mayhew is often left trailing in his wake as his answers turn into monologues."

Asked whether he felt the future of jazz vocal was in good hands, Mark replied, "It is in good hands – yes – in certain places... if we had more time I could detail it more... err... out of people in New York – David Devo who's picked up in four months more than most people pick up in a full six year course with me... and I've heard in my Australian class... there was a couple of wonderful singers... this girl...this (laughter) ... it's difficult to understand, but jazz people as creative people – really for anything else – pretty bonkers ya'know... it's like she stumbled through this first course which had a lyric to remember... a melody to remember... when she came into the second chorus of the improvisation she just relaxed and the whole [indistinct] went da da da... and the rest of the afternoon was just a party... you have to understand that the creative process... I guess... is it the left side of the brain or the right side? – I can't remember... it really screws up the other side of the brain because.. err... it's... you weight it so with this creative side." "Well," replied the baffled Mayhew, "Let's hope both sides of the brain are in good working order tonight, Mark Murphy."

Two days later Bert Warner turned up at Pizza Express in a foul temper. The unpleasantness was reported by *Mark's Times* contributor Barbara King in an article only half-jokingly titled "Nightmare on Dean Street". Warner had lashed himself into another rage over *Song for the Geese*, and was making his opinions known to all and sundry during Mark's performance. Bert was complaining about everyone and everything... "London is boring... I didn't want to come... the train journey was awful... I've only just seen Mark in New York... I don't know why I've come... I felt happier at home... Mark shouldn't have started his set with 'Twisted'... Mark shouldn't have kicked off his new CD with four swingers... the vocal choir is awful... 'Baby It's Just Talk' is just a pop song... the musicians are much better in New York... Peter Churchill is playing too slow...the band's not swinging enough... I really didn't want to come... Alma persuaded me... London's boring, not like New York... oh no, not the Miles Davis tribute... oh no, not 'It's Just Talk'... we've got better musicians back in Whitley Bay... I walked out of the travel agents... I really didn't want to come..."

There was more fun and games on stage, as the band tried to synch up the pre-recorded DAT vocal backing. "They had headphones," recalled Pete Churchill, "and someone was counting the bars in their ear, and the choir would come in on the tape, and another voice was numbering every bar '462, 463, 464', and Mark had no idea of the chaos this caused. Crazy. After a week of this, on the Saturday, we came back in, and found someone else had been using the club. [Drummer Mark] Fletcher had the headphones with the longest lead, and Mark had the shortest lead. But they'd all been plugged back in wrong. After a while Fletcher just tore off his headphones, refused to play with them on. Which meant he was going to get out of synch, because he couldn't hear the bar numbers or the click. So I took mine off as well. Andy kept his on. And then the choir didn't come in because we were out of synch. And Mark just loved it! It was chaotic!"

They set off on tour, starting in the Suffolk village of Boxford, then moving to Wakefield, Leeds, and the Royal Northern Hotel in Manchester. The audience reaction varied according to its age profile: in Wakefield it was a mature crowd who knew him from the old days. But in Leeds, they were younger and wanted to dance because they'd heard Gilles Peterson play "Milestones". Seeing all the frenzied dance floor activity, Mark came sidling up to Churchill during a drum solo and said, "I'm 65 years old and I've become a fuckin' disco queen..."

By the time they reached Manchester, Mark had lost his voice. He was particularly worried because he was flying back to the US the next day to get together with Kurt Elling, Jon Hendricks and Kevin Mahogany for a new project known as the Four Brothers. Said Churchill, "He shut himself in his dressing room and then you heard, 'Water! I want water!' So we ran around and got him some water. And then: 'Chicken soup! I want chicken soup!' And we said, 'Chicken soup? On a Sunday night in Manchester, Mark?' But they found some Indian restaurant that made him some chicken soup. Then he went, 'Peter, come in 'ere! I gotta voice.' So he showed me the set, and it was 'Farmer's Market', 'Twisted', the 'Ding Walls' monologue – stuff where he could carry it just on the rhythm of speech, without much of a voice – and he said, 'We'll open with some jazz haiku. Go out there and play some Japanese shit.' So we got going, and he came on, and he said to the audience, 'Age only matters if you're a cheese.'"

Despite all the shenanigans and setbacks, there is no doubt that from the late Nineties onwards, Mark Murphy's reputation was growing in the USA. Having gone through periods when he felt unwelcome in New York, he now found himself in demand, to the point where tickets for his shows were becoming hard to get. He played Birdland, the Jazz Standard, the Blue Note, the Kitano, the Iridium, and the miniscule Danny's Skylight Room. Audiences were frequently packed with jazz singers – many of them Murphy's own students. Following his Carnegie Hall Nat Cole appearance, he was asked to play at Washington's Kennedy Center in December 1997 – albeit in the Terrace Theater rather than the enormous concert hall – with Lee Musiker on piano, David Finck on bass, Terry Clarke on drums and Menio Acevedo on percussion. The performance, which didn't include anything from *Song for the Geese*, was greeted with two standing ovations. He was also rebooked for two more nights at Birdland for the following October.

After surviving most of the Nineties without Eddie or anyone to take Eddie's place, home comforts seemed more important than ever, and now Mark decided that his real home was not San Francisco or Seattle, but back in the north-east. The following February he wrote to *Mark's Times* to tell them he was moving out of San Francisco. He wanted to be near New York, although not in it, and reckoned he had found the ideal spot in Pike County, Pennsylvania. It was in the Poconos mountains, only two hours' drive from New York City, but a world away in terms of peace and quiet. And property was much cheaper than in San Francisco.

Another big advantage was that there were family and friends nearby: Bill and Judy Mays lived just across the lake. On visiting them, Mark had been reminded of the landscapes of his youth – particularly the woods and lakes. Sheila Jordan lived in the Catskills, a short distance away, and would often invite Mark over for Thanksgiving and cook him a turkey, which he loved. (According to Charles Cochran, Mark liked 'old-fashioned granny food', like leg of lamb with roast potatoes.) Elder brother Doc lived within walking distance of Jordan. And Mark's old friend Ronny Whyte had a house a few miles away in Milford.

Mark took the plunge, buying a modest 1,500 sq ft log house on the lakeshore, at 104 Maple Park Drive, Shohola. Back in San Francisco he packed up his possessions and cleared out the apartment. Moving day was scheduled for Saturday, March 30, 1998. The contents of the apartment would go by truck, while Mark himself planned to travel in the Pacer with Full Voice singer Sandy Anderson as his co-pilot. At one point on the journey, noticing how dirty the windows were, they discovered there was no window washing fluid in the car, and stopped to buy some. On opening the hood, he and Sandy poked around in the engine, and looked at each other. Neither of them had a clue where to put the fluid.

Soon afterwards, they broke down in the Nevada Desert. No parts were available locally, and after three days of waiting, they abandoned the car. Mark managed to get himself to LA, where he booked himself on to a New York-bound plane. The truck carrying his furniture was due to arrive in Shohola by April 6, but on the specified date there was no sign of it, so Mark spent the first couple of nights in his new home without pillows or blankets. It was only on May 1, after Cindy Bitterman had paid for repairs to the Pacer and Mark had made a trip to Brazil and back, that he finally reclaimed the vehicle.

"Mark was probably the least [well] adapted human being that I've ever met to living in this world," said Roger Treece. "Getting along in the everyday practical world was something that he seems to have a singular inability for... The interface with the practical world was just something that was very difficult for him... It was also why things were so difficult after Eddie died, because he didn't have that other half. Eddie was more practical than Mark was... Mark needed a producer. He was very strong on concept and creative details but very weak on technical details."

The San Francisco press wanted to know why Mark had abandoned them, when there was such a vibrant local jazz scene. "Well, my life timing has always been strange," mused Mark. "I asked my psychic in Berkeley if I had been jinxed in a past life, and she said, 'Yes, Mark, you were, back in the 10th century.'"

Perhaps she was right. RCA was now experiencing corporate convulsions. By the end of it, the company president, the head of public relations and many others had gone, including the entire jazz department. There would be no second album for Mark Murphy.

13 The Mother of All Love Songs

Despite his popularity outside the USA with the younger acid-jazz crowd, Mark Murphy still saw himself as part of an older jazz tradition: "I love doing ballads. That's when I feel I can communicate one-to-one with listeners. People tell me it's as if I'm singing directly to them. I've been a part of marriages and divorce settlements, child conceptions and wakes, my fans keep my albums for years. They come up to me at my live shows with these scratchy LPs and ask me to sign them. I never sold a million albums, but those I did sell are still out there. Shirley [Horn], Sheila [Jordan] and I seem to be the last of our generation. But the gold is that when you reach maturity as vocalists, you begin to sing your life. You're not just performing. You're putting your life into your songs."

But the jinx continued. Mark's name was accidentally left out of the *Downbeat* male jazz singers' poll of 1998, prompting a furious letter (which they printed) from Cindy Bitterman and a groveling apology from the magazine. And by the beginning of 1999 there was still no sign of the Benny Green duo album *Dim the Lights*, recorded three years earlier.

Mark decided to take a holiday in Peru, from whence he wrote to *Mark's Times*, the fan club magazine that had been supporting him since 1981: "As I move into a very pleasant and easy, slow moving phrase of my life (which will involve actual – as opposed to early "RETIREMENT") from vocal performances, I need to formally request from you not to use my name on the title of the music journal you put out." After suggesting the magazine be devoted to younger jazz singers and continue publishing online (still a very novel concept in the late 20th century), he hinted that Bert Warner and his wife Alma might prefer to spend more time with their yet-to-be-born grandchildren.

Warner, naturally, was shocked and mystified. "I can understand him wanting to retire, but not in wanting his name off the mag, nor dismissing me from his life after I thought of him as a friend for 32 years. As far as I'm concerned this is unforgiveable! So he's retiring? Well he's just been touring Europe, and has just been in London at the Jazz Café... Then I learn he still intends to make albums and will be appearing at New York's Birdland? A funny sort of retirement," concluded Warner.

Indeed. Long-time US rep for *Mark's Times*, Ron De Armond was equally perplexed at Murphy's brutal Prince Hal-style rejection of Warner. "I've been in shock since I got your letter. I was at a loss for words. He didn't even thank you for all you had done. It's all very strange... I really am anmazed at Mark... can't believe he has not tried to talk to you. I sent him a letter, but he never bothered to respond." Other contributors were equally outraged and baffled at the turn of events. Rosemary Carden, who had been involved in the IMMAS since the beginning, wrote: "I could not believe what I was reading on the back page. I read and re-read it, thinking it was a wind-up. Is that letter <u>really</u> from Mark Murphy? Was the oxygen starvation affecting him?"

Another garbled note from Murphy arrived, this time from his new address in Pennsylvania: "You must not take this personally at all. <u>I cannot go on forever!</u> And when I'm in my new home for a while I get to feeling so good – I even feel younger!! So you can't blame me, eh? (& a kind of music so small in it's returns) <u>Main</u> <u>thing</u> is new singers need this mag to help them!! But Bert, you cannot be given advice by anyone? And are uncriticyable – so you must relax your thinking, maybe?" Warner pointed out that it was only because of Murphy's persistent requests that he had started the magazine in the first place, adding that he could no longer bring himself to play Mark's records. 'Some day I may be able to seperate the man from his music. Meanwhile I'm wondering if my son will let me change his name??' (Mark Warner had indeed been named after his father's idol.)

The singer Ellyn Rucker made excuses for Murphy and seemed to be blaming Warner for the schism. "Stay loyal and try to understand what 50 years in the spotlight feels like, being the focus, under constant scrutiny, loving to sing and perform, but hey, it's hard work too. The pressure to be your best every single time despite everything. It's a huge responsibility with not the greatest returns ... bad sound, bad bread, bad piano, lame players, jet lag, people taking up your break time to tell you how much they hated your last CD."

Meanwhile, in Shohola, Murphy was relaxing on his back porch, watching the birds come to his bird feeder and worrying that the crows were scaring the songbirds away. In 2007, speaking of the break with Bert Warner, he told Ted Panken, "It's harder and harder to please yourself and to please the people who listen to you... I got so mad at the guy who ran my...well, it really was an English fan club, that I had to tell him I don't want to work with him any more. He was really out of bounds with what his... Not to have the attitude. But you don't work for someone and write about them as an editor without first saying, 'I am the editor, but this may not be my favorite of Mark's records,' but you don't come out and slam it, you don't bring it to... He was in the audience at Birdland, going around the room, spitting his opinion all over people. I was pissed off! It took me about a year to compose what I was going to say to him, and I never said, 'Stop the magazine,' all I said was, 'Take my name off it.'"

Dim the Lights finally came out in September 1999, but there was no review in *Mark's Times*, because *Mark's Times* had ceased publication.

Unlike Mark Murphy, Joe Fields never had any intention of retiring. Shortly after selling Muse, he and his son Barney launched a new record label, HighNote. Although Joe had sold the Muse catalogue, he hadn't sold the contracts. "There was literally no transition. We were still in the same office. I took the Muse sign off and put the HighNote sign up, and we just continued to roll." Mark Murphy, a singer without a record label, gratefully signed up.

Before long it was as if he and Joe had never been apart: five HighNote albums were to follow, the first being *Some Time Ago*, which he recorded at New York's M&I Studios in December 1999. His producer this time was Don Sickler, with Lee Musiker as arranger and pianist. The other players included Allen Mesquida on alto sax and Dave Ballou on trumpet (Murphy had met Ballou in Italy while both were teaching there), and all are in dazzling form, the tracks being long enough for them to stretch out. Gone are the experiments with overdubbing and multi-tracked vocals. Among the tunes is Norma Winstone's lyricized version of Jimmy Rowles's "The Peacocks", a terrifyingly difficult tune to sing, which Murphy nailed in one take. He keeps his scatting to a minimum, and amid the thrilling bebop of Cedar Walton's "Life's Mosaic" and "That Old Black Magic", there is also darkness. On the medley of "Why Was I Born" and "I'm a Fool to Want You", the first done as a ballad, the second as a slow rhumba, Murphy sings some desperately sad and lonely *a cappella* lyrics, ruminating on the purpose of a life lived alone.

After years of release hold-ups, several new albums were in the works, and despite the five Grammy failures and a distinct lack of recent product, other accolades were coming in: Murphy was again voted Best Male Vocalist by *Downbeat* readers in both 2000 and 2001.

Some Time Ago was soon followed by another fine album: *The Latin Porter* was a one-off release through the German label GoJazz, agreed before the HighNote contract took effect. This was a live set of Cole Porter songs recorded in January 2000 at the Dakota Bar in St Paul, Minnesota, featuring trumpeter Tom Harrell. As the title suggests, the tunes are all rendered Latin style, with percussion strongly featured. Latin specialist and pianist Peter Schimke came on board to choose the band and take on the role of musical director, and the arrangements were written by the band's trombonist Al Bent. Murphy is in high spirits on the gig. "Cole Porter proved that you don't have to be poor to write a good song," he quips at the start. "Everything that's old is becoming new again – even me, folks."

Right at the end of the year he recorded *Links*, with almost the same personnel as *Some Time Ago*. The album is marred in places by some ugly and intrusive scatting, particularly on Alan Broadbent's "Ode to the Road" and the old Glenn Miller number "The Lady's in Love with You", and there are one or two strained notes. But the choice of tunes is inspired, including Mary Lou Williams's "In the Land of Oo-Bla-Dee" with brilliant, deranged lyrics by Milt Orent, and the Billy Strayhorn ballad "A Flower is a Lovesome Thing" among the best. Murphy wrote three of the lyrics himself and one complete song – the mid-tempo bossa "Breathing". *Jazz Journal* was positive: "Mark moves from Ellington to Brazilian rhythms then to late night mellowness and on to bop. The theme is good songs, good singing and good playing... Another winner from Mark Murphy."

Murphy's third album for HighNote, *Lucky to be Me*, again produced by Don Sickler and arranged by Lee Musiker, was recorded in New York shortly after the 9/11 attacks. As James Isaacs points out in his liner notes, Mark's first words, on "Lonely Town" from an "On The Town" medley, are *New York, New York*. Regarding another track, Jobim's "Photograph", Murphy remarked that, "When I sing it, it's like stepping into a corner of a dimly-lit bar, watching two people practically fucking standing up as they dance. They're the only two people, and the band is playing. Jobim, with all the great things he wrote, I don't think he ever got more tension out of fewer notes; I don't believe he used more than six or seven in the entire melody. It just encapsulates his genius." Added Isaacs: "[Murphy] bends notes into wild shapes, leaps mountain goat-like from baritone to falsetto to yodel, and nimbly deploys slides and pitch fluctuations and gradations." But on "Serenade in Blue" and "Dearly Beloved", the bebopper in Murphy overwhelms the material, the yaps, yelps and slurs an unwelcome distraction from the songs.

That same year, always interested in bringing a jazz approach to new musical genres, Murphy contributed a spoken word piece to an album called *Creating Patterns*. The artists were a pioneering London drum-and-bass outfit known as 4hero, who were looking to explore the territory of nu jazz, broken beat and trip-hop, with guest spots from Terry Callier and Jill Scott as well as Murphy. At the behest of 4hero's Marc Mac, bass player Andy Hamill asked Murphy to write and record a 30-second piece called "Twelve Tribes", concerning the mystical properties of the number 12. This was right up Mark's street. He stayed over with Hamill the night before the recording. Then, on the morning of the session, Mac called Hamill and said, "I know we said 30 seconds, but we'd now like him to speak for the whole track, which is about five minutes." Hamill, who was just about to get in the car to drive Murphy over to the studio, was taken aback. "But Mark actually had written quite a lot of stuff – he'd got all these colored felt pens and underlined words for different emphasis. He'd written it in three sections, and the music also happened to be in three sections, in completely different time feels. The first was floaty, the next bit was a groove, and the third was a different groove. And what Mark had written fitted perfectly – it all came to an end at the same time. And we all fell about laughing for several minutes. Things like that would happen all the time with Mark, that kind of synchronicity, because he was just so creative," said Hamill.

Having worked his last semester at Graz in 2001, Murphy took up a teaching residency at Buffalo State College, a result of his friendship with pop music history professor Charles Mancuso. The latter had been a Murphy fan since his teens, even to the extent of naming his freshman basketball team the Mark Murphys. Over the decades that followed, the singer stayed at Mancuso's house on so many occasions that Mancuso dubbed his guest quarters "The Mark Murphy Room." Interested in the professor's subject, Murphy sometimes sat in class with the students, instantly reverting to adolescence – fidgeting, staring at his handout, and curiously reluctant to volunteer verbal contributions. "Did Al Jolson have any impact on your world?" Mancuso enquired at one point. Murphy was startled, mumbling, "Uh, no, I came to him kinda late..."

One night he was sitting in the lounge at the Buffalo Hyatt, listening to local pianist and singer Jackie Jocko. As Jocko played the intro to "It Don't Mean a Thing", Murphy clambered to his feet. "Let me sing this song for you," he said. But Jocko was having none of it: sitting in was against house rules. Murphy obediently returned to his seat. *It makes no difference if it's sweet or hot*, sang Jocko. Murphy disagreed. "Yes it does," he sang, *sotte voce*, "Yes, it does."

Some of the greatest music of Mark Murphy's career was recorded in Berlin in 2002 with 30-year-old German trumpeter Till Brönner. Hailed in some quarters as a reincarnation of Chet Baker, Brönner had been introduced to Murphy's music by a jazz singer friend. One evening in 2001, on his way back from a radio engagement, Brönner was passing by the A-Trane jazz club and noticed that Murphy was playing that very night. Brönner, whose Baker tribute album, *Chattin' with Chet*, had come out a couple of years earlier, had long been impressed by Murphy's ability to sing like an instrumentalist on albums like *Rah*. Entering the half-empty club and positioning himself in front of the stage, he became aware that Murphy was directing the local trio in a way he had never seen a singer do before. And when Mark sat down alone at the piano to accompany himself on a ballad at the end of the show, Brönner found that tears were rolling down his cheeks.

He waited afterwards for Murphy to come over to the bar, introduced himself, and gave him a copy of *Chattin' with Chet*. Two weeks later the record company called him to say that some desperate character called "Mike Murphy" had been on the phone every day, asking to speak to Till. At the time Murphy was teaching his final semester at Graz. Brönner arranged to meet him there, with the idea that perhaps he could be persuaded to sing on his next waxing, *Blue Eyed Soul*. "It was raining cats and dogs that day. Pino, my brother, and I were in the car with Mark – we picked him up straight from the class he was teaching. We wanted to play the demo of a new song I had, 'Tub of Love'. I played a couple of bars, and he said, 'I could never sing that.' I said, 'What?' He said: 'This I can't sing. *You* should sing that song.'" It is thus Brönner's voice that we hear on the album, albeit with lyrics by Mark Murphy.

The song Mark did sing was "Dim the Lights" – which he had recorded as a ballad for his own album of the same name, but which is here reformulated by Brönner in a trip-hop style. "We brought Mark to Berlin to record his part in my little studio, and of course he was all done in five minutes because he was a first-take guy. It was just perfect. So as he was leaving the studio, I put to him the idea of recording an album in there. He said, 'What kind of album?' I said, 'I remember that evening at the A-Trane, and very few things in life have moved me as much as that performance.' Bear in mind that people expected him to sing like the world champion of scat. And of course, he was one of the few people who could really do it and even make up lyrics while he was doing it. But he wasn't sure about doing a ballad album because he had a very strong image of what people expected him to sing, to be commercially successful."

Brönner persisted. His insight was that Murphy possessed the rare ability to tap into profound, half-buried emotional conflicts, in a way that made his ballad performances extremely moving. "For me, only Frank Sinatra has the same ability to make me feel he is speaking to me when he sings. The others just perform. The songs that Mark sounded so good on were the ones that contained a big unresolved emotion. The mother of all love songs is disappointment, unrequited love, and that's something that you feel you shouldn't show. And in his case, being gay must have given him even more reason to sing [about these emotions]."

This was the beginning of what became the album *Once to Every Heart*. The idea was to aim for a mood of relaxation and intimacy. There would be no hurry, no stress, no clock-watching. Mark would be close-miked, and the only other musician in the studio with him and Brönner would be Frank Chastenier, long-standing pianist with the WDR Big Band, and a player of extraordinary sensitivity. On the recordings, Brönner's own musical lines were as sparse as he had ever played. As he put it, "What could you possibly add after this guy sang?" Following two days in the studio, Brönner did an edit in which he took out all of Murphy's breaths, but he decided in the end to leave them in. "Hearing him breathe made it so personal."

After the session, Brönner offered the recordings to Universal, who showed no enthusiasm, so he kept them in a drawer, reluctant to hand them over for peanuts to yet another small label. "In the meantime Mark gave me a recording he had made with Tim Weston, who had made a whole Rogers and Hammerstein tribute with a beautiful string arrangement." Mark's contribution to that project was "This Nearly Was Mine" from *South Pacific*. He could not recall the name of the woman who had done the string arrangements, but it turned out to be Nan Schwartz, a protégé of Johnny Mandel. "Next time I was in LA I called her and she didn't sound particularly interested. Mark was interested in having strings to make it a little more commercial, and also he had loved the Shirley Horn record with strings. I sent the recordings to her by courier anyway, and about two hours later I got this call from Nan, and she said, 'I apologize for being a bit rude, but I listened to it and I'm absolutely overwhelmed by what I'm hearing, and I have to be part of this production. No matter what kind of budget you have, we'll find a way to do it.'" Counter to normal recording practice, Schwartz arranged the strings to fit around the existing recordings, also adding Christian Von Kaphengst on double bass, along with a pair of flautists, and overdubbed it all in Berlin with the 30-piece Deutsches Symphonie Orchester, which she conducted.

The foundation of *Once to Every Heart* is the unusual degree of rapport between Murphy and Brönner, helped in no small measure by the 70-year-old's road-roughened gravel in combination with the trumpet's high, breathy Baker-like notes. Murphy's wide vocal range is particularly evident here, now that he could descend as far as the E-flat two octaves below middle C. Most of the tunes that he chose for the album were familiar standards. Brönner had been impressed at the singer's unfailing touch when it came to medleys on his recent albums with Lee Musiker, such as "Why was I Born"/"I'm a Fool to Want You" on *Some Time Ago*, and "Lonely Town"/"Lucky to be Me"/"Some Other Time" on *Lucky to be Me*. Accordingly, on *Once to Every Heart*, "When I Fall in Love" segues into "My One and Only Love" via a trumpet line from Brönner that sounds at first like it's going to be a closing phrase but turns out to be the opening melody of the second tune.

But the emotional knife really twists in the songs that immediately follow – a medley of "Skylark", a tune of romantic longing, and "You Don't Know What Love Is", one of anguished loss: *Where someone's waiting to be kissed* is immediately followed by Brönner's tremulous breathy note, like a tongue fluttering in your ear. On *Crazy as a looo-oooooon*, Murphy sends the last note soaring to a falsetto C above middle C in a way that is entirely appropriate to the lyric. As the strings glide upward to match his spontaneous melodic variations and final high note, it becomes clear what an inspired idea it was to design the string arrangements around the voice recording. At the segue, Nan Schwartz inserts very quiet, high, keening strings like a needle into the heart.

The title track was an obscure Jo Stafford B-side from 1952, written by her husband, Paul Weston, with a pencil-written chart that Murphy remembered doing 40 years earlier in his Greenwich Village apartment. Fantastic depth is achieved by piano and muted trumpet on the long intro, with just the right amount of sustain pedal and reverb and gently surging orchestration. The sepulchral "Our Game", Brönner's own song contribution with lyrics by Rob Hoare, maintains the mood with its dark, flamenco-like opening chord. Brönner plays a complete chorus on trumpet, then Murphy does the same with the lyrics, followed by Schwartz's delicate, shimmering strings and faintly warbling flutes on the coda. "Bein' Green", a song written for Kermit the Frog by Joe Raposo, could be Mark Murphy's signature tune, a lighter song than the ones that precede it, with lyrics that provide a wonderful metaphor for being one of life's outsiders.

In the liner notes, Murphy describes the album as "one of the greatest thrills of my career." "I don't ever want to record any other way," he told *Jazz*

Times. "We didn't set out to do a ballad album. Till plays them so naturally and so persuasively that you can't help but go with it. I'd like to make a couple more records like that and see where it leads us."

Once the orchestra had been added, Brönner again offered the project to Universal, owners of the Verve label, and this time they were interested. Joe Fields remembered feeling somewhat snubbed at the time. He could see no reason why Murphy would go off and record for another label. "The only disagreement we ever had had nothing to do with money. I couldn't figure it out – maybe it was something I said. I really have no idea why he sort of pushed away. And then I would hear feedback saying Mark doesn't like you any more, and I really couldn't figure out why. He was a very flighty kind of a guy, and as he got older he got more emotional, more black and white, and you never knew where he was going emotionally." Fields maintained that his dealings with the singer were always straightforward and cordial. "I never got any kind of beef from him, ever. As long as the music was there, he didn't give a shit what went on." Nonetheless, perhaps still a little scarred by his early experiences of dealing with the monolithic Decca and Capitol, Murphy always kept his distance. "He still considered that this was 'the company'." There followed the now-customary delay in releasing *Once to Every Heart*, since Murphy's contract with HighNote still had some way to run.

In June 2002, he appeared on stage at Chicago's Park West as part of a new vocal project known as Four Brothers, a project that had been in the works for five years. The brainchild of Kurt Elling, this 21st-century Rat Pack featured Elling, Murphy, Jon Hendricks and Kevin Mahogany. The collaboration was the retrospective cover story in the following December's *Downbeat*, which focused on the rarity value of four male jazz singers performing together. Four Brothers toured Europe and the US in 2003–4 to much acclaim, with a final performance in the summer of 2005 in Chicago's Millennium Park – a concert which featured Sheila Jordan in the fourth spot and which Elling re-titled Three Brotha's and a Motha.

Two months later, Murphy and his UK trio – bassist Andy Hamill, drummer Mark Fletcher and pianist Pete Churchill – were booked into London's Pizza on the Park for another week of gigs. Churchill had by now married his girlfriend Nikki Iles, and ten days before the residency, their daughter Imogen was born. It soon transpired that the baby was suffering from a serious heart defect. They rushed her into intensive care at London's Great Ormond Street hospital. The Churchills took up residence, but after several days of pacing the corridors, Pete was told by the cardiologists to go out and do something: they themselves were doing everything they could to save Imogen's life. "Mark had heard about this," said Churchill. "I went to Pizza on the Park, and Mark was sitting at the bar with a small glass of white wine, and he had this big bunch of 24 red roses, and he gave them to me with a little card. Inside was written, *If I could give her my heart, I would.* That's the Mark I know."

Four Brothers, North Sea Sea Jazz Festival, 2003 (left to right, Jon Hendricks, Kurt Elling, Mark Murphy, Kevin Mahogany (courtesy Veerle Van de Poel).

The following February, Murphy was back in the studio to record again for HighNote. The album was *Memories of You*, his long-awaited tribute to Joe Williams. It was a collection of blues material, his first since *That's How I Love The Blues!* And this time his arranger was the veteran pianist Norman Simmons, who had played in the Williams trio of the Eighties and Nineties. Throughout his career, Mark's natural extravagance and freedom with the vocal line was not always entirely appropriate to the song he was singing. Many found his renditions too wild, and off-putting. However, with a genre as elastic as the blues, that freedom worked to the advantage of both the artist and music. Here, in the company of this gentle, old-style material, his voice is pleasantly relaxed. Not feeling the need to be hip and experimental, he simply sings the songs. "A very mellow recording experience, I must say," he says in the liner notes. "On this I wanted everything to be copasetic and organic, like the stuff I grew up with. That's a departure. For the last few years I've been bringing in stuff that was new to me, because I liked it or had written it and so on."

One afternoon, having sat in at Sushi-samba in New York's West Village, pianist Misha Piatigorsky was making his way back from the stage when Murphy hailed him from a nearby table. "Hey kid! Come 'ere!" Piatigorsky didn't know Murphy, but it transpired that the singer was in search of a new regular pianist. He invited Misha to come and hear him and his band at Birdland the following week. Soon afterwards they played their first gig together at the Deer Head Inn, about an hour's drive from Murphy's home in the Poconos. This was followed by a week at Birdland.

In June 2004, at another Manhattan club, the Iridium, Mark first met Francesca "Cha Cha" Miano, who was to become a close friend during his later years. Arriving early for the gig, she accosted Mark and nervously asked him to autograph a CD of his greatest hits. The singer shook his head as he looked at it, telling her he'd never seen it before. Unbeknownst to him, Joel Dorn had sold Muse's back catalogue to Savoy Jazz, a subsidiary of Columbia in Japan.

Mark's 2005 tour schedule took in Britain, Finland, Russia, Italy and Japan. In April he again toured Australia, playing nine dates from Newtown to Canberra. While in Helsinki he recorded tracks with the Five Corners Quintet, a retro-groove outfit who released two fine albums featuring Murphy – *Chasin' the Jazz Gone By* (2005) and *Hot Corner* (2008).

After three years, *Once to Every Heart* was finally unveiled. Given his checkered history with album covers, the image of Murphy used for this one is striking; he appears to be banging his head against a brick wall, something he had been doing metaphorically all his life. Some may see a gay subtext in the way he clings to the wall, staring so intently at the camera. "We set up a photo session, which is quite complicated with a guy like Mark. He'd never left the Seventies, that's why he looked like that, a big, muscular guy, with the wig and the moustache, and he wasn't very confident," recalled Till Brönner.

This time the reviewers raved: "A triumphant reminder of the enduring brilliance of a vocalist whose name should be mentioned in the same breath as the Sinatras, Hendricks and Beys of this world..." "The single finest jazz vocal album of 2005..." "Murphy sounds more vulnerable and exposed than ever before. Very close miking reveals every nuance of his voice in minute detail. Sometimes his singing is full bodied and passionate. Far more often it is quiet and very intimate, with silence used to great dramatic effect," said another review.

Brönner felt vindicated by his decision to go with Verve. "It was the same people I had my own deal with, and in fact they did a very good job. Anyway, it sold very well, between 20,000 and 30,000 records. I paid for maybe 80% of the album out of my own pocket, so that had to be reflected in the percentages." He then told the well-worn jazz joke: "That new album of yours – what did you sell?" "Oh, my car, my house..."

Mark Murphy's new-found status as a jazz singer attracted the attention of the *New York Times*, who reviewed a Birdland gig in October of that year. "Unlike almost every male jazz and pop singer you could name, Mr. Murphy... doesn't adopt the usual masculine poses," noted the writer. "Instead of playing the seducer or the comforter when crooning, or the preening, self-assured leader of the pack when swinging, he embodies a wandering post-Beat minstrel, a restless soul, world-weary hipster and die-hard romantic, ruminating on old loves."

In 2006 Mark appeared in Raymond de Felitta's documentary *'Tis Autumn: the Search for Jackie Paris*, about the mysterious life of the eponymous jazz vocalist. The film examines the question of how much one needs to know about an artist's life in order to appreciate his art.

Meanwhile Verve was happy enough with the sales of *Once to Every Heart* to commission a sequel. *Love is What Stays* was recorded in 2006, again at Till Brönner's Berlin studio, with most of the same personnel, although this time, there were problems. "I remember very clearly," said Brönner, "that whatever we achieved with the first record, Mark wasn't super-happy with it. It was very hard to deal with him at the time, to the point where I thought maybe we shouldn't do this new one. He had dark moments..."

On previous albums, the choice of material had always been down to Murphy, but this time Brönner had a few ideas of his own. The singer wanted to be thought of as contemporary, he argued, so why not record "What If," a song by the English band Coldplay? Like Murphy, Brönner had always been interested in using pop material in jazz, reharmonizing where necessary. "With 'What If', I felt this is actually the perfect Mark Murphy lyric. Plus putting out a second record of Mark's, just doing old standards didn't do it for me. I was looking for something from the top 40 that would actually fit Mark's way of singing, and would be on the same level. Same with the Johnny Cash tune, 'So Doggone Lonesome', which he did the greatest job on. So I knew it was going to be difficult, and gave him a list of all the other songs, which he was fine with, such as 'My Foolish Heart'. So once they were done, I said, 'Now

With Till Bronner at A-Trane, Berlin.

Mark, I'd really like you to listen to this one song from Coldplay – they're very successful right now.' And he was like, 'Aaarrgh, come *on*, we don't have to do that pop stuff.' I said, 'No, we don't have to do that pop stuff, and we won't, because it's going to be *your* stuff, the way you do it.' And he said, 'Well, I have to have control over that.' And I said, 'You have control. You can throw it in the garbage can once you've done it. But let's give this a shot.' 'OK, but I'll only do one take on this.' So we listened to the song, and I wrote down the music, but he didn't actually need it. He saw the lyrics and remembered where it was going. It was a ballad so he didn't have to remember that many notes. And he did a wonderful job on it. But the story's not over, because you don't just record a cover of a song by Coldplay. In fact I heard from a publisher that Coldplay doesn't usually give permission. Mark wasn't that bothered because he didn't like it anyway. But I sent it in to the publishers, and the next day they called me and said, 'This is something that's never happened, but we got immediate permission from Coldplay because they liked it so much.'"

Another significant tune on *Love is What Stays* is "Too Late Now". Although it is not featured in the 2005 film *Brokeback Mountain*, Mark felt it perfectly encapsulated both the joy and the doomed passion of the film's central relationship, a romance between two apparently straight cowboys. *Brokeback Mountain* resonated powerfully with him; he claimed to have watched it 15 times, and often referred to it in live performance. As sung by Jane Powell in the 1951 film *Royal Wedding*, "Too Late Now" was a straightforward declaration of love; but Mark, ever the interpreter and reinterpreter of music, heard in the lyrics a darker, more autobiographical meaning. For him it was about lost love – the love that stays even after one has lost it.

Time. Do you have time? he asks on the mainly spoken-word "The Interview", to a background of birdsong and the underfoot sound of leaves and snapping twigs: *Wondering how much more time I have to watch this kaleidoscope of movement wash over me day after night after day...* And on "Did I Ever Really Live", a magnificently obscure ballad from a musical that closed in 1969 after only four performances, Mark calmly stares death in the face: *Too soon you'll hear a distant drum/Too soon the time to go will come.*

Love is What Stays has a valedictory yet serene atmosphere, without histrionics or striving for effect. Alongside *Memories of You* and *Once to Every Heart*, it concludes Murphy's trilogy of late masterpieces. The album contains no fewer than three brief snatches of his signature tune, "Stolen Moments" – the first incorporating some improvised lyrics and scat; the second a more reflective version with only voice and piano; the third an excerpt from a longer take, featuring solos from Frank Chastenier and Till Brönner. "Angel Eyes", also reprised here, had appeared on *Rah*, and "My Foolish Heart" had been on *Mark Time!*

"Another collection of multifarious charms," said *Jazzwise* in its review, "An achingly cool 'Angel Eyes', and swooning 'My Foolish Heart'... plus Johnny Cash's 'So Doggone Lonesome' at a tempo so languorous it seems practically immobile." *AllMusic* called it "a deeply satisfying and, in places, even astonishing reflection on time and its passage. Memory, reverie, regrets, victories, hipster mysticism, and wonderfully canny theatrically poetic wordplay all come to bear."

It was in Berlin that Murphy broke the habit of a lifetime and started smoking tobacco. Said Till Brönner, "I remember Mark having cognac and a cigar in Berlin, and he did that because he was so happy with the result of the record. But I never saw him smoke a cigarette."

14 Much to Do and Not a Moment to Spare

2006, the year that Mark recorded *Love is What Stays*, was the year he turned 74. It was also the year that friends and colleagues began to notice that something wasn't quite right.

Lesley Mitchell-Clarke phoned him for a chat one day. He always called her Blondie. "Hey," she said, "This is Blondie." There was a long pause at the other end. "Which Blondie?" asked Mark, eventually. This set Lesley's alarm bells ringing. Shortly afterwards she learned that he had been diagnosed with Alzheimer's, was wearing a patch that delivered medication, and had a careworker living with him.

When he made one of his regular trips to Holland, Greetje Kauffeld hardly recognized him – he suddenly seemed very old. "Somebody brought him here, just for a visit. It made me so sad to see him like that. You can be 78 and look great, but the way he looked – it hurt me to see him like that. Like someone who was sleeping on the streets – he looked like an old tramp. I was shocked. He looked so tired... He told me he thought it was because of the crack he had been using. He was confused, and spent a lot of time looking for his passport, which he was sure he had lost."

But Mark continued to perform. His February performance at New York's Iridium with Misha Piatigorsky's trio plus percussionist Gilad Dobrecky was filmed by Brad Saville of Cadillac Films, and made into a good quality 43-minute film entitled *A Night With Mark Murphy*. At the same time another filmmaker named Dave Pistoni had been putting together a biography about him entitled *Evolution of an Artist*. "Finally it's completed," said Mark, "and now it's getting the finishing touches on it. I'm hoping it will give me some new energy in the States, and here in the UK too. It starts with my childhood, as you would expect – but I wanted to put lots of things in that people might not expect, things we had on film that we could resurrect. A documentary would get stupid and dull if it just was, 'Oh, he did this and he did that', the kind of things you would expect. So I got together with a drummer friend of mine, and we did some 'word jazz', and instead of doing it the regular way I did it the irregular way. So it's more interesting that way. I made sure there was enough variety. At the end of it I say: 'I'm still here – I must have done something right!'"

But *Evolution of an Artist* never saw the light of day, despite the appearance of a trailer, narrated by Giacomo Gates, on YouTube in January 2007, promising release in April (although the descriptive text below reads February 2008). Despite contributions from the likes of Jon Hendricks, Cleo Laine and Bill Mays, the costs of securing mechanical rights to the songs were prohibitive, and as a result too much music had to be taken out. The filmmakers removed the copyrighted songs and replaced them with three newly-filmed performances of Mark singing his own compositions, but it wasn't enough: a plethora of "talking heads" usually spells death to any documentary, and in any case, Mark Murphy was best-known for the songs he *didn't* write – "This Could be the Start of Something", "Stolen Moments", "Milestones", "Empty Faces". Without enough musical history, even though there were enough examples available on film and video, the documentary no longer made much sense. There was a final cut, but it was never released.

Murphy continued to work, as he had always done, but people were noticing the increased vagueness and the growing eccentricity. At a Brazilian-themed Iridium gig with Misha Piatigorsky's quartet, a reviewer wondered, "Is Murphy in the throes of early senility, so abstract is his poise? Or is this, as has always been the case, his naturally 'stoned' persona, the epitome of hipness and laid-back cool? Don't worry about his apparent inability to find his comb: Murphy's sharp rhythmic command belies a man who knows where things are... So he might shamble distractedly onstage, but in the end, he's always there at the right moment, directing his young quartet in improvised arrangements..."

Through the singer Tessa Souter, Murphy came to know Greek-born guitar player Spiros Exaras, whose friend Manos Tzanakakis was booker for the Gazarte Club in Athens. The guitarist's name carried some weight: as a Greek and as a Blue Note artist, he was known there for his own music – better known, in fact, than Mark Murphy, except among the people there who really knew jazz. Spiros sent his friend some of Mark's music, and Manos was sold. In mid-April 2008 Murphy and Exaras flew to Athens from New York. It was Murphy's second visit to JFK in recent days: he had turned up at a week early by mistake, still wearing his carpet slippers.

Exaras had booked a local bass player and drummer for the Gazarte engagement. German pianist Thomas Rueckert was Murphy's suggestion, someone who was already familiar with his repertoire and approach. There was time for one brief rehearsal the day before the first gig, and an even briefer one the next morning. Typically with Murphy, no songs were rehearsed from beginning to end, just the beginnings and endings. On *Mark Murphy Live in Athens, Greece*, you can hear the degree of improvisation going on – towards the end of "My One and Only Love" the final chord of the second A section hangs in the air, and Murphy exhorts the band, "Next chord, next chord!" so he can go into the bridge.

His last gig with Pete Churchill was at that year's Brecon Jazz Festival in Wales. "He arrived wearing a green shell suit, and he wasn't quite himself. He was forgetting lyrics. I saw him smoking a cigar at the stage door, and I knew this may be the last time... He put his arms round me and whispered, 'I can't do this any more.' And I said, 'Well Mark, just stop. If it's a struggle, no one's going to give you a medal.' We invited him to [our home at] Kings Langley, and I said, 'We'll make you a shepherd's pie' – he was addicted to shepherd's pie. We went for a walk in the countryside and then to a village pub we knew, the Two Brewers in Chipperfield. He sat down in front of the fire. I said, 'What do you want?' and he said, 'A sweet sherry.' And then 'Stolen Moments' came over the speakers! We went back to the house and had some shepherds pie, and chocolate – he had a thing about chocolate as well."

The extended Murphy family had always enjoyed their musical get-togethers, and in September, at the request of the Fulton Music Association, Mark's brother Doc organized a public Friday night concert at Mark's old school in Fulton, now renamed the G. Ray Bodley High School. Several generations of Murphys, Howes, Hinkhouses and Bidwells performed: Mark and his New York trio went on first, in the role of support act to family members including Doc (on upright bass) and his son Mark Edmond Murphy (bass and cello) – both specialists in old-time Appalachian music, sister Sheila (singing "Blue Skies"), sister-in-law Nancy, and cousin Allan Howe playing piano. There was a rousing version of Woody Guthrie's "This Land Is Your Land", featuring Mark Edmond's harmonizing daughters Molly and Sally; "May the Road Rise to Meet You", sung by a 15-piece choir; and Allan's "I'll be Seeing You" and "I'd Rather Drink Muddy Water".

The concert was followed two nights later by a party on the porch at Fair Haven. Everyone was drinking wine and either singing or playing, as Mark – wearing his shag wig, a burgundy shirt and medallion – sat listening quietly at the long refectory table. Nancy Murphy sang "How Come You Do Me Like You Do", and there was a group version of "Don't Get Around Much Anymore". Family friend, singer Nancy Kelly played spoons, then improvised a blues with Mark. When Mark sang "The Very Thought of You", it was electrifying: the entire room went silent. Later there was another, more raucous rendition of "Don't Get Around Much". "This is a time for some contemplative music," announced Nancy solemnly. She and her best friend Betsy Guernsy then sang "The Raccoon Song", a ditty about the different colors of animal shit, to the tune of "Smoke Gets in Your Eyes". Mark sang "Misty", and Nancy Kelly tried to scat but dissolved into peals of laughter and gave up.

Back in Shohola, there were signs that Mark was struggling to cope with living by himself in the log cabin. Calls for help were becoming more frequent. The basement flooded, and Mark Edmond had to go over to replace the hot water heater. His godmother Patti Purcell went to stay part-time, but it didn't work out too well: "They had a funny relationship," said Mark Edmond. "Mark used to call 'Maid! Maid!'" The Jazz Foundation of America then found a caregiver, Michael Barzda, to live there full-time, but it was still felt that sooner or later Mark could have a serious accident.

Said James Gavin, "Mark could not stay in the house in Shohola any more, because he was alcoholic and unhealthy, and endangering himself and possibly other people by staying at home. He was becoming a bit of a menace in the neighborhood. I don't know all the details, but there were stories of him going down the street naked. If Mark had set the house on fire, it was so filled with papers and books, it would have gone up in five minutes. I have a vague memory of stoves being left on... So clearly he was in need of help."

In May of 2009, an email was circulated that officially confirmed that Mark had Alzheimer's, and no forthcoming gigs were listed on his website. Mark was unhappy that word had got out about his condition, and that the world had been told he could no longer perform. Not for the first time in his life, Sheila Jordan came to the rescue. Realizing that things were in danger of falling apart, Jordan contacted her friend the Montreal-based management and booking agent Jean-Pierre Leduc. Via another friend, a second medical opinion was sought on what ailed the great jazz singer. This time the diagnosis was that he did not, after all, have Alzheimer's. In a further irony, it was concluded that the medication he had been taking to combat dementia had succeeded only in making him confused and disoriented: the very signs of someone *with* dementia.

Leduc had some previous experience of helping older artists who were finding it difficult to keep on top of the business side of their music. It had been the same with the veteran pianist and bandleader Hank Jones, who had started double-booking himself into clashing music festivals, hence failing to show up at some of them. Leduc promised nervous promoters that he himself would physically be there to shepherd the artist to the gig, give them their medication, and take care of them in whatever way they needed. Starting with Birdland, he began approaching some of the venues where Murphy had been successful in the past. Owner Gianni Valenti was understandably reluctant at first: like everyone else he had heard the Alzheimer's story. Leduc told him, "Just give me one night, and if it works, we can go from there, but if it doesn't work, I won't ever ask you again." Valenti agreed, and the date was a success. "We even made a little bit of money on it... But it wasn't really about money, it was just to show that [Mark] still had it." "Why did it take us so long to meet?" Mark asked Leduc afterwards.

Next came Harro East Ballroom at the Rochester Jazz Festival, where Murphy brought the house down. "After that we did many, many festivals over a three year period." Leduc was understandably proud of the work he did with the 77-year-old singer. "I was able to... give him back his career which he thought was lost forever." Slowly but surely Murphy resumed international touring, with a run of dates in Istanbul, New Morning in Paris, Berlin, sell-outs at Ronnie Scott's in London and elsewhere. "He felt that there was much to do and not a moment to spare." In Paris he spent the day at the Louvre. "We just got a wheelchair for him and wheeled him all over the museum." In London there was no more sleeping on sofas – they stayed at the beautiful St John Hotel in Chinatown. Later Murphy played the Old Mill in Toronto, with a trio of good-looking young men, "which got him all fired up. Mark had a martini afterwards, even though he was on all this medication," recalled Leduc. His gig at the Quebec City Kerouac festival was recorded for future release.

His health improved to the point where, on July 31 and August 1, 2009, he was able to play four sets at New York's Kitano, a Japanese-owned hotel on Park Avenue and 38th Street. "Reports of Murphy's demise were exaggerated," blogged Will Friedwald. "Although he now walks with a cane and sings sitting down, he looks really good: he's let his beard go white, and has given up the infamous high hair for a tasteful knit cap, and he's neither gained nor lost any weight. His chops are in terrific shape, although his concentration isn't entirely what it used to be... He spends a lot of time scatting, and, beyond that, making wildly nonsensical sounds, but, as always, Murphy extracts more coherent meaning and emotion out of scat phrases that most contemporary singers do with actual words... After being on for 50 minutes or so, Murphy abruptly stopped, took a small bow and walked off. He was, understandably, exhausted after four shows in two nights. (The next day, a Murphy fan emailed me a recording of the earlier Saturday show, which was only slightly longer but included seven different songs, one of which was his own beautiful torch tune, 'Before We Say Goodbye', which, as far as I can tell, he's only recorded in an electronic, acid-jazz setting.) Overall, Murphy sounded great, and it was one of the most moving of all the dozens of performances of his that I've attended."

In October he was honored at Yoshi's in Oakland, during that year's San Francisco Jazz Festival, by many of the singers he had known during his long residence in the Bay area, including Kitty Margolis, Madeline Eastman, Ann Dyer, Laurie Antonioli, Bobbe Norris, and Joyce Cooling. The Jazzschool in Berkeley, which ran a four-year degree course, announced that it was establishing the Mark Murphy Vocal Jazz Scholarship. "He lived here in the 80s when we were cutting our teeth on the local jazz scene," Margolis told *Jazz Times*. "I can remember not only going to see him at his gigs, but him coming to my gigs. Not many older and successful musicians did that. He's always been very generous as a friend and as a teacher." Recalled Ann Dyer, "At the end of the evening, Mark came out, sat on a stool, and it was like – let me show you how it's done. He took the entire room to a whole 'nother level. He still had such facility with his voice. He was eternally hip and eternally sincere in his musical performances." Shortly afterwards, 30-year-old Jua

Howard from Chicago became the first recipient of the Mark Murphy Vocal Jazz Scholarship.

With the aid of Wendy Oxenhorn of the Jazz Foundation of America, a place was found for Mark at a retirement community in Englewood, New Jersey. It was there, in room 111 of the Lillian Booth Actors' Home at 155–175 West Hudson Avenue, that he spent his final years. Mark Edmond Murphy had been granted power of attorney, and bought out the reverse mortgage on the property, which had up to now provided his uncle with some income. This released funds to pay for Mark Sr.'s residence at the actors' home. Like many at his time of life, he was desperate to stay in his own house. "Mark was absolutely miserable about this," said James Gavin. "I know that his nephew was completely devoted to him, but Mark blamed him for getting him out of his beloved home and sending him to this wretched place. That was typical Mark – overreacting and pointing the finger of blame. But it was essential that Mark was moved out of that house, because something terrible was going to happen."

Said Jean-Pierre Leduc, "If he'd had a partner at the end of his life, who was there for him come rain or come shine, then he wouldn't have had to live in that place. But when you're surrounded by people who are staring out the window, or drooling, or whatever, and you've just come back from Paris and London and Berlin, performing to sold-out houses, it's very hard to keep your morale going. I think you can just turn a corner in a bad way, and just give up." James Gavin added, "He didn't want to be there, he never wanted to be there, he hated that place. It has three floors: the upper floor is sunlit and very pretty, and that's the assisted living floor. And so there you're living in small apartments and you're getting help with medications and meals and things. But otherwise you're free to come and go. But the middle and the bottom floors are Alzheimer's and dementia floors, and in those cases you're basically locked in because it's the only way you can remain safe."

Even after Mark Murphy's singing career appeared to be over, he continued to receive visitors and take phone calls. One caller was Jonny Trunk, on the line from London to ask about the digital rights to *This Must be Earth*: "He was speaking exactly like I imagined Mark Murphy from the cover of *Rah* would speak, like a kind of beatnik hipster. He was still using words like 'cat'. He was very excited that I was up for doing something about [*This Must be Earth*]."

The last studio album Mark made under his own name was *Never Let Me Go*, recorded at the instigation of Misha Piatigorsky and drummer Chris Wabich. It was to be something of a labor of love, with no fees for the musicians, and studio costs paid by a friend of Mark's. Piatigorsky and Wabich went to visit him at the actors' home. "It was such a difficult experience for me," recalled Piatigorsky. "It was so painful seeing him there, in this medical white room, with crazy people walking all around, and he had a little keyboard there, and we literally had a little rehearsal. I said, 'Mark, I want to

Recording Never Let Me Go, 2010 (courtesy Misha Piatigorsky).

record anything that you want to sing.' And he just started naming tunes. We talked about how he wanted to it, we talked about keys, and I said, 'I'll write all the arrangements, and we're going into the studio next week, and we're doing it.'"

On January 8, 2010, joined by bassist Danton Boller, they set up in Manfred Knoop's New Jersey studio, which was built into his house. "We picked [Mark] up and drove to the studio. We had the trio in one room, with no separation, and we had Mark in the other room... He sat down on a chair, and we put a mic next to him, and we basically did one take of everything. And it was the most unbelievable musical experience that I ever had. It was this 78-year-old man schooling these little schoolkids how to play, just with his voice... We felt like little schoolboys sitting in a classroom... It was the control he had with his voice."

It was true that Mark had lost none of his skill in communicating with a band. "When you're working with a singer, usually it takes 15 different takes before they're happy... But the only times I stopped the recordings was when *I* fucked up... All the ad-libs that he did, all the outros to the songs, like the Ivan Lins song 'Evolution' – all the arrangements were spontaneous. We would just go into a vamp, none of that was rehearsed or even talked about." On the closing track "Murphy's Vamp", Mark goes into a rambling monologue about the Queen of England and what she might be doing now, sitting up in bed with an electric blanket around her feet, then launches into a repeated phrase about how happy he is to be working with these musicians. Only three of the 11 songs were new to the Mark Murphy canon of recorded music (four

Recording Never Let Me Go, 2010 (courtesy Misha Piatigorsky).

if you don't count his 1955 Decca recording of "Detour Ahead", which was never released). And curiously he included some numbers he had recorded as recently as eight years ago: "I Know You from Somewhere" appears on *Once to Every Heart*. It would be wonderful to say, hand on heart, that *Never Let Me Go* captures the mature Murphy in his stately prime, but there is no escaping the fact that he sounds like a man approaching his 78th birthday.

In June, he played the Zinc Bar in Greenwich Village with the same band that had recorded *Never Let Me Go*. Two days later he appeared at the Rochester Jazz Festival, and was back at Birdland on 24 July, his quartet this time featuring pianist George Mesterhazy.

When Will Friedwald saw Murphy perform in 2011, he noticed a marked improvement in his condition compared to the 2009 Iridium gig. "He was terrific... He moved like an old man, on a very small stage and a very awkward space, but his singing was absolutely fine, the voice was strong, and his head was there. If his singing isn't 100% as good as it ever was, it's still certainly better than it has any right to be."

Much as Misha Piatigorsky loved and respected Mark, he saw that gigs were dwindling to no more than five or six a year, and that Mark's grasp was slipping. "He was slowing down. And there was a drinking problem. In Japan, when we were staying at the Okura Hotel, he got so drunk once he went back to his room and broke the window in his room by falling into it. We were at a jazz club in Yokohama, and usually we would have a set-list. We were playing the second set and some cute little girls were in the club. And Mark forgot what we were going to play. At this point in his life, Mark always had lyrics on a music stand, because he couldn't remember words. Lyrics in big handwriting that he would do for himself. I don't remember what happened... Maybe he couldn't find his lyrics, but the entire set became a blues about the Yokohama Mamas – for about an hour. The Japanese had no idea – they just wanted to see this American show by the great Mark Murphy. But he clearly forgot everything we were going to do because he couldn't find his music."

The sheer weight of decades sometimes made him irascible. That same summer he was interviewed by Melody Breyer-Grell for the *Huffington Post* in the back of a taxi as he headed for another interview at WBGO. Growling about how under-appreciated he was, he no longer harbored any kind thoughts for Kurt Elling. "There is one guy, what's his name in Chicago. He has copied me and is getting all the credit." Breyer-Grell protested that Elling constantly credited him, but Murphy was in no mood to listen. "At his age, Mark does not hold back, vocally or with his opinions. He is of the opinion that he has not been compensated for his work and I don't doubt him, as he has made about 40 some records or CDs. His words are hard ones."

Just before his 80th birthday, on January 30 and 31, 2012, Mark returned to Ronnie Scott's, where he had first appeared nearly 50 years before. Again there were signs that a monumental career was reaching its end. "This was the most painful set I have witnessed since a clearly ailing and confused Anita O'Day had to be helped to hold her microphone at Pizza on the Park during her farewell residency," lamented Clive Davis in *The Times*. "[Murphy] seemed adrift much of the time, his performance not helped by a nagging cough... It was clear that his finely calibrated sense of pitch and timbre had more or less deserted him." But at a belated birthday celebration at the Blue Note on 21 May, he sang and scatted like man half his age. As he told Pete Churchill,

"I'm the first person in the history of the world to recover from Alzheimer's." George Mesterhazy, who had been booked for the Blue Note date, had died from a heart attack a few weeks earlier at the age of 58. "Mark and I never thought this would happen to George. I mean, here we were dealing with this octogenarian, and George was only in his 50s," said Jean-Pierre Leduc. Mesterhazy's place was taken by Alex Minasian.

The singer Amy London had first seen Murphy perform at the Blue Wisp, Cincinnati, in the mid-Seventies. On hearing from her friend Holli Ross of Murphy's move to the Lillian Booth home, which was near Amy's house in Teaneck, NJ, she suggested that they pay the great singer a visit. They found him in low mood. "He was sitting on a bench all dejected and saying, 'Aw, I'm just an old man, nobody wants me.' But I said, 'Come on, man, you're Mark Murphy!' And because I lived so close to him I started taking him to the grocery store, we went shopping for curtains for his room... and we started hanging out a lot." London and Ross persuaded him to start going out with them to jazz clubs and on shopping trips.

London taught on the vocal program at the New School for Social Research in Greenwich Village. Initially she took Murphy to some of her classes simply as a way to get him out of the actors' home, but in December 2011 she found a way to involve him in a student concert. She also invited him to come and teach with her at a summer singing camp at Schroon Lake, in upper New York State; it happened that the Murphy family had a holiday place close by, and Mark was able to stay with his niece Kathy Hinkhouse. "He loved the outdoors," recalled London, "loved his log cabin where he lived by the lake in Pennsylvania. His childhood was very much like that, swimming in the lake and so on."

The Royal Bopsters, London's vocal project with Dylan Pramuk, Holli Ross and Darmon Meader, was intended as a return to the glory days of jazz vocal groups like Lambert, Hendricks and Ross, Manhattan Transfer and Rare Silk. Their debut album would also feature five legendary guest singers, all of whom were approaching the end of their careers: Jon Hendricks, Annie Ross, Bob Dorough, Sheila Jordan, and Mark Murphy. On the recording date, in July 2012, Mark sang six numbers, four of which appear on the resulting album – "Red Clay", "Señor Blues" and "Boplicity", and on "Bird Chasin" he reads an extract from Kerouac's On the Road, as he so often did in concert.

One cold night in October, at a Polish-American social club in Lowell, Massachusetts, with perhaps 75 people in the audience, Mark appeared as part of its annual Lowell Celebrates Kerouac event. Backed by a local band, he was joined on stage by a Beat Generation legend, the multi-instrumentalist David Amram. Another performer that evening was poet, blues musician and Sixties political figure John Sinclair. Amram led the band from the piano, leaving it on occasion to play bop solos on his French horn.

The following month, after playing Cape May Jazz Festival in New Jersey, Murphy made his last ever recordings. The location was the nearby Merion

Inn, where George Mesterhazy had been a regular performer, and the project this time was a four-track EP titled *A Beautiful Friendship: Remembering Shirley Horn*. It had been instigated by writer and Murphy fan Andrew Cartmel, who introduced Jean-Pierre Leduc to Darrel Sheinman of the London-based label Gearbox Records, a boutique label that specialized in new vinyl records as well as lost treasures from the likes of Tubby Hayes and Yusef Lateef.

Leduc produced the recordings in the Merion's wood-paneled restaurant, using vintage Neumann U47 valve microphones. "I was hell-bent on doing this," he said. "I got Till Brönner to overdub two songs – 'Get Out Of Town' and 'But Beautiful'. Curtis Lundy [was] on bass, who played with the great Betty Carter, and Alex [Minasian], and the drummer Steve Williams, who was with Shirley for 25 years."

Istanbul, 2011 (courtesy Jean-Pierre Leduc).

Mark's final professional gig was in November 2012 at the Quebec City Jazz Festival. "Then," said Leduc, "over the Christmas holidays he just lost it, and that was it."

Amy London noticed the big change in Mark in January 2013. By now it seemed likely that his failing memory and motor functions were a result of a series of undetected mini-strokes, the symptoms of which can be similar to Alzheimer's. There was a family history of strokes and related conditions: Mark's own father had suffered them, and so had his late brother Doc, who had passed away in March 2012. His mother had died either from a heart attack or an aneurysm.

On 3 July a special event was held in his honor at Joe's Pub in New York – "Mark Murphy: Celebrating the Life and Career of the Master Jazz Vocalist", the proceeds going towards musicians in need. The event did double duty as the launch for Mark's new EP. Among those who performed at Joe's were Sheila Jordan, Janis Siegel, Jay Clayton and Amy London, backed by the *Beautiful Friendship* line-up, bassist Brandi Disterheft taking the place of Curtis Lundy.

"Mark sang last, and I wheeled him on stage," remembered Sheila Jordan. "He improvised long solos and his voice was the same old Mark. I sang 'Sheila's Blues' and improvised about Mark and what he means to me. It was a lovely evening. I have been through many times with Mark, both good and bad. When his partner died, I was there for him to lean on. He has been to my house upstate and used to come to my dinners on Thanksgiving. He always bragged about my turkey!"

Karlheinz Miklin, now retired from the Graz school, was looking through his tape library one day when he came across the DAT recording he had made with Mark in 1996. Miklin had not heard from him since 2009, and since his website had now disappeared, it took Miklin quite a while to track him down at Lillian Booth. "He was so mentally weak at first that he didn't remember anything. Then he heard the music and said, 'Why did I do this?' But Sheila Jordan was very ambitious – she liked the music and wanted it to come out, and she helped me. She wrote the liner notes, and told me she'd read them to Mark, and he got some tears in his eyes. And finally he remembered a little bit. It was a long procedure to get the rights, but I'm very happy that I did." This was the experimental album released in 2014 as *Shadows*. But the 10th century jinx was still active. "Unfortunately Peter Schmidlin, the owner of TCB Records, died so it didn't have the promotion," added Miklin.

It had never been part of Spiros Exaras's plan to release the recordings of his 2008 Athens gigs with Mark, but when he heard them later, he was struck by their quality. Back in New York, he played one of them to Ken Bloom at Harbinger Records, who agreed to release them. In June 2015, at the suggestion of Mark Edmond Murphy, Exaras took them to play to Mark Sr. at the actors' home. "After about thirty minutes he remembered me, and got so excited and hugged me. I remember that day, I cried so much. So then his nephew put the CD on without telling him what it was, and he said, 'What's that?' And I said, 'It's you.' I said, 'You like it?' He says, 'Yes. Who's playing?' I said, 'You remember the concerts we did in Athens?' He said, 'Yes – let's do them again!' And he starts moving [around] on the bed." Mark gave his approval for the recordings to be released, and whilst Exaras was happy and relieved to have got permission from the horse's mouth, Mark died before the album was finally released in 2016.

Pete Churchill made two visits to the actors' home. The first time, he said, Mark was lucid and remembered all his old friends and colleagues from London. The second time "there was a stage and a grand piano on the ground floor and a microphone, because everyone there did a turn. I walked in and he was in a ring of people in wheelchairs doing exercises in front of a video. So I said, 'Come on, Mark, we're getting out of here' and he said, 'Great, get me outta here.' So we went to the lift and we got to the piano, and I sat at the piano. There were some residents standing in the doorway, and I started to play the old repertoire. And he started to sing, and then he grabbed my right hand... and he carried on singing, joining in with me, and we did 'Too Late Now', and he cried. By this time there must have been 40 people standing around. We went back to his room.... He was in a shared room with a guy who just kept shouting, 'I wanna die, I hate it here!' So I sat down and played him [a recording of our] Dublin gig, and he remembered the gig, and it was lovely. They said, 'He normally sleeps now', so I said my goodbyes, and that's the last time I saw him."

Amongst the last people to see Mark Murphy alive were Sheila Jordan, Francesca Miano, a Brazilian friend Marcelo Maia, and Tessa Souter. By March 2015 Mark could no longer swallow, and was being fed via a tube into his stomach. In June his niece Kathy Hinkhouse and sister-in-law Kate Murphy went to see him. They remembered thinking how beautiful the Lillian Booth home was. "He was kinda lost, not remembering things, and he asked us, 'Does my mother know where I am?' And Kate said, 'You'll get to see her soon.'"

Towards the end, Mark told everybody he wanted to visit Fair Haven, the scene of so many happy family occasions. Sister-in-law Nancy, along with nephew Mark Edmond and cousin Stuart went to see him on what turned out to be the last day of his life. "He couldn't communicate. It was mostly with his eyes. His body was crippled, but he was all dressed up for the visit. We took him outside, where there was a little fountain, and he kept pointing up. He heard a plane, and we figured he just wanted to go up, and leave."

Mark died in his sleep on Thursday October 22, 2015. He was 83. The official cause was complications from pneumonia. He was cremated and his ashes will eventually be buried in Mount Adnah Cemetery in Fulton along with those of Eddie O'Sullivan. Mark expressed a wish to have profile etches of both himself and Eddie engraved on the tombstones in the plot where his parents Dwight and Margaret are buried.

A memorial service was held at 7pm on Monday, March 14, 2016, at St Peter's Church on Lexington Avenue in Manhattan, on what would have been Mark's 84th birthday. As people filed in, Francesca Miano played some of Mark's old singles, some of which had never appeared on an album. They included the rockabilly tune "Daddy Must be a Man", "It's Like Love", "Fly Away My Sadness", "Belong to Me", "Don't Cry My Love", and edited versions of *Rah*'s "Angel Eyes" and "Stoppin' the Clock". Miano wanted to make the point that it had taken Mark until he was 40 to arrive at the style he became known for; prior to that he had experimented with many different types of music.

The performers came next – Nancy Kelly, Carol Fredette, Kurt Elling, Giacomo Gates, Sheila Jordan – who sang "Ballad of the Sad Young Men", and later "Where You At" in a duet with Kurt Elling. Will Friedwald, James Gavin and Michael Bourne spoke. Mark Edmond sang "Happy Birthday" with his children. Every member of his family could sing, Mark used to say.

In her eulogy, Miano said: "The Mark Murphy I came to know had many traits which might be unexpected, by those who only related to him as a singer. He was the man who hipped me to the History Channel show *American Pickers* because he was into antiques. He was obsessed with watching movies, especially classics starring Hedy Lamarr, Joan Crawford and Eleanor Powell. Mark did not read novels only by Jack Kerouac, but also loved to dig into mysteries. (When I gave him a copy of a jazz mystery set in Vegas, he said that Bill Moody's description of the music scene reminded him of his gig at the Four Queens.) He was fascinated with extraterrestrials and folks who had served in World War II. Plus, he never ceased to love nature, in particular, flowers, trees and bodies of water.

"The thing I'll always remember most about Mark, however, was that the music was constantly inside him, as regular as breathing. I was told he once sang to an eagle flying over his log cabin... I personally witnessed him scatting to a tiny frog. Mark would make up songs while crossing the street or waiting for a bus. On one occasion, in 2013, he sat at his regular table in the dining room of the actors' home and sang to me the entire first verse of 'You Are My Sunshine', perfectly.

"Even when illness began to overtake him, Mark never lost his feeling for the music. I would play him CDs and DVDs of singers and instrumentalists, ranging from Miles Davis and Maria Callas to performers new to him. He would react in one of two ways: either smiling broadly with his eyes open and dancing with delight, or else he would close them, as he seemed to drink in what he was hearing. If the tracks were from his own albums, Mark would move his hands, as though he was performing on the stage. He would sometimes move his lips, singing silently to himself. On the Saturday before he passed away, I asked him what he wanted to hear and he responded, 'You know what I like.' So I put on 'Maiden Voyage' by Herbie Hancock, then

'Speak No Evil' by Wayne Shorter. As Mark listened, I looked into his soulful eyes and saw his inner beauty come out.

"Mark Murphy was a great man yet so down to earth, a man and a boy simultaneously. Yet, in spite of all he went through, he never lost his dignity. It was like being in the presence of a great guru, one who exuded music until he took his last breath."

Sheila Jordan said she grieved more over Mark's death than she did over any of her own immediate family.

...

Mark Murphy's reputation will only grow as he recedes into history. His career began when jazz was at its peak of popularity, and continued long after it had been eclipsed in the public mind by other forms of music. His achievements were many, and they were extraordinary. Perhaps the most extraordinary of all was that he survived, eking out a living from his chosen art form, something only a few achieve when that art form is jazz, and of those, almost none without support from the music industry. He lived into old age, while so many of his contemporaries died young, victims to illness, overwork and drug abuse.

Many of those who witnessed his live shows felt that no sound or visual recording medium could do justice to him as a performer. 'He's a hundred times as good as any record that he's ever done,' said Cleo Laine. "He was a total artist," said Richie Cole. "Of course he would have loved to be accepted and famous and all that, but he just followed his natural instincts to put out the best music that he knew. He followed his heart."

At various times in his career Mark was presented with chances to make money, and passed them up. When it came to the crunch, he was simply not prepared to compromise. As Tessa Souter pointed out in her obituary, "To him, it was a 'miracle' that he was able to survive – and even buy a house – without compromising his artistic integrity. ('I don't know that you'll ever find me in K-Mart.') 'Just being a jazz singer is a risk, because it is the world's most unpopular music. You have to dare. You have to get up there. Because you are creating. You are up there making something that wasn't there before and that takes daring. It's not the easiest way of life, but it is interesting.'"

Appendix A: A Jazz Singer Is a Singer Who Sings Jazz

There is more to Mark Murphy's gnomic definition of a jazz singer than one might think. When Michael Bourne interviewed him in 1975, "he… elaborated on the difference between a jazz singer and a cabaret singer. He said there was a singer in New York who used to sing 'Last Night When We Were Young'. And on the same word in every performance, a tear went down her cheek." But real jazz singing, according to Murphy, is not like that. "He said, 'Everything changes as you're even singing the song with musicians. It's like basketball. You're dribbling the ball as you're heading toward the basket, and you have this idea that you're going to shoot a lay-up, and then somebody bumps you, and now you're going sideways, so then you're doing a jump-shot. Things change, as you do them.'"

Forty years later, the British jazz singer Tina May felt that, unlike that New York chanteuse, Murphy was a unique artist who never appropriated anyone else's musical ideas – unlike those who have overtly copied him. If a singer fails to move us, she said, it's because he or she has not internalized the music, instead they have simply learned it, and reproduce it in the same way repeatedly – something Murphy never did. As improvisation is the defining quality of jazz in general, it must be the starting point in how we define a true jazz singer. Controversially, such a definition excludes great singers often associated with jazz, such as Sinatra and Bennett; although they certainly had jazz chops and performed the jazz repertoire, they were pop singers. They introduced small variations to their delivery of songs, for example in the emphasis of lyrics, but they did not improvise in the jazz sense. Murphy, by contrast, performed like a band-leading instrumentalist, who came up with spontaneous variations and extensions to beginnings, endings and solos.

He was also able to place everything he did in context. He thoroughly researched each song he sang – its history, geography and artistic provenance (e.g. from a stage musical or film), its writers, its previous performers. Prior to singing a song, he would often recount these details to audiences, including the circumstances in which he first came across it.

He was already adept at jazz singing by the time he made his first album, with a great natural instrument at his disposal. On top of this he had learned a great deal of singing technique, becoming equally brilliant with swing, blues, Latin and ballads – particularly the latter, later in his career, when he was able to convey emotion to an extraordinary degree. Yet he was primarily what he called a rhythm singer – not simply floating along on top of the instrumental backing, but fully engaged with it as a member of the band, and indeed directing it as bandleader. As the years went by, he developed the individuality that marks out the great from the good, becoming an "abstract expressionist vocalist", according to Wendy Oxenhorn.

His performance skills were second to none, incorporating poetry and the spoken word, and both physical and verbal comedy. Very few singers can do all of these things well. Some struggle even with the basics. Michael Bourne recalls an occasion where both he and Mark Murphy were present at a concert featuring many singers from across the USA. "One after another they got up, and they were all what I would call tremendously adequate. There was nothing about what they were doing that was truly remarkable. Some of them were barely adequate, they sang out of tune, and it was quite embarrassing, in some ways. And Mark was... just hanging there, listening. And I didn't talk to him, but at one point, after a couple of hours of this, he got up, and walked up on to the stage. He was drunk, actually – it was the first time I'd ever seen him drunk. And he staggered on to the stage and just started singing, and blew the roof off. And it was like, *this* is how you do it. And he didn't say anything."

Murphy's voice might be classified as bass-baritone, as agile and resonant, in the words of James Gavin, "as Ben Webster's saxophone, [it] seems to creep from the shadows of some long-ago jazz dive. In person he tends toward wild, boppish deconstructions of jazz standards, but most of his devotees favor his ballads, in which the most idyllic sentiments can sound painfully raw." His voice retained both its accuracy and its extraordinary range into old age. Although his original model was the trumpet of Miles Davis, the voice was more akin to the trombone or French horn. By his seventies, it had acquired a gnarled and leathery maturity that added poignancy to his late recordings, particularly *Once to Every Heart* and *Love is What Stays*. Even as he passed 80, he was able to sing beautifully, although not consistently so.

Perhaps his greatest gift was the ability to truly inhabit the song he was singing. Nancy Kelly commented, "There are two kinds of singers – those who sing from outside and those who sing from inside the song. Every time he did a riff it was motivated by the lyric. It was the most honest, sincere delivery of anyone I've ever listened to. That said, he was completely fearless. He'd take an idea and completely let himself go – he wasn't even on earth when he sang, and he always understood what was going on in the music which allowed him to develop it harmonically." Murphy's approach was often too challenging even for mainstream jazz audiences, but that was because he saw himself principally as a musician, an instrumentalist of the voice. As William Bauer has pointed out, "The same listeners who did not mind if an instrumentalist took off on a melody, or even ignored it completely, as Coleman Hawkins did in his famous rendition of 'Body and Soul'   listeners who in fact counted upon such inventiveness – expected a vocalist to hew closely to the melody's outlines."

Jazz musicians are taught the art of storytelling through music; a solo should take the listeners on an emotional journey. This is even more important with singers, who have lyrics at their disposal as well as a melody. Their task is to interpret these lyrics so as to convey the story, whether a literal narrative or simply that emotional journey. Michael Bourne mentioned the Jobim song "The Waters of March", whose lyrics were written in English. It's a 'catalog' song, running through a seemingly disparate collection of items, places and events – a stick, a stone, the end of the road, a shot in the night. According to Bourne, Mark Murphy believed the song deconstructed a murder scene. This, he thought, was the story.

Having studied acting and performance to degree level, he knew the importance of drama, the nuts and bolts of narrative. Observed one audience member, "He moves his hands, really weaving them as he tells the stories of the songs; and his technique of moving the microphone around in swirls and back and forth in thrusts, so that his voice modulates from soft to loud, also seems part of this getting underneath a song. It is not just dramatics, a singer 'acting' out the song … you can tell Mark's entire being is in the song, immersed in its meaning. He doesn't fake it; he puts himself completely into the body of the song and emotes. He is a consummate storyteller." The potential for storytelling was partly what determined his choice of any particular tune. He told an interviewer, "'When the World Was Young', now that's a whole other thing, that to me is like singing a movie. Or 'Goodbye Pork Pie Hat' is like singing a movie, you've gotta do the words in that and believe them."

A *New York Times* review spelled out clearly how Murphy used all his knowledge, vocal chops, improvisational and performance skills at a Birdland gig late in his career:

"'The Great City', an obscure period jazz ballad by Curtis Lewis that opened Mr. Murphy's set on Thursday, set the mood. The sprawling lament is a lonely-in-the-city depiction of desperate solitude and disappointment, and the songs that followed read like chapters in a novel with that title. Mr. Murphy's rhythmic deconstructions of standards, in which he inched forward in hesitating phrases, and his abrupt tonal leaps, sometimes from a growling lower register to a childlike cry, lent his interpretations a kind of dramatic immediacy few singers would dare attempt to evoke. Flashes of zany humor interrupted the solemnity. 'Skylark' incorporated a sardonic spoken riff in which he imagined the meadow in Johnny Mercer's lyric being turned into a mall in two years. If

Mr. Murphy treads the boundary between dramatic jazz singing and neurotic bellyaching, there is more calculation and rigorous structure in his musical concepts than might appear on the surface. This narrative command, not to mention Mr. Murphy's emotional honesty, kept him on the safe side of mawkishness."

He explored narratives of different kinds. Routines based on his love for film were frequent: Ida Lupino in the 1948 film *Road House* was a favorite. Whole album tracks were done as spoken word, with or without musical backing – "Lord Buckley", "San Francisco", "Ding Walls", "Epilogue", "The Man on the Other Side of the Street", and "Humanity Ltd" on the *Shadows* album. And there were songs with a spoken word element, such as "(Baby) It's Just Talk" on *Song for the Geese*, and the mixture of spoken word and scat that is "The Interview" on *Love is What Stays*. Live, he would perform poetry, such as Johnny Frigo's "Live Jazz" (*Genius put to use / Still comes alive in concert halls / In reverence or abuse*).

Recalled Pete Churchill, "He would do wonderful monologues, underscored by the band. He liked movie scenes. Once at the Royal Northern, Manchester, he lost his voice so just did monologues all night. And the reviews afterwards were great. Another time we played at a half-timbered pub called The Fleece in Boxford, Suffolk. It was a very pretty, chocolate-box type village. Mark arrived in [bassist] Andy Hamill's car, with his knees hunched under his chin, holding his bag of charts. And someone said, 'This is just the sort of place where Agatha Christie would set a murder.' We'd done a soundcheck and we were just about to go on, and Mark said, 'I need a minute', and he went outside. I could see him through the window. He was standing there and it had started to drizzle. He came back in. We started playing the intro to 'Stolen Moments', and he started this monologue. 'I had a vision, outside there. I saw two figures hurrying through the rain to get to this gig. One of them was Miles Davis and the other was Jane Marple. And they bumped into each other, and he said, Hey Jane baby...'"

At another gig, reported one observer, "after singing the line *Thank God I can get oversexed again* he collapsed to the floor and lay horizontal with the mic still in his hand. He lay absolutely motionless for quite a while as the band played on alone; I started to worry whether he was actually acting or not. Then, loud snoring through the mic, and the final lines of the song, and the end of the night....... still horizontal on the floor!"

Early in his career, Murphy learned the importance of rhythm. His chief influences, Peggy Lee and Nat King Cole, were both singers who rode the rhythm of the song. As Anita O'Day put it, "To be this rhythmically in tune you need to have a drummer playing constantly in your head." Murphy always described himself as a time singer, and that made his choice of drummer particularly crucial. "I bounce off the time values. I must have a wonderful drummer who agrees with me on that time conception... That's what generates my motors!" Asked what else he looked for in a drummer, he said, "First, I must have someone who knows how to play brushes. A musician with a wide rhythmic skill set complete with a bunch of mallets and the ability to make it sound like a big band if you want, or a whisper. He has to connect with the bassist and invent a pulse for the pianist to float on. Then, I can float on top of this layer and communicate. I love percussive sounds, that's what your lips are for; the tongue inside the mouth, there are around fifty articulations possible. This came to me bit by bit experimenting through the years."

Said Nancy Kelly, "It was the epitome of conversational singing. No one I have ever heard has the tonal quality or timbre. His instrument is almost flawless in my opinion. He talks a lot on his recordings." The conversational style, of course, was something he had learned from Peggy Lee who, as James Gavin noted, "rarely sang a line that she wouldn't have spoken in the same way. In her case, silence meant as much as words." And Mark too would speak in the same way as he sang – rhythmically, often in staccato phrases.

Understanding the primal links between singing, drumming and dancing, Murphy became an enthusiastic dancer. "[Eddie Jefferson] was a dancer... This is fantastic, because it turns out that my other favorite singer, who had a three-song repertoire, Gregory Hines, was also one of the world's great dancers. And I believe Ella started out as a tap dancer. When I sing, especially when I'm bopping, it's like I close my eyes and I've got Eleanor Powell next to me doing those fantastic things she did with her feet, and I do it with my voice. It's all of those things, and I would say that Eddie must have been one helluva dancer."

"He loved jazz dancers," said Andy Hamill. "There were these guys called the Jazzcotheque Dancers, very fast-footed, almost like breakdancers. Mark would get us to play that kind of music – time, no changes. But he pointed out that the hip ones would be dancing in half time. And the hippest ones of all – which obviously included him – would be dancing in *quarter* time, and he'd do this little dance to illustrate that."

It goes without saying that many singers never write a song. Murphy was not prolific, but his writing was highly accomplished, whether on his own or in collaboration. His songs ranged from the edgy "Come and Get Me", released as a Riverside single in 1962, to "I Know You from Somewhere", about the events of 9/11, recorded for *Once to Every Heart* (2005) and again for *Never Let Me Go* (2010). But mostly he wrote lyrics, describing it as "one of the real pleasures of my life." He first recorded his famous lyric for "Stolen Moments" for Dutch radio in 1970, and it appears again on the *North Sea Sessions* album. "On the Red Clay", from *Mark Murphy Sings* (1975), was one of his more celebrated lyrics. Latterly he penned the words to Sean Smith's "Song for the Geese" (1997), and Alan Broadbent's "Don't Ask Why" from *Links* (2001), among others.

Murphy was progressive by nature, hating to rest on his laurels. The singer Lily Dior pointed out that "he was one of the first male modernists. He modernized the material, he took from people like Eddie Jefferson, especially with scatting and vocalese, but he always wanted to bring new things in, to incorporate what was 'now.'" "He was always trying to keep up to date," said Ari Silverstein, "He even made a rap demo."

This progressive spirit received its first and most important infusion from the work of Miles Davis, who remained a profound influence on him throughout his career. In an interview with John Watson, he said, "Miles Davis... knew the words to the songs, the ballads, he played, and that was – if you like – a circle of who sings and plays. The mystery of it all is explained by the fact that they were just trying to play like singers sing. And now singers are trying to play like Miles Davis. At least I do, and I hope I make it sometimes." Flautist and London club-owner Steve Rubie pointed out that what Mark and others also learned from Miles was the knack of "allowing space into the music – letting it breathe, not being frightened of silence." "If I take any students these days," said Mark, "I say, 'If you want to learn how to sing a ballad, listen to Miles and listen to his ballads, and learn the courage it takes to use space in your work.' I get nervous with too many notes."

He became one of the greatest balladeers of all time, with what Kurt Elling has described as "that savage, ripped-open heart." Part of this expressive ability was physical, bred in the deepening of most men's voices as they get older. "I had to wait for it to get deeper. Now I can really get into a ballad." This increased depth results partly from life experience: on another occasion he said, "Ballad singing is really a very mature art form. You have to have lived at least up to the big 4-0 before you can know. Most of these ballads are about people who've been through some shit. You're not really an adult until you learn to adjust to disappointment, in my opinion." Years later, he added, "It's like Shirley Horn and I, we sing our lives. You end up singing what you've been through. Young people can attempt that and some of them do it very well but you really can't completely do it until you've been there and back." As time went on, Mark's ballad singing became slower and slower. Pianist Misha Piatigorsky, who worked with him near the end of his career, said that Mark would refer to these ultra-slow ballads as being in "the Shirley Horn tempo". Andy Hamill said, "I've never played with anyone who played ballads as slowly as him. You would think, when the hell's the next beat going to come? It was ridiculous, but he always made it work... He would always say, the slower you go, the more you see and learn."

Murphy had originally learned the techniques of ballad-singing from listening to Nat King Cole, recordings such as "For All We Know" from 1949. *For all we know, we may never meet again/Before you go, make this moment sweet again.* In his biography of Cole, Daniel Epstein points out that "that little couplet consumes thirty seconds... This was the tempo so slow that only he [Cole] and Sinatra had the breath control to work it, the breath control and the sense of musical line... [It] had reached a new level of richness and intimacy... His mellow shaping of notes and the precision with which the vibrato diminishes and fades into silence at the line endings is absolutely mesmerizing." "[Mark] has such authority when he sings," commented Lily Dior. 'He commands the song, commands his voice. He'll sing a 'wrong' note with such conviction, that it won't necessarily sound like a wrong note... That's what I loved about Mark: as he got older, he got more experimental, a bit wilder."

In his eulogy written shortly after Murphy's death, Kurt Elling recalled hearing Murphy sing in Minneapolis in the late Eighties, and being profoundly affected by it. "First, Mark was an artist of spontaneity, adventure and edge-of-the-seat thrills. Also, he was a bona-fide hipster, equally as distinctive and quotable offstage as on. But his ballad work closed the deal: Mark was a profoundly dramatic singer whose sets brought out the rumination and the ecstasy and the agony in any song he sang. His performances were raw and real, as though he were vividly reliving some deeply personal backstory. He was an articulate guide to caverns of the Lost Soul. I don't think anybody could touch Mark when it came to heartbreaking ballads. These qualities could put him at odds with some listeners. Mark sacrificed musical precision if it helped him broadcast emotion. His scatting was ... idiosyncratic. And when it came to spontaneous-thought performance, not every audience was ready to bounce around the cosmos, let alone the savage back alleys of the hipster subconscious. If you weren't hip yourself (or willing to pretend), this persona might appear as just plain weird."

Musicians had to work hard to keep up with Mark Murphy, but such was his prowess in communicating what he wanted, it nearly always worked. As Tina May put it, "He had that ability to just switch on a band, wherever he was in the world." This frequently meant diverting the musicians from playing what they usually played in any given circumstance. For example, he didn't always want the piano player to add the usual ornamental flourishes at the end of a tune, once telling Pete Churchill just to play the final chord and no more. But he also liked to be surprised. Murphy told Churchill, "The thing I like about you... everywhere I go in the world, pianists try to give me what they think I want. I get like slow-grade Bill Evans or Wynton Kelly or Red Garland. But I never know how you're gonna play it."

That uncertainty was his bread and butter. His performances were all about spontaneity. "Take an ordinary swing tune like 'The Masquerade is Over," continued Churchill. "He always moved around the stage near to the people he was singing with, so if I was playing an open piano intro he'd move to the well of the piano, just bathing himself in the sound. At the end he'd come out of the bridge. By this time he'd cut me out, and then he'd cut [drummer] Mark Fletcher out, and it was just him and Andy Hamill." Mark would sing the last eight bars with only the bass, and on the penultimate line he would put his hand on Hamill's strings and stop them, then sing the last line unaccompanied.

Churchill remembers with particular fondness a gig at the very short-lived Rhythmic Club in London's Chapel Market, Islington, where Murphy just turned to the band and growled, "C minor" and made a fluttering gesture with his hands. "We had no idea what was coming, and then we heard the verse to 'Where or When', that Andy didn't even know. [Mark] could sing through anything."

The stage was Mark Murphy's laboratory, where anything could happen, depending on how you combined the different musical elements. A fan who had attended a gig in Gainesville, Florida, in January 1998, wrote: "Mark is amazing to watch. His eyes are closed (concentrating) melding himself with the music, standing quietly, moving his microphone to match the dynamics of the music, vowels and consonants. You can understand everything he sings. He occasionally thumps his hand on the piano top, while accenting some unheard or alternate beat running through his mind. His foot occasionally lifts from the floor and performs a counter accent. His eyes flick open wide and look to his left at the drummer, trying to elicit counterpoint and interaction. He coaxes with his eyes, leading and imploring. He moves from words to scat, flicking notes, pouring his soul into the moment. A horn player playing his instrument, but with age-old early language monosyllables. *Unh, unh, wah wah, ahhhhhh*. He soars and swoops, lingering here and there. The voice. I cannot get over the dark [timbre] and control. Clear and confident. So easy, just so damn easy."

Said Murphy, "I learned so much about vocal arranging from being a Peggy Lee freak for so many years. I learned all the possibilities you can do with a trio and ways of keeping an audience's attention by dropping instruments away, suddenly being with just an instrument, suddenly just with drums, using all the aspects of the drums, using percussive elements out of the piano."

He provided an example – "All the Things You Are", which he performed with Richie Cole. "There's a short vocalese intro and then we state the song – I think you've got to do that first – and then Richie and I do an improvisation, he plays while I scat, and then the rhythm section comes in and I do free scat, and then someone else plays and everything stops, and I go back to the verse and do that strictly *a cappella* and out of tempo, and then bring in a completely different tempo. I think I gave everything I could think of to that particular song, which is probably one of the best songs for harmonic possibilities."

Said Andy Hamill, "At a gig, I think in Manchester, he had a bad cold and he'd completely lost his voice, and all he could do was sing very low or very high. And it was one of my favorite gigs – his voice sounded amazing. We had to change most of the keys so it would fit in his range. His biggest influence was Miles Davis, and when he improvised he'd often jump into falsetto, because in his head he was being Miles. On this gig he sang in this really low register and then he'd jump up and improvise with these very high lines, then back down to the low register. He would occasionally forget things on stage, but he would just turn it into something different and it actually helped with the creative process. In the same way Miles Davis would turn a mistake into something positive. Herbie Hancock told the story about playing a wrong voicing, and then Miles using the wrong note as his next idea, and turning it into the right note. It was the same with Mark – he liked it if the tune went off the rails, because it was different, and there was nothing worse than getting stale.

"I liked to surprise him too. The chromatic harmonica is my second instrument, and once I managed to sneak on a spare microphone, and when it came to the bass solo he had his back turned to me, and so I played it on harmonica – he really liked that. And he knew I loved what he did. Mark would always tell [drummer Mark Fletcher] to really go for it, and play the way you would play behind a horn player, not the way you would play behind a singer. Usually if you're playing behind a singer you've got to hold back, so as not to overpower them."

Pete Churchill recalls an occasion at the Underground in Leeds where they were playing "Madalena", and at one point during the tune the band all went off in different directions. "Somebody missed a coda or a sign, or one of those things, and he could hear that we were massively lost. What would a singer do in a situation where there were two different keys involved, and someone was going off to one part and another was going to another part? Chaos. Andy floundering and me thinking, How are we going to get out of this one? And a crowd full of people throwing themselves around. [Mark] turned around, and cut us – the groove was still going but the harmony had gone. And he went, *Letter... B!* And he went straight back in, we all found letter B, and he turned around and carried on singing. Damage limitation. But he felt the best music is often made in those dangerous moments.

"He was also very fast at assessing the strengths and weaknesses of different musicians he found himself playing with all over the world. If he wanted a piece to fire off at some superheated tempo and only the drummer could keep up, he would cut the other musicians out and do something with the drummer. He would do crazy stuff with the mic, like zooming it across in front of him for a certain effect, or rubbing it on his lapel, or stick the mic under his chin for the last low note."

An understanding of harmony is essential for good improvisation, whether instrumental or vocal. Murphy recalled, "I was walking around in Czechoslovakia with a television director. And he said, 'You don't sing the melody, you sing the harmony.' In some sense that's right, I think inside the chord. That's why the harmonics the piano player plays are so important to me."

He also believed that the interpretation and delivery of lyrics varies in importance according to the style of the piece. "[People] ask which is more important, the lyric or the melody? And I always say that in a rhythm song, the music is my primary concern, and in ballads the lyric is primarily my concern... Most of the songs that I sing concern a love lyric, and this gets a bit tiresome from my standpoint, and I imagine from the audience standpoint too. So I'm prone to re-do a lyric, in the sense that I did with 'My Favorite Things."

In the end he seemed to come down on the side of the non-verbal elements of singing, believing that it is not words per se that hit the audience in their emotional center. "A song is first of all a piece of music, and second a piece of literature." He suggested that "the emotion in a song is in the chord changes and in the vowels of the words… Long before we had any languages, the vowels were there saying what people wanted to say."

Learning lyrics is something all singers have to wrestle with, just as actors have to learn lines. Mark, needless to say, had his own method – in this case, one that we might associate with early childhood. According to Albert Amaroso, "When he wanted to learn lyrics, he would act it. If it was *You're breaking my heart*, he would use his hands to break something, and hold his heart. Then he wouldn't forget the lyric. It was wonderful, because he'd learn the tune, and that night we'd be gigging it."

His repertoire roamed far beyond the 200–300 standards which are the shared currency of jazz. As Steve Rubie recalled, "Mark's material changed the whole time. There were a number of great songs I'd never heard before that I heard through him. One example was 'Lazy Afternoon', an obscure song which he discovered and made into one everyone would do." He was interested in the contemporary songwriters he met during his travels, such as Seattle's June Tonkin, and had sufficient faith in their songs to record them. "I get new songs sent to me all the time and I do some writing myself. But it's not as if we're in a golden age. You've got to look for the new Johnny Mandel song or the new Stephen Sondheim song, and they're not writing songs like that anymore."

But he was also famed among singers and knowledgeable audiences alike for his research into the way that older songs had originally been written, often for stage or screen musicals. Songs from the Thirties or Forties often started with a *colla voce* verse – the preamble to the song, the transition from a dramatic part of the performance to a sung part. The verse would set the context for the rest of the song. When these songs were taken up by instrumentalists, they would often omit the verse and begin with the main body of the song. However, Murphy would hunt out the original sheet music, where he knew he would often find an unfamiliar verse written for a familiar tune, standards such as "All the Things You Are", "On Green Dolphin Street", and "Body and Soul". As Fred Bouchard pointed out in his liner notes to *Satisfaction Guaranteed*, "delivering the verse as well as the refrain is delivering the whole song, as the composer intended it to be heard, the whole story."

Mark Murphy understood the mechanics of the mouth and other parts of the body associated with singing. As Dave Gelly points out in his book on Lester Young, "The most precise and delicate movements a human being can make take place inside the mouth, and there, in that secret place, the saxophone player creates his sound." The same is obviously true of singers, and to an even greater extent, since they don't even have a reed to vibrate. Said Murphy, "I developed a repertoire and relaxation with my Cincy [Cincinnati] group. My singing evolved with a feeling of intense relaxation, always using my diaphragm and breathing specifically through my nose. This focuses the air stream as accurate as a hit with drumstick. Dave Lambert, one of my favorites, had that kind of control. He could read music or just blow long solos breathing through his nose with absolute accuracy."

Tobacco smoke was the enemy of the voice, particularly in UK clubs during the Sixties. In 2011 Murphy told Michael Bourne, "When people smoked, I used to go through hell with my voice... but when people stopped smoking, man, my voice came back like an angel." Bourne reminded him that he once kept oxygen at the side of stage when singing in Denver, whose elevation at over 5,000 feet makes life difficult for many singers.

Murphy performed in a huge variety of locations, some more conducive to his art than others, as he explained to Will Friedwald. "For Mark Murphy, the ideal venues are just certain clubs, 'Like Yoshi's in Oakland and another, Sculler's, in Boston where I can call them with conditions. A place in Sydney, Australia, Kinsela's, where I went on a two-week run with a five-piece band. It's a club where you feel that all the staff are behind you. They serve meals quietly, everything runs smoothly. All that matters, knowing the staff are with you. It's hard to achieve, but when you get optimum conditions you can grow so much in one night that you are not the same singer you were the day before. As for singing in noisy, smoky, non-artistic environments. Me!? Seriously, in the 1960s and 1970s, I thought I was losing my voice and I had to stop playing those clubs. But really, when it's noisy, you're not doing your work right. You control the noise. Communicate! If you're not communicating, you've got a problem. But sometimes it's hard and I get nervous. Like those awful afternoon gigs at outdoor jazz festivals when you have to deal with wind and no chance of a sound check and I know if you get 40,000 people only 300 of them know who I am, because I'm still so specialized. That's when I'm nervous.'"

As if battles with the audience and the venue weren't enough, there were also other singers to jostle with. One whom Mark Murphy is often compared to – Betty Carter – did not always meet with his approval; he found her too purist. "In one way she's become a caricature. It's something you can do if you don't keep track of things. She wants to stay in the avant-garde on top of everything but – maybe I'm getting older. It's like a singer who wants to sing too far behind the beat. It's not musical anymore. That's okay if you're doing what Bobby McFerrin's doing. He has a much looser organization. But if you're singing tunes, and you're basing them on tunes, then you've got to stick with those tunes."

As well as an on-off duel with Mel Tormé who, he thought, lacked true passion in his singing, Murphy saw the limits of what was possible with jazz singing in the shape of McFerrin, who took pure sound as far as it could be taken. It caused Murphy to change his own approach. In conversation with Dutch singer Ann Burton, he said, "[McFerrin] affected me by chasing me right back to songs. You can't get any further out with sounds than McFerrin gets, so I went deeper into good songs."

Regarding Betty Carter, he added, "She is one of the greatest bebop singers in the world. I'm certain that Billie Holiday was an innovator, and Satchmo, and Bobby McFerrin. But look – I think it's just as marvelous to be a wonderful singer too... if she could relax a little bit. But I sometimes hear singers being pushed in other directions, by other artists. Like Picasso, who was influenced by trends in painting. In fact, there was a school of painters who had similar influences, so you could say we're a group of singers who feel the same way about this thing called jazz singing. But among us are great differences and subtleties." Ann Burton responded that although Billie Holiday was an innovator, she never seemed to be striving for effect. Murphy replied, "The innovators DON'T. The people who are affected by them give you this feeling of their having to reach."

One area of controversy with Murphy is scat singing. Scatting places great demands on the singer: effective vocal improvisation requires not only an understanding of harmony and chord progression, but a deeper knowledge of the jazz creative tradition, and of course the ability to spontaneously produce coherent melodic lines. Once mastered, scatting not only increases the vocalist's arsenal of effects, but marks the singer out as a *jazz* practitioner, on an equal footing with instrumental soloists. Playing with a trio, a good scat singer can use non-verbal sounds to approximate the function of a horn.

"Scatting is so much fun," Chet Baker once told an interviewer. "You can really extend yourself, and try to come up with some interesting lines that fit in the harmony and chord progressions, but still swing and still have a meaning... It's nothing that's worked out or thought about beforehand; it's completely spontaneous – and very risky."

It is, of course, also possible to scat using lyrics: José James, for example, takes his cue from sampling and other techniques of musical electronica, breaking up and repeating lyrics over and over again on a live gig, chopping them into pieces until they are no more than individual syllables.

But as mentioned earlier, many singers who perform jazz tunes do not improvise, beyond varying the melody and rhythmic emphasis here and there.

Murphy was scatting early: it's there on the fade-out of the first track of his first album ("Fascinatin' Rhythm", from *Meet Mark Murphy*, 1956), on "Falling in Love with Love" (*This Could Be The Start of Something*) and "I Only have Eyes for You" (from *Hip Parade*). He knew that scatting posed a direct challenge to those audiences who liked their singers safe and predictable. "People are used to songs being an unchanging line of storytelling... Scatting or improvising... it makes an audience work harder."

Performed too wildly, scatting can become a liability – not that it ever stopped Murphy. As Francesca "Cha Cha" Miano put it in her blog, "Mark had always paid great attention to clear diction and masterful singing, with a little scatting on the side. As time went on, the scatting became more extravagant, with swoops, shifts of pitch, yodels and growls… Mark had no qualms about letting his voice sound a bit harsh and un-pretty, if he felt it fit the particular mood he was trying to get across."

An interviewer asked him, "Why do you do so much scat?" Murphy replied, "Usually it's because there's no horn. I rarely do more than two choruses. You've got a whole evening to fill out, and I assume people who come to me don't expect me to [sing] ballads all night, and part of the art that I do is scat singing. I would think they'd expect it."

An unsigned article in *Mark's Times* examined Murphy's scat solo on "Boplicity", which contains "ideas which revolve around everything from modal and pentatonic scales to more traditional bebop lines. The way in which Murphy switches from high to low register while working with a variety of 'untraditional' scat syllables is impressive… like 'wambwa', 'dunga', 'whoya da', 'zoinlin lelan' etc., seem to take him beyond the ordinary level of expression in scat and bring him to a whole new level of experimentation with voice texture, slurred melodic passages, and overall vocal and melodic development."

A constant theme of this book has been why Mark Murphy never quite emerged into mainstream consciousness, despite a career spanning seven decades. To put it bluntly, most people have never heard of him. The qualities that set Mark Murphy apart from any other singer were those that simultaneously made him both a great artist and a commercial failure. He did not popularize his art. His unpredictability, his unwillingness to compromise in the struggle between art and entertainment, was the thing that condemned him to obscurity, but also the thing that made him great. With Sinatra or Bennett, you knew in advance what you were going to get. Not so with Murphy. "I've been described as one of the most restless singers there is, because I never settle down. But I think that's what keeps me going, this restlessness to try things different ways and not settle down in any one groove… What's kept me going is not compromising."

In Murphy's hands, wrote the journalist George Varga, "music is like putty, constantly changing form melodically, harmonically and rhythmically. Like a world-class sculptor he carefully shapes and reshapes each note, stretching a phrase with marvelous elasticity here, bending or smearing a lyric there, until he has made a song completely and unmistakably his own."

Appendix B: I Don't Want to Stamp Out Singers Like Cookies

Jazz education has made great strides in recent years, often resulting in extremely high levels of technical ability amongst the young. Perversely, this has created a problem for the professional jazz musician, particularly in New York, where the number of accomplished players greatly outstrips the number of gigs. This, in a simple illustration of the laws of supply and demand, has meant performing for low fees, or no fees at all. In a further irony, jazz education is the one area that has been making real profits since the mid-seventies, expanding greatly since the early nineties.

Teaching has always been a way for musicians to supplement meager earnings, and the natural spontaneity and creativity that Mark Murphy showed as a singer also made him a great teacher. As all who have tried it know, teaching can be as difficult as learning, particularly when the teacher is searching for a simple, practical way to help a struggling student.

As we saw in chapter 7, exactly when Murphy began teaching is uncertain, though it may have been late 1979, at the public community College of the Siskiyous in Weed, northern California, with Dr Kirby Shaw. In 1980, speaking of Weed, Murphy said, "It's funny, you walk around the little town, and you expect to hear a little country-western or maybe some folk music on some soupy station. But then you go into this high school auditorium and the kids are singing bebop, all loving each other's performance. I first noticed it when some kids started hanging around the dock in Tiburon, California, where I sang for ten months. These were kids who work in a high school band and choir in Marin County. They came in one night and all scatted with me, and I was *amazed*. Then I found out, through Herb Wong, about what Kirby is doing up there and started doing clinics for him. I love to do clinic work because it gets me out of nightclubs and it's a way of using another side of your brain. I gave them a little tape lecture on historic jazz singers the other day. I found out that Bessie Smith's teacher was Ma Rainey. Now I have to find out who taught Ma Rainey, and that would take you back to almost 1900.

I teach that jazz is a true fusion of cultures which together have produced an art form. It happened in Louisiana, a Creole, Latin-based culture, but also in Cuba and Brazil, where the African rhythms met the different kinds of European music. Jazz was first vocal, then the instruments came in sounding like voices, and now we've come full circle, with people calling us singers who sound like horns." In the same year, Murphy reported that he had discovered a jazz choir in London, at Goldsmith's College, Lewisham. The following year, through a mutual friend, he was invited to conduct a jazz vocal lecture and demonstration for Jill Heisman's adult music class at Goldsmith's.

The pattern of Murphy's career soon settled into a mixture of gigs and workshops wherever he was working around the world, notably in Graz, near Vienna, and Buffalo in the US, but also in Italy, the UK, Holland, Denmark and elsewhere.

The teaching or mentoring of jazz was very informal in the 1980s, according to Anne Dyer, who knew Murphy in San Francisco. "The teacher-student relationship was not at all definitive then. It was more that you were all part of a scene, where everyone was hanging out together. You would go out to the clubs. In fact you *had* to go out to the clubs, three, four, five times a week. Even if you didn't have a gig, you were hanging out, you were sitting in, your friends were playing. And Mark was very much a part of that scene – the Jazz Workshop, Keystone Korner, The Ramp. That's why I think of him more as a guru than a teacher, because he was involved in our daily lives. He would come to our gigs, he would come to your house for dinner, he was at parties, he was part of your world."

Murphy's teaching approach was more practical than theoretical. "They're trying to put [how to sing jazz] into books now and the books are marvelous, but you can't get the feeling from that," Murphy told an interviewer. "To be a jazz singer it takes a lot of study. You've got to know the chord changes and the words," he said, but was adamant that the only way to learn was by doing it.

John Dankworth and Cleo Laine had started a music education center, then known as The Wavendon Project, in 1970 at their home 50 miles north of London. In 1983, they invited Murphy to teach at a summer school there. A contemporary report illustrates Murphy's knack of finding ways to help individual students. "There were two male singers and one had too much vibrato, the other no vibrato at all, so Mark had them practice together for one to rub off on the other." The writer, a contributor to *Mark's Times*, may have been blind to the innuendo, but what he saw clearly was that Murphy knew how to make learning fun. At the next day's session "one middle-aged female singer was just standing performing by the piano and Mark had her moving around; he started by actually pushing her in different directions. Suddenly she got the hang of it and let herself get into the swing of things; she was transformed from appearing a frumpish middle-aged woman into a very sexy lady whom you could not take your eyes off. Mark pulled one of the younger girls up for not making any facial expressions while singing. 'Nobody likes looking at a blank face all night,' he urged, 'I want you to play Edward G. Robinson and sing out of one corner of your mouth. Then, when I snap my fingers, switch to the other side.' This greatly amused everyone, including the girl concerned, but it worked!"

Some years later another *Mark's Times* contributor was present at a session in central London, and wrote a detailed report on the sequence of events: "At approximately 10:45, we organized ourselves into a circle ready for a series of vocal warm-ups and rhythmic breathing exercises given by singer Anton Browne. Commencing with a gentle loosening of the head and shoulders and then the abdomen, Anton gradually built up the pace with some scalar exercises to his piano accompaniment. An excellent preparation for Mark's arrival. Mark firstly demonstrated a body posture that would soften the front of the throat and thereby minimize stress to the vocal folds and its family of muscles. He next showed us convincingly how much more supportive, and of course natural [it is] for a singer to... breathe in through the nose – still a much disputed topic in singers' circles. Certainly, more air can be drawn in by this "breathing system" referred to by Mark as a 'Working Singer's Lifeline'. [It sounds here as if Murphy was trying to develop a singer's method for circular breathing.]

"Prior to lunch we were guided through exercises designed to develop more 'expression'. These included a round of blues and then scat choruses and exchanges to expert piano accompaniment from Simon Carter, and finally each attendee strolled over to Mark Fletcher and his drum kit to practice vocal percussive interplay. The afternoon was spent very pleasurably, listening to our individual performances in front of the class. Mark listened and watched acutely. I am sure everyone benefitted immensely from his positive advice regarding choice of keys, arrangement, attitude, energy levels, phrasing, diction, and all other minutiae necessary for a convincing performance. The ever versatile Peter Churchill took over on the keys towards the end of the workshop."

In a later interview, Murphy explained what he was doing with posture and breathing: "I've sort of adapted classical technique to the needs of jazz which really is just to take it physically off the front of the throat and redistribute it up into the head tones area and really to stretch it to the back of the neck, because that frees the front so that the [vocal] cords are not in a family of stressed muscles and they just do what they're supposed to do...."

He told Ted Gioia, "Ninety-five percent of people learning to sing haven't a clue what goes on in the physical process of it and none of them knows how to breathe. The breathing is the bottom line. Everyone should learn it or not sing. Jazz singing and grand opera may be the opposite ends of the spectrum but they are the two most difficult kinds of singing and take the biggest amount of time to learn. That's because you have to put not only enormous amounts of technique into it, but also your life. It isn't a music you can fool around with. You can't go into a song with no preparation and think you're going to get away with it." To explain how the issues people had with singing were purely physical, he would often use sporting metaphors, perhaps about boxing or surfing, to suggest the sort of approach they might take. Drinking large quantities of water was another essential, he told them. "At least six pints a day – it will make you run a lot, but it will help your voice."

He offered more general guidelines to would-be jazz singers, recommending "disciplined listening, studying the history and where the music is heading nowadays. Go on an exploration of who's doing what and how they're doing it. See if it's something you can do." Teaching had its frustrations, too: "When I taught at the University of Music and Dramatic Arts in Graz, Austria, first I taught voice technique. But when the students learned good voice technique and would try to be creative and improvise, they'd forget their technique. You have to keep your technique and you have to always be creative, always exploring... It can take almost ten years to original-ize your delivery."

Improvisation was as important to Murphy's teaching as it was to his singing. "I improvise the lesson with each student, because no student is the same as any other. The thing that's worrying me now is that there are more schools and more stunts but fewer artists. It's as if, to get them through school, teachers insist on too much conformity. I try to mess that up – because if you don't mess that up, they won't go to the edge."

Ian Shaw, a fellow baritone, learned from Murphy to "put the words fairly prominently in the songs, get rid of vibrato, or be more selective with vibrato, use my lower register more, listen to the drums." And there was more: "Count off every tune yourself. And sing songs that you're scared of." In Shaw's case these included "What Are You Doing the Rest of Your Life", "Lush Life", "Round Midnight" and "Spring Can Really Hang You Up the Most".

In London, Murphy taught at the Royal Academy of Music, at the Guildhall and at the 606 Club in Chelsea, where the Jazz Singers' Network began organizing sessions in 1992. The club played host to many of his Saturday morning vocal workshops, some observed by owner Steve Rubie. "'He didn't *inculcate* anything... I learned an enormous amount about teaching from Mark, who was one of the best teachers I've ever seen... What was wonderful about Mark was treating each person in the class completely differently. Everyone who does workshops now uses that template." After the warm-ups and general discussion of repertoire, students would come up and perform individually, and Murphy would critique what they did. "But – I choose my words very carefully – he would never *criticize*, he would *critique*, in a very positive way. And he was absolutely brilliant at picking out individual issues. So he would very rarely say the same thing twice to two different singers. For example he might say, 'Your problem is your time', or, 'You're not thinking about the words', or, 'You may need to think about your intonation.' He would introduce this by saying, 'Well that was absolutely brilliant – the only thing I would say is...' He was very good at making people feel good about themselves. I remember there was one woman who had a problem with her breathing, so he said, 'Honey, I think you should lay down on the floor.' It was so she could feel the pressure of her diaphragm."

Murphy's positive attitude was not mere reassurance, but recognition that the performing arts are a source of terror for those lacking confidence, technique or experience. He was able to convince most that they had something that could please an audience. The singer Tessa Souter said, "He presented me at a Mentor concert and forgave me when I had debilitating stage fright. He finally cured me of stage fright by telling me one day: 'These people are just here to have a good time. That is all our job is. It's not about your voice or the performance. You just think, I am here to give these people my love!'"

The audience was indeed the crucial factor. It wasn't simply a matter of standing in the spotlight and emoting with some degree of skill, and expecting people to listen. There also had to be variety, which is why some ability in acting is useful for singers – storytelling, creating characters. "I tell my kids [that the audience] is gonna listen to you in a whole concert, they're gonna listen to you in a whole CD, so I tell them they've got to become different people in each song."

Many otherwise accomplished singers quail at the prospect of scat singing, and with good reason: there is no more painful sound than that of a poorly-executed scat solo. One interviewer asked Murphy how it could be taught."You take it apart," he said, "You put it back together. I divide it into harmonics and percussives. I don't insist that they sing absolute bebop riffs. I've gotten interested lately in pure abstract improvisation. I'll ask them to make sounds, and if you try it a couple of times, if you have the right people, suddenly you have something. I push them to the edge. It's too easy just to be technical. I liken what I do to degrees of painting, where you sketch a figure, then sketch it out, then sketch it back in. You do it with musical brush strokes."

Murphy was far too sophisticated a singer to think that every song had to include vocal improvisation. "It depends on the song. There are certain songs where you don't have to improvise but just sing as it was written. You can [do] improvisation by not singing at all or rhythmical pausing, or hitting a note so squarely in tune that it creates overtones. Some singers never touch the melody. That's not interesting to me – because the composer has written something. I like to hear the melody, or at least a reference to the melody – and then you take it away. I simplify my goals as a singer by only doing what's necessary and by listening when I'm not singing, what I call 'designing your silence'. The hardest thing to teach a singer or a horn player is to shut up! Coltrane once said, 'I can't seem to stop playing.' Miles said, 'Take the horn out of your mouth.' That's how you learn phrasing. I'll take students through four-bar phrases, and I'll tell them to make the first two bars incredibly note-y, then investigate the space in the second two bars. It takes a while to see the importance of *that*. There's really a lot you can do with a song. Of course, not all my students can do it, but I give them a chance to try...."

Rhythm – with or without a drummer – was the key to the sounds one makes when scatting, Murphy would tell his students. To bring home this message he would leave them to sing alone with just the drummer. "Nat [Cole], my God, he would sing so effortlessly and just fracture you with what swing was and what syncopation is. I scream at my kids, 'For God's sake, learn the time step', or 'Bring in some brushes'. Then I put them right up with the drummer and make them watch his hands, and try to make them sing with their voice what he plays with his hands and feet. And it works. Once in a while, it works!"

Murphy not only taught singers, but showed players how to accompany them. This was new even to the eminent head of the jazz department at Graz, Karlheinz Miklin. "We didn't have any singers in Austria before we established the vocal program, but now we have a lot. And I learned how the drummer has to play with a singer. And also my role [as saxophonist] – I was always the soloist, but with a singer you have less space, you have to learn where to play. It's a completely different role between playing with a quartet and playing in a quartet with a singer. We learned this in rehearsal and on stage, and it was a great thing to learn. And the importance of the character of the song. How to phrase something. These were big lessons for me."

Some students just couldn't do it, however hard they tried. "Sometimes," said Murphy, "I simply have to say, 'Look, you are just not right for this, but if you like I can still help you'. Jazz can be very difficult, very taxing to the vocal cords... I have to drum a lot of technique into them."

At a workshop at Leeds College of Music, accompanied by Pete Churchill, the latter noticed that Murphy would devote little time to those singers who seemed relatively uncommitted. He wanted to scatter the seed on the most fertile ground. "One singer turned up late. Mark immediately got her up to the mic to sing. She sang a ballad – 'I Guess I'll Hang My Tears Out to Dry' or something, which everyone thought was pretty good. And he went up and whispered to her, and she went white. He slowed the tempo down and she sang it again, and it was unbelievable. And then she ran from the room, crying." Later on Churchill asked her what had happened, and it turned out Murphy had said, "Imagine you've come home. He's left you, and he's taken all the furniture." "And she said, 'And that's why I was late this morning'. Because that's exactly what had happened."

At another workshop at London's Guildhall, Murphy told a singer to sing "The Nearness of You" saying *Nay* all the way through instead of the lyrics. "She did, and then he told her to sing the lyric with that sound, and it was unbelievable. You could tell she'd never made that sound before. She threw a wobbler, she said, 'No! That's not me! That's not my voice!' and she ran out of the room."

Murphy also knew that you can't do great work if your main motivation is ego. At the same venue, with another now well-known and successful singer whom we shall call Susan Smith, he saw that the problem was over-confidence. "She'd obviously rehearsed her tune 'Yesterdays' with the band beforehand," recalled Churchill. "It was really fast, and she scatted, and when she finished we all went, 'Whoa, amazing!'

"And he went, 'What's your name, darlin'?'

"'Susan Smith.'

"'And how old are you?'

"'Twenty-one.'

"'And what's the song called?'

"'Yesterdays.'

"'OK so you're 21 and you're singing about a time when you were 8 or 9?'

"'Er...'

"'OK, I want you to imagine you're sixty-five and you're singing about a time when you were twenty-one.'

"And then he counted the song in very slowly. And she couldn't do it – because she was twenty-one."

At a workshop at Pizza Express, Murphy asked a participant if she needed her glasses. She said she always wore them. "He said, 'Take 'em off'. She looked like someone who never took off her glasses. And he said, 'Now sing it.' And that was the extent of his advice. She was hiding behind the glasses." Another method was to pair up singers and get them to perform a routine together: "'OK you're a store detective, and you've just been caught shoplifting. Go!' And that was the theme of their scat singing."

As Murphy taught at workshops all over Europe, he began noticing differences in the students. "It's very interesting teaching young people today," he told an interviewer in 1995. "There is a difference between the younger people of southern Europe, and, say, the ones I teach in Holland or Denmark. There is more of a temperament in the people of southern Europe. We call it attitude. It sometimes is not easy to instruct them, you have to wait to find out if the student learns directly or indirectly. Some of them can learn by direct instruction, but some can only learn by listening, you know. So I go with what I hear, I don't demand that everyone learn the same way, because, as I said, there's no really innovative work that I hear vocally or in jazz today. It's all been beautifully learned in music schools but I'm afraid a lot of the individuality got away somewhere. So I don't want to stamp out singers like cookies, I try very hard not to disturb the natural instinct. Although I've got to teach them some technique if I can."

The singer Lily Dior received some private tuition from Murphy. "I had a teacher in Sydney who was very much about 'do it like this and do it like that', but Mark was very much about giving you suggestions and then prodding you in the right direction, rooting it in the rhythm and the moment. I remember I did a ballad, I think it was 'Tenderly', and he said, 'Hmmm, that's very muscular.' I've got quite a deep voice, and at the time I was always trying to prove myself. But if you've got a ballad, you don't have to belt the shit out of it. So he said, 'Be tender, caress the ballad.' The ballad is the hardest thing to do well", she added, "and shows the depth of what's there. I like to get my own students to sing ballads, because not only does it challenge you technique-wise, because you've got to sustain these long notes, it's also the best medium to learn the song in, and to learn vocal technique."

Murphy would also plead with singers to find new material. "He would say, 'The standards are great, but the music has to progress,'" remembered Ann Dyer. "'You have to find new composers, new songs. You can't just keep singing "My Funny Valentine"'. I was a very straight-ahead jazz singer when I started out, but at some point in my career I started being interested in more adventurous, progressive, eclectic music. And the people around me were warning me – 'Be careful, you're getting kind of out there.' [But] Mark actually said, 'You're not taking it far enough, you need to take it to the end of the limb.' That was one reason he got into Brazilian music – new material, new rhythms, new instrumentation."

He became depressed at the lack of seriousness of his students at Buffalo, although his well-honed skills as a teacher ensured positive outcomes. "Here comes this avant-garde jazz star," recalled Ari Silverstein, "who dresses in a peculiar way, is giving them homework and telling them what to do, and they've never been in the presence of someone like him, in the presence of a master. Yet by the time they had to present their songs at the end of the semester, they looked and sounded like jazz singers."

At a 2006 IAJE Conference session on vocal workshops, Murphy told the delegates that from now on people would have to audition for his classes. Soon afterwards he gave up teaching altogether. It wasn't only what he saw as the lack of dedication – breathing was a major stumbling block: he became discouraged that he could not get students to "relax and starting breathing right. Very few of them learned it." Late in life he reached the conclusion that jazz singing could not be taught – either you could do it or you could not. But in this he was surely mistaken. Some people have no gift for music, or jazz, or jazz singing, but for those that do, jazz education is essential. Even had Mark Murphy not been such an inspirational teacher, he was inspirational purely as a singer.

Amy London, a singing teacher at the New School jazz department in New York for 25 years, said she saw him perform "at least 100 times... The major-ity of my teaching methods come from watching Mark Murphy on the stage. Every gig was a masterclass. The way he would conduct, the way he would arrange. He would bring up all these verses. I make all my students learn the verse, if there is one. The way that he swung, the way that he would feel the drums, the way that he would scat, his physical presence, his sound. You have to have a sound; if you don't have a sound as a singer, go back in the shed."

Discography

The principal source for this discography is *The Jazz Discography Volume 15* by Tom Lord (Cadence Jazz Books, 1996), its update on a 2012 CD-ROM, and its online version. I have also consulted a list compiled by Steve Cumming (2008), and the websites discogs.com and allmusic.com.

In recent years the market has been deluged with repackaged out-of-copyright digital releases of Mark Murphy's Decca, Capitol and Riverside work, released with titles like *Jazz Pearls, The Lady in Red, Jazzmatic, Out of This World*, and even *It's Christmas Time with Mark Murphy* (with, of course, no discernible connection to the festive season). These have not been included in this discography. However re-issued complete album collections have, such as the Spanish label Fresh Sound's two-disc compilation of *Playing the Field, Rah* and *That's How I Love the Blues!*.

Unless stated otherwise, the credited artist is Mark Murphy (vocals) and the country of origin is the USA.

INSTRUMENTAL ABBREVIATIONS			
(acc)	accordion	(p)	piano
(arr)	arranger	(perc)	percussion
(as)	alto sax	(pic-tp)	piccolo trumpet (Baroque trumpet)
(b)	acoustic bass	(prod)	producer
(bcl)	bass clarinet	(r)	reeds: various woodwinds, usually
(bs)	baritone sax		doubled by a small group of musicians
(bv)	background vocals	(ss)	soprano sax
(cond)	conductor	(synth)	synthesizer
(d)	drums	(tap)	tapdance
(eb)	electric bass	(tb)	trombone
(ethno-inst)	ethnic (non-Western) instruments	(tp)	trumpet
(fgl)	flugelhorn	(ts)	tenor sax
(fh)	French horn	(tu)	tuba
(fl)	flute	(v)	vocal
(g)	guitar	(vbs)	vibraphone
(hca)	harmonica	(vla)	viola
(kyb)	keyboards	(vlc)	violoncello
(org)	organ	(vln)	violin
		(vtb)	valve trombone

Unreleased recordings
Unidentified orchestra
New York, 1955

One for My Baby
You Don't Know What Love Is
For All We Know
That's All
Detour Ahead
Love Letters
I Dream of You
Alone
I Wanna Be Loved
Like Someone in Love
Long Ago
My Heart Isn't in It

Originally scheduled for Decca DL8379 (catalogue number reassigned)

Meet Mark Murphy – The Singing "M"
Unknown orchestra; Ralph Burns (arr/cond).
New York, June 29, 1956

Give it Back to the Indians ᵇ
You Mustn't Kick it Around ᵇ
Fascinating Rhythm ᵃᵇ
Limehouse Blues ᵇ

New York, August 9, 1956

Guess I'll Hang My Tears Out to Dry ᵇ
A Nightingale Sang in Berkeley Square ᵇ
Irresistible You
If I Could be with You (One Hour Tonight) ᵇ

New York, August 13, 1956

I'm a Circus
I've got Two Eyes
Exactly Like You ᵃᵇ
Two Ladies in de Shade of de Banana Tree

Decca DL8390 – Meet Mark Murphy – The Singing "M"
ᵃ *Decca 9-30101 (single)*
ᵇ *GRP/Decca GRD-670 – Crazy Rhythm: His Debut Recordings*

Unreleased recordings
Unknown orchestra; Ralph Burns (arr/cond).
New York, 1956

Easy to Love
You're Driving Me Crazy
I Dream of You
Everything I Have is Yours
Isn't It a Pity?
You Do Something to Me
Somebody Loves Me
I'm Glad There Is You
There's a Rainbow 'Round My Shoulder

I'm Nobody's Baby
Too Late Now
I've Heard that Song Before

Originally scheduled for Decca DL8595 (reassigned)

Let Yourself Go
Unknown orchestra; Ralph Burns (arr/cond).
New York, April 23, 1957

I Got Rhythm
Takin' a Chance on Love
'Taint No Sin (To Dance Around in Your Bones)
Let Yourself Go (unreleased)

New York, May 3, 1957

Ridin' High
Crazy Rhythm
Elmer's Tune
The Lady in Red

New York, May 22, 1957

Little Jazz Bird
Robbins' Nest
Pick Yourself Up
Lullaby in Rhythm

Decca DL8632 – Let Yourself Go
GRP/Decca GRD-670 – Crazy Rhythm: His Debut Recordings

Single session
New York, June 26, 1957

Goodbye Baby
The Right Kind of Woman

Decca 9-30390

Let Yourself Go
New York, August 15, 1957

Let Yourself Go

Decca DL8632 – Let Yourself Go

Unreleased recordings
Unknown orchestra.
New York, 1957

The Nearness of You
Fever
Blue Star
The Japanese Farewell Song
Honky Tonk
Malagena
Send for Me
Dream
Ol' Man River

The Next Time You See Me
Since I Fell for You
Midnight Earl

Originally scheduled for Decca DL8672 (reassigned)

Unreleased recordings
Unknown orchestra
New York, 1957

What Is There to Say
Why Shouldn't I?
Love Me
Bewitched
I Could Have Told You
For All We Know
Deep in a Dream
I Get Along Without You Very Well
Mam'selle
Try a Little Tenderness
This Love of Mine
I've Got a Crush on You

Originally scheduled for Decca DL8676 (reassigned)

Unreleased recordings
Unknown orchestra
New York, 1957

I Got a Right to Sing the Blues
My Ideal
Why Don't I Get Wise to Myself
I'm Glad for Your Sake
I Love You
A Tree in the Meadow
I Like the Sunrise
There Is No Greater Love
I Can't Escape from You
I'll Be Around
I Surrender Dear
It's the Talk of the Town

Originally scheduled for Decca DL8697 (reassigned)

Single session
Arr Evelyn Roberts, with her Singers (bv); Plas Johnson (ts); Irving Ashby, Renee Hall (g); Ted Brinson (b); Earl Palmer (d)
Capitol Studios, Vine Street, Los Angeles, June 13, 1958

I'll Never be Free (unreleased)
Makin' Whoopee (unreleased)
Looking for Somebody [a]
Don't Cry My Love [b]
Daddy Must Be a Man [a]

[a] *Capitol F4021*
[b] *Capitol F4088*

Single session
Arr Jack Marshall (g); Evelyn Roberts Singers (bv); Kathryn Julye (harp); Gerry Wiggins (org); Art Shapiro (b); Milt Holland (d)
Capitol Studios, Vine Street, Los Angeles, October 7, 1958

Don't Cry My Love (unreleased)
Blacksmith Blues [c]
Belong to Me [b]

[b] *Capitol F4088*
[c] *Capitol CDP 7243 8 33147 2 0 – The Best of Mark Murphy: The Capitol Years*

Sessions Live: Candoli Brothers/Mark Murphy/ Leroy Vinnegar (Stars of Jazz)
Pete Candoli, Conte Candoli (tp); Jimmy Rowles (p); Howard Roberts (g); Red Mitchell (b); Mel Lewis (d)
ABC Studios, Los Angeles, November 24, 1958

That Old Black Magic
Body and Soul

Calliope COL 3025 – Sessions Live

This Could Be the Start of Something
Arr/cond Bill Holman. Stu Williamson, Al Porcino, Lee Katzman (tp); Dick Kenney (tb); Ronnie Lang (fl, as); Richie Kamuca (ts); Jimmy Rowles (p); Bobby Gibbons (g); Joe Mondragon (b); Mel Lewis (d); Charlie Mejia (perc)
Capitol Studios, Vine Street, Los Angeles, December 1, 1958

(medley)
That Old Black Magic [b]
Cheek to Cheek [b]
Jersey Bounce [b]
Sweet Georgia Brown [a] [b]
Lucky in Love [a] [b]
Hit the Road to Dreamland [a] [b]
For Me and My Gal

Arr/cond Bill Holman (ts); Pete Candoli, Conte Candoli (tp); Richie Kamuca (ts); Jimmy Rowles (p); Bobby Gibbons (g); Joe Mondragon (b); Mel Lewis (d); unknown (perc)

Same location, December 15, 1958
This Could Be the Start of Something [a] [b]
Day in – Day Out [b]
The Lady is a Tramp
Mighty Like a Rose [a]
Falling in Love with Love
Just in Time

Capitol T-1177 – This Could Be the Start of Something
[a] *Capitol PRO 1045/1046 (mono promo EP)*
[b] *Capitol CDP 7243 8 33147 2 0 – The Best of Mark Murphy: The Capitol Years*

Mark Murphy's Hip Parade
Prod Tom Morgan, arr/cond Bill Holman (ts); Conte
Candoli, Pete Candoli (tp); Jimmy Rowles (p); Bob
Gibbons (g); Joe Mondragon (b); Stan Levey (d)
Capitol Studios, Vine Street, Los Angeles, August 24,
1959

It's Not for Me to Say
Send for Me [a]
All the Way
Kansas City [b]

Prod Tom Morgan, arr/cond Bill Holman. Lee
Katzman, Conte Candoli (tp); Larry Bunker (vbs, perc);
Jimmy Rowles (p); Bob Gibbons (g); Joe Mondragon
(b); Mel Lewis (d); Gloria Wood, Jud Conlon Singers
(bv) where indicated.
Capitol Studios, Vine Street, Los Angeles, August 26,
1959.

Personality (GW, JCS bv)
Venus (GW, JCS bv)
I Only Have Eyes for You [b]
Lonesome Town (MM v, JM b, GW bv only)

Prod Tom Morgan, arr/cond Bill Holman (bs); Conte
Candoli (tp, perc); Pete Candoli (tp); Larry Bunker
(vbs, perc); Jimmy Rowles (p); Bob Gibbons (g); Joe
Mondragon (b); Mel Lewis (d); Gloria Wood, Jud
Conlon Singers (bv) where indicated.
Capitol Studios, Vine Street, Los Angeles, August 28,
1959.

Firefly (GW, JCS bv)
Catch a Falling Star (GW, JCS bv)
Come To Me [a]
Witchcraft [b]

Capitol T-1299 – Mark Murphy's Hip Parade
[a] *Capitol 45-CL 15117* (UK mono promo single)
[b] *Capitol CDP 7243 8 33147 2 0 – The Best of Mark
Murphy: The Capitol Years*

Playing the Field
Prod Tom Morgan, arr/cond Bill Holman. Conte
Candoli, Ray Triscari, Stu Williamson, Al Porcino
(tp); Frank Rosolino, Lou McCreary, Bob Fitzpatrick
(tb); Joe Maini, Al Thomson (as); Med Flory, Bill
Perkins (ts); Jack Nimitz (bs); Jimmy Rowles (p); Al
Hendrickson (g); Joe Mondragon (b); Shelly Manne (d)
Los Angeles, July 5 and 7, 1960

Put the Blame on Mame [a]
Swinging on a Star [a]
My Gal's Come Back
Playing the Field [a]
Heart and Soul
Love is a Many-Splendored Thing
Honeysuckle Rose
Isn't It About Time

Wishing [a]
As Long as I Live [a]
I Didn't Know About You [a]
But Not for Me

Capitol T-1458 – Playing the Field
[a] *Capitol CDP 7243 8 33147 2 0 – The Best of Mark
Murphy: The Capitol Years*

Rah
Prod Orrin Keepnews, arr/cond Ernie Wilkins. Clark
Terry, Blue Mitchell (tp); Wynton Kelly (p); Art Davis
(b); Jimmy Cobb (d)
Plaza Sound, New York, September 15, 1961

Doodlin'
Twisted
Milestones [b]

Prod Orrin Keepnews, arr/cond Ernie Wilkins. Bernie
Glow, Ernie Royal, Joe Wilder (tp); Jimmy Cleveland,
Urbie Green (tb); Wynton Kelly (p); Barry Galbraith
(g); George Duvivier (b); Jimmy Cobb (d).
Plaza Sound, New York, September 19, 1961

Spring Can Really Hang You Up the Most
Green Dolphin Street
Angel Eyes [a]
No Tears for Me

Prod Orrin Keepnews, arr/cond Ernie Wilkins. Clark
Terry, Ernie Royal, Joe Wilder (tp); Jimmy Cleveland,
Urbie Green (tb); Wynton Kelly (p); Barry Galbraith
(g); George Duvivier (b); Jimmy Cobb (d); Ray Barretto
(perc).
Plaza Sound, New York, September 22, 1961

Li'l Darlin'
Stoppin' the Clock [a]
*I'll Be Seeing You [c]

Prod Orrin Keepnews, arr/cond Ernie Wilkins. Clark
Terry, Ernie Royal, Ernie Royal (tp); Jimmy Cleveland,
Melba Liston (tb); Bill Evans (p); Sam Herman (g);
Wendell Marshall (b); Jimmy Cobb (d); Ray Barretto
(perc).
Plaza Sound, New York, October 16, 1961

Out of This World
My Favorite Things
*My Favorite Things (alt version) [d]

* withdrawn after initial release
Riverside RLP 9395; Fantasy OCJ 141 – Rah
[a] *Riverside R-4511* (single)
[b] *Riverside SE-2066 – The Compositions of Miles Davis
(EP); RLP 3504 – The Compositions of Miles Davis (LP)*
[c d] *Riverside/Milestone SMJ 6064 (Japan)*
[d] *Riverside UCCO-9460 (Japan)*

Various Artists: Everybody's Doin' the Bossa Nova
Orchestra cond Al Cohn.
New York, 1962

> Like Love
> Fly Away My Sadness

Riverside 106905 RIF or R 4537 (single)
Riverside RM 3521 – Everybody's Doin' the Bossa Nova
Not Now Music NOT3CD217 – The Very Best of Latin
Jazz

Single session
Probably New York, 1962

> Come and Get Me
> Love

Riverside R-4519
Riverside/Keepnews Collection RLP 9395 – Rah

Single session
Probably New York, 1962

> Why Don't You Do Right?
> Fly Me to the Moon

Riverside R-4526
Riverside/Keepnews Collection RLP 9395 – Rah

That's How I Love the Blues!
Prod Orrin Keepnews, cond Al Cohn. Nick Travis,
Clark Terry or Snooky Young (tp); Bernie Leighton
or Dick Hyman (org); Roger Kellaway (p); Jim Hall
(g); Ben Tucker (b); Dave Bailey (d); Willie Rodriguez
(perc)
Plaza Sound, New York October 1, December 26 &
27, 1962

> Going to Chicago Blues
> Señor Blues
> That's How I Love the Blues
> Jelly Jelly Blues
> (I'm Left with the) Blues in My Heart
> Fiesta in Blue
> Rusty Dusty Blues
> Blues in the Night
> The Meaning of the Blues
> Everybody's Crazy 'Bout the Doggone Blues
> Blues, You're the Mother of Sin
> Wee Baby Blues

Riverside RS 9441 – That's How I Love The Blues!

Single session
Probably New York, 1962 or 1963

> I Don't Worry About You

> Nothin' But a Fool

Riverside RF 4565

Mark Time! (UK)/A Swingin' Singin' Affair (US)
Orchestra cond Les Reed (p); Tommy Whittle, Roy
Willox, Bill Skeat (fl); Vic Flick or Joe Moretti (g);
Frank Clark (b), Ronnie Verrell (d); unknown strings
and harp.
Probably Philips Studios, Stanhope Place, London W1,
April 8, 1964

> My Foolish Heart
> Happy Days are Here Again
> I'll Be Around
> Come Rain or Come Shine

Orchestra cond Tubby Hayes (vbs?) Kenny Baker, Stan
Roderick, Stan Foster, Eddie Blair (tp); Don Lusher,
Jackie Armstrong (tb); possibly Les Reed (p, org); Vic
Flick, Joe Moretti (g); Frank Clark (b), Ronnie Verrell (d)
Same location, April 9, 1964

> She Loves You
> Iceberg
> Hard-Hearted Hannah (The Vamp of Savannah)
> The Best is Yet to Come

Orchestra cond John Dankworth (as). Kenny Baker,
Stan Roderick, Stan Foster, Eddie Blair (tp); Don
Lusher, Jackie Armstrong (tb); Tommy Whittle, Roy
Willox, Bill Skeat (r); possibly Les Reed (p); Vic Flick or
Joe Moretti (g); Frank Clark (b), Ronnie Verrell (d) +
other unknown musicians?
Same location, April 10, 1964

> Ballyhoo
> I Left My Heart in San Francisco
> Stablemates
> From Time to Time

Fontana TL5217 – Mark Time! (UK) *[US title: A*
Swingin' Singin' Affair]

Single session
London, probably 1964

> And Now You've Gone
> Midnight Train

Fontana TF 489 (UK)

Single session
London, probably 1965

> High on a Windy Hill
> Broken Heart

Fontana TF 572 (UK)

Who Can I Turn To?
Arr/cond Kenny Napper (b); Kenny Baker (tp), Tony
Coe (ts), Alan Branscombe (p), probably Alan Ganley
(d) + others unknown
Probably Philips Studios, London, 1966

Who Can I Turn to?
I Wanna Be Around
What Makes a Girl
Cotton Fields
A Wonderful Day Like Today
You'd Better Love Me
There Is a Time (Le Temps)
My Kind of Girl
This Train
Star Sounds
In Love for the Very First Time
Talk to Me Baby

Immediate IMLP 004 – Who Can I Turn To? (UK)

Single session
London, probably 1967

Ain't That Just Like a Woman
Do You Wonder If I Love You

Fontana TF 803 (UK)

Various Artists: Mezinárodní Jazzovy Praha 1967
Gordon Beck (p); Jeff Clyne (b); Tony Oxley (d).
Recorded live in Prague, Concert Lucerna Hall,
October 17–21, 1967

Stompin' at the Savoy

*Suprafon, Gramofonovy Club SUA 015 0414
– Mezinárodní Jazzový Festival Praha 1967*
(Czechoslovakia)

Midnight Mood
Prod Gigi Campi, arr Francy Boland (p). Jimmy
Deuchar (tp); Åke Persson (tb); Derek Humble (as);
Sahib Shihab (fl); Ronnie Scott (ts); Jimmy Woode (b);
Kenny Clarke (d)
Lindström Studios, Cologne, December 18, 1967

Jump for Joy
I don't Want Nothin'
Why and How
Alone Together
You Fascinate Me So
Hopeless
Sconsolato
My Ship
Just Give Me Time
I Get Along Without You Very Well

SABA SB 15 151 ST – Midnight Mood (Germany)

**Mark Murphy and the Metropole Orchestra:
The Dream**
Prod Joop de Roo/Jerry van Rooyen (arr) and Dolf van
der Linden (cond)
NOB Audio Productions, Hilversum, Holland, January
14, 1969

Hopeless

Jive 2006-2 – The Dream (Austria)

This Must Be Earth
Prod Ken Barnes, assoc Eddie O'Sullivan. Unknown
band, arr/cond Ken Moule,
London, 1969

This Must Be Earth
Cinnamon and Clove
Scarborough Fair
Make Me Rainbows
Misty Roses
Dock of the Bay
What a Wonderful World
Both Sides Now
A Girl I Used to Know
Salt Sea
Let the Rest of the World Go By

Phoenix PMS 1001 – This Must Be Earth (UK)

Single session
London, probably 1969

Come Back to Me
Dear Heart

Pye 7N 17661 (UK)

Various Artists: MPS Jazz Concert '69
Larry Vuckovich (p); Jimmy Woode (b); Kenny Clare (d)
Recorded live in Bremen, Germany, April 11, 1969

C C Rider
Broadway

Center G17048 – MPS Jazz Concert '69

Various Artists: Polish Jazz Vol. 20
Arne Forchhammer (p); Erik Moseholm (b); Jorn Elniff
(d)
Recorded live in Warsaw, October 1969

Broadway

*Polskie Nagrania SXL 0569 – Polish Jazz Vol. 20 Jazz
Jambore '69 – New Faces*
JVR-006 – Polish All Stars Jazz Jamboree '69 (CD
reissue by Polish jazz magazine Jazzi, included with
January 2000 issue)

Mark Murphy and the Louis Van Dyke Trio: North Sea Jazz Sessions Vol. 5
Prod Joop de Roo. Louis Van Dyke (p); Jaques Schols (b); John Engels (d)
VARA Studios, Hilversum, Holland, February 14, 1970

Stolen Moments
Con Alma
The Windmills of Your Mind [a]

As above, September 3, 1970

Bridges
Norwegian Wood
The Lady Is a Tramp [a]

As above, June 3, 1971

I Remember Clifford
Summertime [a]
The Great City

As above, February 9, 1972

As Long as I Live

Jazz World JWD 102.205 – North Sea Jazz Sessions Vol. 5 (Portugal)
[a] *Sonorama S-15 – Happy Samba (EP – Germany)*

Mark Murphy and the Metropole Orchestra: The Dream
Prod Joop de Roo, NOB Audio Productions, Hilversum, Holland, February 9, 1972

So Many Stars

Jive 2006-2 – The Dream (Austria)

Bridging a Gap
Arr David Matthews. Randy Brecker (tp); Michael Brecker (ts); Pat Rebillot (kyb); Sam Brown (g); Ron Carter (b); Jimmy Madison (d)
Basement Studios, New York, November 20 & 21, 1972

Come and Get Me [b]
Sausalito [d]
She's Gone
Steamroller [c]
We Could Be Flying [c]
Sunday in New York [d]
Gee Baby Ain't I Good to You [b]
No More [c]
As Time Goes By [c]
I'm Glad There Is You [a]

Muse MR 5009 – Bridging a Gap
[a] *32Jazz 32036 – Stolen... and Other Moments*
[b] *32Jazz 32063 – Jazz Standards*
[c] *32Jazz 32105 – Songbook*
[d] *32Jazz 32137 – Mark Murphy Sings Nat King Cole... and More*

Mark Murphy and the Louis Van Dyke Trio: North Sea Jazz Sessions, Vol. 5
Louis Van Dyke (p); Jacques Schols (b); John Engels (d).
VARA Studios, Hilversum, Holland, January 9, 1973

He Ain't Heavy, He's My Brother

Jazz World JWD 102.205 – North Sea Jazz Sessions Vol. 5 (Portugal)

Mark II
Prod Helen Keane/arr David Matthews. Ken Ascher (keys); Sam Brown, John Tropea (g); Michael Moore (b); Jimmy Madison (d); Sue Evans (perc)
Probably Basement Studio, New York, December 19–21, 1973.

Chicken Road [c]
Too Much Love
The Unfaithful Servant
Lookin' for Another Pure Love [a]
Barandgrill [c]
Triad [b]
They [c]
Sleeping
Lemme Blues
Truckin'

Muse MR 5041 – Mark II
[a] *32Jazz 32036 – Stolen... and Other Moments*
[b] *32Jazz 32105 – Songbook*
[c] *32Jazz 32137 – Mark Murphy Sings Nat King Cole... and More*

Mark Murphy and the Louis Van Dyke Trio: North Sea Jazz Sessions, Vol. 5
Louis Van Dyke (p); Jacques Schols (b); John Engels (d).
VARA Studios, Hilversum, Holland, February 13, 1974

Happy Samba [a]
Love Sick
'S Wonderful

Jazz World JWD 102.205 – North Sea Jazz Sessions Vol. 5 (Portugal)
[a] *Sonorama S-15 Happy Samba (EP – Germany)*

Mark Murphy and the Metropole Orchestra: The Dream
NOB Audio Productions, Hilversum, Holland, 13 February, 1974

When the World Was Young

As above, December 12, 1974

All in Love Is Fair

Jive 2006-2 – The Dream (Austria)

Herb Geller: An American in Hamburg (Germany)/ Rhyme and Reason (US)
Herb Geller (ss, as, ts, fl); Palle Mikkelborg (tp); Wolfgang Schluter (vbs); Rob Franken, Gottfried Boettger (kyb); Philip Catherine (g); Hans-Lucas Lindholm (b); Alex Riel (d)
Windrose Studio, Hamburg, Germany; January 13, 1975

>   Sudden Senility
>   The Power of a Smile
>   Space à la Mode

Nova 6.2832 DX – An American in Hamburg: The View From Here (Germany, double album)
Atlantic SD-1681 – Rhyme and Reason (USA, single album)

Metropole Orchestra: Plays the Music of Harold Arlen
Ack van Rooyen (tp, fgl); Piet Noordijk (ss, as, cl) + unknown others.
Oslo, 1975

>   Out of This World
>   Let's Fall in Love (with Greetje Kauffeld)
>   Come Rain or Come Shine
>   Get Happy (with Greetje Kauffeld)
>   My Shining Hour (with Greetje Kauffeld)
>   Blues in the Night
>   Between the Devil and the Deep Blue Sea (with Greetje Kauffeld)
>   Medley: This Time the Dream's on Me/Ill Wind (with Greetje Kauffeld)
>   Last Night When We Were Young
>   I've Got the World on a String
>   That Old Black Magic (with Greetje Kauffeld)

Sonorama G C-16 – Plays the Music of Harold Arlen (CD)

Mark Murphy Sings
Prod Helen Keane, arr Dave Matthews. Randy Brecker (tp); David Sanborn (as); Michael Brecker (ts); Don Grolnik (kyb); Joe Puma (g); Harvie S (as Harvey Swartz) (b); Jimmy Madison (d); Sue Evans (perc)
Basement Studio, NYC, June 17–19, 1975

>   On the Red Clay [a]
>   Naima [b]
>   Body and Soul [c]
>   Young and Foolish [a]
>   Empty Faces [a]
>   Maiden Voyage [b]
>   How Are You Dreaming? [c]
>   Canteloupe Island [a]

Muse MR 5078 – Mark Murphy Sings
[a] *32Jazz 32036 – Stolen... and Other Moments*
[b] *32Jazz 32063 – Jazz Standards*
[c] *32Jazz 32105 – Songbook*

Mark Murphy Sings Mostly Dorothy Fields and Cy Coleman
Prod/cond Dick Phipps. Loonis McGlohon Trio – arranged by Loonis McGlohon (p); Terry Lassiter (b); Jim Lackey (d)
Dick Phipps's Music Room, Lake Murray, Lexington, South Carolina, September 1977.

>   I Love My Wife
>   I'm Gonna Laugh You Right Out of My Life
>   When in Rome
>   On Second Thought
>   Seesaw
>   I Walk a Little Faster
>   That's My Style
>   Don't Blame Me
>   Remind Me
>   I'm in the Mood for Love
>   A Fine Romance
>   April Fooled Me
>   Alone Too Long
>   I'm Way Ahead
>   Witchcraft *
>   When Yesterday I Loved You *
>   Where am I Going? *
>   Walking Sad *
>   Exactly Like You *
>   Rules of the Road *
>   The Best Is Yet to Come *
>   Real Live Girl *
>   Sometimes When You're Lonely *
>   Doodlin' *
>   Lovely to Look at *

Audiophile AP 132 – Mark Murphy Sings Dorothy Fields and Cy Coleman
*Audiophile ACD 132 – Mark Murphy Sings Mostly Dorothy Fields and Cy Coleman (CD – additional tracks)

Stolen Moments
Prod/arr Mitch Farber. Warren Gale (tp); Mark Levine (vtb); Richie Cole (as); Smith Dobson (p); Jim Nichols (g, eb); Chuck Metcalf or Paul Breslin (as noted) (b), Vince Lateano (d); Jack Gobetti (perc)

Filmways/Helder Studio, San Francisco, June 1, 1978

>   Stolen Moments [a]
>   Again (PB b) [c]
>   Farmer's Market [b]
>   D.C. Farewell (PB b) [d]
>   Waters of March [a]
>   Sly (PB b) [b]
>   We'll Be Together Again (PB b) [c]
>   Don't Be Blue [c]
>   Like a Lover (O Cantador) [a]

Muse MR 5102 – Stolen Moments
[a] *32Jazz 32036 – Stolen... and Other Moments*
[b] *32Jazz 32063 – Jazz Standards*

^c *32Jazz 32105 – Songbook*
^d *32Jazz 32137 – Mark Murphy Sings Nat King Cole…
and More*

Satisfaction Guaranteed

Prod/arr Mitch Farber. Tom Harrell (tp); Slide
Hampton (tb); Richie Cole (as); Ronnie Cuber (bs);
Mike Renzi (p); Gene Bertoncini (g); Mark Egan (b);
Jimmy Madison (d); Ray Mantilla (perc) as noted.
Nola Recording Studio, New York, November 21, 1979

> Satisfaction Guaranteed ^a
> Eleanor Rigby ^c
> Medley: Don't Go to Strangers/Don't
>   Misunderstand ^c
> Bijou (RM perc) ^b
> All the Things You Are ^c
> Welcome Home ^d
> Waltz for Debby ^b
> I Return to Music ^d

Muse 5215 – Satisfaction Guaranteed
^a *32Jazz 32036 – Stolen… and Other Moments*
^b *32Jazz 32063 – Jazz Standards*
^c *32Jazz 32105 – Songbook*
^d *32Jazz 32137 – Mark Murphy Sings Nat King Cole…
and More*

College of the Siskiyous Choir with guest artist
Mark Murphy

28–29 January, 1980

> A Tribute to Duke [Solitude]
> Stolen Moments

KM 4842

Wild and Free

Paul Potyen (p); Peter Barshay (b); Jack Gobetti (d);
Babatunde Lea (perc)
Recorded live at Keystone Korner, San Francisco, June
1980

> I Return to Music
> Farmer's Market
> Medley: It Might as Well Be Spring/Spring Can
>   Really Hang You Up the Most
> Stompin' at the Savoy
> You Fascinate Me So
> Bijou
> Fiesta in Blue
> Body and Soul
> Waters of March
> Medley: Laugh Clown Laugh/Send in the Clowns
> Charleston Alley
> Blues in the Night
> I've Got You Under My Skin
> Don't Be Blue

HighNote HCD7310 – Mark Murphy Wild and Free

Bop for Kerouac

Prod/arr/cond Bill Mays (kyb); Richie Cole (as, ts);
Bruce Forman (g); Bob Magnusson, Luther Hughes (b);
Roy McCurdy, Jeff Hamilton (d); Michael Spiro (perc)
Sage and Sound Studios, Hollywood, March 12, 1981

> Be-bop Lives (Boplicity) ^a
> Goodbye Pork Pie Hat ^b
> Parker's Mood ^a
> You'd Better Go Now ^c
> You've Proven Your Point (Bongo Beep) ^a
> The Bad and the Beautiful ^c
> Down St Thomas Way ^d
> Ballad of the Sad Young Men ^a

Muse MR 5253 – Bop for Kerouac
^a *32Jazz 32036 – Stolen… and Other Moments*
^b *32Jazz 32063 – Jazz Standards*
^c *32Jazz 32105 – Songbook*
^d *32Jazz 32137 – Mark Murphy Sings Nat King Cole…
and More*

Jeff Hamilton Quintet: Indiana

Lanny Morgan (as); Bob Cooper (ts); Biff Hannon (p);
John Clayton (b); Jeff Hamilton (d).
San Francisco, January 1982

> Split Season Blues

Concord CJ 187 – Indiana

Mark Murphy and the Metropole Orchestra:
The Dream

Rob Pronk (arr).
NOB Audio Productions, Hilversum, Holland,
February 2, 1982

> (I'll Build a) Stairway to Paradise

Jive 2006-2 – The Dream (Austria)

The Artistry of Mark Murphy

Prod/arr Dave Matthews. Tom Harrell (tp, fgl); Gerry
Niewood (r); Ben Aronov (kyb); Gene Bertoncini (g);
George Mraz (b) or Mark Egan (eb) as noted; Jimmy
Madison (d); Sue Evans (perc)
Sear Sound, New York, April 2 & 3, 1982

> The Odd Child (GM b) ^a
> I Don't Want to Cry Anymore (ME eb) ^a
> Moody's Mood (GM b) ^a
> Trilogy for Kids: Babe's Blues/Little Niles/Dat Dere
>   (ME eb) ^b
> I Remember Clifford ^b
> Autumn Nocturne (GM b) ^c
> Close Enough for Love ^c
> Medley: Long Ago and Far Away (Gershwin)/Long
>   Ago and Far Away (Taylor) (ME eb) ^a

Muse MR 5286 – The Artistry of Mark Murphy
^a *32Jazz 32036 – Stolen… and Other Moments*

ᵇ *32Jazz 32063 – Jazz Standards*
ᶜ *32Jazz 32105 – Songbook*

Mark Murphy featuring Viva Brasil: Brazil Song
Prod Mark Murphy/Lupe de Leon, arr Jay Wagner
(synth). Michael Austin-Boe (p); Claudio Amaral (g);
Rubens Moura Jr (d); Chalo Eduardo, Michael Spiro
(perc); Julia Stewart (bv) as noted
Russian Hill Recording, San Francisco, March 21 & 22,
and August 2 & 4, 1983

> Desafinado ᵇ
> Two Kites ᵃ
> The Island ᵇ
> Bolero de Sata (JS bv)
> She
> Someone to Light Up My Life (Se Todos Fossem
>   Iguais A Voce) ᵃ
> Nothing Will Be As It Was Tomorrow ᵇ
> October (Outubro) (JS bv) ᵇ
> Bridges ᵇ

Muse MR 5297 – Brazil Song
ᵃ *32Jazz 32036 – Stolen... and Other Moments*
ᵇ *32Jazz 32105 – Songbook*

**Mark Murphy Sings the Nat King Cole Songbook,
Vols. 1 and 2**
Prod Mark Murphy/Steve Zegree. Gary Schunk (kyb);
Joe LoDuca (g) all vocal/instrumental duets, as noted.
(GS kyb)
Western Sound Studios, Kalamazoo, Michigan,
October 8–10, 1983

> Love Letters/Serenata (JLD g) ᵃ ᵉ
> Oh You Crazy Moon (GS kyb) ᵃ ᵉ
> 'Tis Autumn (JLD g) ᵃ ᵉ
> I Keep Going Back to Joe's (GS kyb) ᵃ ᵉ
> Lush Life (JLD g) ᵃ ᵈ
> Never Let Me Go (GS kyb) ᵃ ᵉ
> These Foolish Things (GS kyb) ᵃ ᵉ
> Don't Let Your Eyes Go Shopping (JLD g) ᵇ ᶜ ᵉ
> More Than You Know (GS kyb) ᵇ ᵉ
> Maybe You'll Be There (JLD g) ᵇ ᵉ
> Portrait of Jennie/Ruby (GS kyb) ᵇ ᵉ
> Blue Gardenia (JLD g) ᵇ ᵉ
> For All We Know (GS kyb) ᵇ ᵉ
> The End of a Love Affair (JLD g) ᵇ ᵉ

Bob Magnusson (b)
Sage & Sound Studio, Hollywood, CA, November 1,
1983

> Medley: Nature Boy/Calypso Blues ᵃ ᵉ
> Tangerine ᵃ ᵉ
> Medley: Until the Real Thing Comes Along/Baby
>   Baby All the Time ᵃ ᶜ
> Look Out for Love ᵇ ᵉ
> Medley: Walkin' My Baby Back Home/Breezin'
>   Along with the Breeze ᵇ ᵉ

ᵃ *Muse MR 5308 – Mark Murphy Sings the Nat King
Cole Songbook Volume One*
ᵇ *Muse MR 5320 – Mark Murphy Sings Nat's Choice:
The Nat King Cole Songbook Volume Two*
ᶜ *32Jazz 32036 – Stolen... and Other Moments*
ᵈ *32Jazz 32063 – Jazz Standards*
ᵉ *32Jazz 32137 – Mark Murphy Sings Nat King Cole...
and More*

**Mark Murphy and the Metropole Orchestra:
The Dream**
Orchestra includes Piet Noordijk (as); Rob Pronk (arr);
Dolf van der Linden (cond)
NOB Audio Productions, Hilversum, Holland, October
19, 1983

> Since I Fell for You
> Down Here on the Ground

Jive 2006-2 – The Dream (Austria)

Bobbe Norris: Close-Up/Out of Nowhere
Larry Dunlap (kyb, arr); Frank Tusa (b); Bobbe Norris
(v)
Menlo Park, CA, Dec 4, 1983

> My Baby Likes to Bebop (duet) ᵃ
> Invitation (duet) ᵇ

ᵃ *Céleste CMY 6147 – CloseUp (Japanese release only)*
ᵇ *Four Directions FDR-2004 – Out of Nowhere*

Living Room
Prod Mark Murphy/David Braham (org, kyb); Ted
Curson (tp, fgl); Gerry Niewood (ts, fl); Harry Leahy
(g); Jimmy Lewis (b), Ed Caccavale (d); Grady Tate (d,
v on "Midnight Sun" only; Caccavale (d) on all other
tracks); Lawrence Killian (perc)
Van Gelder Recording Studio, Englewood Cliffs, NJ,
December 10–21, 1984

> Living Room ᵃ
> Our Love Rolls on
> LA Song Circle: LA/LA Breakdown/The Way It
>   Was in LA ᵇ
> There'll be Some Changes Made
> Ain't Nobody Here But Us Chickens ᵃ
> Medley: Misty/Midnight Sun ᵃ
> Charleston Alley ᵃ
> Full Moon
> Maxine ᵇ

Muse MR 5345 – Living Room
ᵃ *32Jazz 32063 – Jazz Standards*
ᵇ *32Jazz 32137 – Mark Murphy Sings Nat King Cole...
and More*

Blossom Dearie: Chez Walberg Part One, Vol. 9
San Francisco, summer 1985

> Love Dance (duet)

Just Being Here (duet)

Daffodil BMD 109 – Chez Walberg Part One, Vol. 9

Beauty and the Beast
Prod/arr/cond Bill Mays (kyb). Brian Lynch (tp, fgl); Lou Lausche (vln); Steve LaSpina or Michael Formanek, as noted (b); Joey Baron (d)
Classic Sound Studio, New York, September 10 & 11, 1985

> Beauty and the Beast [b]
> I Can't Get Started (MF b) [d]
> Doxy [c]
> Effendi [c]
> The Lady Who Sang the Blues (MF b)
> Along Came Betty [c]
> *Spring Friend (MF b) [a e]
> *Memphis Blues (MF b) [a]

Brian Lynch (tp); Bill Mays (kyb); Lou Lausche (vln); Mike Formanek (b); Joey Baron (d)
Classic Sound Studio, New York, November 23, 1986

> Poem: Beauty and the Beast
> Vocalise

* omitted from original release
Muse 5355 – Beauty and the Beast
[a] *Vogue VG 651 600606 (France) – Beauty and the Beast*
[b] *32Jazz 32036 – Stolen... and Other Moments*
[c] *32Jazz 32063 – Jazz Standards*
[d] *32Jazz 32105 – Songbook*
[e] *32Jazz 32137 – Mark Murphy Sings Nat King Cole... and More*

Mark Murphy, Azymuth, Claudio Roditi, Frank Morgan: Night Mood
Prod Richard Bock, assoc prod Lupe DeLeon, arr Jose Roberto Bertrami (kyb, bv); Azymuth: Alex Malheiros (eb, perc, bv); Ivan 'Mamao' Conti (d, perc, bv); Frank Morgan (as); Claudio Roditi (tp, fgl); Maria Marquez, Claudia Gomez (bv)
Fantasy Studios, Berkeley, CA, June–August 1986

> Nightmood (Lembra)
> Madalena
> Ticket (Bilhete)
> Dinorah Dinorah
> Before We Lose Tomorrow (Antes Que Seja Tarde)
> Sails (Velas Içadas)
> Love Dance (Lembrança)
> Mãos de Afeto
> Believe What I Say (Daquilo Que Eu Sei)

Milestone MCD-9145-2 – Night Mood: The Music of Ivan Lins

Kerouac, Then and Now
Prod John Goldsby (b), arr Bill Mays (kyb); Steve LaSpina or John Goldsby, as noted (b); Adam Nussbaum (d)
Hillside Studio, Englewood Cliffs, NJ, November, 1986

> Blood Count (JG b) [a]
> Medley: Eddie Jefferson/Take the A Train [a]
> Ask Me Now [b]
> San Francisco (JG b) [a]
> Lazy Afternoon [c]
> If You Could See Me Now [b]
> November in the Snow [a]
> Lord Buckley (JG b) [a]
> Medley: The Night We Called it a Day/There's No You [c]

Muse MR5359, MCD5359 – Kerouac, Then and Now
[a] *32Jazz 32036 – Stolen... and Other Moments*
[b] *32Jazz 32063 – Jazz Standards*
[c] *32Jazz 32105 – Songbook*

Ann Burton: That's All
Rob Agerbeek (p); Harry Emmery (b); Frits Landesbergen (d); Ann Burton (v)
Recorded live at Nick Vollebregt's Jazz Café, Laren, the Netherlands, April 23, 1987

> Medley: Moments Like This/My Buddy
> I Wish I Were in Love Again

Blue Jack BJJR 0221 – That's All (Japan)

September Ballads
Prod Larry Dunlap (p, v), co-prod Lupe De Leon. Art Farmer (fgl as noted); Donald Bailey (hca as noted); Bob Mocarsky (synth); Oscar Castro-Neves (as noted), Larry Coryell (g); David Belove, Jeff Carney; Scott Steed (b, as noted); Vince Lateano (d); John Santos (perc, as noted)
Fantasy Studios, Berkeley, CA, September 15–17, November 8 and 22, 1987

> September Fifteenth (OCN g, DB b, JS perc)
> When She Is Mine (AF fgl, DB hca, SS b)
> When this Love Affair is Over (DB hca, SS b)
> Night Life (DB hca, SS b)
> Sack Full of Dreams (AF fgl, JC b, JS perc)
> Crystal Silence (OCN g, DB b, JS perc)
> I Never Went Away (AF fgl, OCN g, DB b, JS perc)
> Sausalito (JC b, JS perc)
> Para Nada (OCN g, DB b, JS perc)
> Spring Is Where You Are (JC b)

Milestone M-9154 – September Ballads

Bop for Miles
Allan Praskin (ss, as); Peter Mihelich (p), Achim Tang (b); Vito Lesczach (d)
Recorded live at the Nachtkaffee, Vienna, Austria, May 10, 1990

> All Blues
> Summertime
> Autumn Leaves
> Bye Bye Blackbird
> On Green Dolphin Street
> My Ship
> Farmer's Market
> Goodbye Pork Pie Hat
> Parker's Mood
> Milestones

HighNote HCD 7126 – Bop For Miles

Various Artists: BP Club All-Stars 1991
Allan Praskin (ss, as); Peter Mihelic h (p), Achim Tang (b); Vito Lesczach (d)
Recorded live at the BP Club, Zagreb, Croatia (then Yugoslavia). Same period

> My Ship

Jazzette (Yugoslavia) BCP 11— BP Club All-Stars 1991

What a Way to Go
Prod/arr Larry Fallon (synth); Danny Wilensky (ts); Pat Rebillot (p); John Cobert (synth), David Spinozza (g); Francisco Centeno (b); Alan Schwartzberg, Chris Parker (d); John Kaye, Sammy Figueroa (perc)
Sound on Sound Studio, New York, September 1990

> What a Way to Go ^c
> Ceora Lives ^b
> I Fall in Love Too Easily ^c
> Saxophone Joe ^b
> All My Tomorrows ^c
> Jamaica (a Little Island of Calm) ^d
> I Never Noticed Until Now
> Clown in My Window
> Ding Walls ^a

Muse MCD 5419 – What a Way to Go
^a *32Jazz 32036 – Stolen... and Other Moments*
^b *32Jazz 32063 – Jazz Standards*
^c *32Jazz 32105 – Songbook*
^d *32Jazz 32137 – Mark Murphy Sings Nat King Cole... and More*

Madeline Eastman: Mad About Madeline!
Phil Woods (as); Cedar Walton (p); Tony Dumas (b); Vince Lateano (d); Madeline Eastman (v)
Berkeley, January 1991

> You're the Dangerous Type

Mad Kat MKCD 1003 – Mad About Madeline!

Various Artists: BP Club All-Stars 1991
BP Club, Zagreb, Croatia, 1991

> Señor Blues

Jazzette BPCD-011 – B.P. Club All Stars '91 (Croatia)

Sue Maskaleris: Unbreakable Heart
Big band featuring Andrew Lippman (tb); Darmon Meader (ts, v); Sue Maskaleris (p, v); Eddie Gomez (b); Lenny White (d). Murphy also contributed sound samples to this track
New York/Brazil, 1991–1998

> Scat!

Jazilian J103-71 – Unbreakable Heart

Sheila Jordan/Mark Murphy: One for Junior
Prod Sheila Jordan (v), Mark Murphy. Bill Mays (synth, p); Kenny Barron (p); Harvie S (as Harvie Swartz) (b); Ben Riley (d)
Sears Recording Studio, New York, September 23–26, 1991

> Where You at? ^a
> Medley: Round About/It All Goes Round ^c
> One for Junior
> Trust in Me ^c
> Medley: The Bird/Tribute (Quasimodo)/
>   Embraceable You ^b
> Aria 18 (BM synth, p)
> The Best Thing for You ^b
> Eastern Ballad (BM synth, p) ^c
> Medley: Don't Like Goodbyes/Difficult to Say
>   Goodbye

Muse 5489 – One For Junior
^a *32Jazz 32036 – Stolen... and Other Moments*
^b *32Jazz 32063 – Jazz Standards*
^c *32Jazz 32137 – Mark Murphy Sings Nat King Cole... and More*

Mark Murphy and the Metropole Orchestra: The Dream
Orchestra includes Cor Bakker (p); Erno Olah (vln); Rob Pronk (arr, cond)
NOB Audio Productions, Hilversum, Holland, 12 November, 1991

> Laura
> This Is New
> Sometimes When You're Lonely
> I See Your Face Before Me

Jive 2006-2 – The Dream (Austria)

I'll Close My Eyes
Prod Larry Fallon. Claudio Roditi (tp); Pat Rebillot (p); Cliff Carter (kyb); John Basile (g); Dave Finck (b); Peter Grant (d); Sammy Figueroa (perc)
Unknown studio, New York, December 16 & 17, 1991

> I'll Close My Eyes [b]
> If
> Happyin'
> Miss You Mr Mercer [b]
> Small World [c]
> There Is No Reason Why
> Time on My Hands [a]
> Ugly Woman
> Not Like This

Muse MCD 5436 – I'll Close My Eyes
[a] *32Jazz 32036 – Stolen... and Other Moments*
[b] *32Jazz 32063 – Jazz Standards*
[c] *32Jazz 32137 – Mark Murphy Sings Nat King Cole... and More*

MHS Big Band: Klangdebuts
Recorded live at Festival 'Vocal Nights', Orpheum, Graz, 9 April 1992

> Don't get Around Much Anymore
> Detour Ahead

MHS G 3 – Klangdebuts (Austria)

Balcony Big Band: Seasoned to Taste
Bill Carmichael, Skip McAuliffe (tp,fgl); Ralph Guzzi (tp, fgl, pic-tp, arr) Bob Riddle, Mark Snyder, Milt Orkin, Fran Duffy Snyder (tb) Dave Piecka (fh); Greg Grenek, Nick Dialoiso, Matt Ferrante, Vince Ruffini (r); Max Leake (p); Brian Stahurski (b, eb); H.B. Bennett (d); George Jones (perc)
Audiomation, Pittsburgh, April–July 1992

> I Concentrate on You
> My Romance
> You Don't Know What Love Is

Corona Music CD-70620 – Seasoned To Taste

George Gruntz/Allen Ginsburg: Cosmopolitan Greetings
Don Cherry (tp, ethno-inst); Andy Haderer, Rob Bruynen, Klaus Osterloh, John Marshall (tp); Ray Anderson (tb, v); Dave Horler, Ludwig Nuss, Bernt Laukamp, Roy Deuvall (tb); Howard Johnson (tu, bs, v) Heiner Wiberny, Harald Rosenstein, Olivier Peters, Rolf Romer, Steffen Schorn (r); George Gruntz (p, cond); Mike Richmond (b); Danny Gottlieb (d); Freddie Santiago, Christoph Eidens (perc); Sheila Jordan, Renee Manning (v); WDR Big Band
Kölner Philharmonie, May 26, 1992

> Funny Death
> Prophecy

7th Avenue Express Blues
Those Two and Maturity

Musikszene Schweiz MGB CD 9203 – Cosmopolitan Greetings (Switzerland – double album)

Another Vision
Prod Jack Van Poll (p); Ack Van Rooyen (flg) as noted; Turk Mauro (ts) as noted; Martin Wind (b); Hans Van Oosterhout (d)
Studio 44, Monster, Holland, July 3–4, 1992

> The Masquerade Is Over (AVR fgl)
> Medley: I Wish I Knew/A Ghost of a Chance
> The More I See You (TM ts)
> People Will Try Again
> Nobody Else But Me
> You're a Weaver of Dreams (TM ts)
> Quiet Now
> Speak Low (TM ts)
> Love Locked Out
> Medley: Pieces of Dreams/You Must Believe in Spring
> Epilogue/Never Never Land

September CD 5113 – Another Vision (Belgium)

Just Jazz
Karlheinz Miklin (r); Claus Raible (p); Ewald Oberleitner (b); Heimo Wiiderhofer (d)
Recorded live at 'Jazz' Club, Graz, Austria, 1993

> Stolen Moments
> Parker's Mood
> Along Came Betty
> Vera Cruz
> Bolero de Sata
> Going to Chicago
> Charleston Alley
> I Remember Clifford
> Prism
> Body and Soul.

Jazzette BPCD 027 – Just Jazz (Croatia)

Mark Murphy and the Metropole Orchestra: The Dream
Rob Pronk (arr, cond)
NOB Audio Productions, Hilversum, Holland, 20 May, 1993

> The Dream
> Gone
> Estate
> We Can Try Love Again

Jive 2006-2 – The Dream (Austria)

Mark Murphy and Nine: Very Early
Prod/arr Oliver Groenewald, exec prod Harry
Huber. Steve Gut (tp); Andreas Pesendorfer, Oliver
Groenewald (tp, fgl); Michael Burgbaur (tb); Marko
Lackner (as, ss); Klemens Pliem (ts, fl); Thomas
Rottleuthner (bs, bcl); Emil Spanyi (p); Thorsten
Zimmermann (b); Franz Trattner (d); Ewald Gaulhofer
(perc)
Pink Noise Recording Studio, Klagenfurt, Austria, 1993

> The Song Is You
> Early Autumn
> A Sleepin' Bee
> Without Form
> I'm All Smiles
> Duke Ellington's Sound of Love
> Love Came on Stealthy Fingers
> I Cover the Waterfront
> Very Early
> Everything Happens to Me
> Hello Young Lovers

West and East Music 220022-2 – Very Early (Austria)

**United Future Organization: No Sound is
Too Taboo**
Gil Manly (v); Mikiko Sakai (turntable)
London, 1994

> Future Light

*Brownswood Records/Talkin' Loud 522 271-2 – No
Sound Is Too Taboo* (UK)

Various Artists: Last Night When We Were Young
Fred Hersch (p)
New York, 1994

> Last Night When We Were Young

*Classical Action 1001 – Last Night When We Were
Young: The Ballad Album*

Guido Di Leone: Hearing a Rhapsody
1994

> Like Someone in Love
> The Nearness of You

Modern Times MDT 30133 – Hearing a Rhapsody
(Italy)

The Baker Boys: Facin' Our Time
Niklas Fredin (tp,v); Jan Lundgren (p); Hans Andersson
(b); Lars "Baker" Andersson (d)
Malmö, Sweden, January 29, 1995

> Angel Eyes (duet)
> Bye Bye Blackbird (duet)

Sittel SITCD 9221 – Facin' Our Time (Sweden)

Song for the Geese
Prod Charlie Ellicott, exec prod H.K. 'Bud' Miller.
Rick Mandyck (ss, ts); Marc Seales (p); Doug Miller
(b); John Bishop (d); Larry Bouleau (perc); Full Voice:
Roger Treece, Sandy Anderson, Lincoln Briney (bv)
Triad Studios, Redmond, WA, April 1995

> You Go to My Head
> Sugar
> Baltimore Oriole
> Do It Again
> (Baby) It's Just Talk
> You're Blasé
> Song for the Geese (Terna Para Los Gansos)
> Everybody Loves Me
> Lament
> I Remember
> We Two (Nos Dois)
> I Wish You Love (Que Reste-t-il De Nos Amours)

RCA Victor 74321-448652-2 – Song For The Geese

United Future Organization: United Future Airlines
London, 1995

> Stolen Moments (UFO Remix)

Talkin' Loud TLKX 54 – United Future Airlines (EP)

Mark Murphy/Benny Green: Dim the Lights
Prod Kirk N. Loeffler. Benny Green (p)
Calgary, early 1996

> Your Red Wagon
> Rules of the Road
> Street of Dreams
> Medley: Beautiful Love/Lullaby of the Leaves
> Softly as in a Morning Sunrise
> A Quiet Place
> Dim the Lights
> See You Later
> Two Lonely People
> It Amazes Me
> North Sea Night
> Time All Gone
> Medley: I Never Know When to Say When/I'm in
>   Love Again
> Medley: Ravel Concerto/How Insensitive/Corvocado
> The Man on the Other Side of the Street

Millennium MILCD 001 – Dim the Lights (Canada)

Fernando Correa: Em Contraste
Lilian a Bollos (p); Fernando Correa (g, v); Ewald
Oberleitner (b); Duskan Norakor (d)
Maribor, Slovenia, April 13–14, 1996

> Where Could Love Have Gone?
> Time All Gone
> Lilianne

LiCord Music 964-01 – Em Contraste (Austria)

Shadows
Exec prod Peter Schmidlin. Karlheinz Miklin (r); Fritz
Pauer (p); Ewald Oberleitner (b); Dusan Novakov (d)
Studio RTV, Maribor, Slovenia, June 12–13, 1996

> Dawn
> If I Should Lose You
> Empty Room
> Next Page
> Lilac Wine
> Hodnik
> Shadows
> Humanity Ltd

TCB 33802 – Shadows (Switzerland)

Rinaldo Donati: Jardim Botanico Oceanico
Rinaldo Donati (g, synth, v); Marco Brioschi (tp, flg);
Antonio Zambrini (p); Jochen Stendel (kyb); Tito
Mangialajo (b); Carlo Virzi (d); Kal dos Santos (perc)
Maxine's Studio, Milan, Italy, 1996

> Nata
> Jardim Botanico (Oceanico)
> Nos Otros Tambem
> Aguaviva

Maxine MXN 0033 – Jardim Botanico Oceanico (Italy
– double CD)

Edouard Ferlet: Escale
Claus Stotter (tp, fgl); Simon Spang-Hanssen (ss, ts);
Gary Brunton (b); Gregor Hilbe (d)
Paris, June 24 & 25, 1996

> K do en poins au nez (Sweet Poison)

Quoi de Neuf Doctor DOC 041 – Escale

Barbra Sfraga: Oh, What a Thrill
David Berkman (p); Bruce Saunders (g); John Hébert
(b); Eric Halvorson (d)
Acoustic Recording, New York, June 17, 1998

> I'll Call You

Naxos Jazz 86047-2 – Oh, What a Thrill (Germany)

Ellen Hoffman: Daydreams
Ellen Hoffman (p)
Oakland, CA, November 22, 1998

> Day Dream

No label or number – *Daydreams*

Bop for Miles
Prod Joe Fields. Peter Mihelich (p)
M&I Studio, NYC, July 30, 1999

> Miles

HighNote HCD 7126 – Bop For Miles

Some Time Ago
Prod Don Sickler, arr Lee Musiker (p); Dave Ballou
(tp); Allen Mesquida (as); Sean Smith, Steve LaSpina
(b); Winard Harper (d)
M&I Recording Studios, New York, December 1999

> There's No More Blue Time
> Peacocks
> Bohemia After Dark
> With Every Breath I Take
> You're My Alter Ego
> Life's Mosaic
> Some Time Ago
> That Old Black Magic
> Why Was I Born/I'm a Fool to Want You

HighNote HCD 7048 – Some Time Ago

The Latin Porter
Prod Leo Sidran. Tom Harrell (tp); Al Bent (tb); Peter
Schimke (p); Mark Van Wageningen (b); Daniel
Gonzalez (d); Esther Godinez (perc)
Dakota Bar, St. Paul, Minnesota, January 19 & 20, 2000

> I Get a Kick Out of You
> In the Still of the Night
> Dream Dancing
> Get Out of Town
> Looking at You
> I've Got You Under My Skin
> All of You
> Everything I Love
> Experimental
> Confluence

GoJazz GO 6051-2 – The Latin Porter (Germany)
GoJazz GO 6047-2 – The Latin Porter

**Tenth and Parker featuring Mark Murphy:
Kool Down**
Fantasy Studios, Berkeley, CA, 2000

> Kool Down (4 different mixes)

Disorient SUSHI 23 – Kool Down (EP – UK)

Various Artists: Something Wonderful
Prod Tim Weston, arr Nan Schwartz

> This Nearly Was Mine

*WHD Entertainment 622800 – Something Wonderful:
Rodgers and Hammerstein Tribute Album*

Links
Arr Lee Musiker (p); Dave Ballou (tp); Allen Mezquida (as); Steve LaSpina or Sean Smith (b); Winard Harper or Tim Horner (d); Memo Acevedo (perc)
M&I Recording Studios, New York, December 27 & 28, 2000

    In the Land of Oo-Bla-Dee
    The Lady's in Love with You
    Don't Ask Why
    Wheelers and Dealers
    Taming of a Rose
    Breathing
    A Flower is a Lovesome Thing
    Ode to the Road
    Medley: Daydream/In a Sentimental Mood
    I'm Through with Love

HighNote HCD 7077 – Links

Tenth and Parker featuring Mark Murphy: Disorient Sushi 25
Fantasy Studios, Berkeley, CA, 2001

    Millennium Riddle Song (2 versions)

Disorient Sushi 25 (UK single)

4 Hero: Creating Patterns
Dollis Hill Studio, London, 2001

    Twelve Tribes

Talkin' Loud 5862122 – Creating Patterns (Australia)

Live in Italy, 2001
Prod Bruno Nochvelli, exec prod Luigi Naro. Marco Tamburini (tp, flg); Mario Piacentini (p); Piero Leveratto (b); Marco Tonin (d); Mark Murphy (p, as noted)
Recorded live, Prima Rassegna Jazz Letteratura at Teatro Franciscarum, Brescia, May 18, 2001

    All Blues
    Summertime
    Bye Bye Blackbird
    Miles
    Milestones
    Do Nothin' Till You Hear from Me (MM p)
    On Green Dolphin Street
    My One and Only Love
    Parker's Mood

Splasc(H) Records CDH GS 5003.2 – Mark Murphy Live in Italy 2001 (Italy)

Andy Hamill: Bee for Bass
Anita Wardell (v, kazoo) as noted; Shea Seger (v, tap) as noted; Andy Hamill (b)
Alchemy Studios, London, June 2001–January 2003

    The Planet Formerly Known as Moon (AW, SS)

    Love and Money Don't Mix

Emu 03 – Bee for Bass (UK)

Lucky to be Me
Prod Don Sickler, arr Lee Musiker (p); Scott Wendholt (tp, fgl); Bobby Porcelli (as, fl); Jay Leonhart or David Finck (b); Tim Horner (d); Memo Acevedo (perc)
M&I Recording Studios, New York, December 26 & 27, 2001

    Medley: Lonely Town/Lucky to Be Me/Some
      Other Time
    Dearly Beloved
    Then I'll Be Tired of You
    Photograph
    Serenade in Blue
    Just As Though You Were Here
    I Ain't Gonna Let You Break My Heart
    Blues for Frances Faye
    Medley: I Wonder What Became of Me/If Love
      Were All

HighNote HCD 7094 – Lucky to be Me

Jan Lundgren Trio Plays the Music of Jule Styne
Jan Lundgren (p); Mattias Svensson (b); Morten Lund (d)
Sun Studio, Copenhagen, February 26, 2002

    What Makes the Sunset
    The Things We did Last Summer

Sittel Records SITCD 9288 – Jan Lundgren Trio Plays the Music of Jule Styne (Sweden)

Till Brönner: Blue Eyed Soul
Berlin, 2002

    Dim the Lights

Verve 016 879-2 – Blue Eyed Soul (Germany)

Once to Every Heart
Prod Till Brönner (tp, flg), arr/cond Nan Schwartz. Christian Raake, Tilmann Dehnhard (fl); Frank Chastenier (p,arr); Joris Bartsch Buhle, Brigitte Kaser, Martin Essmann, Anne Feltz, Anna Mogunowa, Daniel Draganov, Ralf Zettl, Barbara Sadowski, Hannes Neubert, Michiko Pryslasznik, Susanne Tribut (vln); Christoph Starke, Reinald Ross, Atsuko Matsuaki, Martin Schaller, Gabriel Tamayo, Holger Herzog (vla); Volkmar Welche, Agnieszka Antonina Bartsch, Ulf Borgwart, David Hausdorf (vlc); Christian Von Kaphengst (b, as noted), Markus Rex, Martin Schaal, Igor Prokopec (b).
Berlin, 2002

    I'm Through with Love (CVK b)
    When I Fall in Love/My One and Only Love
    Skylark/You Don't Know What Love Is (CVK b)

Our Game (CVK b)
I Know You from Somewhere (CVK b)
Bein' Green
Once to Every Heart (CVK b)
It Never Entered My Mind
Do Nothing 'Till You Hear from Me (MM p, v;
    FC out)
Love Is Here to Stay

Once To Every Heart – Verve 06024 9872410, Verve 5476

United Future Organization: V
2002

    No Problem

Exceptional EXLPCD0204 – V (UK)

Memories of You
Arr Norman Simmons (p). Bill Easley (ss, ts); Paul
Bollenbeck (g); Daryl Hall (b); Grady Tate (d)
New York, February 4, 2003

    The Comeback
    In the Evenin'
    Everyday
    Memories of You
    Just Squeeze Me
    If I Were a Bell
    Close Enough for Love
    Love You Madly
    I Got It Bad (and That Ain't Good)
    Sposin'
    A Man Ain't Supposed to Cry

HighNote HCD 7111 – Memories of You

Ian Shaw: A World Still Turning
Eric Alexander (ts); Billy Childs (p); Paul Bollenbeck
(g); Peter Washington (b); Mark Fletcher (d)
Avatar Studios, New York, June 2003

    Soon as the Weather Breaks (duet)

441 Records FFD-0020 – A World Still Turning

**George Gruntz/Peter O. Chotjewitz: The Magic of
a Flute**
Tobias Weidinger, Ingolf Burkhardt, Claus Stotter,
Reiner Winterschladen (tp, fgl); Joe Gallardo, Dan
Gottshall, Stefan Lottermann (tb); Ingo Lahme (b
tb, tuba); Fiete Felsch, Peter Bolte, Christof Lauer,
Lutz Buchner, Frank Delle (r); Vladyslav Sendecki (p,
kyb) Stephan Diez (g); Lucas Lindholm (b); Danny
Gottlieb (d); Marcio Doctor (perc); Renee Manning,
Lauren Newton, Ian Shaw, Marcelino Feliciano, Sandie
Wollasch, Yvonne Moore, Kitty Margolis (v); Peter O.
Chotjewitz (comp); George Gruntz (cond)
"Menuhin Festival", Gstaad, Switzerland, August 8, 2003

Musiques Suisses MGB CD 6219 – The Magic of a Flute
(Switzerland)

Lindberg Hemmer Foundation: Inside Scandinavia
2003

    Little Things

*Raw Fusion Recordings RAFCD 001 – Inside
Scandinavia* (Sweden)

**Five Corners Quintet featuring Mark Murphy:
Chasin' the Jazz Gone By**
Jukka Eskola (tp,fgl); Lalli Koylio, Heikki S. Tikkanen
(fh); Timo Lassy (ts); Severi Pyysalo
(vbs); Mikael Jakobsson or Kim Rantala (p) as noted;
Maria Daroczy, Eeva Salminen, Elina
Kuronen, Paulina Anttila, Emilia Markkanen, Ake
Jarvinen (vln); Matti Lindholm, Sini
Hypponen (vla); Samuli Hyvarinen, Borje Holopainen
(vlc); Antti Lotjonen (b); Teppo
Makynen (d,perc); Abdissa "Mamba" Assefa (perc)
Nuspirit Helsinki Studio and Quad Studios, New York,
2005

    This Could Be the Start of Something (MJ p)
    Before We Say Goodbye (KR p)
    Jamming (With Mr Hoagland) (MJ p)

*Ricky Tick Records RTCD01 – Chasin' the Jazz Gone
By* (Finland)
Columbia (Finland) 520264 – Chasin' the Jazz Gone By

Brother K: Degeneration Beat
2006

    The Subterraneans

Cromo Music – Degeneration Beat (Italy)

Love is What Stays
Til Brönner (tp,.fgl); Gregoire Peters (fl, ts, bcl); Lee
Konitz (as) as noted; Peter Weninger (ss, ts); Frank
Chastenier (p); Don Grusin (el p) as noted; Arne
Schumann (acc) as noted; Kai Brückner , Johan
Leijonhufvud, Karl Schlöz and/or Chuck Loeb (g) as
noted; Christian von Kaphengst (b); Sebastian Merk
(d); Deutches Symphonie Orchester; Nan Schwartz
arr/cond, as noted
Berlin, 2006

    Stolen Moments (KB g)
    Angel Eyes (JL g)
    My Foolish Heart (LK as, DSO)
    So Doggone Lonesome (KS,KB g, AS acc)
    What If (DG el p, CL g, DSO)
    The Interview (DSO)
    Once Upon a Summertime (DSO)
    Stolen Moments (1ˢᵗ reprise)
    Love is What Stays* (DSO)

Stolen Moments (2nd reprise) (KB g)
Too Late Now (DSO)
Blue Cell Phone
Did I Ever Really Live

Verve UCCM 1107 – Love is What Stays
* *Verve 06025 1724256* (single)

Three Minutes with Mark Murphy: VIE 018CDR
2006

Secrets (four versions)

Vienna Scientists Recordings – VIE 018CDR (Austria)

Live in Athens, Greece
Thomas Rueckert (p); Spiros Exaras (g); George
Georgiadis (b); Alex Drakos (d)
Recorded live at Gazarte Club, Athens, Greece, April
18–20, 2008

My Funny Valentine
All Blues
On Green Dolphin Street
Summertime
Autumn Leaves
Medley: When I Fall in Love/My One and Only
    Love
Bye Bye Blackbird
Miles
Milestones
Red Clay
Medley: Inutil Paisagem/Dindi

Harbinger HCD 3202 – Mark Murphy Live in Athens,
Greece

Five Corners Quintet featuring Mark Murphy:
Hot Corner
Jukka Eskola (tp, fgl); Timo Lassy (fl, ts, bs); Mikael
Jakobsson (p); Antti Lotjonen (b); Teppo Makynen (d,
perc)
Nuspirit Helsinki Studio, 2008

Kerouac Days in Montana
Come and Get Me

Ricky Tick Records RTCD09 – Hot Corner (Finland)

Gill Manly: With a Song in My Heart
Guy Barker (tp); Simon Wallace (p); Mark Hodgson
(b); Ralph Salmins (d); Gill Manly (v)
Underhill Studios, London, February 20 & 29, 2008

I Keep Going Back to Joe's

Linn Records BKD 328 – With a Song in My Heart
(UK)

Guillaume de Chassy/Daniel Yvinec: Songs from
the Last Century
Guillaume de Chassy (p); Daniel Yvinec (b); Paul
Motian (d)
New York, March 2008

I'll Walk Alone
Then I'll Be Tired of You
Taking a Chance on Love
I Wish You Love

Bee Jazz BEE009 – Songs from the Last Century
(France)

Never Let Me Go
Prod/arr Misha Piatigorsky (p); prod Chris Wabich (d);
Danton Boller (b)
River Edge, NJ, January 8, 2010

Evolution
Never Let Me Go
Detour Ahead
Don't Ask Why
I Know You from Somewhere
Useless Landscape
The Great City
Photograph
I've Got You Under My Skin
Turn Out the Stars
Murphy's Vamp (Just Kickin' Back and Havin' Fun)

No label – Never Let Me Go

The Royal Bopsters Project
Prod Amy London (v); Holli Ross, Darmon Meader,
Dylan Pramuk (v); Steve Schmidt (p); Sean Smith (b);
Steve Williams (d); Steven Kroon (perc), as noted
Water Music, Hoboken, NJ, June 12, 2012 & July 6–7,
2012

Red Clay (SK perc)
Señor Blues (SK perc)
Boplicity
Bird Chasin'

Motéma 182 – The Royal Bopsters Project

A Beautiful Friendship: Remembering Shirley Horn
Till Brönner (tp) as noted; Alex Minasian (p); Curtis
Lundy (b); Steve Williams (d)
Merion Inn, Cape May, NJ, November 2012

A Beautiful Friendship
But Beautiful (TB tp)
Get Out of Town (TB tp)
Here's to Life

Gearbox GB 1515 – A Beautiful Friendship:
Remembering Shirley Horn (UK EP)

Notes

MT = Mark's Times
DB = Downbeat
BB = Billboard

Foreword: It's Compromise, Don't Bother

could not be happier... Interview with Spiros Exaras 4.28.16

ungenerous headline... San Diego Union, 9.5.86

the way he sings... James Gavin, *From New York With Love*, 2010
http://www.jamesgavin.com/page7/page251/page251.html

the people I do appeal to... Interview with Steve Edwards, Jazz FM, reprinted in MT, no.41, August 1991, pp.36–37

don't have the patience ... MT, no.64, July 1997, p.5

it's compromise, don't bother... He was speaking of his problems with Capitol Records around 1960 when they dropped him from the label. Interview with Bob Rusch, 6.21.84, *Cadence*, October 1985, p.13

Dianne Reeves and Kurt Elling... Will Friedwald. *A Biographical Guide to the Great Jazz and Pop Singers* (Knopf Doubleday, 2010), p.348

better than almost anyone... One good example is his album *Mark Murphy Sings Dorothy Fields and Cy Coleman*, recorded in September 1977

raw oysters and aquavit... Lee Jeske, *New York Post*, 3.1.91, reprinted in MT, no.40, June 1991, p.23

beluga and snails... Rex Reed, *New York Observer*, 3.11.91, reprinted in MT, no.40, June 1991, p.26

not a household name... Interview 1.24.92 with Bob Protzman, *Saint Paul Pioneer Press*, reprinted in MT, no.44, April 1992, p.11

desert of critical neglect... Kevin Lynch, 12.2.2015
http://nodepression.com/article/jazz–singer–mark–murphy–1932–2015–next–sinatra–
did–it–his–way Lynch's sources include Gary Giddins' two large volumes of seemingly definitive *Visions of Jazz: The First Century* (690 pages), *Weatherbird: Jazz at the Dawn*

of its Second Century (632), Whitney Balliett's anthology *Collected Works of Jazz 1954–2000* (873), largely from *The New Yorker*.... James Lincoln Collier's *The Making of Jazz: A Comprehensive History* (543)... *A New History of Jazz* by Alan Shipton (965)... Ted Gioia's *A History of Jazz (*444), and Henry Pleasants' eclectic 1974 *The Great American Popular Singers: Their Lives, Careers & Art* (384)

President Bill Clinton... Martin Weil, *Washington Post*
http://elvispelvis.com/bettycarter.htm#obit

playing the saxophone... Lester Young is reputed to have been the first to use the word "cool" in this sense

jazz's greatest instrumentalists... Mel Tormé. *It Wasn't All Velvet* (1988)

something you probably don't... John Leland. *Hip: The History* (Harper Collins, 2004), pp.5–6. In addition, the Wolof *dega* means "to understand", source of the colloquial "dig," and *jev* ("to disparage or talk falsely"), supposedly evolved into "jive."

that's hip, right?... Harry the Hipster was a comic performer who recorded songs such as "Who Put The Benzedrine In Mrs Murphy's Ovaltine?" and appeared on the same bill as leading beboppers like Parker and Gillespie in the 1940s. Ted Gioia. *West Coast Jazz* (OUP, 1992), p.16

tear the walls down... Interview transcribed in MT, no.72, March 1999, p.22

like Miles's trumpet... William R. Bauer. *Open the Door: The Life and Music of Betty Carter* (University of Michigan Press, 2002), pp.74–5

both socially and literally... Prior to a 2003 Supreme Court ruling, same-sex sexual activity was still illegal in 14 US states. In the UK, the Sexual Offences Act of 1967 was the first legislation to allow limited homosexual practice

devoid of cynicism... Interview with Gilles Peterson, 4.8.16

1 That's When It Bit Me

died of starvation... Also known as the Irish Potato Famine

Mrs James Murphy... Letter from Neil Murphy in MT, no.51, May 1994, p.76. Kathy Hinkhouse has the ship's manifest (interview 5.6.16)

arrived in the United States... Interview with Randy Dempsey 4.28.16.

lead the Methodist congregation there...
http://jazzriffing.blogspot.co.uk/2014_04_01_archive.html

largest woolen mill... Interview with Randy Dempsey 4.28.16

City the Great Depression Missed...
https://www.ny.gov/sites/ny.gov/files/atoms/files/Fulton.pdf

assistant county attorney... *The Fulton Patriot*, 6.19.41

Nuremberg Trials... Kate Murphy memorial service eulogy 3.14.16

on two occasions... Interview with Mark Edmond Murphy 6.2.16

short distance from Fulton...
http://wc.rootsweb.ancestry.com/cgi–bin/igm.cgi?op=GET&db=brendablack&id=I4182

Magnificent Ambersons ... David Ritz in MT, no.42, November 1991, p.4. *The Magnificent Ambersons* is a 1942 Orson Welles film about a wealthy family in genteel decline

Voorhees Park... Email from Allan Howe 6.3.16

administering the bankruptcy... Email from Nancy Murphy 8.28.16

little Elliott ("Billy"), the youngest... Fair Haven Register obit, 8.29.40

And that's it... Family 8mm movie compilation (courtesy of Allan Howe)

until they're ninety... MT, no.62, March 1997, p.54

to draw or read... Interview with Kate Murphy 6.4.16

fishing trips to Canada... Interview with Nancy Murphy 8.28.16

friends on his boat... ibid

at sporting events... Kate Murphy eulogy

around those days... Jazz Times, 1.21.11 http://jazztimes.com/articles/27063–mark–murphy–ready–to–sing. The Chautauqua movement was a Methodist creation, founded in New York state in the 1870s with the object of training Sunday school teachers, but it gradually expanded to teach self-improvement to the rural masses through bible study, discussion of current affairs and political reform. In between the lecturing and speechifying, a certain amount of respectable entertainment was permitted, in the form of music. In the days before radio became ubiquitous, the Chautauqua circus would travel from town to town, setting up their distinctive brown tents

The Last Rose of Summer... MT, no.62, March 1997, p.54. The singer on the soundtrack of *The Dead* is uncredited

Duke Ellington came to town... Herald American, Syracuse, 5.15.88, reprinted in MT no.31, December 1988, p.18

he's talking to you... Ritz, op cit

doctor in London... Email from Allan Howe 6.3.16

for a year or two... Email from Nancy Murphy 8.28.16

time with his mother... Interview with Kathy Hinkhouse 5.6.16

hunting, fishing and sailing... ibid

rest of the family talked... Email from Kate Murphy 10.13.16, and from her eulogy

conflicts with his father... Ritz, op cit

Bing Whittaker... Herald American, Syracuse, op cit

Lullaby of Rhythm... J-Voice interview, early 2012 http://skylinepro.com/jvoice/?page_id=101

over and over again... MT, no.44, April 1992, p.4

ingenuity at the piano... Brian Priestley. The Life and Legacy of Charlie Parker (OUP, 2005), p.27

hooked ever since... Jazz Times interview with W. Royal Stokes, January 1984

tentatively at the time... Gunther Schuller. The Swing Era (OUP, 1989), p.817, quoted in Nat King Cole by Daniel Mark Epstein (Farrar, Straus and Giroux, 1999), p.114

in that kiddie sense... Ted Panken interview, Jazziz, 6.6.03 https://tedpanken.wordpress.com/2015/10/22/r–i–p–mark–murphy–march–14–1932–oct–21–2015/

Fulton High School... Now G. Ray Bodley High School

the Rotarians or someone... Herald American, Syracuse, op cit

copying what he heard... J-Voice op cit

one early favorite… James Gavin, February 1997, reprinted in MT, no. 67, January 1998, p.29

Marian McPartland in 1999… Interview with Marian McPartland, transcribed in MT, no.72, March 1999, p.24

knew how to teach… Bruce Crowther and Mike Pinfold. *Singing Jazz: The Singers and their Styles* (Blandford 1997), p.53. Amy London says Murphy did actually study opera and classical singing at Syracuse, and that he agreed it was "great for your chops" (WBGO interview with Michael Bourne 3.13.16)

slightly abstract songs… James Gavin. *Is That All There Is? The Strange Life of Peggy Lee* (Atria, 2014), p.100

hilarity all 'round… Email from Nancy Galusha Thomas, 4.21.16

whenever he sang… W. Royal Stokes, op cit

big band classics… Document courtesy of Allan Howe

artists like George Shearing… W. Royal Stokes, op cit

Charlie Parker and cool stuff… Mark Bialczak, *Syracuse Post-Standard* , 7.1.08 http://blog.syracuse.com/listenup/2008/07/syracuses_own_mark_murphy_tour.html

anybody but Peggy Lee… Liner notes for *The Artistry of Mark Murphy*

Teddy's sister Annamarie… Email from Barbara Nies Mezzatesta, 10.27.17

Lake Ontario resorts… BBC *Jazz Scene* interview 4.26.64

the Royal Arms… http://buffalo.com/2015/11/02/news/music/in–buffalo–mark–murphy–bopped–from–the–shadows–to–his–own–beatnik–beat

born to be in shadow land… ibid

course at Syracuse University… MT, no.53, February 1995, p.16

part of the course… Mark Gilbert interview, *Jazz Journal*, July 2009

because I swung… *Herald American,* Syracuse, op cit

in the formings of jazz… https://tedpanken.wordpress.com/2015/10/22/r–i–p–mark–murphy–march–14–1932–oct–21–2015/

"developed" singers… ibid

This is art… *J-Voice*, op cit

The Embassy Club… Mark misremembered it as The Ebony Club. MT, no.44, April 1992, p.7

sing a tune?… MT no.28, March 1988, p.13. Although Murphy usually told interviewers that this took place in 1953, according to Hal Webman's liner notes for *Meet Mark Murphy* it was summer 1952.

play it to Allen… http://jazzsceneusa.blogspot.co.uk/2013_06_01_archive.html The interview, with Oscar Brown Jr., took place in 1962 on the TV show Jazz Scene USA.

developed into a correspondence… Suzi Price interview http://www.jazzreview.com/jazz–artist–interviews/mark–murphy.html

I ever worked with… Gene Lees, DB, 11.7.63, p.20

jobs he hated… James Gavin, *Village Voice,* 28 January 1997, reprinted in MT, no.62, March 1997, pp.14–15

2 Dues-Paying Days

never got sea-sick... Interview with Nancy Murphy 8.28.16

girl of great regret... Quoted in Gavin, *Peggy Lee*, p.166

acting or singing... Liner notes for *Meet Mark Murphy*

total opposite of Mark... Interview with Sheila Jordan 4.25.16

11th Avenue... Email from Nancy Murphy, 8.28.16

$8 per month... Kate Murphy eulogy

want to go in there, lady?... Family memorial interview tape (courtesy of Allan Howe)

lettuce for sixty-five cents... Dan Wakefield. *New York in the 50s* (Houghton Mifflin, 1992), p.116–17

back in the old country... ibid p.127

hotels as a bellhop... Liner notes for *Meet Mark Murphy*

Wallingford, Connecticut... Casey at the Bat was based on Ernest Thayer's mock-heroic 1888 poem about a baseball match

jazz singing and playing... BBC *Jazz Scene* interview op cit

after-hours joints... James Gavin, February 1997, reprinted in MT, no. 67, January 1998, p.29

piano-singers and piano trios... Panken, op cit

those same eyes... Ritz, op cit

beginnings of Birdland... MT, no.62, March 1997, p.53

new medium of television... David Meeker, "Jazz on the Screen" (Library of Congress) http://memory.loc.gov/diglib/ihas/html/jots/jazzscreen–overview.html

Broadway and cabaret gigs... Liner notes for *Memories of You*

Kelly's Stable... Gavin. *Peggy Lee*, p.217

Art Blakey sometimes appeared... ibid, p.311. Murphy recorded Oscar Pettiford's tribute to the club, "Bohemia After Dark", on his *Some Time Ago* album

the way Mark sang... Ellen Johnson. *Jazz Child: A Portrait of Sheila Jordan* (Rowman and Littlefield 2014), p.33

this wonderful mystery... Suzanne Lorge interview, *All About Jazz* – "Mark Murphy: Inside The Mystery", July 31, 2009 https://www.allaboutjazz.com/mark–murphy–inside–the–mystery–mark–murphy–by–suzanne–lorge

ideas for song arrangements... MT, no.44, April 1992, p.10. He was still doing occasional gigs with Ernestine Anderson in 1983 (MT no.10 September 1983, pp.2–4)

village that we all loved... Liner notes for *One for Junior*

I just learned by doing... Gilbert, op cit, p.3

New York in 1954... Doc was teaching at the Fort Dix army band training school at the time. http://www.legacy.com/obituaries/dailygazette/aspx?pid=156862378

fit the big band thing... Rusch, op cit, p.12

seen the light of day... The Jazz Discography Volume 15 by Tom Lord (Cadence Jazz Books, 1996). The catalogue numbers have since been re-assigned, and what has happened to Murphy's recordings is anyone's guess – see Discography

signed Peggy Lee… Gavin. *Peggy Lee*, p.128

know what they wanted… ibid, p.154

sing the way I sing… Interview 15.4.88 with WICN Worcester, MA, reprinted in MT no.34, Winter 1989, pp.16–17

he was in his teens… Interview with Charles Cochran 9.13.16

*if it had been known…*Gene Lees. *Friends Along the Way* (Yale University Press, 2003), p.249

Berkeley Square…. MT, Sept. 82, no.6, p.16

he'd had it permed… Interview with Michael Bourne 3.18.16

hair round the sides… Interview with James Gavin 8.29.16

so there you were… Rusch, op cit, p.12

equally good show material… BB, 22 Dec 12.22.56

especially with hip deejays… Quoted in Jordi Pujol's Liner note to Fresh Sound Records double CD re-release of Murphy's first two Decca albums, 2013 http://www.freshsoundrecords.com/mark–murphy–albums/5934–the–complete–decca–recordings–2–lps–on–1–cd.html

like my mother did… Lee Mergner interview, *Jazz Times*, 1.21.11 http://jazztimes.com/articles/27063–mark–murphy–ready–to–sing

very very touching… MT, no.62, March 1997, p.54

now he's making millions… http://www.jazzdisco.org/stars–of–jazz/discography/session–index/

did not move very much… Interview with Charles Cochran 9.13.16

bass on some tracks… Rusch, op cit, p.12

fans will like… BB, 5.19.58

Newport Jazz Festival… Interview with Pete Churchill, 8.2.16

Miles Davis's band… Peter Pettinger. *Bill Evans: How My Heart Sings* (Yale Univ Press, 1988), pp.42 and 58

not a happy one… John Watson interview, Jazz Camera http://www.jazzcamera.co.uk/index.php?page=mark–murphy–––doing–it–right

blue and green… Interview with Mark Edmond Murphy 6.2.16

another eight years… Mark later said he had a $67.50 per month fifth-floor walk-up apartment on Sullivan Street – quite a way from 11th Avenue

multitrack recordings… Interview with Pete Churchill 8.4.16

with a shotgun… Interview with Randy Dempsey 4.28.16

little by little… MT, Sept. 82, no.6, p.16

desperate plan to work… Interview with Kate Murphy 6.4.16

3 All the Bases Were Loaded

physical comedy act… Ira Gitler, Liner notes for *Rah*

offensive language… New York Times 12.2.2007 http://www.nytimes.com/2007/12/02/arts/television/02wein.html?_r=1

after that, nothing... Interview with Bill Steigerwald, *Los Angeles Times*, 2.14.81. The other career low that he occasionally mentioned was getting booed off the stage at a jazz festival in Bremen

starved to 149lbs... MT, no.65, September 1997, p.5

literal starvation... Interview with James Gavin 8.28.16

show him their etchings... MT, June 1983, no.9, p.19–20. Despite being networked in 1958, and winning an Emmy, *Stars of Jazz* was cancelled in January 1959 due to low ratings, and Seligman ordered the tapes of the 130 episodes to be erased so they could be reused. Fortunately many were preserved and are now stored In the UCLA Film library. http://jazzprofiles.blogspot.co.uk/2011/12/bobby–troup–stars–of–jazz.html One of the Murphy shows was released on DVD by Jazz Legends

recordings from Stars of Jazz... http://www.jazzdisco.org/stars–of–jazz/discography/

from Meet Mark Murphy... http://www.tv.com/shows/the–steve–allen–show/episodes/

Steve Allen Playhouse... The website tv.com does not state what songs Mark performed on these shows. http://www.tv.com/shows/the–steve–allen–playhouse/episodes/

Come and Get Me... He recorded "Come and Get Me" three times: for Riverside in 1962, again for the *Bridging a Gap* album in 1972, and again half a century later with Finnish retro-groove combo the Five Corners Quintet, on their *Hot Corner* album (2008)

someone like Mark... Interview with James Gavin 8.28.16

male version of his idol... Liner notes for *The Best of Mark Murphy: The Capitol Years* by James Gavin, February 1997

Peggy Lee's favorite arrangers... Gavin. *Peggy Lee*, p.259

credit should go to him... Gavin. *Best of Mark Murphy*, op cit

drummer Mel Lewis... Anita O'Day. *High Times Hard Times* (Corgi 1983), p.182

sensitivity at the keys... Gavin. *Peggy Lee*, p.152

George Shearing... Gavin. *Best of Mark Murphy*, op cit

Frank Sinatra... BB, 6.29.59 – the result apparently "indicating that more will be heard of this lad"

dig something out of herself... Interview by Stan Britt, *Perfectly Frank*, nos. 71 and 72, 1964

Barnum and Bailey... Interview with Lesley Mitchell-Clarke 9.8.16

he's attractive, single... Liner notes for *Mark Murphy's Hip Parade*

ambiguous aside... Gavin. *Peggy Lee*, p.45

problem city... ibid, p.5

what to do with these... ibid, p.226–7

jockey programming item... BB, 2.1.60

direction and seasoning... Gavin. *Best of Mark Murphy*, op cit

kind of traumatized... ibid

years of his life... Interview with James Gavin 8.28.16

Kapp Records... Gavin. *Best of Mark Murphy*, op cit

place that wasn't overcrowded... Panken, op cit

audience back east... According to Ira Gitler's Liner notes for the *Rah* album

Galvis and Young... These previously hard-to-find tracks were re-released in 2016 on a compilation album – *The Very Best of Latin Jazz* (Not Now Music)

with the Bill Evans Trio... Pettinger, op cit, p.110

LaFaro was adamant... Interview with Pete Churchill 8.2.16

both men were killed instantly... http://www.geocities.ws/chuck_ralston/10slfchr–61.htm – the "Scott LaFaro home page", maintained until 2009 by Charles A. Ralston, who in turn appears to have obtained his information from LaFaro's sister, Helen LaFaro-Fernandez

before making the journey... Interview with Pete Churchill 8.2.16

crashing the car on the way... Ralston, op cit

a congenial collaborator... Some repackaged versions of the album add an unwarranted exclamation mark to the title

a down stud, as they say... DB, 11.7.63

began managing Evans... Pettinger, op cit, p.119

written for Mary Martin... Rusch, op cit, p.13

when I'm feeling sad... Lyrics printed on liner of 1974 Japanese re-release (SMJ 6064)

My Favorite Things (short ver.)... Lord. *The Jazz Discography* CD-Rom (2012)

insulting Cole Porter... MT, no.6, September 1982, p.17

eponymous 1958 album... Confusingly, the track was originally titled "Miles", and was changed to "Milestones" on later editions of the album. This added another layer of confusion: there was already a tune called "Milestones", first recorded in 1947. It was written by John Lewis *for* Miles Davis but erroneously credited *to* Davis. And if that weren't confusion enough, Murphy much later recorded his own ballad entitled... "Miles"

off the shelf... MT, no.74, September 1999, p.25

he told Bob Rusch... Rusch, op cit, p.13

the arranger's pen... DB, 4.12.62

understand jazz... MT, no.3, December 1981, p.73

not in tune... Interview with Ronny Whyte 10.10.16. Years later (1999) Murphy recorded Whyte's lyric to "Bohemia After Dark" for the *Some Time Ago* album

the Village Vanguard... Pettinger, op cit, p.120

something more catchy... http://www.nytimes.com/2004/02/23/arts/bart–howard–88–songwriter–known–for–fly–me–to–the–moon.html?_r=0

indigo and so forth... Jazz Journal, May 1965, p.15

easily make a dent... BB, 3.23.63, p.40

accepted as such... Gene Lees interview, DB, 11.7.63

26 episodes in 1962... Eight shows were issued on VHS by Shanachie Entertainment Corp. Some of these were also issued on DVD, and interested parties can seek them out online

God Bless The Child... The "God Bless the Child" performance can be viewed on YouTube: https://www.youtube.com/watch?v=3IpH_yvS5D8

Dave Lambert... http://jazzsceneusa.blogspot.co.uk/2013_06_01_archive.html

stupid, in my opinion... Reprinted in MT, no.1, June 1981, pp32, 38

a little bit haywire... Interview with Charles Cochran 9.13.16

outcats... Francis Davis. *Outcats: Jazz Composers, Instrumentalists and Singers* (OUP, 1990), intro, p.ix

5 That's What I Like About London

he recalled in 1980... Bill Moody. *The Jazz Exiles: American Musicians Abroad* (Univ of Nevada Press, 1993), p.90

Chris Connor at Atlantic... Will Friedwald. *Jazz Singing: America's Great Voices from Bessie Smith to Bebop and Beyond* (Quartet, 1991), p.311

in the first place... Bauer, op cit, p.96

nostalgic for a lost era... Francis Davis quoting Greg Sandow in "Real Stuff In Life to Cling To", published in *Bebop and Nothingness: Jazz and Pop at the End of the Century* (Schirmer Books, 1996), p.215

I didn't like it... Wakefield, op cit, p.158

The Beatles... O'Day, op cit, p.250

took up hairdressing to survive... ibid, p.249

Detroit supermarket... Bauer, op cit, p.106. Carter didn't actually show up on the day she was due to start

a way to survive... Moody, op cit, pp.i–ii

becomes a different person... ibid, p.94

none of them got results... Gavin. *Best of Mark Murphy* notes

James Gavin... interview with James Gavin 8.29.16

scatter again and wait... Leonard Feather, *Los Angeles Times*, 11.25.89 http://articles. latimes.com/1989–11–25/entertainment/ca–301_1_mark–murphy

the attention I got... Pat Brand, *Crescendo* September 1964, p.19

on to BBC radio... Jonathan Schwartz on WNEW, NYC, August 1986. Reprinted in MT, no.24, March 1987, pp.29–30

everything went poof... Remarks no.1, reprinted in MT, no.1 June 1981, pp.6–7

The Umbrellas of Cherbourg... Interview with James Gavin 8.28.16. *The Umbrellas of Cherbourg* was directed by Jacques Demy with a through-composed score by Legrand

and never got out... *Huffington Post* interview by Melody Breyer-Grell. "Conversation With Mark Murphy – The Last Word in Vocal Jazz?" 7.21.11

Burkhardt's suggestion... *Cleveland Plain Dealer*, 5.6.88, reprinted in MT no.31, December 1988, p.20. Also Moody, p.90

It was fantastic... Remarks, op cit

a place to stay... Interview with Kathy Hinkhouse 5.6.16

dirty and run down... Brand, op cit

there's no comparison... MT, no.14, September 1984, p.20

expanding my brain... Gilles Peterson interview, BBC Radio London, November 1987, reprinted in MT no.28, March 1988, p25

broadcasting in the UK... Brand, op cit

Gerrard Street, Soho... The club moved to its present base in Frith Street at the end of 1965

Miles's All Blues... Britt, op cit

Mack the Knife... Crescendo, March 1964, p.29

attention in the States... Brand, op cit

he couldn't get a gig... BBC *Jazz Scene*, April 1964

career going so long... Ritz, op cit

Covent Garden... Piet Schreuders, Mark Lewisohn, Adam Smith. *The Beatles' London* (Portico 1994), p.74

live music... MT, no.18, September 1985, p.17

BBC radio shows... genome.ch.bbc.co.uk

wide lapels and flares... MT, no.46, October 1992, p.53

brother who takes dope... Britt, op cit

some different audiences... Roy Carr, *Crescendo*, January 1964, pp.23–24

get through after all... John Bloom was an English entrepreneur, best known for his role in the "Washing-Machine Wars" of 1962–64, when he drastically reduced prices via direct sales that cut out the retailers

a very lonely man... Email from Les Reed 11.10.16

but it's beautiful... Brand, op cit

incredibly complimentary... Email from Les Reed 11.10.16

national exposure... *Remarks*, op cit

reviewer who heard it... Review by Fred Nolan and Stan Britt of Murphy's 1964 Scott's appearance, reprinted in MT no.2, pp.37–38

outside the jazz sphere... Liner notes for *Mark Time!*

got so bored with... Brand, op cit

broaden Murphy's appeal... MT, no.4, March 1982, p.98

night club audiences... Crescendo, January 1964, p.3

the real thing comes along... Sunday Telegraph, June 1964 (exact date unknown)

Jazz 625 soon emerged... With 625 scanning lines, the quality of the BBC2 picture was higher than that of the existing BBC1 and ITV channels, with 405

Betty Bennett... Simon Spillett. *The Long Shadow of the Little Giant: The Life, Work and Legacy of Tubby Hayes* (Equinox Publishing, 2015), p.184

A Lot of Livin' to Do... Meeker, op cit

Ronnie Scott... genome.ch.bbc.co.uk

Secret Love... Meeker, op cit

recordings have been lost... the transition from film to videotape was the probable cause. *Jazz 625* was first recorded on film, then tape; but tape was expensive, and many shows simply got wiped when the tape was reused

added Voce... Jazz Journal, January 1965, p.18. Murphy continued to work with the Brian Dee Trio until at least 1991

trips to this country... Sinclair Traill, *Jazz Journal*, May 1965, p.14

6 He's As Good As I Am

King's Road, Chelsea... Interview with Ian Shaw, 4.14.16

Andy Williams... and Mark Murphy... http://www.britishrecordshoparchive.org/soho–record–centrealex–strickland.html

Town Records... Bay Area Reporter, October 1989

had to be over 21... Text of the Sexual Offences Act – http://www.legislation.gov.uk/ukpga/1967/60/pdfs/ukpga_19670060_en.pdf

the Murphy repertoire... Interview with Francesca Miano 3.15.16

with a lover... Interview with Michael Bourne 3.18.16

Respighi... Ottorino Respighi (1879–1936) was an Italian violinist, composer and musicologist

cucumber salad!... Bristow also managed Dusty Springfield and the group Episode 6

Natural History Museum... Address ("c/o O'Sullivan") listed in Leonard Feather's *Encyclopedia of Jazz in the Sixties* (Quartet, 1978), p.218

trees and shrubs... Possibly this was Eddie's place to begin with. According to the electoral register he was living there in October 1965. However by 1968 his name was no longer listed

swift exit... Email from John Jack, 4.5.16

Anita O'Day ever made... London Life magazine, March 1966

driving a camper van... Email from Nancy Murphy, 8.28.16

Eddie was his 'flat-mate'... Interview with Kate Murphy, 6.4.16

thought he was straight... Kate Murphy eulogy, op cit

his hero Jack Kerouac... Interview with Charles Cochran 9.13.16

Leslie Bricusse... Obituary by Brian Willey in *The Independent*, 6.3.94

appearance is also planned... Fred Dellar in *Mojo*, March 1999, reprinted in MT, no.73, July 1999, p.5. The author has been unable to trace *The Mark Murphy Show*

Melody Maker's readers' poll... Remarks op cit; Tom Schnabel, op cit

above five million... http://www.teletronic.co.uk/tvratings_60s.htm

glamorous Blackpool... genome.ch.bbc.co.uk

firing a crossbow while blindfolded... Meeker, op cit

too often to mere sounds... Benny Green. *Jazz Decade: London Ten Years at Ronnie Scott's* (Kings Road Publishing, 1969), p.27

firmly in control... DB, 8.10.67

segregated performances... http://www.independent.co.uk/arts–entertainment/obituary–dusty–springfield–1078196.html

played by Clive Dunn... The entire film can be viewed on YouTube at https://www.youtube.com/watch?v=GslQEIkzCis Mark appears at 00:33:15 ('Let's Take A Chance') and 1:09:16 (title tune)

under the new regime... genome.ch.bbc.co.uk

playing in the north-east... MT, no.6, September 1982, p.5. Warner added that Mark never offered him any money for his board when staying with them, and would often walk away when restaurant bills were presented, leaving someone else to pay. Interview with Bert Warner 3.27.16

back to London... ibid

sing and act... Remarks, op cit

best he ever made... Liner notes for *Midnight Mood* by Keith Lightbody

wasn't released yet... Remarks, op cit

Mark was gay... Note from Nancy Kelly 1.15.17

week-long residency... MT, no.46, October 1992, p.53. Photographs of this gig suggest it took place in 1968

he's as good as I am... James Gavin, February 1997, reprinted in MT, no. 67, January 1998, p.29

This Must Be Earth... Trunk Records re-released the album digitally in 2017

entertainer Roy Castle... MT, no.31, December 1988, p.39

Murphy had in mind... Gavin, *Strange Life,* p.391

one Sunday morning... MT, no.6, September 1982, p.7

Murphy himself agreed... Interview with Jonny Trunk 6.7.16

off his tits at the time... ibid. This British expression usually refers to heavy drug use

jazz fans can be dangerous... Moody, op cit, p.92

back to North America... ibid, p.93

No question... Interview with Charles Cochran 9.3.16

modern American life... genome.ch.bbc.co.uk

endowing clichés with significance... Gillian Reynolds, *The Guardian,* 4.10.72

cash from an Arab... Interview with Bert Warner 3.27.16

under construction... Interview with Ian Shaw, 4.14.16

police were on their tail... Interview with Bert Warner 3.27.16

unpaid tax... Interview with Pete Churchill 8.2.16

7 Ready for Anything

in an ambulance... http://www.locateancestors.com/margaret–murphy–born–in–1900/

Margaret was dead... Email from Nancy Murphy, 8.28.16

for the funeral... ibid

wonderful things for myself... Interview with Kate Murphy 6.4.16

fourth career relaunch... Jazz Review op cit

top 40 material... Ritz, op cit

picked up with them again... Remarks, op cit

club called The Scene... Interview with Albert Amaroso 2.16.17

his living situations... Interview with Charles Cochran 9.13.16

somewhere safe... Interview with Albert Amaroso 2.16.17

the easy-going Cochran... Interview with Charles Cochran 9.13.16

nine months... O'Day, op cit, p.261

macho world of jazz... Lees, op cit, p.281

between her front teeth... Interview with Joe Fields 5.3.16

Latin and fusion ... Andy Thomas http://daily.redbullmusicacademy.com/2015/04/muse–records–guide

music school in Cincinnati... Interview with Dave Matthews 8.9.16

no time for mistakes... Interview with Richie Cole 2.3.17

they'd tell a story... Interview with Joe Fields 5.3.16

lovingly caressing "you"... Michael Bourne, DB, January 2016, p.8

complained Downbeat... DB, 11.10.73

Louis van Dijk Trio... Liner notes for *North Sea Jazz Sessions vol.5*

between 1969 and 1993... Liner notes for *The Dream*

Dancing to Midnight... genome.ch.bbc.co.uk

nothing to the originals... DB, 5.22.75

Sweet Caroline... Gavin, *Strange Life*, p.356

trumpet with words... Liner notes for *Mark Murphy Sings*

rhythm section... Interview with Dave Matthews 8.9.16

experience the songs... Liner notes for *Mark Murphy Sings*

his curly locks... Interview with Michael Bourne 3.18.16

fresh viewpoint... DB, 8.12.76

commercial for IBM... Interview with Albert Amaroso 2.16.17

no further than the pilot... Mark Murphy with Michael Bourne, WBGO Newark NJ. 7.18.11. http://www.wbgo.org/blog/mark–murphy–with–wbgos–michael–bourne

do you *think* so... Interview with Kathy Hinkhouse 6.5.16

American Popular Song... Published by OUP, 1972

large houseplants... David Demsey's introduction to the annotated edition of his memoir *Letters I Never Mailed: Clues to a Life* (University of Rochester Press, 2005), p.24

Wilder demanded to know... James Gavin Liner notes for *Mark Murphy Sings Dorothy Fields and Cy Coleman* CD http://jamesgavin.com/page66/page197/page197.html

thank the good lord... ibid

ballads and standards... Fred Bouchard's Liner notes for *Satisfaction Guaranteed*, quoting WBUR-FM host and Murphy enthusiast Tony Cennamo

all marvelous... Liner notes for *September Ballads*

best performances... When Wilder's health started to fail, he nominated as his successor Marion McPartland, whose *Piano Jazz* series replaced it, running until 2011

state of emergency... https://en.wikipedia.org/wiki/1977_Blizzard

a musical model... Ritz, op cit

US residency... Interview with Albert Amaroso 2.16.17

she was not happy... Interview with Kate Murphy 2.27.17

for crying out loud... Interview with Albert Amaroso 2.16.17

Van Ness Avenue, San Francisco... Email from Kate Murphy 10.13.16

The Heart is a Lonely Hunter... Kate Murphy eulogy

Richie Cole... New Musical Express, 4.25.87, p.9, reprinted in MT no.25, June 1987, p.27

Still on the Planet... Interview with Richie Cole 2.3.17

got off on a technicality... http://elvispelvis.com/gunshot.htm#2

killing him instantly... Echoes, 4.25.87, reprinted in MT no.25, June 1987, pp28–29

next to each other... Interview with Richie Cole 2.3.17

always asking... Watson, op cit

guys were going to get... Interview with Joe Fields 5.3.16

yet it doesn't drag... Liner notes for *Stolen Moments*

Mitch Farber's mix... Tom Schnabel, DB, February 1980, p.52

played it constantly... Interview with Francesca Miano, 3.15.16

young people... ABC Australia podcast 2004 http://mpegmedia.abc.net.au/rn/podcast/2015/11/msw_20151101_1110.mp3

I tell a story... Interview with Richie Cole, 2.3.17

Tony Cennamo... MT no.3, December 1981, p.55, in which Ms Hines is wrongly identified as Rosemary Hines. Cennamo, known as The Old Bebopper of Boston, broadcast from the city's university for 25 years

booked for the date... Interview with Greetje Kauffeld 6.10.16

Frank DeMiero... MT no1, June 1981, p.20

Dutch radio show... Interview with Greetje Kauffeld 6.10.16

Skymasters... Interview with Ack Van Rooyen 2.10.16

decided to contact him... Email from Kirby Shaw, 3.9.17

what's going on here... MT, no.62, March 1997, pp.46–55

world's greatest singers... Interview with Bert Warner, 3.27.16

a little newsletter... MT, no.20, March 1986, p.117

jazz in general... MT, no.40, June 1991, p.2

writing a screenplay... MT, no.15, December 1984, pp.43–44

Pope of Greenwich Village... Mark was presumably referring to Mickey Rourke. If it still exists, the script may be buried somewhere in his nephew's basement in Shohola, PA

8 Where Fountains Drip in a Forgotten Tempo

came to New York... According to Albert Amaroso, Murphy and Kerouac knew each other in the Fifties

Five Corners Quintet... "Kerouac Days in Montana", from the *Hot Corner* album (2008)

home town of Fulton... MT, no.28, March 1988, p.12

rhythmic writing... ABC Australia podcast http://www.abc.net.au/radionational/programs/musicshow/mark–murphy–remembered/6893300 MM uses the word "dig" in the sense of "understand" rather than "appreciate"

so inspiring... Why Kerouac Matters by John Leland (Viking 2007), pp.119–120 *path to wisdom...* Davis, op cit, pp.32–33

person-to-person thing... Rusch, op cit, p.90

creating pure language... Leland, *Why Kerouac Matters*, p.134

letters and notebooks... ibid p.135

magic was happening... James Gavin. *Deep In A Dream: The Long Night Of Chet Baker* (Vintage, 2003), p.90

steaming coffee urns... MT, no.48, May 1993, p.5

he was pretty loose... Interview with Bill Mays, 3.12.16

forlorn rags of growing old... Kerouac himself cut spoken word albums in 1958 and 1959 – *Poetry for the Beat Generation*, with Steve Allen on piano; *Blues and Haikus*, with Al Cohn and Zoot Sims; and unaccompanied on *Readings by Jack Kerouac on the Beat Generation* (Francis Davis, "Talking Kerouac" [1990] in *Bebop and Nothingness*, p.257ff.) Mark Murphy also wrote a number of "jazz haikus" (see pp.??)

Beat Generation... Kuh was a local San Francisco character and proprietor of the legendary Old Spaghetti Factory nightclub at 478 Green Street in North Beach. "In the heyday of the Beatnik period, from the mid-'50s until the early '60s, the place was renowned not only for serving bargain-priced pastas but was an incubator and magnet for local talent." http://www.sfgate.com/news/article/OBITUARY-Frederick-Walter-Kuh-2796413.php

underdog kind of hero... Interview with Richie Cole 2.3.17

the best of Mark... Interview with James Gavin 8.29.16

some funny bank... Rusch, op cit, p.6

two opening tracks... MT, no.2, September 1981, pp.41–2

back in London... MT, no.4, March 1982

in the past... MT, no.5, June 1982, p.12

another man entirely ... MT no.2, September 1981, p.29

more adventurous... Francesca Miano's blog: http://www.jazzsaints.blogspot.co.uk/ 2009/05/fearless–singer.html

patients had wandered over... Interview with Ari Silverstein 2.25.16

an IMMAS member... MT, no.9, June 1983, p.20

cameramen seemed confused ... MT, no.8, March 1983, p.11

lose 10lbs... MT, no.9, June 1983, p.2

Equmina beach... he meant Ipanema; *Lagos* is actually Lagoa

it was something else... MT, no.12, March 1984, p.1

everybody yells in Rio... Liner notes for *Brazil Song*

release of The Artistry... Sun-Herald (Australia), 2.6.83

Basie's orchestra... Interview with Bill Mays 3.12.16

most familiar name... MT, no.9, June 1983, p.2

electrified the world... MT, no.47, February 1993, p.40

strange collapse... Insert with MT, no.10, September, 1983. MM's account appeared with the handwritten headline STAR LETTER OF THE MONTH!

hot weather... Rusch, op cit, p.12

Gang Show... he meant Chuck Barris's *Gong Show*

admiring a sunset... Interview with Steve Rubie 3.22.17

write a bad song... Liner note to *Brazil Song*

established working group... MT, no.12, March 1984, p.1

story of my life... MT, no.10, September 1983, p.7

9 It's Hot, It's Red Lights, It's Exciting!

South London schoolboy ... Interview with Gilles Peterson 8.4.17

acid jazz was born... https://www.youtube.com/watch?v=MMH-__-QHck – there's a brief history in this extract from a TV documentary made for a series called *01 For London*, a late-night ITV show from the late 1980s

acid house music... Interview with Gilles Peterson 4.8.17

A Night in Tunisia... Straight No Chaser, no.2, Autumn 1988, p.30

two-tone spats... http://www.theartsdesk.com/new–music/snowboys–history–uk–jazz–dance–scene

Dingwalls dancehall... http://www.bbc.co.uk/radio1/gillespeterson/biography.shtml

bewildered by it... Interview with Gilles Peterson, 4.8.16

Jazz Horizons... MT, no.1, June 1981, p.19. Open letter from Mark Murphy dated 4.28.1981

Canvey Island... MT, no. 21, June 1986, p.41. Probably refers to longstanding Canvey Island club, The Goldmine

cool jazz... MT, no.15, December 1984, pp.43–44

jitterbugging and going crazy ... Dan Ouellette, DB, April 1997, p.26ff

Bass Clef... The Hoxton (London) based club Bass Clef was founded by bass player Peter Ind in 1984. Its success was partly due to the jazz dancing craze

reported an observer... MT, no.25, June 1987, p.36.

New Musical Express... 4.25.87, p.9, reprinted in MT no.25, June 1987, p.27. The Wag, in Soho's Wardour Street, was an acronym of the name of the previous club on the premises, the Whisky-A-Go-Go, a Sixties night spot

one female dancer... *Straight No Chaser*, op cit, p.33

all of them were packed... MT, no.29, June 1988, p.47

Yusef Lateef... MT, no.42, November 1991, p.13

the Six... Interview with Steve Rubie 3.22.16.

singing workshops... See appendix B

Dingwalls on Sunday afternoon... Interview with Gilles Peterson, 4.8.16

collection of old clocks... Interview with Bert Warner 3.27.16

very masculine... Interview with Ann Dyer 3.31.16

domestic arrangements... Interview with Kate Murphy 6.4.16

Nat King Cole freak... Liner note to *Mark Murphy Sings the Nat King Cole Songbook Volume One*

each song from within... *Cadence* Magazine, August 1985, reproduced in MT, December 1985, no.19, p.19

Benny Miller Quartet ... MT, no.19, December 1985, p.16

Another micro budget... Interview with Bill Mays, 12.3.16

I love it, no problem... According to Albert Amaroso, Mark was frustrated that Alice Coltrane would not allow him to use some lyrics he written to some of her late husband's tunes

do all the work... Rusch, op cit, p.6

my ancient RV... MT, no.21, June 1986, p.30

Another Night in Tunisia... www.grammy.org

the contemporary Jobim... Interview in *Pulse* (undated) by Eliot Tiegel, reprinted in MT, no.26, September 1987, p.4

Frank Morgan... https://www.allaboutjazz.com/frank–morgan–frank–morgan–by–brandt–reiter.php?pg=2

Lins's songs... Liner notes for *September Ballads*

Barbara Glass... MT, no.24, March 1987, pp.58–64

Lord Buckley... Richard Myrie "Lord" Buckley was a proto-beatnik who worked as a stage performer from the 1930s to the end of the 50s. In live situations, Buckley was an improviser to rival the most adventurous jazz musician. In her autobiography *High Times, Hard Times* (Corgi, 1983), Anita O'Day details some of Buckley's more outrageous exploits during the 1930s at Planet Mars, Chicago, featuring acrobatic leaps, nudity and overt drug-taking

synthesized version... Interview with Bill Mays 3.12.16

Mark nailed it... Interview with Richie Cole 2.3.17

the Shearing sound... Interview with Bill Mays 3.12.16

very expensive album... MT, no.37, June 1990, p25a

whoozie-whatzit... John Rockwell, *International Herald Tribune*, 6.15.88

trying to sing jazz... Johnson, op cit, p.52

smells of smoke... Posted on Amazon by Dr. Harry Smallenburg, November 11, 2008. Mark can be glimpsed in this brief German documentary about *Cosmopolitan Greetings*: https://vimeo.com/10229398 A recording of the opera was eventually released in 1993 on the Musikszene Schweiz label

Don Ellis Big Band... MT, no.37, June 1990, p.9

Brothers... MT, no.32, Spring 1989, pp.16–17

10 I Remember Less and Less, Except You Baby

Sheila Jordan... Interview with Sheila Jordan 4.25.16

Golden Gate Bridge... Email from Kate Murphy 10.13.16

his sick-bed... Interview with Kate Murphy 6.4.16

aged 50... Bay Area Reporter, November 1989

stitched together... Interview with Kate Murphy 6.4.16.

over the years... Interview with Francesca Miano, 3.15.16

the consummate optimist... Kate Murphy eulogy

the blizzard of '77... Rusch, op cit

blubbering on the streets... Interview with Steve Edwards, Jazz FM, reprinted in MT no.41, August 1991, pp.36–37

For All We Know... Interview with Kate Murphy 6.4.16

in whom it specialized... Interview with Tina May 9.10.16

original fortnight... MT, no.36, April 1990, p.50

telling him in advance... ibid, p.54

heard with a singer... MT, no.38, October 1990, p.41

Larry Fallon... MT, no.40, June 1991, p.21

not liking the synthesizers... MT, no. 43, February 1992, p.3

images in sound... Mary Ellison, *Jazz Times*, June 1991, no.60

Murphy as a replacement... Interview with Sheila Jordan 4.25.16

distinctly uneasy... Interview with Karlheinz Miklin 7.18.16

Jeff Zygmont ... MT, no.43, February 1992, pp.32–33

one kind reviewer... *Jazz Magazine* no.24, May/June 1994, p.27

turned out better... Letter to MT, no.43, February 1992, p.64

never to be home... ibid

road zombie... MT, no.45, June 1992, pp.10–18

On the Road vagabond... Interview with James Gavin 8.28.16

stopped using crack... Interview with Amy London 2.27.16

Cosmopolitan Greetings... Interview 1.24.92 with Bob Protzman, *Saint Paul Pioneer Press*, reprinted in MT, no.44, April 1992, pp.10–11

my favorite singer... MT, no.62, March 1997, p.52

inquiry about more gigs ... MT, no.45, June 1992, p.4

about six years... ibid, pp.10–18

part of my life... ibid, p.33

future appearances... MT, no.50, December 1993, p.4

new program controller... The full story was told in a *Guardian* article by John Fordham and Ronald Atkins, reprinted in MT, no.46, October 1992, p.28

three-night booking... MT, no.46, October 1992, p.40

economic insecurity... MT, no.48, May 1993, p.54

announced the closure... ibid, pp.2–3

Easy Does It... genome.ch.bbc.co.uk

jazz haikus... Interview with Tina May 9.10.16. There were plans for Murphy to record some of his haikus, but he became too ill and it never happened. Tina May recorded them herself with Lutter for 33 Records, under the title *Café Paranoia*. Murphy heard the tracks and gave his seal of approval before he died. He can be heard, recorded on Lutter's cellphone, on the final, untitled track of the album, released in 2017

have you met someone?... Interview with Pete Churchill 8.2.16

Smollensky's... Several reports in MT, no.50, December 1993

viewing conditions... MT, no.58, June 1996, p.7

Jazzcoteque dancers... MT, no.59, September 1996, p.14

different kind of album... Liner notes for *Song for the Geese*

You Go To My Head... MT, no.55, September 1995, pp.5–6

that disqualified him... Interview with Roger Treece 9.15.16. Murphy alluded to this in a letter to Mark's Times: 'The fact that I'm not a soul brother doesn't help...' MT, no.53, February 1995, p.7

ADAT... Alesis Digital Audio Tape

in the driver's seat... Interview with Roger Treece 9.15.16

Take 6... technically dazzling a cappella gospel group whose first album released in 1988 went platinum

Europe's a different matter... MT, no.51, May 1994, p.13

George Wein... impresario who founded the Newport Jazz Festival

Pat Metheny song... MT, no.51, May 1994, p.51

things were changing... ibid, p.24

mainly local musicians... ibid

tired of San Francisco... MT, no.54, June 1995, p17

north, to Seattle... MT, no.58, June 1996, p.27

end of the year... MT, no.61, February 1997, p.46

projected his gloom... MT, no.54, June 1995, p.17

heading to the UK ... MT, no.51, May 1994, pp.12–14

Basement in Sydney... ibid, p.50

business was wonderful... ibid

Amazing YEAH... MT, no.52, November 1994, p.4. Mark also recorded "Stolen Moments" with the group, but the version on this album is instrumental. For the vocal version, see the Remix album released in 1995

no distributor... MT, no.55, September 1995, p.5

Steely Dan... Interview with Pete Churchill 4.8.16

delighted with Full Voice... MT, no.55, September 1995, pp.5–6

glorious mono... A mono mix was still needed on occasions. Even in 1995 some American AM stations were not able to broadcast in full stereo. As a result, some material, such as jingles, had to be mixed within a narrow audio field that was close to being mono, to avoid losing some of the sound

it's a bit humorous... MT, no.56, April 1996, pp.6–9. Since he didn't actually have a record company he was probably referring to the duplication plant

Decidedly Jazz Danceworks... MT, no.55, September 1995, p.8

his own role... Undated report by Alison Mayes in *Calgary Herald*, probably Jan. 1995, reprinted in MT, no.54, June 1995, p.75

press release... Dated May 18, reprinted in MT, no.54, June 1995, pp.73–4

huffin' and puffin'... MT, no.55, September 1995, pp.6–7

finance the project... Dan Ouellette, DB, April 1997, p.26ff. The show can be viewed here: https://www.youtube.com/watch?v=GiSrR5fDC8s&list=PLjEkVLib3ZysZN1Dy2dQoxM57 hGrRkDVY&index=51&t=358s

ecstatic reviews... MT, no.54, June 1995, p.61

The Dream... MT, no.55, September 1995, p.17 18

her epiphany... ibid, p.43

24 of his albums... ibid, p.29

if this is a religion... ibid

Very Early... ibid, pp.17 and 51

watching Mark work... ibid, p.48

loving care... Interview with James Gavin 8.31.16

Charlie Ellicott... MT, no.56, April 1996, p.3

STOP THE PRESSES... MT, no.55, September 1995, p.25

12 Age Only Matters If You're a Cheese

it's brand new... MT, no.58, June 1996, p.41

Betty Carter's trio... MT, no.72, March 1999, p.42

sign up with us... MT, no.63, June 1997, pp.30–31

hodnik... It means "corridor"

experimental... Interview with Karlheinz Miklin

Best Male Singer... Oullette, op cit

two-pronged efforts... Email from Samir Köck

Erling Kroner... MT, no.63, June 1997, p.52

sold out to Fantasy... Interview with Joe Fields 5.3.16

chicken soup... MT, no.62, March 1997, pp.16–23

Peg... Gavin, *Strange Life*, p.427

tickets were sold... MT, no.65, September 1997, pp.28–33

longtime label Capitol... MT, no.66, December 1997, p.7

Kurt Elling... Oullette, op cit

Bill Traut... MT, no.64, July 1997, pp16–17

Mark did that first... Interview with Lily Dior 3.2.16

professional publicist... Interview with Lesley Mitchell-Clarke 9.8.16

Turner Classic Movies... Interview with Michael Bourne 3.8.16

cummerbund... Paul de Barros, unknown publication, reprinted in MT, no.67, January 1998, p.78

Buddy Rich... MT, no.66, December 1997, p.61

sales figures... ibid, p.4

DAT machine... Interview with Duncan Hopkins 11.22.16

DJ Helen Mayhew... Philip Annis in MT, no.66, December 1997, p.74

Nightmare on Dean Street... MT, no.66, December 1997, p.89

It was chaotic... Interview with Pete Churchill 8.4.16

disco queen... Interview with Pete Churchill 1.29.16

reputation was growing... Friedwald, *Biographical Guide*, p.348

Kennedy Center... MT, no.68, April 1998, pp.6–7

his real home... ibid, p.15

cook him a turkey... Singer Kitty Margolis recalled once preparing an elaborate dinner for Mark, which he took one look at and asked whether she had a hamburger

singer Sandy Anderson... Interview with Roger Treece 9.15.16

without pillows or blankets... MT, no.69, July 1998, p.25

reclaimed the vehicle... Interview with Lesley Mitchell-Clarke 9.8.16

back in the 10th century... Dan Ouellette http://www.sfgate.com/entertainment/article/Hipster–Back–in–the–Limelight–2978659.php

13 The Mother of All Love Songs

love doing ballads... Oullette, DB, op cit

holiday in Peru... MT, no.72, March 1999, p.70

Rosemary Carden... MT, no.73, July 1999, pp.62–74

change his name... ibid, pp.72

Ellyn Rucker... ibid, p.92

scaring the songbirds away... ibid, pp.22–24

break with Bert Warner... Panken, op cit. Mark seems to have misremembered where Bert Warner's 'Nightmare on Dean Street' took place

nailed in one take... Tessa Souter http://www.londonjazznews.com/2015/11/tribute–tessa–souter–remembers–mark.html

another winner... *Jazz Journal*, July 2002 review by David Lands

Twelve Tribes... Interview with Andy Hamill, 4.11.16

Charles Mancuso... http://buffalonews.com/2015/11/02/in–buffalo–mark–murphy–bopped–from–the–shadows–to–his–own–beatnik–beat/

rolling down his cheeks ... Interview with Till Brönner 5.29.16. He could not remember which ballad it was, but thought it was one of Murphy's own compositions. Alternatively it might have been "Too Late Now", a ballad he regularly played solo at the end of shows after Eddie O'Sullivan died, and which he later recorded for *Love is What Stays*

protégé of Johnny Mandel... Friedwald. *Biographical Guide*, p.353

the Shirley Horn record... *Here's To Life* (1992)

pencil-written chart... According to a page on the Verve Music website, since removed

ballad album... Andrew Gilbert, *Jazz Times* Jan/Feb 2006. "Mark Murphy: Always the Beat Generation"

straightforward and cordial... Interview with Joe Fields 5.3.16

contract with HighNote... Price, op cit

Four Brothers... The name refers to the Jimmy Giuffre tune played by Woody Herman's "Second Herd", designed to exploit the sound of one baritone and three tenor saxophones. (Lees, op cit, p.244)

cover story... John McDonough, DB, Dec 2002

Three Brotha's and a Motha... http://kurtelling.com/band/

daughter Imogen... Interview with Pete Churchill, 2.8.16

Sushisamba... Interview with Misha Piatigorsky 7.4.16

greatest hits... Interview with Francesca Miano, 3.15.16

he again toured Australia... *Sydney Jazz Scene*, April 2005

reviewers raved... *Jazzwise* (UK), October 2005; *Jazz Times*, December 2005; *Jazz Rag* (Birmingham, UK), Winter 2005

masculine poses... Stephen Holden, *New York Times*, 1.11.05. "A World-Weary Soul Singing Like a Post-Beat Minstrel"

'Tis Autumn... imdb.com

Love is What Stays... Interview with Till Brönner 5.29.16

Too Late Now... http://jamesgavin.com/page66/page123/page123.html

multifarious charms... Peter Quinn, *Jazzwise*, May 2007, p.50; http://www.allmusic.com/album/love–is–what–stays–mw0000478548

14 Much to Do and Not a Moment to Spare

blondie... Interview with Lesley Mitchell-Clarke 9.8.16

trips to Holland... Interview with Greetje Kauffeld 10.6.16

A Night with Mark Murphy... https://vimeo.com/4487895

Evolution of an Artist... Watson, op cit

trailer... https://www.youtube.com/watch?v=LyTTL3E42uI

mechanical rights... Interview with Mark E Murphy 6.2.16

final cut ... Email from Francesca Miano, 3.16.16. Dave Pistoni confirms this information (email 2.16.17). A short extract may be viewed here: https://vimeo.com/21661145

Iridium gig... https://www.allaboutjazz.com/mark–murphy–at–the–iridium–nyc–mark–murphy–by–martin–longley.php

Gazarte Club... Interview with Spiros Exaras 4.28.16. See chapter 1 for more about these gigs

carpet slippers... Interview with Sheila Jordan 4.24.16

Brecon... Interview with Pete Churchill 8.2.16

Fulton Music Association... http://oswegocountytoday.com/sept–26–murphy–family–event–concert–in–fulton–also–features–singers–brother–son–family–members/; family video courtesy of Allan Howe

party on the porch... ibid

struggling to cope... Interview with Mark E Murphy 6.2.16

in need of help... Interview with James Gavin 8.29.16

Alzheimer's... Interview with Jean-Pierre Leduc 3.9.16

Kitano... Will Friedwald. http://www.jazz.com/jazz–blog/2009/8/4/mark–murphy–at–the–kitano

an electronic, acid-jazz setting... on the Five Corners Quintet album *Chasin' the Jazz Gone By* – see Discography

Yoshi's... Lee Mergner, *Jazz Times*, 10.13.09 http://jazztimes.com/articles/25168–mark–murphy–to–be–honored–at–event–at–yoshi–s–in–oakland

whole 'nother level... Interview with Ann Dyer 3.31.16

This Must Be Earth... Interview with Jonny Trunk 6.7.16. The album is available as a download from Trunk Records but at the time of writing there is not yet a vinyl version

Never Let Me Go... Interview with Misha Piatigorsky 7.24.16

marked improvement... quoted in Mergner, op cit

weight of decades... Breyer-Grell, op cit

painful set... The Times 2.3.12, p.12

in the mid-Seventies... Interview with Amy London 2.27.16

French horn... John Basile blog http://bourne.wickedlocal.com/article/20151030/ENTERTAINMENTLIFE/151039396

valve microphones... Conversation with Darrel Sheinman 3.13.17

Mark sang last... Johnson, op cit

last day of his life ... Nancy Murphy, at family memorial

he was cremated... Email from Nancy Murphy 8.28.16

his family could sing ... Interview with Francesca Miano 3.15.16

in her eulogy... http://www.jazzsaints.blogspot.co.uk/search/label/Mark%20Murphy, 3.20.16

immediate family ... Interview with Sheila Jordan 4.25.16

Cleo Laine... https://vimeo.com/21661145

obituary... http://www.londonjazznews.com/2015/11/tribute–tessa–souter–remembers–mark.html

Appendix A: A Jazz Singer Is a Singer Who Sings Jazz

definition of a jazz singer... Interview with Michael Bourne 3.18.16

overtly copied him... Interview with Tina May 9.10.16

researched each song... Interview with Steve Rubie 3.22.16

abstract expressionist vocalist... Speech at memorial service 3.14.16

tremendously adequate... Interview with Michael Bourne 3.18.16

agile and resonant... James Gavin, *Village Voice*, January 28, 1997, reprinted in MT, no.62, March 1997, pp.14–15

two kinds of singers... Interview with Nancy Kelly 1.15.17

Coleman Hawkins... Bauer op cit, p.64

The Waters of March... Interview with Michael Bourne 3.18.16

one audience member... Larry Prager in MT, no.40, June 1991, p.34

singing a movie... Rusch, op cit

New York Times... Holden, op cit

monologues... Interviews with Pete Churchill, 1.29.16 and 8.2.16

Anita O'Day... Friedwald. *Jazz Singing,* p.225

choice of drummer... Herb Wong's liner notes for *Stolen Moments*

how to play brushes... J-Voice, op cit

conversational style... Gavin. *Strange Life,* p.94

Gregory Hines... Panken, op cit

jazz dancers... Interview with Andy Hamill 4.11.16

pleasures of my life... *Herald American,* Syracuse, op cit

what was "now"... Interview with Lily Dior 3.216

rap demo... Interview with Ari Silverstein 2.25.16

Miles Davis... Watson, op cit

frightened of silence... Interview with Steve Rubie 3.22.16

too many notes... Panken, op cit

ripped-open heart... Interview with Kurt Elling 5.6.15

get into a ballad... MT, no. 22, Sept 1986, p.11

mature art form... ibid, p.10

Shirley Horn tempo... Interview with Misha Piatigorsky 7.24.16

more you see and learn... Interview with Andy Hamill 4.11.16

biography of Cole... Epstein, op cit, p.194

wrong note... Interview with Lily Dior 3.2.16

affected by it... https://jazztimes.com/departments/farewells/
kurt–elling–remembers–mark–murphy/

switch on a band... Interview with Tina May 9.10.16

liked to be surprised... Interview with Pete Churchill 8.2.16

amazing to watch... Steve Weeks in MT, no.68, April 1998, p.26

in Manchester... Interview with Andy Hamill 4.11.16

different directions... Interview with Pete Churchill 8.4.16

understanding of harmony... Rusch, op cit

piece of literature... BBC *Jazz Scene* 4.26.64

emotion in a song... *Billy Taylor's Jazz* http://www.npr.org/programs/btaylor/archive/
murphy.html [undated]

new Johnny Mandel song... Ted Gioia. *The Jazz Standards* (Oxford UP 2012), p.111

creates his sound... Dave Gelly. *Being Prez: The Life and Music of Lester Young* (Equinox, 2007), p.89

repertoire and relaxation... J-Voice, op cit

when people smoked... Michael Bourne, WBGO, op cit

Yoshi's in Oakland... Friedwald, *Jazz Singing,* p.56

she's become a caricature... MT, no.24, March 1987, p.42

McFerrin affected me... MT no.26, September 1987, p.33

scatting is so much fun... Quoted in Gavin, *Deep in a Dream*, p.243

musical electronica... Technology can also help the modern jazz singer to improvise in live performance: José James has sometimes used a looping device live to build up layers of voices and clapping. Trumpeter and singer Arve Henriksen often sings into his instrument; electronics are then used to manipulate the resulting sounds

audience work harder... Gioia, op cit, p.133

trying to get across... Miano, op cit

so much scat... MT, no.22, Sept 1986, p.9

scat solo on Boplicity... MT, no.19, December 1985, p.9

music is like putty... '30 LPs and still obscure', by George Varga, *San Diego Union*, 9.5.86

Appendix B: I Don't Want to Stamp Out Singers Like Cookies

no fees at all... Stuart Nicholson. *Jazz and Culture in a Global Age* (Northeastern University Press, 2014), pp.5–11

Herb Wong... jazz historian and long-time broadcaster on KJAZ

clinic work... Schnabel, op cit

Goldsmith's College... Moody, op cit, p.95

teacher-student relationship... Interview with Ann Dyer 3.31.17

Keystone Korner... In 2017, HighNote released *Wild and Free*, a Mark Murphy live set recorded at Keystone Korner in 1980

books are marvelous... Lorge, op cit

blind to the innuendo... MT no.10, September 1983, p.7

sequence of events... Report by Paul Pace in MT, no.63, June 1997, p.17

posture and breathing... MT, no.72, March 1999, p.27

ninety-five percent... Gioia, op cit, p.119

purely physical... Interview with Pete Churchill 8.4.16

six pints a day... Rusch, op cit, p.7

no student is the same... MT, no.64, July 1997, pp.4–5

fellow baritone... Interview with Ian Shaw 4.14.16

London's 606 Club... Interview with Steve Rubie 3.22.16

Mentor concert... Tessa Souter, *London Jazz News*, 11.3.15 http://www.londonjazznews. com/2015/11/tribute–tessa–souter–remembers–mark.html

different people in each song... MT, no.64, July 1997, p.20

you take it apart... ibid, pp.4–5

it depends on the song... MT, no.64, July 1997, pp.4–5

just the drummer... DB, December 2002, p.26

didn't have any singers... Interview with Karlheinz Miklin 7.18.16

very taxing... Feather, *Los Angeles Times*, op cit

workshop at Leeds College... Interview with Pete Churchill 8.4.16

teaching young people ... MT, no.54, June 1995, p.17

individual lessons... Interview with Lily Dior 3.2.16

the standards are great ... Interview with Ann Dyer 3.31.16

lack of seriousness... Interview with Ari Silverstein 2.25.16

IAJE Conference... International Association for Jazz Education. https://www.youtube.com/watch?v=3pdPWOb3VyU

could not be taught... Michael Bourne, WBGO, op cit

go back in the shed... Royal Bopsters interview WBGO 3.13.16

Index

4hero, 140
52nd Street, 13
606 Club, 181
9/11: 140

ABC Records, 84
Abbott, John, 131
Abeona, The, 1
Abominable Dr Phibes, The, 54
Acevedo, Memo, 134
acid jazz, xiii, 91, 137, 154
Adams Willis, Vicki, 119
Adamson, Harold, 7
ADAT, 115, 118
African Waltz, 46
Again, 75, 97, 127
AIDS, 103–4
Ain't Nobody Here But Us Chickens, 96, 104
Airto, 93
*Alec Wilder and Friends: American Popular
    Song*, 71–72
All Blues, ix, x, 43, 47, 97
All the Things You Are, 97, 104, 172, 174
Allen, Steve, 9, 10, 23–25, 29, 37, 83
Alley Cat, The, 98
Allmusic, 149
Alone Too Long, 72
Altamont, NY., 50
Alzheimer's, 150, 153, 155, 159, 161
Amaroso, Albert, 63, 70, 71, 73, 174
Amato Opera House, 13
AMC Pacer, 132, 135
American Pickers, 163
*American Popular Song: the Great
    Innovators*, 71
American Woolen Mills, 2

Amram, David, 159
And Now You've Gone, 45
Anderson, Ernestine, 14, 76, 89
Anderson, Gaye, 114
Anderson, Sandy, 132, 135
Angel Eyes, 120, 148, 163
Anglo Saxes, The, 44
Annie's Room, 43
Another Night in Tunisia, 98
Another Vision, 111
Antonia's, 87
Antonioli, Laurie, 154
Apollo moon missions, 59
Apollo Theatre, 12
Appalachian music, 152
Arlen, Harold, 23, 36, 76
Artistry of Mark Murphy, The, 86, 87, 97
As Time Goes By, 67, 97
Astaire, Fred, 59
Astor Hotel, 41
Athens, ix–x, 151, 161–2
Atlantic Records, 39
A-Trane, The, 141–2
Audiophile Records, 72
Autumn Leaves, 97, 112
Avalon, Frankie, 26, 27, 40
Avengers, The, 54
Avia 18: 107
AVRO, 76, 77
Aznavour, Charles, 45, 52
Azymuth, 98

(Baby) It's Just Talk, 118, 119, 130, 133, 168
Bacharach, Burt, 68, 108
Bad and the Beautiful, The, 83, 84
Baker, Chet, 81, 141, 143, 176

Baker, Jimmie, 22
Baker, Kenny, 51, 52
Baker Street Jazz Club, 119
Baker's Keyboard Lounge, 74
Ball, Kenny, 46
Ballad of the Sad Young Men, 83, 84, 119, 163
Ballou, Dave, 139
Ballycastle, 1
Ballyhoo, 45
Bancroft, Anne, 71
Banks, Tommy, 119
Barandgrill, 68
Barber, Chris, 46
Barnes, 85, 92
Barnes, Ken, 59
Barretto, Ray, 31
Barron, Kenny, 106
Barry, Jerry, 92
Barzda, Michael, 153
Basement, Studios, 67, 69
Basement, The, 84, 116
Basie, Count, 9, 19, 32, 33, 36, 52, 87
Basilio, Carmen, 23
Bass Clef, The, 93
Bassey, Shirley, 48, 50, 52
Baubles, Bangles and Beads, 27
Bauer, William, 167
Baverstock, Jack, 45–46
BBC Radio, 41, 43, 57–58, 68, 90; Home
        Service, 44; Light Programme,
        55, 75; Third Programme, 60, 81;
        reorganization, 55; 77; Radio 1–4,
        55; Radio 3, 60; live recordings, 79;
        cutbacks, 60; drama productions, 82;
        Radio London, 91–2; Radio 1, 117;
        cuts big band, 110, Radio 2, 111
BBC Television, 42; BBC1, 53, 60; BBC2, 47,
        52, 60
Beatlemania, 39
Beatles, The, 40, 46
Beautiful Friendship, A, 160–1
Beautiful Love, 124
Beauty and the Beast, 97, 98
BeBop Lives, 83, 97
Beck, Gordon, 55
Becker, Walter, 118
Before We Say Goodbye, 154
Bein' Green, 143
Belong to Me, 24, 163
Belvedere Arms, 93
Bendell, Barry, 110
Bennett, Betty, 47
Bennett, Richard Rodney, 59, 76, 101
Bennett, Tony, 27, 35, 37, 40, 52, 71, 99, 114,
        165, 177

Benny Goodman Story, The, 23
Benny Hill Show, The, 52–3
Benson, George, 76
Bent, Al, 139
Bergman, Marilyn and Alan, 59
Berklee College of Music, 106
Berkeley, Calif., 135, 154
Berlin, 60, 141–3, 147, 149, 154, 155
Berlin, Irving, 68
Bernhardt, Warren, 31
Bertoncini, Gene, 76, 86
Best, Lennie, 85
*Best of Mark Murphy, The Capitol Years,
        The*, 24
Bethel Baptist church, 2
Bey, Andy, 146
Bidwell family, 152
Bidwell, Sheila (née Murphy, sister), 1, 4, 17,
        21, 71, 99, 152
Big Bertha, 63, 64, 70, 72, 74, 98
Big Lulu, The, 126
Big Sur, 100
Bijou, 47
Bilk, Acker, 46
Billboard magazine, 16, 19, 26, 29, 36, 87
Bing Crosby Show, The, 27
Bird Chasin', 159
Birdland (song), 74
Birdland (club), 13, 17, 44, 108, 126, 130, 131,
        134, 138, 145, 146, 153, 158, 167
Birds Eye, 2
Birmingham, 85, 113
Birth of the Cool, xiii
Bitterman, Cindy, 120–123, 125–131, 135,
        137
Black Coffee, 11
Blacksmith Blues, 24
Blakey, Art, 13, 92, 124
Blanchard, Terence, 124
Blood Count, 99
Bloom, John, 45
Bloom, Ken, 161
Blue Eyed Soul, 141
Blue Gardenia, 96
Blue Monk, 47
Blue Note (Jakarta), 117
Blue Note (New York), 134, 158–9
Blue Note Records, 123, 127, 128, 151
Blue Skies, 152
Blue Wisp, The, 159
Blues in the Night, 23, 36, 57, 104
BMG Ariola Records, 126
Body and Soul, 23, 47, 69, 167, 174
Bogart, Humphrey, 129
Boileau, Lois, 84

Boland, Francy, 56–57
Boller, Danton, 156
Bongo Beep – see *You've Proven Your Point*
Boone, Pat, 40
Bop for Kerouac, 81–84, 86, 87, 92, 99, 119
Bop for Miles, 104, 111, 112
Boplicity, 82–84, 159, 177
Borgnine, Ernest, 71
Bosnian War, 111
bossa nova, 31, 52
Boston, Mass., 3, 63, 89, 105, 175
Bouchard, Fred, 174
Bouquet of Blues, 11
Bourne, Michael, 16, 35, 49, 67, 70, 126, 129,
    163, 165, 166, 167, 175
Bowie, David, 51
Boxford, 134, 168
Bracknell, 85
Braham, David, 96
Brand, Pat, 46
Branscombe, Alan, 51
Brasil '66: 59
Braunstone Hotel, 84
Brazil Song, 87, 89, 90, 92
Brazilian music, 31, 48, 52, 59, 89, 90, 99,
    140, 151, 185
Breathing, 140
Brecker Brothers, 67, 69
Brecker, Michael, 70
Brecker, Randy, 69
Brecon Jazz Festival, 152
Brel, Jacques, 42
Bremen, 60
Breyer-Grell, Melody, 158
Bricusse, Lesley, 51, 52
Bridges, 90
Bridgewater, Dee Dee, 101, 131
Bridging a Gap, 66–68, 83, 85, 97
Brighton, 90
Bristol, 90
Bristow, Gloria, 49
Britt, Jimmy, 34
Britt, Stan, 27
Broadbent, Alan, 139, 169
Broadway, 13, 41, 42, 76, 106, 111
Brokeback Mountain, 104, 148
Broken Heart, 45
Brönner, Pino, 141
Brönner, Till, 141–144, 146–149, 160
Brother Can You Spare a Dime?, 43, 110
Brother John, 93
Brothers, 102
Brown, James, 66, 67
Brown Jr, Oscar, x, 37, 43
Brown, Ray, 124

Brown, Reuben, 105
Brown, Ruth, 127
Brown, Sam, 67
Brubeck, Dave, 23, 52
Bruce, Lenny, 22
Bryn Mawr, 5
Buckley, Lord, 100, 128
Buddah Records, 64
Buffalo, N.Y., 9, 71, 72
Buffalo Hyatt, 141
Buffalo News, 9
Buffalo Philharmonic, 76
Buffalo State College, 85, 141, 179, 185
Bull's Head, The, 85, 92
Burkhardt, Fred, 42
Burns, Ralph, 15, 16, 18, 19, 28, 33, 34, 45
Burrett, Hugh, 8
Burton, Ann, 176
But Beautiful, 160
Bye Bye Blackbird, 97
Byrd, Charlie, 31, 89
Byrd, Donald, 128
Byrds, The, 68

Cadence magazine, 96
Cadillac Films, 150
Café Bohemia, 13
Café Continental, 117
Café Paranoia, 112
Calder, Tony, 51
Calgary, 119–120
Callas, Maria, 163
Callier, Terry, 140
Calliope (record label), 23
Calypso Blues, 96
Camden, 91, 92, 94, 110
Canandaigua, N.Y., 32
Canberra, 146
Candoli, Conte, 25
Candoli, Pete, 25
Can't Buy Me Love, 46
Canteen, The, 84
Cantaloupe Island, 70
Canvey Island, 92
Cape May Jazz Festival, 159
Capitol Records, 24–26, 28–30
Carden, Rosemary, 138
Carnegie Hall, 127, 134
Carnegie Recital Hall, 72
Carson, Johnny, 40
Carter, Betty, xi, xii, xiii, 37, 39, 40, 124, 160,
    175, 176
Carter, Ron, 67
Carter, Simon, 180
Cartmel, Andrew, 160

Casablanca Club, 8
Casey at the Bat, 12
Cash, Johnny, 147, 148
Cassady, Neal, 80
Castle, Roy, 59
Castronari, Mario, 110
Catskills, 135
Cava Bob, 60
CBS Records, 59
CDM, 85
Cecil, Malcolm, 43
Cennamo, Tony, 76
Central Line, 91
Chandler, Raymond, 120
Charles, Ray, 33, 37, 52
Chasin' the Jazz Gone By, 146
Chastenier, Frank, xi, 142, 148
Chattin' with Chet, 141
Chelsea, 48, 50, 93, 181
Cherry, Don, 101
Chicago, 16, 60, 100, 123, 127, 144, 155, 158
Chicago 7 Conspiracy Trial, 60
Chicken Road, 68
Chihuahua, 89
Chipperfield, 152
Christie, Agatha, 168
Christy, June, 6, 24
Chumley's, 12
Churchill, Imogen, 144
Churchill, Pete, 112, 113, 133, 134, 144, 152,
       158, 162, 168, 171, 173, 180, 183, 184
Cincinnati, Ohio, 63, 66, 69, 97, 159, 175
Cinnamon and Clove, 59
Clark, Frank, 63
Clark University, 3
Clarke, Terry, 134
Clarke-Boland Big Band, 56
Classic Sound, 97
Clayton, Jay, 161
Clayton, Peter, 46
Clementi, Pierre, 60
Cleveland, Ohio, 63
Clinton, Bill, xii
Club 43: 47
Cobb, Jimmy, 33, 109
Cochran, Charles, 15, 18, 38, 51, 60, 63, 64,
       135
Cocker, Joe, 51
Coe, Tony, 51, 52
Cohn, Al, 31, 33, 36
Coldplay, 147–8
Cole, Nat 'King', xi, 6, 27, 36, 93, 95, 96, 98,
       104, 114, 127, 128, 134, 168, 170, 183
Cole, Richie, 67, 73, 74, 76, 82, 83, 92, 100,
       164, 172

Coleman, Cy, 72
Coleman, Ornette, 41
College of the Siskiyous, 77, 178
Collins, Joyce, 87
Cologne – see Köln
Coltrane, John, 33, 69, 182
Columbia Records, 64, 146
Columbia University, 5, 35
Come and Get Me, 24, 36, 67, 169
Come to Me, 27
Como, Perry, 40
Conlon, Jud, 26, 27
Connor, Chris, 39
Cooling, Joyce, 154
Coots, J. Fred, 104
Copenhagen, 41
Cosmopolitan Greetings, 101, 109
Corso, Gregory, 83
Coryell, Larry, 101
Cosby, Bill, 40
Craig, Wendy, 54, 55
Cranfield Institute, 90
Crawford, Joan, 163
Crazy Rhythm, 18
Creating Patterns, 140
Crescendo magazine, 41, 44, 46
Crescendo, The, 44
Critchinson, John, 85
Crosby, Bing, 59
Crosby, David, 68
Cross, Milton, 5
Crystal Illusions, 59
Culver City, Calif., 98
Cuyahoga Community College, 106

Daddy Must be a Man, 24, 163
Dakota Bar, 139
Dalto, Jorge, 93
Damone, Vic, 35
Dancing to Midnight, 68
Dankworth, John, 43, 45, 46, 47, 51, 179
Dankworths, 90
Danny's Skylight Room, 134
DAT, 119, 130, 131, 133, 161
Dating Game, The, 57
David, Hal, 68, 108
Davis, Bette, 129
Davis, Clive, 158
Davis, Francis, 38, 80
Davis, Miles, xiii, 13, 19, 33, 34, 35, 36, 43,
       52, 53, 82, 84, 92, 96, 128, 133, 163,
       166, 168, 170, 172, 173, 182
Davis Jr, Sammy, 9, 10, 48, 105
Dearie, Blossom, 37, 76
De Armond, Ron, 78, 138

De Felitta, Raymond, 147
De Koenigswarter, Pannonica ('Nica'), 122
De Line, Alan, 8
De Line, Jim, 9
De Roo, Joop, 58, 60, 61, 68, 76, 111
De Vol, Frank, 96
Dead, The, 5
Dearly Beloved, 140
Decca Records, 14–16, 19, 22–25, 30, 31, 34, 45, 51, 111, 144, 157
Decidedly Jazz Danceworks, 119
Dee, Brian, 44, 47, 86, 104
Deer Head Inn, 146
Dell, Alan, 44
DeMiero, Frank, 76
Denver, Colo., 120
Depression (1930s), 2
Desert Inn, The, 44
Detour Ahead, 157
Deuchar, Jimmy, 57
Deutsches Symphonie Orchester, 143
Devo, David, 133
Devon, 3
Diamond, Neil, 69
Did I Ever Really Live, 148
Die Presse, 126
Difficult to Say Goodbye, 107
Diller, Phyllis, 129
Dim the Lights, 124, 137, 139, 142
Ding Walls, 94, 105, 134, 168
Dingwalls dancehall, 92, 93, 94
Dior, Lily, 128, 169, 171, 184
Disterheft, Brandi, 161
Dirty Harry, 132
Do It Again, 118, 129, 130,
Do You Wonder If I Love You, 48
Dock of the Bay, 59
Dobrecky, Gilad, 150
Dobson, Smith, 74
Don't Cry My Love, 24, 163
Don't Get Around Much, 152
Don't Go to Strangers, 97
Don't Like Goodbyes, 107
Don't Misunderstand, 97
Doodlin', 43, 47, 50
Dorham, Kenny, 31
Dorn, Joel, 126, 146
Dors, Diana, 23
Dorsey, Jack, 44
Dorough, Bob, 159
Dougan, Jackie, 47
Down Argentine Way, 88
Down St Thomas Way, 92
Downbeat magazine, 14, 18, 26, 29, 31, 35, 36, 65, 68, 70, 120, 144; voted New

Star of the Year in, 39; report on South African tour, 54; voted Best Male Singer in, 125, 127, 128, 139; left out of poll, 137
draft-dodging, 41
Drakos, Alex, ix
Dream, The, 109, 111, 120, 121, 123
Drew, Martin, 85, 90
Duff, Edwin, 97
Duke, Vernon, 19
Dunlap, Larry, 100, 117
Dunn, Clive, 54
Dunn, Maurice, 92
Dutch Metropole Orchestra – see Metropole Orchestra
Dyer, Ann, 95, 154, 179, 185
Dylan, Bob, 40
Dysart, Dave, 119

Earth, Wind and Fire, 91
Eastern Ballad, 107
Eastman, Madeline, 95, 154
Eastwood, Clint, 132
Easy Does It, 111
Easy to Love, 16
Eckstine, Billy, 6, 8, 36
Ed Sullivan Show, The, 36, 40
Edmonton Journal, 81
Edmunds Community College, 76
Edwards, Steve, 104, 110
El Morocco, 101
Electric Ballroom, 91–94
Elias, Eliane, 101
Ellicott, Charlie, 123
Elling, Kurt, xi, 123, 127, 128, 131, 134, 144, 145, 158, 163, 170, 171
Ellington, Duke, 5, 140
Elliott, Don, 19, 23
Ellis, Stanley, 105
Elmer's Tune, 18, 19
Embassy Club, 9
Embers, The, 13
Emerald Centre, 94
EMI Records, 51
Empty Faces, 59, 63, 70, 90, 92, 93, 112, 119, 151
Englewood, N.J., 99
Englewood Cliffs, N.J., 96
Epilogue, 168
Epstein, Daniel, 170
Erie canal, 2
Esquire magazine, 13
Essex Music, 51
Evans, Bill, 19, 31, 32, 33, 36, 43, 64, 66, 76, 81, 98, 101, 171

Evans, Gil, 34, 36, 82
Evans, Sue, 86
Evening with George Shearing and Mel Tormé, An, 87
Every Day I Have the Blues, 32, 57
Everybody Digs Bill Evans, 31
Everybody Loves Me, 130
Everybody's Crazy 'bout the Doggone Blues, 36
Everybody's Doin' the Bossa Nova, 31, 34, 90
Everything I Have Is Yours, 7
Evolution, 156
Evolution of an Artist, 150–151
Exactly Like You, 15, 16
Exaras, Spiros, ix–x, 151, 161–162

Fabian, 26
Fagen, Donald, 118
Fain, Sammy, 33
Fair Haven, NY, 3, 4, 6, 11, 17, 118, 152, 162
Falling in Love with Love, 25, 176
Fallon, Larry, 105, 107
Fame, Georgie, 52, 53, 60
Famous Door, 13
Fantasy Records, 84, 98, 101, 126
Farber, Mitch, 74–75
Farmer, Art, 75, 101, 113
Farmer's Market, 75, 97, 109, 110, 134
Fascinatin' Rhythm, 15, 16, 23, 176
Feather, Leonard, 41
Felice, Dee, 63
Ferguson, Maynard, 41
Ferlinghetti, Lawrence, 83
Fields, Barney, 139
Fields, Dorothy, 18, 72
Fields, Joe, 64–67, 69–71, 74, 75, 81–84, 95, 105, 107, 126, 139, 144
Filmways/Helder Studios, 74
Finck, David, 134
Firefly, 27
Firestone Hour, The, 5
Firestone, Irene, 73, 95
Fitzgerald, Ella, 6, 8, 25, 57–58, 93, 131
Five Corners Quintet, 80, 146
Five O'Clock Club, 52
Five Spot, NYC, 40
Fleece, The, 168
Fletcher, Mark, 133–4, 144, 171, 173, 180
Flower is a Lovesome Thing, A, 140
Fly Away My Sadness, 31, 163
Fly Me to the Moon, 36, 39, 53, 100
Fontana Records, 45–46, 48
For All We Know, 96, 104, 170
For Heaven's Sake, 47
Ford, Tennessee Ernie, 68

Forge, Patrick, 92
Forman, Bruce, 82
Formanek, Mike, 97
Fort Dix army band, 14
Four Brothers, 134, 144–145
Four Freshmen, The, 24
Four Queens Hotel, 109, 163
Fourie, John, 54
Fredette, Carol, 163
Freeman, Russ, 81
Friedwald, Will, xi, 154, 158, 163, 175
Frigo, Johnny, 168
Fuest, Robert, 54
Franks, Michael, 91
Full Voice, 114, 118, 131, 132, 135
Fulton, NY, 1–3, 6, 7, 9, 11, 20; Rotary Club, 3; Pleasant Point Club, 3; Emerick Park Association, 3; Voorhees Park, 3; friends in, 6; High School, 8; marching band, 8; civic groups, 17; radio station, 8; Chamber of Commerce, 17; Home Appliance, 17; hospital, 62; similarity to Lowell, 80; Music Association, 152; G. Ray Bodley High School, 152; Mount Adnah cemetery, 162
Future Light, 117

Gabler, Milt, 14–16
Gainesville, Fla., 172
Gale, Warren, 74
Galusha, Helen, 8
Galusha, Jim, 8
Galusha, Nancy, 8
Galvis and Young, 31
Gang Show – see Gong Show
Garland, Red, 110, 171
Garner, Errol, 33, 98
Garside, Ernie, 47
Gates, Giacomo, 151, 163
Gavin, James, 12, 16, 22, 24, 27, 30, 41, 42, 69, 83, 108, 112, 120, 122, 130, 153, 155, 163, 166, 169
Gay, Al, 85
Gazarte Club, ix, 151
Gearbox Records, 160
Geier, Werner, 126
Geller, Herb, 60
Gelly, Dave, 174
Geneva, NY, 32
Genovese, Annamarie, 8
Genovese, Teddy, 8
Gerde's Folk City, 40
Gerry and the Pacemakers, 44
Gershwin, George, 23

Gershwin, Ira, 23
Get Out of Town, 160
Getz, Stan, 32, 52
Gilbert and Sullivan, 9
Gillespie, Dizzy, 77, 80
Ginger Bread Boy, 128
Ginsberg, Allen, 101
Gioia, Ted, 180
Giorgiadis, George, ix
Glass, Barbara, 99
Glenn, Tyree, 5
God Bless the Child, 37
GoJazz label, 139
Golden Apple, The, 100
Golden Gate Bridge, 73, 103
Golden Shot, The, 53
Goldman, Leo, 60
Goldsby, John, 99
Goldsmith's College, 179
Gong Show, 89
Goodbye Baby, 18
Goodbye Pork Pie Hat, 83, 84, 97, 167
Goodman, Benny, 6
Goody Goody, 43
Gordon, Dexter, 128
Gotham Hotel, 13
Grable, Betty, 88
Grade, Lew, 71
Grammy Awards, xii, 76, 84, 87, 89, 98, 101,
    104, 130, 131, 139
Granby, 3
Grant, Alan, 109
Grapes, The, 85
Grauer, Bill, 31, 41
Graz – see University of Music and
    Performing Arts
Great American Music Hall, San Francisco,
    85
Great American Songbook, The, 59, 67
Great City, The, 47, 167
Great Famine, 1
Great Ormond Street Hospital, 144
Greco, Fred, 8
Green, Benny (critic), 43, 53
Green, Benny (pianist), 124, 137
Green, Johnny, 122
Green Mill, The, 127
Green, Urbie, 33
Greene, Burton, 57
Greenwich Village, 11, 14, 35, 40, 79, 143,
    158, 159
Greys Club, 55
Grolnik, Don, 70
Gruntz, George, 60, 101, 103, 105, 107, 109
Guernsy, Betsy, 152

Guildhall, 181, 183
Guess I'll Hang My Tears Out to Dry, 15, 183
Guthrie, Woody, 152
Guys and Dolls, 9

Haley, Bill, 15, 40
haiku, 112, 113, 134
Hall, Lani, 59
Hamburg, 60
Hamburg State Opera, 101
Hamill, Andy, 140, 144, 168, 169, 170, 171,
    172
Hammerstein, Oscar, 33, 142
Hampton, Lionel, 9
Hampton, Slide, 41
Hancock, Herbie, 69, 70, 163
Handy, W.C., 36
Happy Bachelor, 47
Happy Days Are Here Again, 46
Happyin', 108
Hard-Hearted Hannah, 46
Harbinger Records, 161
Harrell, Tom, 86, 101, 139
Harrington, Mike, 40
Harro East Ballroom, 153
Harrods, 50
Hartman, Johnny, 37, 71
Hasselback, John, 63
Havens, Richie, 40
Hawkins, Coleman, 167
Hayes, Tubby, 45, 46, 47, 104, 160
Haymes, Dick, 6, 37, 78, 98,
Heart is a Lonely Hunter, The, 73
Henderson, Joe, 101
Hershey Hotel, 101
Hefti, Neal, 34
Hello Young Lovers, 43
Helsinki, 146
Hendricks, Jon, 9, 19, 20, 41, 43, 60, 92, 98,
    115, 123, 134, 144, 145, 146, 151, 159
Hentoff, Nat, 14
Here's That Rainy Day, 105
Herman, Woody, 9, 15, 52
Hey Look Me Over, 47
Hi-Lo's, The, 33
HighNote Records, 111, 139, 140, 144, 145
Hillside Sound, 99
Hilversum, 58, 68, 76, 77, 88, 111
Hilversum Greets Radio 2, 111
Hines, Earl, 36
Hines, Gregory, 109, 169
Hines, Rosetta, 76
Hinkhouse family, 152
Hinkhouse, David, 71
Hinkhouse, Kathy (niece), 10, 18, 71, 159, 162

Hip Parade – see *Mark Murphy's Hip Parade*
History Channel, 163
Hoare, Rob, 143
Hodnik, 125
Hoffman, Don, 123
Hoffman, Richard, 14
Holiday, Billie, 13, 15, 25, 97, 176
Hollywood, Calif., 82, 101,128
Holman, Bill, 24–26, 29, 33, 34, 88
Holy Grail of Jazz and Joy, The, 105
homosexuality, laws concerning, 48
Hopeless, 57
Hopkins, Duncan, 131
Horizon Radio, 91
Horn, Shirley, 137, 142, 160, 170
Horne, Lena, 13, 23, 76
Hot Corner, 146
House Is Not a Home, A, 108
How High the Moon, 105
Howard, Bart, 36
Howard, Jua, 154
How Come You do Me Like You Do, 152
Howe, Abraham (ancestor), 3
Howe, Allan (cousin), 18, 20, 152
Howe, Elizabeth ('Betty') (aunt), 4, 14, 59
Howe, Elliott ('Billy') (uncle), 4, 16, 29
Howe, Katherine ('Katie') (aunt), 4, 29
Howe, Priscilla ('Sally') (aunt), 4, 14
Howe family, origins, 3; sexual equality, 5; concert, 152
Howe, John Harroun (grandfather), 3, 5
Howe, Margaret (mother) – see Margaret Murphy
Howe, 'Nana' (grandmother), 3, 15, 17
Howe Tavern, 3
Hubbard, Freddie, 53, 69
Huffington Post, The, 42, 158
Humanity Ltd, 125, 168
Humoresque, 6
Hunt, Marsha, 86
Hunter Ceiling Fans, 2
Huston, Anjelica, 5
Huston, John, 5

I Believe in You, 47
I Cover the Waterfront, 122
I Got Rhythm, 18, 19
I Keep Going Back to Joe's, 104
I Know You from Somewhere, 157, 169
I Left My Heart in San Francisco, 67
I Never Went Away, 101
I Only Have Eyes for You, 176
I Remember Clifford, 47, 97
I Return to Music, 78

I Walk a Little Faster, 72
I Wish You Love, 129
IAJE, 185
IBM, 70
IDJ, 92
I'd Rather Drink Muddy Water, 152
If You Could See Me Now, 82, 99
Iles, Nikki, 113, 144
I'll Be Seeing You, 33, 34, 152
I'll Close My Eyes, 107
I'll Never Be Free, 24
I'm a Circus, 16
I'm a Fool to Want You, 139, 143
I'm Glad There is You, 16, 67, 83
I'm in the Mood for Love, 72, 73
I'm Old Fashioned, 105, 110
In the Fast Lane, 93
In the Land of Oo-Bla-Dee, 140
Immediate Records, 51
Independence, 11
International Mark Murphy Appreciation Society, The (IMMAS), 78, 79, 86, 92, 120, 132, 138
Interview, The, 148, 168
Iridium, 134, 146, 150, 151, 158
Irresistible You, 15
Is That All There Is? The Strange Life of Peggy Lee, 27
Isaacs, James, 140
Islington, 171
Isn't It A Pity?, 16
Israels, Chuck, 36
Istanbul, 154
It Might As Well Be Spring, 104
It's Like Love, 31, 34, 163
It's Not for Me to Say, 27
ITV (UK), 42
I've Got You Under My Skin, 43

Jack, John, 49
Jackie and Roy, 130
Jack's, San Francisco, 44
Jackson, Michael, 57
Jagger, Mick, 43
Jakarta, 117
Jamal, Ahmad, 124
James, José, 176
Jarreau, Al, 82, 91, 115
Jarrdical, 105
Jazz (club), 111
Jazz 625, 47
Jazz 90, 94
Jazz At Night, 44
Jazz Café, 110, 111, 138
Jazz Club, 44

Jazz Composers, The – see *Beauty and the Beast*
Jazz Discography, The, 14, 34
Jazz FM, 104, 110, 132
Jazz Foundation of America, 153, 155
Jazz Horizons, 92
Jazz Journal, 47, 140
Jazz Messengers, 124
Jazz Scene, The (UK), 44
Jazz Scene USA, 37
Jazz Session, 44
Jazz Singers' Network, 181
Jazz Standard, The, 134
Jazz Times, 154
Jazz Unlimited, 6
Jazz Workshop, 179
Jazz World (record label), 111
Jazzcoteque dancers, 113, 169
Jazzette (record label), 111
Jazzland, 126
Jazzschool, 154
Jazzwise magazine, 148
Jefferson Airplane, 68
Jefferson, Eddie, 66, 73, 74, 76, 92, 100, 123, 126, 169
Jelly Jelly Blues, 36, 43
Jesus of Nazareth, 71
Jive Records, 111
Jobim, Antonio Carlos, 87, 90, 98, 140, 167
Jocko, Jackie, 141
Joe's Pub, 161
Johannesburg, 54
Johnson, Ellen, 13
Johnson, Lowell, 54
Jones, Etta, 97
Jones, Hank, 153
Jones, Jack, 30, 76
Jones, James Earl, 71
Jones, Philly Jo, 41
Jones, Salena, 52
Jones, Thad, 41
Jordan, Louis, 96
Jordan, Sheila, 11, 13–14, 101, 103, 105–107, 109, 111, 135, 137, 144, 153, 159, 161, 162, 163, 164
Joual, 81
Junior – see Helen Meyer
Just in Time, 25
Just Jazz, 111
Just Like a Woman, 48, 54, 55

Kahal, Irving, 33
Kalamazoo, Mich., 95
Kapp Records, 30
Kameron, Pete, 14, 51

Kansas City, Mo., 71, 83, 127
Kansas City, 47
Kauffeld, Greetje, 76, 150
Kay, Monte, 14, 51
Keach, Stacy, 71
Keane, Helen, 33, 64–66, 68
Keepnews, Orrin, 31, 33, 98
Keepnews, Peter, 68
Kellam, Colin, 92
Kellaway, Roger, 76
Kelly, Gene, 59
Kelly, Nancy, 152, 163, 166, 169
Kelly, Wynton, 33, 171
Kelly's Stable, 13
Kennedy Center, 134
Kennedy, John F., 41
Kent, Stacey, 113
Kenton, Stan, 6, 9, 24
Kermit the Frog, 143
Kern, Jerome, 18, 76
Kerouac Festival, 154
Kerouac, Jack, 51, 80–84, 97, 99, 100, 104, 105, 108, 112, 127, 128, 159, 163
Kerouac Then and Now, 102, 103, 132
Keystone Korner, 179
Kimball's, 115
King, Barbara, 133
King, Morgana, 14, 66
King, Peggy, 122
Kings Cross, 93
Kings Langley, 152
King's Road, Chelsea, 48, 93
Kinsela's, 117, 175
Kinsey, Tony, 44
Kirk, Elsie, 14
Kirk, Lisa, 14
Kitano, 134, 154
KJAZZ (London), 91
KJAZZ (Long Beach), 109, 115
Knight, Gladys, 64
Knoop, Manfred, 156
Köck, Samir, 126
Köln, 56, 88
Krall, Diana, xi, 128
Kroner, Erling, 126
Kuh, Fred, 83

LA Reader, 99
Lady Be Good, 8
Lady in Red, The, 18, 120
Lady is a Tramp, The, 25
Lady Who Sang the Blues, The, 97
Lady's in Love with You, The, 139
Laine, Cleo, 43, 45, 52, 76, 78, 151, 164, 179
Lake Murray, 71

Lake Placid, 19, 50
LaFaro, Scott, 31–33, 36
Lamarr, Hedy, 163
Lambert, Dave, 9, 19, 20, 37, 43, 60, 115, 159, 175
Lambert, Hendricks and Ross, 60, 115, 159
Lambrinos, Phil, 8
Landesman, Fran, 83, 84
Landesman, Jay, 83, 85
Landmark Records, 126
Lane, Burton, 7
Laren, 77
Las Vegas, Nev., 109, 163
LaSpina, Steve, 97, 99
Last Night When We Were Young, 165
Last Rose of Summer, The, 5
Lateano, Vince, 74, 75, 117
Lateef, Yusef, 93, 160
Late'n'Lazy, 44
Latin Porter, The, 139
Laughton, Charles, 24
Laura, 109
Lausche, Lou, 97
Lazy Afternoon, 99, 100, 174
Le Café, 84
Le Temps, 52
Leduc, Jean-Pierre, 153–155, 159–161
Lee, Lawrence, 83
Lee, Peggy, 6, 8, 9, 11, 15, 24, 25; attempted seduction by, 27–29; 36, 37, 50, 52, 59, 76, 96, 127, 168, 169, 172
Leeds, 134, 173
Leeds College of Music, 183
Lees, Gene, 15, 31, 32, 36, 39, 64, 76, 90
Legrand, Michel, 41–42
Leicester, 84
Leonard, Jack E., 23
Leonhart, Jay, 127
LeSage, Bill, 44
Less and Less, 112
Let Yourself Go, 18, 22, 23
Let's Take A Chance, 54
Level 42: 91
Levesley, Leonard, 50
Levine, Mark, 74
Lewis, Curtis, 167
Lewis, Jerry Lee, 40
Lewis, Mel, 25
Lewis, Ramsey, 124
Lewis, Sam, 104
Lewisham, 179
Lexington, S.C., 71
Liberace, 128
Life magazine, 13
Life's Mosaic, 139

Like Love, 34
Lillian Booth Actors' Home, 155, 159, 161, 162
Linardos, Patti, 108
Lincoln Tunnel, 89
Lindström Studios, 56
Links, 139, 169
Lins, Ivan, 98, 99, 156
Lissack, Selwyn, 54
Little Jazz Bird, 18
Little Richard, 40
Little Sodus Bay, 4
Liverpool, 1
Living Room (album), 96
Living Room (dance sequence), 120
Living Room, The (club), 12
Livingston, Joric, 14
LoDuca, Joe, 95
Logan, Freddie, 47
London, Amy, 109, 159, 161, 185
London Bridge, 91
London, Julie, 23, 25
London Tara Hotel, 60
Lonely Town, 140, 143
Long Beach, Calif., 115
Lookin' for Another Pure Love, 68
Looking for Somebody, 24
Lord Buckley, 100, 168
Lord, Tom, 14
Lost and Found, 107
Lot of Living to Do, A, 43

Louis', NY, 12
Louvre, The, 154
Love, 36
Love is What Stays, 147, 148, 150, 166, 168
Lowell, Mass., 80, 159
Lowell Celebrates Kerouac, 159
Lucas, Isabelle, 60
Lucky to Be Me, 140, 143
Lullaby in Rhythm, 18
Lullaby of the Leaves, 124
Lundy, Curtis, 160, 161
Lupino, Ida, 75, 97, 168
Lush Life, 104, 181
Lutter, Andy, 112, 113
Lynn, Gloria, 105
Lyttelton, Humphrey, 104

Mac, Marc, 140
Mack the Knife, 43
Mad on Jazz, 91
Madalena, 119, 173
Madison, Jimmy, 67, 69, 76, 86
Magaro, Polly, 14

Magnificent Ambersons, The, 3
Magnusson, Bob, 95
Magog, 10
Mahogany, Kevin, 134, 144
Maia, Marcelo, 162
Maiden Voyage, 97, 163
Main Man, The, 73, 74
Mainly Millicent, 53
Makin' Whoopee, 24
Man on the Other Side of the Street, The, 168
Manchester, 47, 90, 134, 168, 172
Mancuso, Charles, 141
Mandel, Johnny, 59, 142, 174
M&I Studios, 139
Manhattan School of Music, 11
Manhattan Transfer, 98, 159
Manne, Shelly, 23, 82
Manning, Jane, 60
Margolis, Kitty, 95, 154
Maria, 37
Marie's Crisis Café, 13
Mark II, 68–69, 130
Marlborough, Mass., 3
Marion McPartland's Piano Jazz, xiii
Mark Murphy Sings, 59, 69–71, 90, 97, 169
*Mark Murphy Sings Dorothy Fields and Cy
    Coleman*, 72
*Mark Murphy Sings Nat's Choice: The Nat
    "King" Cole Songbook Volume Two*,
    96, 98
*Mark Murphy Sings the Nat King Cole
    Songbook Volume One*, 96
Mark Murphy's Hip Parade, 26–29, 176
Mark Murphy Room, The, 141
Mark Murphy Vocal Jazz Scholarship, 154
Mark Murphys The, 141
Mark Time!, 45–46, 48, 52, 53, 148
Mark's Times, vii, 78, 79, 84, 85, 88, 90,
    98, 99, 105, 107, 111, 115, 120, 123,
    124, 127, 130, 133, 135; closure of,
    137–139; 177, 179, 180
Marple, Jane, 168
Marquee Club, 47
Marsalis brothers, 124
Martha Cohen Theatre, 119
Martin, Dean, 26
Martin, Mary, 33
Martin, Millicent, 53
Mason, Barry, 45
Mathis, Johnny, 18, 27, 48
Masquerade Is Over, The, 171
Matthew, Brian, 44
Matthews, Dave, 63, 66–69, 74, 86
Matthews, Francis, 54
Matthewson, Ron, 85, 90

May the Road Rise To Meet You, 152
May, Tina, 165, 171
Mayfield, Curtis, 64
Mayhew, Helen, 132–133
Mays, Bill, 81, 82, 87, 97–101, 107, 117, 135,
    151
Mays, Judy, 82, 135
Mays, Lyle, 101
McCorkle, Susannah, 128, 130
McCullers, Carson, 73
McDougal, Dick, 6
McDuff, Jack, 93
McFarland, Gary, 101
McFerrin, Bobby, 98, 102, 105, 175, 176
McGlohon, Loonis, 71, 72
McGowan's restaurant, 40
McHugh, Jimmy, 76
McPartland, Marion, xiii, 7, 128
Meader, Darmon, 159
Meadowlane Enterprises, 37
Meaning of the Blues, The, 36
Mercer, Johnny, 23, 36, 52, 127, 167
Mercer, Mabel, 71
Meet Mark Murphy, 14–18, 22, 23, 37, 55,
    176
Melbourne, 117
Melody Maker, 52
Memories of You, 145, 148
Mendes, Sergio, 59, 90
Merion Inn, 159, 160
Mesquida, Allen, 139
Messenger, The, 128
Mesterhazy, George, 158–160
Metheny, Pat, 101, 115
Methodist church, 1–3
Metro's Midnight Music, 76
Metropole Orchestra, 68, 76, 109
Metropole Orchestra, The (radio show), 111
Meyer, Helen ('Junior Morrow'), 14, 107
Miami, 87
Miano, Francesca, 85, 146, 162; eulogy, 163;
    176
Middlesbrough, 59
Midnight Mood, 56–57, 69, 90
Midnight Strings, The, 44
Mihelic, Peter, 111
Miklin, Karlheinz, 105–106, 111, 124–125,
    161, 183
Miles Ahead, 36
Milestone Records, 98, 100
Milestones, 34, 47, 70, 92, 93, 97, 134, 151
Milestones (club), 96
Millennium Park, 144
Millennium Records, 124
Miller beer, 2

Miller, Benny, 123
Miller, Bud, 115, 126
Miller, Glenn, 139
Millionaires' Club, The, 85–86
Minasian, Alex, 159, 160
Ministry of Sound, 117
Minton's Playhouse, 12
Miranda, Carmen, 88
Misty, 152
Mitchell, Blue, 33
Mitchell, Joni, 68, 83, 84
Mitchell, Red, 41
Mitchell-Clarke, Lesley, 28, 62, 123,
    128–131, 150
Mondragon, Joe, 25
Modern Jazz Quartet, The, 50
Mombasa, 117
Monheit, Jane, xi
Monk, Thelonious, 31, 43, 80, 122
Monro, Matt, 42, 52
Montgomery, Wes, 31, 43
Montmartre Club, 95
Moody, Bill, 40, 60, 78, 163
Moody, James, 66, 73
Moody's Mood, 76
Moody's Mood for Love, 73, 97, 104
Mooney, Art, 31
Moore, Dudley, 51, 53
Moore, Mike, 69
Morgan, Frank, 99
Morgan, Tom, 24, 33
Moriarty, Dean, 80, 87
Morrow, Junior – see Helen Meyer
Motian, Paul, 31
Move, The, 51
MPS record label, 56
Mulligan, Gerry, 33, 82
Mure, Billy, 31
Murphy, Ann (ancestor), 1
Murphy, Dwight Louis – 'DL' (father), 1, 3,
    4–5, 17, death, 20–21; 162
Murphy, Dwight 'Doc' (brother), 1, 3, 6, 8,
    11, 14, 20, 21, 50, 51, 135, 152
Murphy family, vii: Celtic/Scots-Irish roots,
    9, 80; home movies, 4; concert, 152
Murphy, James (great-grandfather), 1
Murphy, Kate (née Rogers, sister-in-law), 21,
    50, 51, 62, 63, 73, 95, 103, 104, 162
Murphy, Margaret (née Howe, mother), 1, 4;
    resemblance to Duchess of Windsor,
    5; doesn't believe son is gay, 51; death,
    62; 162
Murphy, Mark: achievements, vii; Athens
    concerts, ix–x; 'Marf Murky', xi,
    132; critical neglect, xii; 'cool', 'hip',
xii–xiii; birth, 1; childhood shyness,
5; conflicts with father, 5; vocal
range, xii, 143; moves to New York,
11; baldness and wigs, 16, 70, 71, 85,
129–130, 146, 152; sexuality, 8, 15,
19, 28, 48–49, 62, 95; moves to LA,
22; moves to London, 42; London
flat, 49–51; moves to San Francisco,
72; moves to Shohola, 135; bothered
by smoke, 56, 117, 175; discontent
with Europe, 60; writes screenplay,
79; taste in clothes, 85–86; collapse,
88; scat singing, 97, 108, 154; grief
and addiction, 102, 103, 108, 109,
110; considers retirement, 109, 110;
decline in health, 150, 152–153;
moves to actors' home, 155; revival,
153–160; death, 162; memorial
service, 163–164
Murphy, Mark Edmond (nephew), 152, 153,
    155, 161–163
Murphy, Mary (ancestor), 1
Murphy, Molly, 152
Murphy, Nancy (née Purcell, sister-in-law),
    19, 20, 50, 51, 62, 152, 162
Murphy, Patrick (ancestor), 1
Murphy, Paul (DJ), 91
Murphy, Richard D. (grandfather), 2
Murphy, Richard Kevin (brother), 1, 4, 10,
    17, 20–21, 50–51, 63, 73
Murphy, Sally, 152
Murphy, Sheila (sister) – see Sheila Bidwell
Murphy, Stuart (cousin), 162
Murphy's Vamp, 195
Muse Records, 57, 64–68, 83, 86, 92, 96,
    105–108, 125, 126, 139, 146
Music Around Midnight, 44
Music Before Midnight, 44
Music From Midnight, 44
Music to Midnight, 44, 68
Music Through Midnight, 44
Musicians' Union (UK), 43
Musicians' Union (USA), 8
Musiker, Lee, 134, 139, 140, 143
My Favorite Things, 33, 34, 43, 47, 174
My Foolish Heart, 147, 148
My Funny Valentine, ix, 185
My Kind of Girl, 52
My Old Friend, 109
My One and Only Love, 143, 152
My Ship, 57, 97

Nachtkaffee, 104, 111
Naima, 69
Naples, Italy, 11

Napper, Kenny, 51, 52, 54
Nascimento, Milton, 59, 70, 89, 90
National Public Radio (NPR), 71
Natural History Museum, 49
Nature Boy, 95, 128
NDR Big Band, 101
Nearness of You, The, 183
needle time, 43
Nelson, Oliver, 74
Neruda, Pablo, 60
Nestlé, 2
Nevada Desert, 89, 135
Never Let Me Go, 96, 120, 155–158, 169
Never Never Land, 111
New Jersey turnpike, 89
New Morning, 154
New Musical Express, 93
New Orleans Restaurant and Jazz Café, 114
New School for Social Research, 159, 185
New Stories, 114
New York, New York, xii
New York Sun, 2
New York Times, 146, 167
Newcastle, 55, 56, 78
Newley, Anthony, 51
Newman, Paul, 12
Newport Jazz Festival, xii, 19, 32
Newtown, 146
Niagara Hilton, 104
Nichol, Althea, 2
Night Beat, 44
Night in Tunisia, A, 92
Night Mood, 98–99
Night Ride, 55
Night We Called it a Day, The, 99, 100
Night with Mark Murphy, A, 150
Nightingale Sang in Berkeley Square, A, 15, 16
No Sound Is Too Taboo, 117
No Tears for Me, 34
Nobody Knows You When You're Down and Out, 43, 110
Nola Studios, 76
Nordring Festival, 76, 88
Norris, Bobbe, 95, 154
North Sea Jazz Sessions Volume 5, 111
Nothing Will Be As It Was Tomorrow, 90
Novakov, Dusan, 125
November in the Snow, 100
Nunez, Flip, 108
Nuremberg Trials, 3, 5
Nussbaum, Adam, 99

Oakenfold, Paul, 91
Oakland, Calif., 116, 154, 175

O'Day, Anita, 6, 25, 34, 38, 39, 40, 50, 60, 64, 158, 168
Ode to the Road, 139
Odetta, 40
Okura Hotel, 158
Old Folks, 37
Old Mill, The, 154
Old Piano, 110
Oldham, Andrew Loog, 51
On Broadway, 47
On Green Dolphin Street, x, 97, 174
On the Red Clay, 69, 159, 169
On the Road, 80, 81, 83, 84, 99, 100, 108, 159
On the Town, 140
Once to Every Heart, 96, 142–144, 146–148, 157, 166, 169
One for Junior, 107
One Step Down, 105
Ontario, Lake, 1, 3, 9
Open House, 52
Orent, Milt, 140
Origins of the Beat Generation, The, 83
Oslo, 76
O'Sullivan, Eddie, first meeting, 48; 49–51, 56, 59–61, 63, 68, 71; marriage of convenience, 73; living in San Francisco, 73, 94–95; 72, 78, 96; illness and death, 102–104; 108, 110, 112, 113, 118, 129, 134, 135, 162
Oswego Country Club, 3
Oswego River, 1
Ottley, Frank, 32
Ouellette, Dan, 125, 127
Our Game, 143
Out of This World, 34, 35
Outubro, 89
Oxenhorn, Wendy, 155, 166
Oxford University, 5

Pablo's Place, 60
Pacer – see AMC Pacer
Page Three, The, 13, 14, 107
Panken, Ted, 138
Papandreou, George, ix
Para Nada, 101
Paradise, Sal, 80
Paris, 41, 110, 154, 155
Paris, Jackie, 147
Park West, 144
Parker, Charlie, 6, 8, 80, 83, 84, 122
Parker's Mood, 83, 97, 104
Parnell, Jack, 53
Passion of Christ, The, 71
Pauer, Fritz, 106, 124, 125

PBS, 101
Peacocks, The, 139
Pearls, 116
Peg, 127
Perfectly Frank, 37
Perth, 84
Petaluma, Calif., 123
Peter Pan, 111
Peterson, Gilles, 57, 91, 92, 93, 94, 105, 117, 134
Peterson, Oscar, 124
Philadelphia, 5, 37, 101, 122
Philips Records, 42, 45, 49
Phipps, Dick, 71
Photograph, 140
Piatigorsky, Misha, 145, 150, 151, 155–158, 170
Piazzola, Astor, 126
Picasso, Pablo, 176
Pick Yourself Up, 18
Pike, Dave, 41
Pike, Midge, 54
pirate radio, 42, 55, 91
Pistoni, Dave, 150
Pizza Express, 132, 133, 184
Pizza on the Park, 104, 105, 109, 113, 144, 158
Planet Formerly Known as Moon, The, 112
Playboy magazine, 13
Playing the Field, 29
Platz, David, 51
Plaza Sound Studios, 33
Poconos Mountains, 135, 146
Ponty, Jean-Luc, 93
Pope of Greenwich Village, The, 79
Porter, Cole, 34, 49, 76, 139
Portrait in Jazz, 31
Portuguese language, 89
Powell, Bud, 80, 124
Powell, Eleanor, 163, 169
Powell, Jane, 148
Powell, Robert, 71
Power, Tyrone, 70
Prague, 56
Pramuk, Dylan, 159
Praskin, Allen, 104
Prayer for Mr Davis, 128
Presidio, The, 132
Presley, Elvis, 40, 44
Prestige Records, 64, 126
Previn, André, 24
Price, Lloyd, 27
Procol Harum, 51
Protestants, 1, 2
Providence, R.I., 63

Prysock, Arthur, 6
Purcell, Nancy – see Murphy, Nancy
Purcell, Patti, 153
Puritans, 3
Put the Blame on Mame, 29
Pyne, Mick, 104

Quebec City Jazz Festival, 161

Rachmaninoff, Sergei, 97
Raccoon Song, The, 152
Radiance and Death of Joaquin Murieta, 60
Radio Caroline, 42
Radio Invicta, 91
Radio London (pirate station), 43
Radio Nederland, 68
Radio Times, 61
Rah, 19, 32–35, 36, 65, 98, 141, 148, 155, 163
Rainey, Ma, 178
Raksin, David, 83, 109
Ramp, The, 179
Rampling, Danny, 91
Raney, Sue, 24
Raposo, Joe, 143
Rare Silk, 159
Rays, The, 110
RCA Records, 126, 136
Reagan, Ronald, 81
Rebillot, Pat, 67, 105
Record Retailer, 51
Red Clay – see *On the Red Clay*
Red Drum, The, 83
Redding, Calif., 115
Reed, Les, 45
Reed, Rex, 130
Remarks, 78
Renzi, Mike, 76, 127
Reeves, Dianne, xi
Resistible Rise of Arturo Ui, The, 60
Respighi, Ottorino, 49
Reynolds, Gillian, 61
Rhythm Addiction, 119
Rhythmic Club, 171
Rickles, Don, 22
Ridin' High, 18
Right Kind of Woman, The, 18, 45
Riley, Ben, 106
Rio de Janeiro, 87
Riverside Records, 31–34, 36, 41–43, 49, 84, 98, 169
Road House, 97, 168
Roar of the Greasepaint, the Smell of the Crowd, The, 52
Robinson, Edward G., 180
Robbins' Nest, 18

Roberts, Evelyn, 24
Rochester Jazz Festival, 153, 158
rock and roll, 13
Rodgers, Richard, 33, 34, 43
Roditi, Claudio, 99
Rogers, John, 109
Rolling Stones, The, 51
Roney, Wallace, 126
Ronnie Scott's, London, 43, 49, 51–53, 57,
    58, 78, 85, 92, 93, 110, 154, 158
Ronnie Scott's, Birmingham, 113
Ross, Annie, 9, 20, 34, 43, 50, 52, 60, 75, 159
Ross, Holli, 159
Ross, Ronnie, 44
Round Midnight, 181
Roundabout, 44
Route 66: 23, 104
Rowles, Jimmy, 25, 37, 139
Royal Arms, 9
Royal Bopsters, The, 159
Royal Festival Hall, 57
Royal Northern Hotel, 134, 168
Royal Oak, 117
Royal Roost, The, 25
Royal Wedding, 185
Royal York, 91
Rubie, Steve, 89, 93, 170, 174, 181
Rucker, Ellyn, 126, 138
Rueckert, Thomas, ix, 151
Rugg, May, 3
Rusch, Bob, 35, 83, 84
Russian Hill Recording, 88

S (Swartz), Harvie, 69, 70, 106
Sack Full of Dreams, 101
Sackville-West, Vita, 51
Sage and Sound Studios, 82
St George's Table, 63
St John Hotel, 154
St Louis Blues, 36
St Paul, Minn., 139
St Peter's Church, 163
Salmins, Ralph, 110
Salt Sea, 59
Salzburg, 135
Samba de Flora, 93
San Francisco, 99, 168
San Francisco Jazz Festival, 154
Sanborn, David, 69
Sanders, Pharoah, 93
Satchmo – see Louis Armstrong
Satisfaction Guaranteed, 76, 78, 97, 174
Sausalito, 67, 101
Saville, Brad, 150
Savoy Jazz label, 146

Scala Cinema, 93
Scene, The, 63
Schimke, Peter, 139
Schmidlin, Peter, 161
Schroon Lake, N.Y., 159
Schunk, Gary, 95, 96
Schwarzenegger, Arnold, 57
Schwartz, Nan, 142, 143
'Sconsolato, 57, 90
Scott, Jill, 140
Scott, Ronnie, 45, 47, 56, 57
Scott, Tony, 14, 54
Sculler's, 175
Sear Sound, 86, 106
Seattle, Wash., 76, 105, 114, 116, 117, 134, 174
Secret Love, 47
Seligman, Selig J., 22
Selleck, Tom, 57
Send for Me, 27
Señor Blues, 36, 47, 131, 159
Sentimental Journey, 8
September (record label), 111
September Ballads, 100, 101
September Fifteenth, 101, 119
September in the Rain, 100
Serenade in Blue, 140
Sessions Live, 23
Shadows, 125, 161, 168
Shakespeare, 9
Shaw, Ian, 181
Shaw, Dr Kirby, 77, 178
Shaw, Marlena, 109
She Loves You, 46
Shearing, George, 8, 26, 80, 87, 100
Sheila's Blues, 161
Sheinman, Darrel, 160
shellac records, 13
Sherman Oaks, Calif., 84
Shihab, Sahib, 57
Shipley School, PA, 5
Shohola, 135, 138, 152, 153
Short, Bobby, 71
Shorter, Wayne, 97, 98, 164
Showplace, The, 35
Shrine Auditorium, 87
Sickler, Don, 139, 140
Siegel, Janis, 161
Silver, Horace, 36, 67
Silverstein, Art, 85, 170, 185
Simmons, Norman, 145
Sinatra, Frank, 12, 15, 24, 25, 26, 29, 35, 36,
    37, 48, 50, 52, 69, 78, 82, 95, 114, 120,
    121, 128, 130, 142, 146, 170, 177
Sinatra Society, The, 165
Sinclair, John, 159

Sing a Song of Basie, 20
Singing M, The, 4, 17, 18
Sissinghurst Castle, 51
Sixteen Tons, 68
Skylark, 104, 143, 167
Skymasters, The, 77
Slate Brothers, 22
Sleepy People (Don't Cause Revolutions), 112
Smith, Bessie, 101, 178
Smith, Howlett, 108
Smith, Lonnie Liston, 93
Smith, Sean, 114, 118, 169
Smoke Gets in Your Eyes, 152
Smollensky's, 113
So Doggone Lonesome, 147, 148
Softly as in a Morning Sunrise, 124
Soho Record Centre, 48
Solar Radio, 91
Some Nice Things I've Missed, 69
Some Other Time, 143
Some Time Ago, 139, 143
Someone to Love, 47
Something's Comin', 37
Somewhere, 37
Sondheim, Stephen, 174
Song for the Geese, 103, 114, 115, 117, 123,
    124, 125, 126, 128–134, 168, 169
Song of Norway, 9
Sophocles, 49
Souter, Tessa, 151, 162, 164, 182
South Carolina Educational Radio, 71
South Hill Park, 85
South Pacific, 142
Speak No Evil, 164
Spitalfields Market, 59
Spring Can Really Hang You Up the Most, 34,
    50, 104, 181
Springfield, Dusty, 54
Springtime in the Rockies, 88
Stablemates, 53
Stafford, Jo, 25, 143
Stamford, Conn., 2
Stapleton, Maureen, 12
Star Sounds, 52, 90
Starr, Kay, 24
Stars of Jazz, 13, 22, 23, 37
Staton, Dakota, 24
Steed, Scott, 117
Steely Dan, 118, 129
Stephenson, Ronnie, 43
Steppenwolf, 60
Stereo Review, 83
Steve Allen Playhouse, The, 24
Steve Allen Show, The, 10
Stewart, Rod, 129

Stigers, Curtis, xi
Still on the Planet, 74
Still Small Softcell, 60
Stillman, M.B., 99
Stitt, Sonny, 66, 82, 83, 126
Stockholm, 41
Stolen Moments, 74, 75, 76, 77, 91, 97, 104,
    110, 112, 119, 120, 148, 151, 152, 168,
    169
Stolen Moments (dance show), 119
Stoppin' the Clock, 163
Storyville, 116
Straight No Chaser, 47
Strasberg, Susan, 57
Strathallan Hotel, 85
Strayhorn, Billy, 13, 15, 99, 100, 140
Streisand, Barbra, 100
Strickland, Alan, 48
Stories of the Road, 82
Styne, Jule, 15, 76
Subterraneans, The, 83
Summertime, 97
Sunday in New York, 67
Sunday Telegraph, 46
Sunderland, 56
SUNY – see Buffalo State College
Sushi-samba, 145
Sutton Public Library, 91
Swartz, Harvie – see Harvie S
Sweet Caroline, 69
Sweet Smell of Success, The, 12
Swingin' Singin' Affair, A, 45
'S Wonderful, 37, 47
Sydney, 84, 116, 175
Syracuse, 1, 5, 8–12, 15; University, 9;
    Suburban Park, 9; day jobs in, 10

T'ain't No Sin, 18, 19
Take 6, 115
Taking a Chance on Love, 18
Talbot, Kenneth, 71
Talk To Me Baby, 52
Talkin' Loud and Sayin' Something, 92
Tangerine, 127
Tanya, 128
Tate, Grady, 96, 127
Tatum, Art, 6
Taylor, Art, 41
Taylor, Cecil, 41
Tea for Two, 58
TCB Records, 161
Teagarden, Jack, 15
Tenderly, 184
Terrace Theater, 134
Terry, Clark, 33

Tesser, Neil, 95
That Old Black Magic, 23, 139
That's How I Love the Blues!, 36, 37, 42, 145
There Is No Greater Love, 15
There Is No Reason Why, 108
There's No You, 99, 100, 120
These Foolish Things, 96
They, 68
Thigpen, Ed, 41
Third Floor Media, 128
This Could be the Start of Something, 23, 25, 26, 29, 151, 176
This Land Is Your Land, 152
This Must Be Earth, 58, 59, 68, 90, 155
This Nearly Was Mine, 142
This Train, 52
Thomas, Dylan, 49
Three Brotha's and a Motha, 144
Three Rivers Inn, 10
Tiburon, Calif., 73, 178
Tie a Yellow Ribbon 'Round the Ole Oak Tree, 69
Time Out magazine, 110
Times, The, 158
Tin Palace, The, 74
'Tis Autumn: the Search for Jackie Paris, 147
Toast, The, 12
Tobin, Christine, 113
Tokyo, 117
Tonight, 37
Tonight Show, The, 23, 40
Tonkin, June, 105, 174
Too Late Now, 104, 148, 162
Top Gear, 44
Top o' the Senator, 131
Tormé, Mel, xii, 15, 35, 37, 39, 76, 77, 78, 87, 89, 114, 175
Toronto, 6, 60, 87, 131, 154
Tortorelli, George, 9
Town Records, 48
Town and Country Club, 92
Tracey, Stan, 43, 44, 47
Traut, Bill, 128
Travessia – see *Bridges*
Treece, Roger, 114, 115, 118, 119, 130, 132, 135
Triad, 68
Tribute to Miles, A, 96
Tropea, John, 68
Troup, Bobby, 13, 23
Trunk, Jonny, 59, 155
Try a Little Tenderness, 15
Tub of Love, 141
Turing, Alan, 48
Turner, Big Joe, 36

Turner Classic Movies, 129
Twelve Tribes, 140
Twisted, 34, 97, 133, 134
Two Brewers, 152
Two Kites, 90, 92
Two Ladies in de Shade of de Banana Tree, 16, 23, 96
Tynan, John A., 35
Tzanakakis, Manos, x, 151

UFO, 117
Ugly Woman, 108
Umbrellas of Cherbourg, The, 42
Underground, 173
Universal Records, 142, 144
University of Music and Performing Arts (Graz), 104–106, 111, 117, 124, 125, 141, 161, 179, 181, 183
Uptight Records, 126

Valenti, Gianni, 153
Van Dijk, Louis, 68, 111
Van Gelder, Rudy, 96
Van Heusen, Jimmy, 76
Van Rooyen, Jerry, 88
Van Rooyen, Ack, 88
Varga, George, 177
Vaughan, Sarah, 6, 8, 52, 64
Venus, 27
Vera Cruz, 59, 112
Verve Records, 39, 64, 144, 146, 147
Very Early, 111, 122,
Very Thought of You, The, 152
Vienna, 104, 110, 111, 116, 126
Vietnam War, 41
Village Gate, The, 39, 117
Village Vanguard, The, 13, 32, 36, 39
Vine Street Bar & Grill, 101
vinyl records, 13, 59, 96, 160
Viva Brasil, 88, 90
Vocalise, 97
Voce, Steve, 47
Von Kaphengst, Christian, 143

Wabich, Chris, 155
Wag Club, The, 93
Wagner, Lindsay, 57
Wakefield, 134
Waldron, Mal, 41
Walk On By, 46
Wall Street, 12; the Crash, 3
Wallingford, Conn., 12
Walton, Cedar, 139
Waltz for Debby, 76
Warner, Alma, 88, 133

Warner, Bert, vii, 35, 55, 56, 61, 78, 79, 85, 94, 111, 120, 130, 133, 137, 138
Warner, Mark, 138
Warner Brothers, 71
Washington D.C., 74, 89, 134
Waters of March, The, 167
Watson, John, 170
Wavendon, 90, 179
Waymans, Little Willie, 11
Wayne's World, 132
WBGO, 158
WBUR, 76
WDR Big Band, 142
Webster, Ben, 41, 166
Weed, Calif., 77, 178
Wein, George, 115
Weinstock, Bob, 126
Welcome Home, 76
West and East Music (record label), 111
Weston, Paul, 143
Weston, Tim, 142
Wee Baby Blues, 36, 47, 97
West Side Story, 37
Western Sound Studios, 95
What a Way to Go, 94, 105, 108
What are You Doing the Rest of Your Life, 181
What If, 147
When I Fall in Love, 143
When the World Was Young, 167
Where Are You?, 47
Where or When, 172
Where You At?, 163
Whisper Not, 47
White Horse Tavern, NYC, 12, 40
Whiting, Margaret, 127
Whitley Bay, 56, 78, 133
Whittaker, Bing, 6
WJZZ, 76
Who Can I Turn To?, 49–52, 90
Why and How?, 57
Why Don't You Do Right, 36, 39
Why Was I Born?, 139, 143
Whyte, Ronny, 35, 135
Wilder, Alec, 40, 71, 72, 76
Wiley, Lee, 6, 37
Wilkins, Ernie, 32, 34, 35, 41

Williams, Andy, 48
Williams, Joe, 9, 26, 32, 36, 37, 114, 145
Williams, Mary Lou, 140
Williams, Steve, 160
Willow Weep for Me, 13
Wilmington, NC., 5
Wilson, Cassandra, xi
Wilson, Hal, 69
Wimbledon, 70
Winstone, Norma, 139
Witchcraft, 27
Wolf, Tommy, 83
Wolof, xiii
Wonder, Stevie, 68
Wong, Herb, 75, 178
Wood, John, 23
Woode, Jimmy, 57
Woods, Phil, 41
Woodruff, Mary (aunt), 1, 6, 17
Woolf, Virginia, 51
Worcester, Mass., 2, 101
Worcester Manufacturing Company, 2
World War II, 88
Wright, Leo, 41, 60
WRVR, 75
Wynn, Keenan, 23

Yesterdays, 184
Yokohama, 158
Yoshi's, 116, 175
You Are My Sunshine, 163
You Don't Know What Love Is, 104, 143
You Go to My Head, 114
Youmans, Leonard, 8
Young and Foolish, 69
Young, Lester, 83, 174
Young, Phil, 104
(You've Got) Personality, 27
You've Got To Have Freedom, 93
You've Proven Your Point, 83, 84, 107

Zanzibar Club, 9, 122
Zawinul, Joe, 74
Zeffirelli, Franco, 71
Zinc Bar, 158
Zygmont, Jeff, 107